Dorsey Armstrong, Ph.D.

Associate Professor of English
and Medieval Literature
Purdue University

Professor Dorsey Armstrong is Associate Professor of English and Medieval Literature at Purdue University. She received her A.B. in English and Creative Writing from Stanford University in 1993 and her Ph.D. in Medieval Literature from Duke University in 1999. Before joining the English department at Purdue in 2002, she taught at Centenary College of Louisiana and California State University, Long Beach. Her research interests include medieval women writers, late medieval print culture, and the Arthurian legend, on which she has published extensively. Her book *Gender and the Chivalric Community in Sir Thomas Malory's "Morte d'Arthur"* was published by University Press of Florida in 2003, and her *Sir Thomas Malory's "Morte Darthur": A Modern English Translation* will be published by Parlor Press in 2009. In January 2009, she became editor in chief of the academic journal *Arthuriana*, which publishes the most cutting-edge research on the legend of King Arthur, from its medieval origins to its enactments in the present moment. In her current research project—*Mapping Malory's "Morte"*—she explores the role that geography plays in Malory's version of the story of King Arthur. ■

D1158835

Table of Contents

The Medieval World

Dorsey Armstrong, Ph.D.

THE
GREAT
COURSES™

PUBLISHED BY:

THE GREAT COURSES
Corporate Headquarters
4840 Westfields Boulevard, Suite 500
Chantilly, Virginia 20151-2299
Phone: 1-800-832-2412
Fax: 703-378-3819
www.thegreatcourses.com

Table of Contents

Table of Contents

Table of Contents

The Medieval World

Scope:

Welcome to *The Medieval World*, a course that aims to explore as fully as possible the many facets of the period of history we have come to call the Middle Ages. Over the next 36 lectures, we will explore medieval social and cultural institutions and the historical events that shaped this incredibly important period in human history. Although 36 lectures may sound like ample time to cover what is exciting and interesting about the medieval world, the Middle Ages was such a complex and varied period that we will, in some cases, barely scratch the surface. I mention this because any study of the medieval world has to begin with an understanding of how multifaceted this period is; any such study must recognize the diverse range of cultures, institutions, and belief systems that are encompassed under the single descriptor "medieval."

For the sake of convenience, most scholars define the medieval period as lasting roughly 1,000 years, from 500 to 1500, and being geographically located in the place we generally refer to as Western Europe. As one might suppose when considering the number of societies and eras included under the rubric "medieval," the Middle Ages should not properly be thought of as a single period in time with a uniform cultural consciousness. Certainly Britain in the year 700 and Italy in the year 1350 were vastly different in terms of language, social structure, literature, government, trading activities, and more. Perhaps even more significantly, if we compare two Western European medieval societies that existed at the same time—such as Spain and France in the year 900—so, too, we will find the differences more striking than the similarities.

As different as the various communities of the Middle Ages were in relationship to one another, the difference between then and now is in many ways far greater. Still, there are many similarities to be found—both among medieval societies themselves and between the Middle Ages and our own period. The medieval world—strange and foreign as it may seem at first to those of us living in the 21st century—is a world that is on its way to becoming our own. So much of what we consider key aspects of our modern ideas of religion, government, science, technology, and social structure can be traced directly to origins in the medieval world.

This course is slightly different in focus from other courses on the Middle Ages. Very often, the study of the medieval period presents a daunting challenge because it seems that there are so many wars and kings and plagues to keep track of. Of necessity, this course will spend considerable time on the major historical events and people who shaped this period, but at the same time it aims to bring the medieval world to life. What was daily life like for a peasant in the 14th century? What did medieval people eat? What kind of houses did they live in? What did they wear? What did they do for entertainment? What kind of literature did they like? To explore these questions and others, the course will be structured in two ways. We will move through the period roughly sequentially, but from time to time a lecture will be more thematic in nature, allowing us to explore in depth certain ideas or events we could not fully understand by moving through them chronologically.

Likewise, we will also seek to situate the medieval world in a broader geographical, social, and temporal context. We will spend time exploring how the late antique period—the time of the Roman Empire—transformed into what we now call the Middle Ages and how the Middle Ages itself developed into what we think of as the modern period. Likewise, we will spend considerable time beyond the borders of Western Europe, exploring how interactions with different cultures and religions—Eastern Europe, the Byzantine Empire, the Middle East, Islam, and Asia—profoundly influenced and shaped the medieval world. Approaching the study of the Middle Ages from multiple perspectives—shifting from a chronological approach to a thematic approach, from a broad overview to a specific case study, from a Christian to a Muslim perspective—helps us to better understand this fascinating period and its many unique characteristics and nuances. ■

The Medieval World
Lecture 1

The Middle Ages is such a complex and varied period. … Any study of the medieval world has to begin with an understanding of how multifaceted this period is and needs also to recognize the diverse range of cultures, institutions, and belief systems that are encompassed under the descriptor "medieval."

T o those living in Europe in what we now call the Middle Ages, the period was not in the middle of anything; in fact, many thought they were living in the last days of the world. In one respect this was true: With the collapse of the Roman Empire in the 5th century, European social and cultural institutions underwent dramatic shifts. Yet, although many people believe that the Middle Ages was one long dark age, nothing could be further from the truth. The medieval world was a rich and varied place,

© 2009 JupiterImages Corporation, a Getty Images company.

Far from being a "dark age," the Middle Ages gave birth to the great universities of Europe.

3

encompassing a vast diversity of peoples, cultures, languages, and traditions; so to explore it, we must first try to define it.

More for convenience than anything else, most scholars think of the Middle Ages as lasting roughly 1,000 years—from A.D. 500 to 1500—and as including most of what we think of today as Western Europe. Scholars further divide the medieval period into three subperiods: the early (500–1000), High (1000–1300), and late Middle Ages (1300–1500). Although most scholars agree to these boundaries, ideas and institutions we might call medieval can be identified from well before 500 and lasting well past 1500. Similarly, regions outside Western Europe—particularly the Byzantine Empire and the Islamic world—significantly affected the development of the medieval world.

While it is true that by modern standards the Middle Ages was a trying time in which to live, it also brimmed with life.

While it is true that by modern standards the Middle Ages was a trying time in which to live, it also brimmed with life and was marked by exciting social, political, artistic, and scientific developments that have profoundly affected modern society. The university system has its origins in this period, when students hungry for knowledge would gather around a renowned scholar to learn from him. Some of the greatest works of world literature were composed in the Middle Ages, including *Beowulf*, *The Canterbury Tales*, Dante's poetry, and stories of King Arthur. Many seemingly modern ideas about legal rights have medieval origins. The Magna Carta, for example, set the stage for later thinking about the limits of a leader's power. Great strides were made in architecture at this time, seen particularly in the construction of breathtaking cathedrals and churches during the High Middle Ages.

For the majority of people living in the medieval world there was only one faith—Christianity—and there was no distinction between secular and religious life. Faith informed politics, national identity, and almost every aspect of daily life, and it was regarded by most people as proper that this should be the case. Still, the roots of ideas such as the separation of church and state and religious dissent such as that seen in the Protestant

Reformation can be found in the Middle Ages. Although Christianity was the dominant religious force in the medieval world, Judaism and Islam both played important roles in shaping these societies, particularly in the areas of economics and the sciences. Medieval Christianity experienced its fullest and most devout expression in the many monastic orders that developed during the Middle Ages and in the practice of pilgrimage. ∎

Suggested Reading

Cantor, *The Civilization of the Middle Ages*.

Linehan and Nelson, *The Medieval World*.

Questions to Consider

1. In what ways is the adjective "medieval" a useful and accurate descriptor for the period spanning roughly 500–1500 in Western Europe? How does it fall short?

2. What seem to be the most striking differences between medieval culture and modern culture, generally speaking?

The Medieval World

Lecture 1—Transcript

Welcome to *The Medieval World*, a course that aims to explore as fully as possible the many facets of the period in history that we have come to call the Middle Ages. My name is Dorsey Armstrong, and I am a professor at Purdue University, where I teach courses on medieval literature and culture. My particular specialties and interests include the legend of King Arthur, medieval women, and the impact that the development of printing had on late medieval society. Over the next 36 lectures, we will explore these and other topics—examining medieval social and cultural institutions and the historical events that shaped this incredibly important period in human history. Although 36 lectures may sound like ample time in which to cover most of what is exciting and interesting about the medieval world, the Middle Ages is such a complex and varied period that we will, in some cases, barely scratch the surface. I mention this because I feel that any study of the medieval world has to begin with an understanding of how multifaceted this period is—and needs also to recognize the diverse range of cultures, institutions, and belief systems that are encompassed under the descriptor "medieval."

This course is a little different in focus from other courses on the Middle Ages. Very often, the study of the medieval period seems daunting because it seems that there are so many wars, kings, and plagues to keep track of. Of necessity, this course will spend considerable time on the major historical events and people who shaped this period—but at the same time, this course aims to bring the medieval world to life, as it were. What was daily life like for a peasant in the 14th century? What did medieval people eat? What kind of houses did they live in? What did they wear? What did they do for entertainment? What kind of literature did they like? As we explore these questions, we will move through the period roughly sequentially—but from time to time, we will stop to explore in-depth certain ideas or events that we couldn't fully understand if we simply moved through them chronologically.

But before we get started talking about the Middle Ages, we need to be able to define it, both geographically and temporally, and we need to identify the cultures and traditions from which it developed. For the sake of convenience, most scholars define the Middle Ages as lasting roughly 1,000 years— from about 500 to 1500—and geographically, the term "medieval" is most commonly used to refer to what we think of today as Western Europe. That's a lot to cover in terms of both time and space, and that's before we even take into consideration the often-times pronounced cultural differences of the various societies of medieval Europe.

In order to make the study of the medieval world a little more manageable, we can further subdivide the Middle Ages in terms of time and geography, and this course will do some of both. Generally speaking, however, scholars broadly divide the period into three periods: the early Middle Ages, from approximately 500 to 1000; the High Middle Ages, from approximately 1000 to 1300; and the late Middle Ages, from approximately 1300 to 1500. Although we necessarily use these dates as a matter of convenience, I cannot stress enough that most scholars are very cautious about relying too much on such artificial boundaries. With a few rare exceptions, one really can't say that the world was one way, for example, in the year 499, and then suddenly became completely different in the year 500.

Historians who work on medieval England, for example, have pretty much agreed to say that the Middle Ages in England end in 1485. They pick that year simply because it marks a change in dynasty; 1485 is the year that the last Plantagenet king, Richard III, was ousted by his distant cousin Henry Tudor, who became King Henry VII. Although scholars have agreed to identify that change as marking the end of the Middle Ages, we can be certain that the values and beliefs of the English people did not suddenly change overnight. Likewise, it would be wrong to suggest that the Renaissance or early modern period did not suddenly spring into being all of a sudden in the 16th century; those who study such things can see that many of the ideas and philosophies considered inherently Renaissance or early modern actually have their origins in the Middle Ages.

It is also important to realize that medieval people didn't think they were living in the middle of anything. The terms "medieval" and "Middle Ages" come into use after this period and were used by early scholars of history as a handy descriptor for a period that they regarded as being between two much more remarkable historical periods—that of the Roman Empire, or as it's often called the late antique world, and the so-called Renaissance, or early modern period. People actually living in the Middle Ages were more likely to regard themselves as living at the end of days; in one respect, this was partially true, as the Roman Empire had effectively come to an end, and with it many of the social and cultural institutions that had been a hallmark of the empire ceased to function as effectively as they once had—and in some cases, ceased to function at all. So, in order to understand the Middle Ages, then, it is necessary to talk a little bit about the Roman Empire and its legacy, and we will do that in our next lecture.

But why, one might ask, should one bother to study the Middle Ages at all? Very frequently I encounter people who assume that this period was all one dark age. Life was difficult. People didn't live long due to wars, and famine, and plague. There was no understanding of hygiene. It was a time of superstition and ignorance. Women had no power and were completely subject to the whims of their husbands, etc., etc., etc. In other words, the Middle Ages is this long nothing between the glory of the Roman world and the incredible learning and innovation that would take place with the Renaissance in the 16th century. Certainly some of the charges leveled against the medieval period are fair—by our modern standards, life was difficult for most people—but many of the things we regard as fundamental aspects of modern life have their origins in the Middle Ages. Indeed, most medievalists will tell you that they detest the term "Dark Age" or "Dark Ages" because, in fact, in many respects this was a period of incredible learning and progress.

For example, the university system as we know it today has its origins in the Middle Ages. It begins probably sometime in the late 11th century—when students would gather around the home of a noted scholar, or rhetorician, or philosopher in order to learn from him. An organized infrastructure had to come into being in order to cope with students who needed a place to live, and who wanted well-known scholars to agree to a certain number of hours of instruction. I always emphasize this to my students when I discuss the rise of the university system: The students in the Middle Ages—many of whom traveled long distances in order to learn from these masters—demanded more education, more hours of instruction, than what the masters were originally willing to give. They also wanted a standardized system of fees—and gradually, what had been an informal arrangement between a scholar and student grew into the great institutions of learning such as Oxford and Cambridge Universities; the University of Paris, or the Sorbonne; and the Italian Universities of Bologna and Padua. Although this burning desire on the part of students to be accepted by a master in order to learn from him may strike us as rather different from the attitudes of many of today's university students, other evidence also suggests that students then and students now are, in many respects, similar. For example, when he was a student at the University of Paris in the 15th century, the poet François Villon was routinely in all kinds of trouble for playing pranks with his comrades—some of which involved stealing the signs of taverns and other businesses. On one famous occasion, he and his friends liberated a large stone that was called, for reasons unknown, "The Devil's Fart" from private property, and they placed it in front of the entrance to one of their classrooms, making it impossible for either students or instructor to enter and have class.

The medieval world, it is true, was a much more difficult world to live in than our modern world in many ways, but that didn't mean that medieval people didn't have a sense of humor. As the exploits of students at various universities suggests, practical jokes were a perennial favorite. Riddles were also quite popular, particularly among the Anglo-Saxons, the Germanic peoples who immigrated to the Isle of Britain from the continent in the 5th century. One riddle that survives in the manuscript known as the *Exeter Book*, which dates from about the middle of the 10th century, goes as follows, as translated from the original language by scholar Elaine Treharne: A curious thing hangs by a man's thigh, under the lap of its lord. In its front it is pierced, it is stiff and hard, it has a good position. When the man lifts his own garment above his knee, he intends to greet with the head of his hanging object that familiar hole which is the same length, and which he has often filled before.

What's the answer to the riddle? Why, a key, of course. Were you thinking of something else maybe? In Anglo-Saxon culture, keys were worn on a belt around the waist, and they were often worn under an outer tunic, necessitating the need to lift the outer garment if one was going to place the key into the lock. Obviously, the real joke here is the sexual double entendre, but you'd be amazed how many students, when they encounter this riddle, assume that the Anglo-Saxons were not trying to be suggestive, and that the bawdy undertones are entirely accidental—as if these medieval people were so busy worrying about wars, and famine, and plague, there was little time for joking, and certainly there was no time to make jokes that were a little risqué in nature.

Jokes were not the only things being composed in the Middle Ages—some of the most beautifully crafted and enduring works of literature were created during this time. The story of Beowulf, Geoffrey Chaucer's *Canterbury Tales*, the poetry of Dante, the legends of King Arthur—all of these came into being during the medieval period. While it is true that levels of literacy were low, and that books were few in number—those books that were produced during this period were true works of art. Called manuscripts, which means literally "written by hand," these texts were painstakingly crafted—usually by monks, especially in the early part of the Middle Ages. There was no paper as we know it today, so the process of creating a book was amazingly involved. First, one needed to slaughter an animal, usually a cow or a goat; skin the animal; stretch, scrape, and otherwise treat the hide to make it workable; cut it into sheets; rule and prick those sheets, which simply means marking them in such a way that a writer could have some sort of guide as he worked, and that's before we've even gotten to the mixing of ink, which was often made from walnut galls, and the plucking and sharpening of a quill. The forming of letters was also a painstaking process—much more painstaking than it is today. For example, the writing of just the letter *m* in a high-quality manuscript from the 14th century could involve as many as 12 different pen strokes, just for that one letter. It is not surprising that, given the amount of labor involved, the copying of a manuscript was often considered a form of prayer by those monks who labored in the scriptorium, preserving histories and literary texts for future generations.

One benefit of medieval manuscripts is, indeed, their toughness. Barring any calamitous events, like fire, they have endured remarkably well and should justifiably be considered treasures—in no small measure because so many of them include breathtaking images and pictures, both as the main subject of a page and also in the margins. Famous manuscripts—such as The Book of Kells, a lavishly decorated edition of the Gospels found (in all places) in a bog in Ireland, where it had probably been thrown to hide and protect it from marauding Vikings; and the Luttrell Psalter, a family prayer book that includes some of the most accurate and detailed depictions of medieval daily life in the pictures rendered in its pages—make clear that medieval people had an appreciation and talent for art on par with that of any modern person. So valuable were these manuscripts, that often they might be bound within jeweled covers, and any household or monastery lucky enough to have these manuscripts, these books would be displayed on a lectern, so that their jeweled covers were visible—rather than standing them on a shelf with only the spines visible, as is typical today. But even if it seems that many medieval people are like us in that they valued books and learning, we only have to look at a surviving letter—written from one monastery to another— to remind ourselves that the world that they inhabited was in many ways different from ours. In this letter, one abbot asks another if his monastery might borrow an important text in order to make their own copy for, you see, a bear had gotten into their scriptorium and eaten their only copy of this text.

At the height of its renown and reputation, the monastery of Monkwearmouth Jarrow in England, known for being an exceptional repository of learning, had about 300 volumes. Many people today have that number or more in their own houses. What makes it possible in part for all of us today to enjoy such a delightful excess of words is the invention of moveable type and the printing press, which comes into being in Europe in the late Middle Ages and is usually attributed to one Johannes Gutenberg. With the advent of print in Europe, books become more accessible to—and affordable for—a large portion of the population. While proponents of the early modern period, which begins in the 16th century, argue for this time as a renaissance of learning, literacy, and education, the roots of this movement are to be found firmly planted in the Middle Ages.

Likewise, modern ideas about legal rights—indeed, some would say the very foundation of the American legal system—arguably can be traced back to a day in 1215 at the meadow beside Runnymede when 25 barons of the realm forced England's King John to sign the Magna Carta—or the Great Charter. We will talk about this document and its significance at length in a later lecture—but here, among other important items, we see the establishment of the writ of habeas corpus and limits placed on the powers of a leader of the people. There are also, you might be surprised to learn, clauses that deal with issues such as the rights of people to set fish weir, or fishtraps, in the

River Thames and standards of weights and measures for food, drink, and cloth—but we will deal with these and many other fascinating aspects of the Magna Carta a little bit later in the course.

The medieval period is also one of the great periods for architectural innovation. Although it is true that the majority of the population of Europe during the Middle Ages lived in simple dwellings, usually made of wood, this is also the age of cathedral building. These soaring, massive stone structures are a testament to medieval ingenuity and understanding of architectural principles, and they also demonstrate a sophisticated grasp of mathematics and physics. The labor required to produce these glorious buildings was enormous and demanding—both in terms of the physical manpower required for their construction and the delicate artistry that provided the finishing touches on these marvels. A stone worker might labor for weeks or even months on a portion of a cathedral that, when set into place, might only occasionally be seen by human eyes—and in some cases, might never be seen, depending on its location. Many cathedrals took decades to build, meaning that the architects—or master builders—who began the project might not be alive to witness its completion. When one looks at the number of cathedrals scattered throughout Europe and how well they have endured, and when one considers that these edifices were constructed without benefit of modern equipment like cranes or modern drafting techniques, one can appreciate that the medieval minds responsible for their existence were certainly as clever, subtle, and sophisticated as those of any modern architect or builder today.

One of the driving forces that made such a huge undertaking possible was religious faith—and here, I think, it is safe to say that the medieval world is different from the modern United States. One has to remember there is no such thing as separation of church and state in the Middle Ages—in many instances, in fact, they seem to be one and the same. Religion permeated all aspects of life in the medieval period. Another thing that we need to keep in mind is that for most of the Middle Ages and for most medieval people, there is only one religion, and that is Christianity—and specifically, that branch of Christianity that we call Catholicism today. In fact, because the Catholic Church so dominated medieval life, I often tell my students that when speaking of Christianity and the Middle Ages, it is not correct to say "the Catholic Church." When we use that phrase today, we are usually distinguishing one kind of Christianity from others, notably those that came into being during the Protestant Reformation, which most people think of as beginning sometime in the 16th century or after the medieval period. Because there is really only one acceptable faith for the majority of people in the medieval period, I tell my students that they should refer to the major religious institution of the Middle Ages as simply "the church," or maybe "the Western Church," in order to distinguish it from Eastern Christian traditions that start to develop in the world around the city of Constantinople after the fall of the Roman Empire.

This is not to say, however, that there was not significant religious tension and even dissent during the Middle Ages, because there certainly was. In fact, the roots of both the Protestant Reformation and the debate about the separation of church and state are to be found in the medieval period. For example, on Christmas day in the year 800, the pope crowned Charlemagne, ruler of the Carolingians, as Holy Roman Emperor. A debate ensued: Did the pope's move serve simply to acknowledge the power that Charlemagne had won for himself, or did the act demonstrate that the church was the higher authority and had the right to grant the power to rule over men? The relationship of secular rulers with religious authorities would be a contentious one throughout the Middle Ages and will be something we explore in some depth as our course progresses. We will also look at movements of religious dissent that laid the groundwork for the Protestant Reformation—movements like Lollardy, also called Wyclifism, which was a significant element in 14th-century Britain.

The Lollards and the man often identified as their leader, John Wyclif, believed that people could have a direct relationship with God, without the need for the intermediary services of the church. In the medieval period, you see, church services were performed in Latin, and the Bible and its interpretation was the domain of ecclesiastical leaders. The idea was that ordinary or "lay" people lacked the training and knowledge to properly understand the message of the Bible, and priests were needed to guide and instruct the people so that they did not misinterpret something—and thus, needlessly fall into sin through an error of understanding. Wyclif and his followers believed that the Bible should be translated into English and be made available to anyone—and also that anyone, even women, could be religious leaders and teachers. For their trouble, many Lollards were excommunicated, burned, or otherwise severely punished.

Although the church is everywhere in medieval society and is, for all intents and purposes, the only game in town when it comes to Christianity, Jews and Muslims and their cultural and religious beliefs are incredibly important in the medieval world. Jewish communities served several important functions in medieval society—unfortunately, one of those functions was often to play the role of scapegoat or villain. The Muslim world would profoundly affect Western Europe in a variety of ways—from architecture, to literature, to cooking. This course will spend considerable time exploring contacts between and among Christian, Jewish, and Muslim communities in order to demonstrate that although the church dominates medieval life, its relationships with various groups and members of the societies of the Middle Ages is more nuanced and less monolithic than has often been considered the case.

We can see the multifaceted nature of medieval religious belief in part through an examination of those most devoted of Christian practitioners, monks and nuns. There are several different kinds of religious or monastic orders that come into being in the Middle Ages, each with its own ideas about proper devotion to, and worship of, God. We will learn about the various communities of men and women who sought to forsake earthly pleasures and serve God by gathering in communities where they would work and pray for the glory of the Lord. Then there are those religious figures who sought a higher form of devotion and would have themselves enclosed or essentially buried alive in small cells, which were usually attached to churches. These people—most frequently women who were called anchoresses, anchorite being the masculine equivalent—might live out their days in a small room with barely enough room to stretch out. Very often, their cell—or anchorhold—would have a small window, which would allow them to see the altar of the church to which their enclosure was attached, and they might have another small window to the outside world, where they might converse with religious pilgrims seeking counsel and also receive food—although numerous accounts of anchoresses suggest that many of them lived on little more than the occasional communion wafer and communion wine, as fasting and deprivation were considered exemplary forms of prayer and devotion.

Spiritual athletes such as these occasionally made it to sainthood, and the veneration of saints is another important aspect of medieval society that we will explore in some detail. One of the most important literary masterpieces of the Middle Ages, Geoffrey Chaucer's *Canterbury Tales*, takes as its framing motif the journey of a group of religious pilgrims to the Shrine of St. Thomas Becket at the Cathedral of Canterbury. Making a religious pilgrimage was a popular activity in the Middle Ages, and people did so for a variety of reasons, including to atone for sins or to seek a cure for illness or injury. Some also seem to have gone on pilgrimages as a kind of vacation or social activity, as the opening lines of Chaucer's masterpiece suggest. He tells us in the English of 14th century London:

> Whan that aprille with his shoures soote, the droghte of March hath perced to the roote, And bathed every veyne in swich licour, Of which vertu engendred is the flour; Whan Zephirus eek with his sweete breeth Inspired hath in every holt and heeth The tendre croppes, and the yonge sonne Hath in the Ram his halve cours yronne, And smale foweles maken melodye, That slepen al the nyght with open ye (So priketh hem nature in hir corages); Thanne longen folk to goon on pilgrimages.

What Chaucer is essentially saying here is that after the rains of April have fallen, and spring has come, and the sun is warm, and the fields and meadows are in flower, and the birds are singing, then people desire to go on pilgrimages—in other words, making a pilgrimage to atone for sins is all well and good, but most people prefer to travel to a shrine when the weather is nice, thank you very much.

So we can see that the medieval world and its inhabitants are, in many respects, just like us—they have a sense of humor; they want their leaders, both secular and religious, to treat them fairly; they're capable of amazing feats of artistry and innovation. At the same time, the medieval world is a place that can seem utterly foreign to us in the 21st century. It is hard for many of us today to imagine what it must have been like to live in a world completely permeated by religion; to live in a world where a woman might give birth to 10 children and only see 2 of them make it past the age of 5, if she was lucky; to live in a world where society was divided into hierarchies between which it was usually impossible to move; to be constantly aware that just one or two years of bad harvests could mean the difference between starvation and well-being.

I could go on and on, discussing the differences between our world and that of the Middle Ages—but to put it simply, this is what makes the medieval world so fascinating. It is, in so many respects, utterly alien to our 21st-century sensibilities, but at the same time, it is a foreign culture within which lie the seeds of our own. For this reason alone, it is incredibly important that we understand the Middle Ages so that we can also understand the source of many of the institutions and customs we regard as fundamental to our society today.

In order to understand the medieval world, we have to understand its origins, and that means we need to understand the legacy of the Roman Empire and the late antique world in the West. In our next lecture, we will discuss the end of the Roman world and how its cultural systems, institutions, and beliefs gave rise to the society that we refer to as medieval.

The Legacy of the Roman World
Lecture 2

Rome became more than just a geographical locus; Romanization, or the spread of Roman ideas and customs, became important throughout the empire. ... The various cultures that sprang from the Roman Empire are viewed by most scholars as interesting hybrids of Roman, Germanic, and Christian elements.

The legacy of the Roman Empire shaped and influenced the early Middle Ages, particularly in terms of the so-called Crisis of the Third Century, the responses of Emperor Diocletian to the crisis, and the significance of the rule of Emperor Constantine. The customs and institutions of Rome gave rise to the many societies of the Middle Ages. To understand how this transformation happened, we need to understand the geographical, political, and cultural nature of the empire.

The empire was astonishingly large, including Europe as far west as Britain and as far north as the Rhine and Danube rivers. It extended into the Middle East, and it included much of North Africa in its embrace. The desire for natural resources—for example, Britain's tin—led to much of the empire's expansion, and the justly famous Roman military, a wonder of order and precision, led that expansion. The idea of *romanitas*—literally, "Romanness"—spread throughout the empire; every major town tried to turn itself into a mini-Rome, mimicking the customs, political system, and buildings found in the capital.

Current scholarship rejects the idea of a single, cataclysmic fall of Rome and tends to see the Roman world transforming, rather than collapsing, into the medieval world. This transformation began long before the so-called end of the Roman era. In the 3rd century, the empire was seriously overextended in terms of both manpower and resources, and it was threatened in four main areas: the military, the political arena, the economy, and social upheaval. Emperor Diocletian, who took the throne in 285, set out to solve these problems by establishing the emperor as a deity; dividing the empire into two administrative areas, each with its own emperor and caesar (the tetrarchy);

and scapegoating (and persecuting) Christians. Emperor Constantine, who came to the throne in 306, helped transform Christianity from the most persecuted to the most favored religion in the empire by issuing the Edict of Toleration, protecting Christians from persecution, in 313.

In the 4th and 5th centuries, the Roman Empire continued to feel pressure on its borders, particularly to the north, beyond which lay Germania and the Visigoths. The Goths had, at various times, served the empire, particularly as paid members of the military. At the end of the 4th century, pressured out of their homeland by the advancing Huns, the Goths requested asylum within the empire but were denied because the Roman economy was too stretched to accommodate them. In 410, they sacked Rome, and their leader, Alaric, was made emperor. Thus began the Germanization of the empire. The devastating effects of the sack of Rome and of Germanization are perhaps seen most clearly in Britain. Abandoned by the empire, it turned to Anglo-Saxon mercenaries for defense against the Picts and Scots, only to be invaded and conquered by those same Anglo-Saxons.

Diocletian's division of the empire into eastern and western halves would have significant repercussions throughout the Middle Ages.

Diocletian's division of the empire into eastern and western halves would have significant repercussions throughout the Middle Ages and beyond. Scholars speak of the "barbarization" (i.e., Germanization) of the West and the "Hellenization" (i.e., Greek influence) of the East. The population of the West stagnated, even fell in some areas; urban centers went into decline; violence increased; trade withered; literacy rates dropped; and centralized power decreased, shifting into the hands of local leaders. ∎

Suggested Reading

Linehan and Nelson, *The Medieval World*.

Rosenwein, *A Short History of the Middle Ages*.

1. How did Diocletian's reform pave the way for the Roman society that would eventually transform into the medieval world?

2. Were there any positive effects of the Germanization of the Roman Empire?

The Legacy of the Roman World
Lecture 2—Transcript

Welcome back. In our last lecture, we discussed some of the broad similarities and differences between our modern world and the medieval world, and how many of the institutions and ideas that we consider modern, in fact, have their roots in the Middle Ages. As I noted last time, medieval people didn't think they were living in the middle of anything. The terms "Middle Ages" and "medieval" were applied to the period much later and were used primarily by scholars who thought that this period—which we define as spanning roughly 1,000 years, from 500 to 1500—was a sort of Dark Age, a long space between the glory that was the Roman Empire and the Renaissance or early modern period—which was, in the minds of many, a rebirth or rediscovery of classical learning and artistic flourishing that hearkened back to the days of the empire.

It is certainly true that if we want to understand the Middle Ages, we have to spend some time exploring the legacy of the Roman Empire, as early medieval societies—and I'm deliberately using the plural here—developed out of the social, religious, and political customs and institutions of the empire. Most people today, even if they haven't studied the period, have some sense of what the Roman Empire was. For our purposes in this course, it is most important to understand three aspects of the Roman world, and these are the geographical, the political, and the cultural nature of the empire. Geographically, the empire was astonishingly large—especially when one considers that this massive territory all had to be managed and controlled without the use of telephones, or faxes, or any other modern conveniences of communication. It included Europe all the way west to Britain and north to the Rhine and Danube rivers. To the east, the empire extended well into the area we know as the Middle East today, fluctuating around the natural boundary of the Euphrates River. To the south, the empire extended into northern Africa.

Politically speaking, the empire had been built largely by physical (i.e., military) force. The Roman military is justly famous as an incredibly efficient, effective, well-oiled fighting machine. Their superior training, coordination, and significantly sophisticated battle tactics—not to mention sheer numbers—made it possible for them to easily conquer, subdue, and maintain control over many realms they wished to bring into the embrace of the empire. They wished to bring many of these realms under their control not because the leaders of the empire were necessarily power hungry—although there were a few leaders who did seem to exhibit a desire to conquer and rule just for the sake of doing so—but very often, it was the desire for natural resources and making those resources easily available that led to their expansion. For example, one reason the Romans were interested in Britain was because it was rich in tin, a metal that was useful for a variety of purposes and easy to work with.

During the reign of the Emperor Caracalla, around the year 212, all free inhabitants of the empire—not just those living on the Italian peninsula, but those out in the provinces as well—could be considered full Roman citizens. This would have a lasting impact: We see peoples in the far west of the empire, in north Africa and the Middle East, still identifying themselves as Roman citizens into the 5th century—by which time the Roman Empire had essentially ceased to exist. With Roman citizenship and identity being significantly extended in the 3rd century, all the power that had once been concentrated on the Italian peninsula and in the city of Rome itself started to diffuse. Indeed, by the 3rd century, Roman emperors could come from the provinces and not just Rome itself. For example, the emperors Trajan and Hadrian both came from the region that today we call Spain.

So geographically, we have an empire that covers a large territory and a variety of different peoples who, no matter their original ethnicity, however we might choose to define that phrase, would also identify as Roman. Politically speaking, power begins to be spread and dispersed away from the Roman center in the 3rd century. Part of what makes this possible is that third important factor I mentioned a moment ago—Roman culture. The culture of the empire has its own word—*romanitas*—to describe it. What *romanitas* essentially means is "Romanness." Rome became more than just a geographical locus—Romanization, or the spread of Roman ideas and customs, became important throughout the empire. Each town within the Roman Empire became a sort of mini-Rome, mimicking institutions—like the Roman Senate found in the capital. Other aspects of Roman culture were also re-created everywhere the Romans established themselves. Go to the south of France and you can find aqueducts, like the Pont du Gard. In London, you can see the remains of the original wall around the city from when it was called Londinium. In the English town of Bath you can visit—no big surprise here—the Roman baths. One of the greatest things that efficient, well-oiled Roman military did was build roads. The main reason for this was practical: Rome wanted to be able to move its legions from place to place as quickly as possible when needed, but the workmanship was such that 1,000 years after the Romans left Britain, for example, the best roads were still in many cases those laid down by the Romans. Today, in many parts of Europe, major highways and arteries follow what is essentially the original route laid out by the Romans.

At its height, the Roman Empire was one of the most awesome institutions of man the world has ever seen. All good things must come to an end, however—and for a long time, professional scholars, arm-chair historians, and lay people alike held the belief that the end of the empire had been a dramatic, cataclysmic event. This idea was common by the time Edward Gibbon wrote his famous *Decline and Fall of the Roman Empire* in the late 18th century. Gibbon claimed to have been inspired to write his book while sitting among some ruins in the city of Rome. He and many other historians saw a contrast between Roman civilization and the barbarians in the North. The area beyond the Danube was called Germania by the Romans, and the people living there were long regarded as uncivilized barbarians.

Although it was once accepted by most scholars that the Roman Empire had experienced a relatively sudden disintegration, today most historians working on what we call the late antique period prefer to think of the period from the 3rd to the 5th centuries as more of a transformation than a decline and fall or collapse. Experts are more likely to see Rome as transforming as it accommodated various groups outside its borders. Specifically, the various cultures that sprang from the Roman Empire are viewed by most scholars as interesting hybrids of Roman, Germanic, and Christian elements. We can see this transformation beginning during what many scholars have called the crisis of the 3rd century. By the 3rd century, the Roman Empire was seriously overextended in terms of both manpower and resources, and we can see this evidence in four areas: In terms of military threats (number one), (number two) political problems, (number three) economic issues, and (number four) social upheaval. In the 3rd century, the empire was threatened on almost every one of its borders. These threats came from Germanic tribes in the North, the Persian Empire in the East, and Berber tribes in Africa—in the southern part of the empire. Most of these threats on the borders were not from peoples who wished to conquer Rome or any of its territories, but rather most frequently what these people wanted—at least initially, in most cases—was to be let in to the empire, to become citizens.

Within the empire itself, Rome was threatened by the fact that it lacked a clear system of imperial succession—so successful rule really depended upon the personal presence and command of the emperor. This guy absolutely had to be charismatic enough to hold the loyalty of his subjects in general and, most importantly, of those in the military. Between the years 235 and 285, there were at least 20 emperors—with several more men who could be considered pretenders to the throne. All but one were murdered, killed in battle, or died while imprisoned. It doesn't take a genius to see that if this issue were to continue to go unresolved, it would have a seriously negative impact on the stability of the empire.

Adding to these other problems was an economic downturn. To begin with, the Roman economy, especially in the West, was not particularly sophisticated or stable. The economy was primarily agrarian, based on agriculture and farming—and thus, was subject to serious problems should bad weather or other factors cause significant crop failures. Because of the increased threats along the borders, additional taxes needed to be levied in order to pay the military. When this wasn't sufficient, currency devaluation became necessary—which only exacerbated, rather than alleviated, the economic problems.

Contributing to these issues—or perhaps because of them in part—a new ruling class rose during this period. Their strength was militarybased, which meant that the Roman Senate and those high-ranking citizens back in Rome proper were losing status. Many noble Roman families who had long had power and influence found themselves shunted aside by relative upstarts who had gained a high social position through service to, and command of, the military. It was the Emperor Diocletian, who reigned from 285 to 305, who provided the most effective and significant responses to the Crisis of the Third Century. His solutions had as their main goal the preservation of *romanitas*, but the empire was definitely different politically, socially, and culturally after his reforms—which he enacted in three key areas. The first was in the area of religion. What we need to remember here is that the Romans at this time are still polytheistic pagans, worshipping many gods. To the pantheon of official gods and those so-called diverse household gods revered in outlying areas of the empire, Diocletian added the cult of the emperor—sometimes called the genius of the emperor—emphasizing the power and divinity of the emperor in an attempt to solidify his authority.

The second area in which Diocletian made some changes was in terms of the daily administration of the empire—and here the most important thing he did was restructure the office of emperor. Diocletian recognized that one person could not possibly oversee the entire Roman Empire and do a good job, so he sought to solve the control issue and the succession issue with one move: He divided the empire into two halves—the western and the eastern—and then developed a tetrarchy, which literally means "rule of four." In this system, he would remain emperor, but he would have a co-ruler—called an Augustus—and there would also be two junior deputies, one for each emperor, and these would be called caesars. The idea was that the caesars could help share the burden of ruling while being trained to take over as heirs to the imperial thrones. Diocletian claimed the eastern half of the empire for himself for reasons that we'll discuss in a moment, and his co-ruler took the western half.

As Diocletian's choice suggests, the eastern half of the empire was more attractive than the West in the early 4th century. There were a number of reasons for this. First, the eastern half of the empire contained more and larger cities—such as Alexandria, Thessalonica, and Athens—which were quite prosperous. Second, unlike the West, the Eastern economy did not have all its eggs in the agrarian basket, so to speak—there was a strong commercial, mercantile economy in the East. The population of the eastern half of the empire was also significantly larger than that in the West—which meant, among other things, that there was a significant amount of manpower for military and other projects, and there was also a significant tax base. In addition to all these other plusses, the borders of the Eastern Empire were less frequently attacked than those in the West, which meant a relatively more peaceful, stable civilization.

In 305, Diocletian and his co-Augustus Maximian abdicated in favor of the caesars, but instead of the orderly succession for which Diocletian had hoped, civil war ensued. Finally, Constantine—son of the Caesar Constantinus—successfully claimed the throne of emperor in 312. Constantine, an incredibly ruthless and ambitious man, is also very significant to any study of the medieval period for two main reasons: The first is his establishment of a new capital called Constantinople, located in Byzantium on the Black Sea, which would become a new Rome for the eastern half of the empire; and the second is his championing of Christianity.

As I said earlier in this lecture, the societies that emerged from the dissolution of the Roman Empire are considered to be hybrids of Roman, Germanic, and Christian ideals, and the status of Christianity as a powerful influence can be in large measure attributed to Constantine—for it is during his reign that Christianity goes from being a persecuted religion to the major religion of the empire. As we have already discussed, Roman paganism was comfortably polytheistic. Religion was also tied to patriotism, so religious practice in essence was also a way of expressing or displaying one's Roman citizenship. A religion that was a problem for the empire was Judaism. They were a problem in that they were, obviously, emphatically monotheistic, worshipping one god, and there was no way to truly comfortably accommodate their beliefs within the religious spectrum of ideologies that were acceptable in the empire. But for the most part, the Jews were tolerated, allowed to practice their religion, and lived in relative harmony with the other citizens of the empire—although at the same time, the striking difference in their religious practices from the rest of the empire did set their communities apart and made those communities very close-knit.

Christians, on the other hand, were a much more significant problem in the eyes of the empire. Here, one of the most important things to understand about the earliest days of the Christian religion is, number one, it wasn't considered Christian at all—rather, it was just another sect of Judaism. Number two, this new Jewish sect proselytized and recruited in a way that Jews traditionally had not. Jews had been tolerated because they did not really seek converts; by contrast, Christianity in the early empire was regarded as an aggressive cult, and it was not seen so much as a religion as it was a subversive political movement.

The result of this was a series of persecutions. In particular, in about 303, we have the beginning of what has come to be called the Great Persecution of Christians. All of this changes, however, during the reign of the Emperor Constantine, who ruled from 306 to 337. It is estimated that when Constantine came to the throne about 10 percent of the population of the Roman Empire was Christian. What changes everything for Christianity and the empire—and thus has a profound effect on the medieval period—is the conversion of the Emperor Constantine. One of the key moments in the process of his conversion was an event in 312 known as the Battle of Milvian Bridge. The night before the battle, the story goes, Constantine has a vision in which he's told to paint a certain symbol on his shield. That symbol is known as the Chi Rho, and these two characters were the first two letters of Christ's name in Greek. Constantine does this and wins the battle. It is believed that this inspires Constantine to issue something called the Edict of Toleration in the year 313. What this does is prohibit persecution of Christians. We don't know exactly what Constantine himself believed or how devout or sincere any conversion of his own might have been—but what we do know is that over the course of the next century, paganism and Christianity essentially reversed positions, and the Christian faith went from being a minority religion to the religion of the empire.

So, by the end of the 4th century, we have a Roman Empire that is Christian, that has instituted some rather drastic measures to try and ensure its survival, and that is increasingly threatened on many of its borders. One of the biggest threats comes from the region that the Romans called Germania—which, as I noted, is essentially everything north of the Danube River. One thing that we absolutely need to remember is that these so-called barbarians were, first of all, not at all one unified group of people. They were disparate tribes who would think of their particular group as distinctly different from, say, a tribe whose community was centered just a few miles away. But in terms of cultural practices, religious beliefs, and language, they were similar—although they would not have understood themselves as all belonging to a single group that today we might call Germanic.

There are all kinds of groups moving through Europe in the 4th and 5th centuries, and these movements put considerable pressure on the borders of the empire, but the most important group for our purposes today are the

Goths—and that's the group we're going to focus on now. We know about the Goths primarily from the writings of a 6th century man named Jordanes. When he describes the Goths, Jordanes makes some interesting comments. He identifies them as coming from Scandinavia. When he describes their movements during the 4th and early 5th centuries, he describes military conquest as a motivation—but also notes that in many cases what we have is families who are moving to new territory and settling down. We have migrations into towns, and we have plenty of trade and contact with other peoples, including the Roman Empire. He characterizes the Goths as fierce and warlike, but also says that they are "nearly like the Greeks," suggesting that they had a highly developed and sophisticated culture. In the year 376, the Visigoths request asylum inside the empire—as they are being forced out of their own territories in the East by the Huns. Asylum is denied to them, and it is more out of desperation than any desire for conquest that they attack and defeat the Roman army at the Battle of Adrianople in the year 378. This battle is significant for several reasons. One is that the emperor of the western half of the empire, a man named Valens, is killed there. From this point on, the Visigoths are variously allies and enemies of Rome. They serve in the Roman army from time to time—and when they were of some use to Rome, they were quite welcome in that they could assist Rome in fighting many of their other enemies who were pressing against their borders. In 402, under the leadership of a man named Alaric, the Visigoths entered the Italian peninsula. They asked, in return for their support and alliance, that Rome give them land and gold. The Romans stalled—and in frustration, in the year 410, the Goths marched south and sacked Rome itself, and Alaric became emperor.

Although the city of Rome itself had declined in terms of prestige, the psychological ramifications of this are profound for those people living within the empire and who thought of themselves as Roman citizens. There is really no other option but for the empire to accommodate the Visigoths. As allies of Rome, they fight against the Huns, who are led by the infamous Attila—and Galla Placida, the daughter of the Emperor Theodosius, actually marries Alaric's successor, Atauf, in 414. This accommodation of the Visigoths sets a dangerous precedent, in that it paved the way for other so-called barbarian tribes to settle within the empire and become citizens—

although these people did tend to become Romanized, to adopt *romanitas* as an ideal. The result was that the empire was also becoming Germanized.

One place that became Germanized in emphatic fashion was Britain. The Romans had managed to bring much of Britain under control of the empire, and most of the people living in Britain, with some important exceptions, were Roman citizens from the year 43 AD until the 5th century—so for almost four centuries. Think of that—400 years. That's significantly longer than the United States has even been in existence.

Even though they were on the edge of the empire, many of what we might call the Romano-British had embraced *romanitas*. As we discussed in our last lecture, the Romans did what they always did when they took over an area— they re-created Roman culture. They built baths, and villas, and temples, and roads and put an administrative bureaucracy in place to manage the territory more efficiently. In fact, although many parts of the Roman Empire had gone into a decline in the 4th century, this was actually a period of relative prosperity for Britain—the archaeological evidence, for example, shows large agricultural villas in existence around this time. But as I mentioned earlier, Rome itself was under threat in the early 5th century, and in 406, an over-extended empire called the legions stationed in Britain back to Rome to address the increasing threat from the Goths.

Even after this, however, the British still considered themselves Roman citizens and expected that should they need protection, Rome would provide it. Very soon after the withdrawal, the Romano- British began to be attacked by some people called the Picts, who come down from the north from what is today Scotland—and they were attacked also by the Scots, who, confusingly, at this time don't come from Scotland, but rather come from Ireland. In response to these attacks, the Britons sent a letter to the Roman consul Aetius, just across the channel in Gaul, which is modern-day France. The letter begins with the writers telling the consul that they are sending him "the groans of the Britons." The letter goes on to ask for help, saying: "The barbarians drive us to the sea, the sea drives us to the barbarians; between these two fatal threats we are either slain or drowned." The answer that comes back is essentially: You're on your own. The Rome of which the Britons believe they are citizens, for all intents and purposes, no longer exists.

In response to this threat, one of the many leaders of the Britons, a man named Vortigern, hires a group of mercenaries who hail from the area around present-day Germany to come to Britain and help the Romano-British fight off their enemies. According to tradition, in the year 449 A.D., three boatloads of Germanic sea-faring warriors—led by two brothers with the marvelous names of Hengest and Horsa—land on the shores of Britain, and they fairly quickly do what Vortigern hired them to do—that is, they push back the Picts and the Scots. But then after this, they take a look around and see that Britain is a pretty nice place to live and its people have no means of military resistance. They send word back to the Continent, and pretty soon you have a full-scale migration—usually called the Anglo-Saxon invasion of Britain. Members of the tribes of the Angles and Saxons were heavily represented in this invasion, but the invaders also included members of other Germanic groups, like the Jutes and the Frisians—still, today, for the sake of convenience, we refer to this group collectively as the Anglo-Saxons. As you might imagine, there is no way the Britons are going to be able to fight off the people they paid to fight off the people they were unable to fight off—so the Anglo-Saxons very quickly establish themselves as a power on the island.

As a general rule, medieval scholars dislike the phrase "Dark Ages," but if ever there were a period that could be called a dark age, the 5th century in Britain is it. This is a period often referred to as sub- Roman Britain to indicate the influence of at least the idea of Rome and *romanitas* that lingered for much of the populace—although the reach of the empire actually no longer extended that far. As part of the Roman Empire, Britain had had scholars and scribes—many of whom were religious men, like monks and priests— because, like the rest of the empire, early Britain had been Christian. With the arrival of the Germanic Anglo-Saxons, who were polytheistic pagans and members of a preliterate culture, Britain is plunged into a period of darkness, about which we know very little. Writing and recordkeeping essentially disappear. People are concerned with simply staying alive, and there's not room for much else.

As we head toward the 6th century, something similar to what has occurred in Britain with the invasion of the Anglo-Saxons and in the capital of Rome itself with the sack by the Visigoths is occurring all throughout the western part of the empire. The impact of Diocletion's division of the empire into two halves would continue to be felt well into the Middle Ages. To put it simply, the two halves of the empire went in different directions. The legacy of this divided empire resulted ultimately in what many scholars have described as the barbarization of the West (meaning that societies in the western half of the empire became more like the non-Roman groups that had been living on its fringes and borders) and the Hellenization of the East (meaning that the eastern half of the empire came to resemble what we think of generally as the culture and ideals of Greece and the Greek-influenced ancient world).

The West is where most of our focus is going to remain throughout these lectures—although the eastern half of the Roman Empire will continue to be important, at least as an idea. As we look ahead to our next lectures, there are several aspects of this transformation of the Roman Empire in the West that we need to keep in mind as we start to think about the early Middle Ages. First—in the face of a series of migrations, invasions, and other upheavals—the population either remains stagnant or declines. Second, we have urban centers—cities—beginning to wither. There are also several eruptions of violence. So, not surprisingly, trade declines, as does what we might call cultural life—in particular, levels of literacy among the population decrease. In the aftermath of the Roman Empire, power becomes localized—meaning that people are no longer looking to a distant capital or center, Rome, as a model, or for guidance, or directives, or laws—but rather, local warlords and those who are able to control the economy are the ones with power.

In our next lecture, we will examine in greater detail how the cultures that emerged from the Roman Empire were hybrids of Roman, Germanic, and Christian elements—and how all these elements found expression in such seemingly diverse areas as politics, architecture, art, and literature.

The Christianization of Europe
Lecture 3

"Like some new Constantine, he stepped forward to the baptismal
pool, ready to wash away the sores of his old leprosy and to be cleansed
in flowing water from the sordid stains which he had borne so long. …
King Clovis confessed his belief in God the Almighty."

—Gregory of Tours, *The History of the Franks*

A lthough at its end the Roman Empire was officially Christian, many
European communities, especially in so-called Germania, were
not. Once the empire dissolved into various small kingdoms, the
Christianization of medieval Europe began in earnest. This lecture goes
back to the 4th century, when Christianity became the dominant religion
of the Roman Empire, to explore how it changed after Roman rule ended,
focusing in particular on the conversion of various communities. We will pay
particular attention to accounts of conversion given in the Venerable Bede's
Ecclesiastical History of the English People and Gregory of Tours's *History
of the Franks*, examining the strategies and stumbling blocks of medieval
Christian missionaries.

Within 100 years of the Edict of Toleration, Christians had become the most
favored religious group within the empire, but the process of Christianization
was far from simple or easy. During its persecution, Christianity was seen as
a threat to the empire because it was an aggressive, proselytizing religion and
its adherents wished to institute reform. Once it became a protected religion,
Christianity's success was due in part to its willingness to incorporate pagan
traditions and symbols into the new faith, making the transition easier for
many pagans.

Two case studies of the conversion process—those of the Franks and the
Anglo-Saxons—offer an idea of the realities attendant on bringing pagan
peoples into the fold of Christianity in a practical, everyday sense. The group of
Franks known as the Merovingians had settled in Gaul (modern-day France)
by the 4th century. Their conversion was recorded by a near contemporary,

Gregory of Tours, in his *History of the Franks*. Merovingian King Clovis married Clothild, a Christian from the Burgundian royal family, and she tried to persuade him to convert. Clovis agreed to convert if Christ granted him victory over the Alemanni. This, of course, is what happened. While Gregory takes pains to paint Clovis as a "new Constantine," Gregory likely manipulated the facts to write a providential history, one focused on proving that God is the ultimate source and cause of all things. It seems more likely that Clovis was already a Christian, albeit a heretical one—an Arian.

Like Gregory of Tours, Bede's agenda was promoting Christianity, which makes his inclusion of accounts of early conversions that seem somewhat less than sincere all the more remarkable.

Like the Merovingians, the Anglo-Saxons in Britain were Germanic, linguistically and culturally. With their conquest of Britain in the mid-5th century, they almost entirely wiped out its Romanized and Christian society. The Anglo-Saxon kingdom was one of the last former realms of the empire to remain pagan. In 597, Pope Gregory the Great sent a missionary team, led by Augustine of Canterbury, to convert them. Most of what we know of this process comes from an 8th-century British monk and scholar, the Venerable Bede, who recorded the events in his monumental *Ecclesiastical History of the English People*. Like Gregory of Tours, Bede's agenda was promoting Christianity, which makes his inclusion of accounts of early conversions that seem somewhat less than sincere all the more remarkable. Bede describes how the majority of the East Saxons converted to Christianity simply because their king, Ethelbert, did so in 604. He also relates how King Edwin of Northumbria was persuaded to convert by his chief pagan priest.

While these conversion narratives reveal much, remember we are seeing evidence from only a small proportion of the upper echelons of society. We have no real idea about the religious practices and beliefs of up to 95 percent of the population. These narratives also serve to caution us about working with contemporary sources, as Gregory and Bede each obviously had an agenda. Objectivity as modern historians think of it was largely unknown in the medieval world. ■

Suggested Reading

Geary, *The Myth of Nations*.

Rosenwein, *A Short History of the Middle Ages*.

Questions to Consider

1. What do early conversion narratives suggest about the depth and sincerity of religious belief in the early Middle Ages?

2. How did early Christians draw on Roman traditions and ideals to establish and support their new faith?

The Christianization of Europe
Lecture 3—Transcript

Welcome back. In our last lecture, we discussed the legacy of the Roman Empire, particularly the fact that the cultures that emerged from what was left of Rome tended to be hybrids of Christian, Roman, and Germanic elements. Today we're going to talk a little bit more about how the process of Christianization continued after the decline of the empire—particularly among those groups of peoples who lived beyond the traditional bounds of the Roman Empire in the region that the Romans referred to as Germania.

The process of the Christianization of the Roman Empire is complex—indeed, we could do a whole lecture series just on this topic alone—but I'm going to try and give you a brief, somewhat simplified overview of that process. One reason Christianity spread throughout the empire is that, unlike the Jewish traditions from which it sprang, Christianity was a belief system that actively sought to recruit adherents, to spread the message of Jesus. The refusal of Christians to participate in the worship of pagan gods or the cult of the genius of the emperor was considered a major problem by the Roman State. Concentrated and deliberate persecutions of Christians began in the 1st century under the Emperor Nero and escalated into the 3rd century. By the year 250, the Emperor Decius had identified Christians as enemies of Rome. This belief was underscored by Diocletian's reaction to the Crisis of the Third Century. The Christians presented an obstacle to one of his solutions to the crisis—the renewed emphasis on the divinity of the emperor—because of their unshakeable monotheism. In the year 298, on an occasion when Roman priests were performing a pagan sacrifice in the presence of the emperor, it was thought that favorable omens did not result because some Christians were present, and they had made the sign of the cross during the pagan ritual. Events such as these led eventually to the Great Persecution, which began in 303 and continued for about the next decade until Constantine, as we discussed last time, offered protection to Christians in 313 with the Edict of Toleration, which he issued after his victory at the Battle of Milvian Bridge—a victory he felt had been made possible through divine intervention.

Over the course of the next century, Christianity and paganism essentially switched positions within the empire. What we should understand about Christianity in the empire is that it is not so much a triumph of one belief system over another as it is a successful compromise—many older pagan traditions were incorporated into the practices of the new religion, and traditional imperial symbols were reinterpreted in a Christian calendar. The reality is that most people probably held a sort of combination of Christian and pagan beliefs—and very often, Christian celebrations and feasts were simply substituted for pagan ones. The most obvious example of this would be the celebration of the birth of Christ in December. Many scholars are convinced that the historical Jesus was actually born in late summer. So why celebrate his birthday in late December? That had traditionally been the time of the celebration of the pagan Saturnalia, an event that usually coincided with the winter solstice, or the longest night of the year. In other words, this was the time when people celebrated the fact that the days were finally about to start getting longer and the nights shorter. If you think about it, this would really be something to celebrate in the days before electricity. Although I'm greatly oversimplifying and perhaps being a little flippant here, it makes sense that if you're going to ask people to give up many of their traditional religious beliefs, you could at least let them keep the celebration that provided some entertainment and merriment at the darkest time of the year. That, in a nutshell, is why Christmas is celebrated when it is.

Once the church became the favored religion of the empire, it was able to build wealth and consolidate its position locally, in the area around the Mediterranean. At the start of the 5th century and well into the 6th, however, the church's attention shifts to northwestern Europe, and today we're going to focus on two occurrences of conversion—paying particular attention to narratives that described the conversion process among the Franks, whose kingdom included most of what is modern-day France; and the Anglo-Saxons, who eventually became the people we know as the English.

The Frankish people, also known as the Merovingians—so-called after one of their legendary leaders, Merovech—were a Germanic people who, by the 4th century, had settled within the Roman Empire in the region known as Gaul. They had served in the Roman Army, but they were different from other Germanic tribes in that they settled in one place and then began to expand their power, rather than continuing to move throughout Europe. We know about the Merovingians primarily from a history written by a man called Gregory of Tours. Gregory's chronicle, the *History of the Franks*, is one of the most readable texts from the early medieval period. At times he becomes downright chatty, and he provides us with an invaluable look at a region that was transforming from Roman Gaul into Merovingian France. His text is a first-hand observer's record of the social, religious, and political life of a community at a crucial point in history—when Rome no longer existed in the West, but could still be remembered, and that memory was still potent.

Gregory was born in the middle of the 6th century and was the son of an aristocratic Gallo-Roman family. His family had been influential in the region of the city of Tours for some time, dominating the religious offices of this episcopal see—a term that refers to the domain of the authority of a particular bishop. Gregory's text is important not only for what it tells us in terms of historical events and important figures, but also because it demonstrates quite clearly how history could be manipulated to serve a particular agenda. Gregory's goal was to write what we call a providential history—in other words, a chronicle that detailed how God is the ultimate cause of all things. Gregory worked quite closely with the Frankish kings, whom he saw as instruments of divine providence—and in writing his history, he also wanted to provide kings of his day with what he considered to be good examples of kingly behavior.

Perhaps the most important example of this is Gregory's treatment of the Merovingian King Clovis, who ruled from 481 to 511. We'll talk at greater length about Clovis and the Merovingian dynasty as a whole in our next lecture, but for our purposes today I want us to focus on how Gregory represents him in his text. Gregory of Tours presents Clovis as a pagan who takes as one of his wives a woman named Clothild, who was of a Burgundian royal family. Clothild tries to persuade Clovis to convert, but with little effect. She has their first son, Ingomer, baptized, but Ingomer dies shortly thereafter, and Clovis places the blame for this on her God. A second son is born and baptized—and he, too, becomes sick. Clothild prays over him, and he recovers, but this is not enough to persuade Clovis to take up this new religion.

What does the trick, finally, is what worked in the case of Constantine, and this is essentially a battlefield conversion. The Franks were at war with a people known as the Alemanni, and Clovis's troops were being slaughtered left and right. He prays to Christ and asks for victory; in return, Clovis will accept baptism and become a Christian. Needless to say, he wins the battle and then prepares himself for baptism. According to Gregory, he meets with Bishop Remigius, who had been summoned by the queen—and although he tells the bishop that he is ready to convert, he is concerned that his people will be unwilling to give up worshipping their gods. So he arranges a meeting with his people to discuss this new religion with them, but before he can say a word, according to Gregory, they all with one accord and one voice announce that they are ready to forsake the worship of pagan gods and to accept this new religion. With that settled, Clovis goes to be baptized, and in the words of Gregory of Tours:

> Like some new Constantine, he stepped forward to the baptismal pool, ready to wash away the sores of his old leprosy and to be cleansed in flowing water from the sordid stains which he had borne so long … King Clovis confessed his belief in God the Almighty, three in one. He was baptized in the name of the Father, the Son, and the Holy Ghost, and marked in chrism with the sign of the cross of Christ.

There are a few problems or issues with Gregory's account of Clovis's conversion. First of all, this narrative, as we will see, is a kind of set piece that is retold in various forms in several conversion narratives throughout the Middle Ages—and as such, it contains four elements that we will see repeatedly. These include the role of a Christian queen in converting her pagan husband, the power of the Christian God to bring victory in battle, the king's concern over his peoples' willingness to follow him in his conversion—and then the conclusion, in which the king and all his people convert.

One of the biggest issues scholars have with Gregory of Tours's account is the fact that we have ample evidence that before this moment, Clovis was already Christian, but he was an Arian Christian. What does this mean? What we have to remember is that in the early days of Christianity it was still very much a work in progress. The tenets and practices of the faith were still being worked out by various important church fathers, such as the famous Saint Augustine, bishop of Hippo from North Africa. Early on in the Christian tradition, we see people following beliefs that will eventually be condemned as heresies. What we have to remember, however, is that until they are officially condemned, such beliefs are regarded as completely legitimate and orthodox by many; Arianism is one of these beliefs. In a nutshell, Arianism was the belief that although Christ was divine, he could not be as divine as God the Father—in part because he had been human for a time, and because as the Son, he had not existed co-eternally with the Father. The issue was one of those taken up and dealt with at the Council of Nicea, which Constantine himself had overseen. Thus, Gregory's attempt to characterize Clovis as a new Constantine is significant in that he seems to be trying to rewrite Clovis's conversion, making him a convert directly from paganism to the true Christian faith—and representing his people as ready, willing, and eager to convert with him.

Arianism is just one of many heresies that appear as Christianity establishes and cements its belief systems and rituals in the early Middle Ages. Another important heresy of the period is Pelagianism. Named for a British monk, Pelagius, this was the belief that original sin had not irrevocably tainted humankind, and that one could earn one's way into heaven by performing good works. Pelagius essentially argued that Adam had set a bad example for humankind, but that the good example set by Jesus served to counter Adam's actions. According to Pelagianism, humans had full control over their salvation or damnation, as each individual was fully responsible both for his or her good or sinful actions. It was Saint Augustine who most soundly condemned Pelagianism, arguing that humans were saved only by the grace of God—no one person could save himself by performing good works. Although Pelagianism was condemned at several church councils, especially in the 5th century, it persisted for quite some time—even popping up again in the late Middle Ages.

Because Pelagius was British, it is no surprise that this heresy was particularly popular in Britain. Pelagius himself was a Roman Christian. We need to remember that during the greatest part of his lifetime—which scholars say is roughly from about 354 to 420 or so—Britain is part of the Roman Empire, and with Constantine's conversion to Christianity, the Romano-Britons had, for the most part, followed suit.

But as we've already discussed at some length about the arrival of the Germanic Anglo-Saxons had a profound impact on the Romano- Christian culture of Britain. The invasion of these early English peoples effected Germanization of a culture that had embraced *romanitas*, even though it was at the edge of the empire, and which had become Christian while part of that empire. The Anglo-Saxon invasion for a time looked as if it would effectively wipe out the Roman and Christian legacy of the empire in Britain.

But in 597, Pope Gregory the Great sent missionaries to England, led by a man whom history now calls Augustine of Canterbury; this is confusing because we have just been talking about Gregory of Tours and Augustine of Hippo, one of the most important early Christian church fathers. But these are a different Gregory and a different Augustine, and this Gregory and Augustine are both at least a century or two later in history than those earlier similarly named important Christian figures.

Anglo-Saxon England was one of the last former Roman outposts to be re-Christianized. The Franks, just across the channel in what is modern-day France, had been Christian for at least a century when Pope Gregory the Great sent Augustine to the Anglo-Saxons. According to the first biography of Gregory, which was written in the British monastery of Whitby in the 8th century, Gregory became inspired to send missionaries to the Anglo-Saxons after seeing some young Anglo-Saxons—probably slaves—in Rome. He was struck by their appearance—according to tradition they were fair-haired and looked unlike most people living in the area around the Mediterranean basin—and he asked them who they were. According to the story, a series of bad puns then follow. The slaves answer that they are Angles, to which Gregory responds, that no, rather, they look as if they were angels. He asks them the name of their king, and they tell him that they are subjects of Alle; Alleluia, Gregory responds: "God's praise must be heard in your kingdom." Then he asks the name of their kingdom, and they tell him that they are from Deira, spelled D-E-I-R-A, which in Latin, when split in two, becomes de ira, which can mean "from wrath," and Gregory says they shall flee from the wrath of God and come to the Christian faith.

This is a very cute story, but it is more likely that Gregory had long been thinking of the need to convert the English, as their kingdom was the last of the kingdoms that rose from the Roman Empire to remain pagan. Most of what we know of the conversion process of the Anglo-Saxons comes from perhaps the most important text of the 8th century, and this is a massive chronicle written by a monk known as the Venerable Bede, and his work is *The Ecclesiastical History of the English People.*

We don't know much about Bede himself, but the bare facts of what we do know are fascinating and compelling. Bede was most likely born in the region of Britain known as Northumbria sometime around 672. When he was just seven years old, Bede was given by his family to the British Monastery of Monkwearmouth Jarrow, also in Northumbria. These were originally two separate monasteries that eventually joined together. This so-called donation of a young boy was not an unusual practice, and many families gave young children into the keeping of a monastery in the hope that there they would have a safe and secure life as a member of the church. Such children were called oblates, and many of them did, indeed, spend the rest of their lives living as monks in a monastery.

Probably the earliest reference to Bede is in an anonymous text that chronicles the lives of several important church figures, including the Abbot Ceolfrith of the monastery of Jarrow. In the year 685, we know that a deadly plague swept through the area, and according to the account of the life of the Abbot Ceolfrith, everyone died except for the abbot and one small boy. Alone, these two struggled to perform the religious services that were required, a daunting task usually shared out among several in the monastery.

Based on what we know of Bede's life and the date of the text, it seems quite clear that this young boy, who alone of all the members of the monastic community besides the abbot survived the plague, was Bede. It's not hard to imagine that after watching the older monks and the other young boys with whom he lived, and studied, and played at the monastery die, Bede might have thought himself to have been saved by God for some important task. He became a deacon at age 19—highly unusual, as church standards called for someone to reach the age of 25 before becoming a deacon. He went on to be a scholar—whose writings reveal a lively, curious, intelligent, and, of course, deeply devout mind. Modern scholars are forever grateful to Bede for writing his *Ecclesiastical History*, for without this one text, there are many pre-8th-century British historical events and figures about whom we would know exactly nothing.

One thing he writes about at great length is the process of the conversion of the English. Although Bede understood himself to be writing a history, he was not writing history in the way that modern people think of it—most modern scholars make every effort to be objective, to avoid passing judgment whenever possible, to try and avoid any appearance at least of bias. Such things were not the primary concerns of medieval historians. Within this text, Bede demonstrates, rather obviously, that in addition to recording history, he wishes to promote the church—and in this respect he is very like Gregory of Tours, who had a similar agenda to promote. It seems quite clear, for example, that Bede expected that his text would be copied, sent to various places throughout Britain, and read aloud to large groups of people. We have to remember literacy is very low in medieval Europe—maybe 5 to 10 percent of the population at best could read—so gathering to hear texts read aloud was an activity that was actually quite common. Although Bede wrote his text originally in Latin, the language of scholarship in the Middle Ages, it was translated into Anglo-Saxon or Old English—making it accessible to a larger potential audience. Bede's hope, evidently, was that the account of events narrated in his history would inspire his readers and listeners to greater faith and devotion.

So, it is a little surprising that when we read some of these accounts, it seems quite clear that in the early stages, conversion to Christianity was not sincere in the way that we today might think of it—to us, many of these conversions might not seem real. Bede was very conscious that as the king went, so went his people—so he sought most earnestly to make sure that his text made it to the court of important rulers. Many of the conversion narratives he relates tell of how a king's conversion to Christianity precipitated, almost immediately, the conversion of all of his subjects. Again, we see the similarities and connections with Gregory of Tours's account, in which Clovis's subjects have miraculously decided that they wish to give up worshipping their pagan idols at the exact moment Clovis is contemplating Christian baptism.

When Bede relates the story of how the East Saxons converted in following the example of their King Ethelbert in 604, he admits that many of Ethelbert's subjects probably converted because they were afraid of the king and what he might do if they did not follow his lead. Another famous conversion narrative Bede tells is that of King Edwin of Northumbria. Edwin's wife was a Christian—another similarity to the conversion narrative told by Gregory of Tours—and when this Christian princess, Ethelberga, married Edwin of Northumbria, she brought with her her bishop, Paulinus, and this Paulinus is recorded by Bede as going to great lengths to persuade Edwin to convert. The rest of this story has a bit of everything and certainly echoes the elements that we've seen in the account of Clovis's conversion. There is victory in battle granted by God. There are prophetic dreams and mysterious signs, letters from the pope himself urging the queen to continue to exert herself in order to persuade her husband to convert—but the final persuasive moment is offered to Edwin by, of all people, his chief pagan priest, a man by the name of Coifi. Edwin has called a council to discuss this new religion of Christianity, and Bede offers his readers and listeners speeches from the mouths of the pagan priest and other of the king's retainers that display both poetic beauty and a breathtaking misunderstanding of the nature of faith and Christian devotion in particular.

At the council, Coifi says essentially: Look, as your chief priest, no one has been more devoted to our gods than I have, and yet there are lots of other people who are wealthier and enjoy higher status than I do. You would think that if anyone would be getting rewards from our gods, I would be that person, since I've served them so devotedly. So, obviously, our gods don't have a lot of power, and if this new god might be better, let's go with him. In other words, Coifi thinks perhaps the Northumbrians should switch religions because the pagan gods have not given him much in the way of material wealth and status. As a motive for conversion, this is not the highest. But Bede knew that such logic might well be effective for some reading, or most likely listening, to this account. If they could be persuaded of the ineffective nature of the pagan gods, they might be willing to try another religion. Although their conversion to Christianity might not be as devout and fervent as one might wish, once they were brought into the fold, so the thinking went, they could gradually be re-educated into true Christians. Similar thinking led to pagan temples being re-consecrated as Christian churches. Even though they had changed religions, people could go to the same place to worship as they always had—and it led also to pagan holidays, such as the Saturnalia and the Spring Festival of the Goddess Eostre being re-christened, literally, as Christmas and Easter.

But for those of his more philosophical readers, Bede offered another argument in favor of Christianity from the mouth of one of King Edwin's retainers. According to Bede, this man said: Your majesty, when we compare the present life of man on earth with that time of which we have no knowledge, it seems to me like the swift flight of a single sparrow through the banqueting hall where you are sitting at dinner on a winter's day with your thanes and counselors, In the midst there is a comforting fire to warm the hall; outside, the storms of winter rain or snow are raging. This sparrow flies swiftly in through one door of the hall, and out through another. While he is inside, he is safe from the winter storms; but after a few moments of comfort, he vanishes from sight into the wintry world from which he came. Even so, man appears on earth for a little while; but of what went before this life or of what follows, we know nothing.

Therefore, if this new teaching has brought any more certain knowledge, it seems only right that we should follow it. This eloquent comparison of the transitory nature of human life with a swallow's flight through a great hall in winter has both logic and poetry going for it, and in narratives such as these, we see Bede's cleverness and his fervent desire to bring more people into the embrace of the church. In one conversion narrative, he has offered numerous proofs and arguments for Christianity that could potentially work on multiple levels.

But as Bede himself acknowledges, the conversion process for the Anglo-Saxons would hardly be simple or direct. Many new converts to Christianity simply added an altar to Jesus next to their pagan shrines, thinking that it couldn't hurt to pray to this god as well as to those to whom they had always prayed. Bede also tells of King Redwald of East Anglia, who converted to Christianity, but later converted back to paganism due to the influence of his wife—who, according to Bede, seduced her husband back to the dark side.

While Bede's history is full of singular moments and fascinating events, it is also—as you may have noticed—a bit narrow in focus. In the histories of both Gregory of Tours and Bede, we hear a lot about kings and a lot about the true Christian faith. We don't hear much about exactly what it was these kings converted away from. Neither Bede nor Gregory wants to give us too much information about pagan practices—and we don't really get to see much about what life was like for the ordinary person, the average Joe or man on the street. This is incredibly frustrating for scholars, because when histories focus on people at the top of the social order—royalty and the like—we have to remember that we're not getting the full story; what we're getting from these histories is a slanted view of maybe 5 percent of the population. It's the other 95 percent that we would really like to know about. But these 95 percent were usually poor in terms of both wealth and status. They were usually illiterate, and in the early period in particular, they didn't keep records, and their deeds only rarely came to the attention of those that did. Still, we can get some sense of their lives from other sources—like archaeology and the occasional mention in a chronicle. Although Bede and Gregory of Tours paint a picture of people who joyfully convert en masse to the new Christian faith, other kinds of evidence suggest to us that among the common people, what we would call pagan practices took a very long time to die out, if ever. Rather than Christian practices replacing pagan ones, what we more often sense is that there's a kind of accommodation happening, in which certain pre-Christian rituals become adapted and acceptable, and Christianity itself is practiced alongside older religious ritual. To put it simply, this would be why many people today who are Christians celebrate the resurrection of Jesus with festive activities that center around a rabbit who lays different colored eggs—the egg having long been a pagan symbol of fertility.

This kind of accommodation would have some surprising and occasionally stunning results when we consider again the ways in which the societies that developed out of the Roman Empire were hybrids of Christian, Roman, and Germanic culture. In our next lecture, we will examine some of the cultural and artistic texts and pieces of art that demonstrate this synthesis.

After the Roman Empire—Hybrid Cultures
Lecture 4

With the Christian missionaries sent from Rome came literacy. Although it seems clear that the Anglo-Saxons had a very rich oral storytelling tradition during the time before their conversion, it is only afterward that much of that lore is set down on parchment—and most likely it was written down by monks, who often seem to wish to put their own Christian interpretation on a poem that may have had no Christian elements in its original oral form.

M any scholars agree that the societies that developed out of the Roman Empire should be considered hybrids of Roman, Christian, and Germanic elements. Literature, art, and architecture in Anglo-Saxon England demonstrate how the values and ideals of these three different cultures were being combined in new and interesting ways. In support of these claims, we can read Old English poems such as "The Wanderer," "The Dream of the Rood," and *Beowulf*; study archaeological treasures found at the Sutton Hoo burial, including the famous Franks Casket; and examine illuminated manuscripts, such as the Lindisfarne Gospels.

Christianity gained a strong position within the empire in part by accommodating pre-Christian customs and traditions. Administratively, the early church imitated the bureaucratic institutions and hierarchy of the empire, dividing various realms into provinces, dioceses, and parishes. The title of the supreme leader of the

The 7th-century artifacts discovered at Sutton Hoo point to a hybrid of Christian and pagan cultures in Anglo-Saxon Britain.

church—*pontifex maximus*, or pope—was the same as that used by the head pagan priest in Rome's pre-Christian days.

The blending of Christian ideals with Roman administrative practices was further underscored at the church council of Nicaea in 325. Significantly, it was headed not by the pope but by the secular ruler of Rome, the Emperor Constantine. Bishop Ambrose of Milan, one of the early church fathers, explicitly described a connection between the kingdom of God and the physical realm of the Roman Empire on Earth, but he also believed that religious authority trumped that of secular leaders.

What happened when Christian and Roman ideals came into contact with Germanic culture? Early medieval Britain presents some of the most interesting evidence of cultural hybridization. The Franks Casket, unearthed at the Sutton Hoo archeological dig, depicts a series of scenes from both Christian and pagan traditions. The poetry of Anglo-Saxon England reflects this cultural synthesis, particularly in topic selection and treatment of religious subjects. The only original copy of the pre-Christian poem "The Wanderer" contains a later Christianizing addition, while "The Dream of the Rood" envisions Christ as a heroic (i.e., Germanic) warrior.

Bishop Ambrose of Milan, one of the early church fathers, explicitly described a connection between the kingdom of God and the physical realm of the Roman Empire on Earth.

Perhaps the most famous literary work from the Anglo-Saxon period showing this cultural fusion—and the unease and disjunction it sometimes created—is *Beowulf*, with its pagan characters and Christian narrator. The illuminated manuscripts from this period also demonstrate in their illustrations a cultural synthesis of Roman, Germanic, and Christian elements. While the earlier texts show a blending of styles with an emphasis on the British, by the 8th century the style is strongly Roman. ∎

Suggested Reading

Geary, *The Myth of Nations*.

Rosenwein, *A Short History of the Middle Ages*.

Questions to Consider

1. What specific elements of Roman, Christian, and Germanic cultures seem to have been dominant in the new hybrid cultures to which they gave rise?

2. How useful is it to look to artistic and literary production as a means of understanding a culture as a whole?

After the Roman Empire—Hybrid Cultures
Lecture 4—Transcript

Welcome back. In our last lecture we discussed how the process of Christianization occurred in the early medieval world, focusing in particular on the conversions of the Merovingian Franks and the Anglo-Saxons. We saw how the historians who wrote about such things—specifically the Venerable Bede and Gregory of Tours—had a particular agenda each wished to promote. This would be the support of the church, and as such, their narratives are full of accounts of conversions, and these are usually stories of how a king is persuaded to convert, and all of his subjects then follow suit. As told by both Bede and Gregory, these conversion narratives become set pieces—we very often have a Christian princess married to a pagan king who initiates the conversion process. Usually, she brings with her a bishop or priest, who does most of the theological heavy lifting. There are also several instances in which the Christian God seems to provide victory in battle, or major players in these narratives have prophetic dreams—and finally, their people express a desire that the king convert so that they may as well. As canned as some of these accounts might seem, the ultimate message of their histories is correct—peoples who had been pagans converted to Christianity, and the church becomes one of the most important elements in our attempts to understand the nature of the medieval world. As I have said in the past, in the Middle Ages there is no such thing as a separation of church and state—very often, they are one and the same—although debates about the nature of secular versus religious power and position would occur quite frequently and will be the subject of some of our future lectures.

For the next several lectures, our primary focus will be on Western Europe, or the culture that developed from the western half of the Roman Empire, but it will be important that we keep in mind the significance of the split of the empire into East and West, and how the two halves of the former Roman Empire were going in different directions around the 5th century. Many scholars refer to the barbarization of the West, meaning that societies in the western half of the former Roman Empire were becoming, in many respects, much like the Germanic—or so-called barbarian—cultures that had long existed beyond the natural borders of the Rhine and Danube rivers. Scholars refer also to the Hellenization of the East, meaning that what we think of today as mostly Eastern Europe and the area around Constantinople were becoming more like Greece and Greek culture. Although our focus will be on the West for the next great while, we can never forget the potential and significance of the East.

In an earlier lecture, I discussed the importance of the idea of *romanitas*, or Romanness, in the empire—especially in terms of the Crisis of the Third Century. In our last lecture we looked at the conversion process for two groups of people—the Franks and the English—and how the accounts of these conversions, by Gregory of Tours and the Venerable Bede, worked to promote a particular agenda and support the church. Today we're going to talk a bit more about Roman Christianity and its legacy for the medieval world, and we're also going to examine more closely those Germanic elements that are significant aspects of the societies that evolved out of Rome, focusing on the hybrid nature of those cultures.

As I mentioned last time, the appropriation of pagan holidays, festivals, and feasts is one way that Christianity managed to establish itself in the empire. In terms of its administrative structure, the early church also essentially copied imperial offices and subdivisions—like the idea of the province, diocese, and parish—and here we can really see how early medieval cultures are hybrid cultures. Early churches are usually built in the shape of a basilica, the form of Roman administrative buildings, and the basis of canon law was the Roman legal code. In fact, the title taken by the bishop of Rome—the highest ranking official in the church—was *pontifex maximus*—what we could call pope today—and this was the same title that had been used by the chief priest of pagan Rome. The first pope was held to be Saint Peter, who is always listed first among the disciples of Jesus. Peter and Paul were now held up as replacements for Romulus and Remus—the mythical founders of Rome who had been suckled by a she-wolf.

This linking or blending of the ideals and infrastructure of the Roman Empire with those of Christianity was further emphasized by the Emperor Constantine and the early church father Bishop Ambrose of Milan. The theology of the early church was very much a work in progress, and different groups—all calling themselves Christians—often held very different beliefs, and on some very key, central issues. The Council of Nicaea, which convened in 325, is hugely important in the early development of Christianity because it was the first attempt to work through some of these thorny issues and achieve some measure of consensus by means of an assembly of Christian leaders who were understood to function as representatives of all Christendom. Among the many issues that were debated and attempted to be resolved at this council were those of the Arian heresy—which, simply put, held that although Jesus was divine, he could not be as divine as God the Father, and which we discussed in our last lecture. The Council of Nicea also debated the proper date for the celebration of Easter—which was a complex matter for reasons I'll discuss in greater detail later—and they discussed also the nature of God the Son in relationship to God the Father.

These are all very important issues, but what I want to stress here is not the theological debate that ensued at the Council of Nicaea, but rather, the fact that it was the Emperor Constantine—and not a religious leader—who served as the head of the council. It seems fairly clear that what Constantine wished to do was make the emperor the de facto head of the church. Bishop Ambrose of Milan seemed to agree insofar as he saw a way to join the infrastructure of the empire with the mission of the church. In the year 394, Ambrose wrote:

> In the beginning of the Church, God diffused the power of the Roman Empire throughout the whole world, and brought together in his peace minds in discord and divided lands. Living under one earthly empire all men learnt to confess by faith the rule of the one omnipotent God.

At the same time, however, Ambrose wanted a clear acknowledgment that the power of the church trumped the secular, administrative power of Rome. We see this in a confrontation between the Emperor Theodosius and Ambrose. In the year 390, there was rioting in the Greek city of Thessalonica, which infuriated the emperor. He punished the population by ordering their massacre, for which action Ambrose promptly excommunicated him. The emperor was not allowed back into the fold of the church, as it were, until he had done public penance. In what seems a somewhat surprising move, Theodosius agreed—in doing so, he essentially was acknowledging that even the emperor had to answer to God. Not surprisingly, however, this reconciliation would be far from the last word on the matter.

So we can clearly see how Roman and Christian traditions and values are blending as we head towards the 6th century, but we see some of the most interesting cultural and religious intersections when we examine Germanic culture in relationship to Christianity and *romanitas*. As we've already discussed, the Germanic peoples were polytheistic, and the culture was what we would call preliterate. Although they had a rich oral tradition of storytelling that included the occasional risqué joke, they didn't have a system of writing that was commonly practiced, aside from runic inscriptions—these would be angular, easy-to-carve letters made up of individual characters that were known as runes—and these would be placed most often on important monuments, usually made out of stone. It would be wrong to think of Germanic people as all self-identifying as belonging to the same group— they would have been more likely to identify themselves in terms of tribal affiliations. For instance, last time I mentioned that the different tribes of the Angles, Saxons, Jutes, and perhaps some Frisians were involved in what we now call the Anglo- Saxon invasion of Britain—and although they spoke a similar language, there were probably some distinct linguistic variations among the various tribes.

When the Anglo-Saxons settled in England, they established several separate kingdoms, and geographical names in place still to this day give us a clue as to what group settled where. When its various peoples were at the height of their powers, there were seven distinct kingdoms in Anglo-Saxon England. Starting at the North, we have—logically enough—the kingdom of Northumbria, called so because it was where certain Angles had settled north of the River Humber. Below that, on the east coast of what is today England, was the kingdom of East Anglia—also populated by Angles and which includes modern Norfolk and Suffolk. West of East Anglia was the kingdom of Mercia, occasionally called Southumbria—indicating that it was the land of the Angles who had settled south of the River Humber. South of East Anglia was the kingdom of Essex, land of the East Saxons, which includes London. To the west and south were, as you might suppose, the kingdoms of Wessex, the West Saxons, and Sussex—the South Saxons. To the far east and sort of sandwiched in a bit between Essex and Sussex was the kingdom of Kent. On several occasions I have and will speak of Old English, or Anglo-Saxon, poetry or prose texts—but just to drive home the point that these Angles, Saxons, and Jutes who invaded Britain regarded themselves as different peoples, I should note that there are really four distinct dialects of what we call Old English. These are Northumbrian, Mercian, Kentish, and West Saxon. For reasons that will become clear later, the bulk of Old English writing survives in the West Saxon dialect—so really, when I say Old English, I'm talking about texts that are most frequently found in the West Saxon dialect.

As I mentioned last time, England provides a great example of how the cultures that emerged from the end of the Roman Empire were essentially hybrids of Roman, Christian, and Germanic elements. In our last lecture, we discussed how Roman Britain became Germanized in the 5th century, a process that seemed at first as if it would wipe out the Christian and Roman components of the culture in Britain. But relatively quickly after their conquest of Britain, the Anglo-Saxons converted to Christianity—and as we have seen already, Christian and Roman culture were deeply intertwined by the time the empire came to an end. It is from Anglo-Saxon England that we have some of the most compelling artistic and literary evidence of the way in which the elements of the Roman, Christian, and Germanic came together to create a new hybrid culture.

For example, there is an astonishing item known as the Franks Casket—so called after its best-known owner—that displays how Germanic traditions were becoming combined with Roman and Christian ones. The casket is a small box made of panels of whalebone. Scholars have determined that it was most likely made in the kingdom of Northumbria sometime in the early 8th century—and they base this on the Anglo-Saxon runic inscriptions that are carved into the casket. There are also several scenes carved into the sides and top of the casket, not all of which have been conclusively identified. We do know what is represented in most of the panels, however, and these scenes are highly suggestive and significant. For example, the panel usually identified as the front panel includes two scenes—on the left is a depiction from the Germanic legend of Wayland the Smith, an important figure in Norse mythology.

Although the documented evidence is scanty, it is safe to assume that the polytheism practiced by the Anglo-Saxons before their conversion to Christianity was directed toward a pantheon of gods very similar—if not identical to—what we think of today as the figures of Norse mythology: Thor, Odin, etc. In fact, the names for many of our days of the week come from the Norse tradition—Wednesday, for example, just means "Woden's day," Woden being another name for Odin, the most important of the Norse gods. Thursday means "Thor's day."

So, on the left front of the panel, we have a scene from Germanic, pre-Christian legend, and on the right—a depiction of the Adoration of the Magi, the moment when the three wise men, or magi, come to honor the newborn Christ child. On the left panel of the box, we have a scene depicting the mythological founders of Rome—the twins Romulus and Remus, who, according to legend, were suckled by a she-wolf. The rear panel of the casket depicts the story of the destruction of Jerusalem by Titus in the first Jewish-Roman War. The lid of the casket shows another figure from Norse legend—the archer Egil. So, on this one small object, we have represented elements from Roman mythology, Roman and Jewish history, Norse mythology, and the Christian tradition. There is no better example of the synthesis of Germanic and Mediterranean, Christian and pagan, cultural ideas.

An archaeological dig at a place known as Sutton Hoo—which is in present-day Suffolk, England—has yielded a trove of treasures that demonstrate a blending of Christian and Germanic elements. In particular, the burial of one high-ranking individual—whose coffin was an actual ship dragged up from the river, filled with grave goods and then buried—shows how pre-Christian traditions, like a ship burial with treasure to carry into the next life, might still be a fitting way to say goodbye to a Christian Anglo-Saxon leader. Within the ship were placed astounding and skillfully made pieces of art, including what has become known as the Great Gold Buckle and the Sutton Hoo Helmet—the two objects that are most likely to be on the cover of almost any edition of the poem *Beowulf*. Also found were two spoons—one with the name Saul, and the other Paul. As those who study Christianity know, Saul was the name of the apostle Paul before he converted to Christianity. The presence of these objects, along with some others, suggests that the person buried here was a convert to Christianity, with many scholars believing it to be the grave of the 7th-century King Redwaeld of East Anglia, who famously kept shrines to both Jesus and the pagan gods.

The poetry of Anglo-Saxon England similarly demonstrates how these cultural elements were blending in new ways from the 6th century on. Almost all surviving Anglo-Saxon literature, we must remember, was written down after the Anglo-Saxons converted to Christianity—with the Christian missionaries sent from Rome came literacy. Although it seems clear that the Anglo-Saxons had a very rich oral storytelling tradition during the time before their conversion, it is only afterward that much of that lore is set down on parchment—and most likely it was written down by monks, who often seem to wish to put their own Christian interpretation on a poem that may have had no Christian elements in its original oral form.

A good example of this is the poem called *The Wanderer*, about which there has been much scholarly debate. In this poem, which exists in only one version in a single manuscript known as the *Exeter Book*, it seems that a man bereft of friends and community laments his current state in a monologue. In perhaps some of the most famous lines of Anglo-Saxon poetry, he bewails his situation by crying out:

> Hwær cwon mearg? Hwær cwom mago? Hwær cwom matthumgyfa? Hwær cwom symbla gesetu? Hwær sindon seledreamas? Eale beorht bune! Eala byrnwiga! Eala theodnes thrym! Hu seo thrag gewat, genap under nihthelm, swa heo no wære.

Which means:

> Where has gone the horse? Where has gone the rider? Where has gone the treasure giver? Where have gone the seats at the feasts? Where are joys of the hall? Alas the bright cup! Alas the mailed warrior! Alas the majesty of the prince! How that time departed, grew dark under the helm of night, as if it never was.

The values expressed here are hardly obviously Christian and reflect the structure of Anglo-Saxon society in which one of the worst things to have happen would be to lose your lord, to have no one to serve. Treasure is important in Anglo-Saxon society primarily as a way of cementing bonds between a lord and his loyal retainers, or *thanes*—also sometimes called his comitatus. This group of men would feast and drink together in the great hall, which was the center of any Anglo-Saxon community. This hall is usually known as the mead hall—as mead, a kind of fermented honey, was the beverage of choice there. The comitatus would also fight together, and at the end of any battle, the thanes would be rewarded by their lord, their treasure-giver, as the poem says. Some other Anglo-Saxon poetry—notably that piece called *The Battle of Maldon*—take this devoted relationship between lord and thane to its utmost expression, suggesting that a lord's thanes would rather die in battle once their lord has been killed and would sacrifice themselves in order to "lie beside their lord on the earth." In reality, this was probably not practicable, but the ideal of sacrificing oneself for one's lord is clearly a strong one.

The speaker of *The Wanderer* laments all these earthly pleasures he has lost, but then at the end of the poem, there seems to be a comment by the narrator, the poet, or scribe, and his comment is something like: "He who finds himself in such a situation would do well to seek solace from the Father in heaven, in whom all our security resides." In other words, when these earthly pleasures are all gone—pleasures and values that remain from our pre-Christian, pagan days—one would do well to turn to Christ.

As you might have gathered from the information I've given you so far, the Anglo-Saxons were not turn the other cheek kinds of people. Although I'm over-simplifying a bit here, it would not be wrong to say that theirs was a culture in large measure dominated by war. Bravery, prowess in battle, and the ability to make a boast in the mead hall and then fulfill it on the battlefield were traits that were admired. How, then, to bring them to accept Christianity when Christ himself seems in so many ways to be the antithesis of all the Anglo- Saxons admired? One answer is that they found in the Old Testament plenty of examples of behavior they could admire—eye for an eye, tooth for a tooth: That they got. But in another example of the blending of cultural values, they also wrote a version of the crucifixion in which Christ is most definitely not a meek pacifist who humbly submits to his death. In the poem known as the *Dream of the Rood*, the crucifixion is rewritten in a decidedly Anglo-Saxon style.

The word "rood" itself is an Old English word that means "cross," and the poem is just what the modern title suggests—it is the account of a dream in which the cross on which Christ was crucified figures prominently. But what might be startling to modern readers is that in this poem, the dreamer and the cross have a conversation in which the Rood tells the story of the crucifixion. There was a strong tradition in Anglo-Saxon storytelling in which inanimate objects could speak. The Anglo-Saxon riddles are perhaps the best example, but there are others as well—notably the poem often called *The Husband's Message*, in which a piece of wood carved with runes speaks. So, in the *Dream of the Rood*—an obviously Christian poem—we have a hearkening back to a literary tradition that most likely predated the coming of Christianity to the Anglo-Saxons. We also have an unusual representation of Christ. The speaking rood describes Christ thusly: "Ongyrede hine Tha geong hæleth—thæt wæs God ælmihtig—strang and sithmod; gestah he on gealgan heanne, modig on manigra gesyhthe, tha he wolde mancyn lysan." Or in my modern English translation: "Then the young warrior stripped himself—that was God almighty—strong and resolute; he mounted the high gallows, brave in the sight of many, when he wished to ransom mankind." In this poem, Christ strips himself for battle and mounts the cross, where he bravely wages a war for the souls of mankind.

But perhaps the most famous literary intersection of the Christian with the Germanic is in the Old English epic poem called *Beowulf*, the greatest surviving literary work from the Anglo-Saxon period. The single manuscript copy of this poem is dated roughly around the year 1000 (although there's been a lot of debate about that date), but the story it contains is—in its basic plot points—much older.

Although the poem is written in English, the story is set not in England, but in the Germanic homeland—with Denmark being the site of most of the poem's action. It tells the story of a young warrior, Beowulf, who along with his comitatus—or group of loyal thanes—crosses the sea to Denmark to offer assistance to King Hrothgar, whose community is being destroyed by a solitary monster named Grendel, who regularly comes at night into the mead hall and snatches up a sleeping thane or two and usually eats them alive. As I've already mentioned, the mead hall was the center of any Anglo-Saxon community, and it was not only the place where the king and his thanes would feast, but it's also where the comitatus would essentially live. After the feast, the thanes might spend the night on the floor of the great hall. This was not just a case of people having too much to drink and simply sleeping where they fell—although that certainly might happen on occasion. This sharing of communal space with the king was a mark of honor—and eating, drinking, sleeping, and going to war together were all elements that worked toward the building of bonds of fellowship. Indeed, Grendel's attack is particularly monstrous because he chooses the mead hall, at the center of the community. There are any number of undefensible homesteads on the edges of the community, but Grendel's hatred is such that he passes up the easy pickings to go right for the most important members of the community, who are also its defenders. Beowulf arrives to deal with Grendel in part to repay a debt of his father's by helping out King Hrothgar, but he also quite plainly indicates that he has taken up this quest in order to make a name for himself—to build up a reputation. In Anglo-Saxon society, an eagerness to win fame or glory seems to have been considered a worthwhile and laudable value; one rarely sees the virtues of humility extolled in Old English literature.

But what is fascinating about *Beowulf*—in the form that we have it today—is that all the main characters are pagans, and the narrator of the poem is a Christian. The sense one gets is that the narrator admires Beowulf for his remarkable feats of prowess, but at the same time is full of sorrow because this great man is most certainly in hell—as he died without ever knowing anything about Christ. So, here we see a story that, in its earliest form, may have been a rousing tale of adventure and derring-do, but in its current form offers lessons of caution and admonition. The combination of the Germanic and the Christian has produced something completely new to both cultures.

This cultural synthesis happens not only in words written on a page, but also occurs in the decoration around those words that we find in many texts from the early medieval world. I talked a little bit about the amount of labor that went into making a manuscript—a text written by hand—in my first lecture. One thing it is important to remember is that medieval manuscripts were far more than simply texts. Illustrated manuscripts, known as illuminated manuscripts, contained pictures in the margins, and sometimes all on their own—what is called a carpet page, meaning that it has only an illustration and no text. "Illuminated" is definitely the right word to use to describe these manuscripts, as so many of the images are glorious almost explosions of light and color. One manuscript in particular, known as the Lindisfarne Gospels, is a breathtaking example of both the artistic possibilities of early manuscript illuminators and the blending of traditions that occurred after the end of the Roman Empire. These Gospels, produced in the north of Britain sometime in the late 7th century, make use of an artistic style that scholars tend to call Hiberno-Saxon, and this style is what we'd call non-representational and somewhat abstract. In other words, figures—such as people, or animals, or plants—are not rendered realistically.

There is very little use of depth, or foreshortening, or other elements of what we might think of as a realistic style. Rather, we have a more linear, flat style, and this tradition delights in rendering convoluted lines that twist, and turn, and overlap, and interlace in what has often been called the endless knot style. An example of this style is very evident on the famous Chi Rho page of the Book of Kells. But the Lindisfarne Gospels synthesize this Hiberno-Saxon non-representational style with a more realistic, figurative style more typical of the area around the Mediterranean and Rome itself. Just a century later, the blending of styles demonstrated by the Lindisfarne Gospels and other similar manuscripts is nowhere to be seen in a manuscript known as the Codex Amiatinus. Although we know this manuscript was produced in the British Isles—at the monastery of Monkwearmouth Jarrow in the 8th century to be precise—its style is decidedly Mediterranean. The distinction between this manuscript and others like the Lindisfarne Gospels and the Book of Kells serves as a reminder that although Rome seemed at times to be a world away from the far-flung reaches of the former empire, its influence still carried— especially as it became the center of power for the church in Western Europe. In our next lecture, we'll examine one of the many expressions of religious piety to be found within the church: monasticism.

Early Monasticism

Lecture 5

Benedict considered obedience to be the most important principle of monastic life. He also did not see the monastery as a retreat away from the world—the monastery was a place where the monks were, in fact, engaged in saving the world through the work of prayer.

This lecture examines one extreme form of pious expression that became fairly popular in the medieval period: monasticism. Most early medieval monastic institutions followed the Rule of Saint Benedict, which divided a monk's day between manual labor and prayer. However, this was not the only type of monasticism popular in the early Middle Ages; the Irish followed a different model, which led to some notable debates between what came to be called the Roman and Celtic churches.

Monasticism would significantly affect the culture of the Middle Ages in myriad ways. It existed in two main forms—eremitic and cenobitic monasticism. "Monastic" comes from the Greek *monos*, meaning "alone," and eremitic ("hermit") monasticism, as practiced by the Desert Fathers, was a true example of solitary living. The second and more familiar type of monasticism is cenobitic ("community") monasticism. A community of men would be known as monks, and they lived in a monastery; women who adopted this way of life were called nuns and lived in a nunnery, or convent.

There were more than a few reasons why people chose to forsake secular life and all the things—marriage, children, and the ability to own property, to name a few—that went with it. The main reason was undoubtedly because of religious faith. Although piety was expected of everyone, the self-sacrifice of monasticism provided a much more rigorous test of faith. At the same time, and somewhat contradictorily, monastic life was attractive to people who, for whatever reason, were denied the possibility of a successful secular life. Although it was possible for peasants to join an order, for the most part the ranks of monks and nuns were drawn from the upper echelons of society. Many were younger sons, widows, and widowers of wealthy families.

The Rule of Saint Benedict served as a guide to all aspects of monastic life. Saint Benedict of Nursia believed quite strongly that all monastic communities should be self-supporting, so manual labor was an important component of his rule. He also felt the monastery should be run like a family, with a father figure, called an abbot, at the head. Thus obedience was a prominent part of the rule. Although in many respects removed from secular life, Benedict viewed the monastery as very much engaged with the world, because one of the main tasks of the monks was to pray for the sins of others.

Although strict in many respects, the prologue and 73 chapters of Benedict's rule show flexibility and the recognition that exceptional situations might occur within the monastery. The rule addresses all practical facets of monastic living, like clothing, sleeping arrangements, and food allotment. Dictates concerning prayer comprise some of the most rigorous and demanding parts of the rule and reveal that medieval monks interrupted work and sleep to attend to this most important labor. The monastic day was divided by prayers called Matins, Laud, Prime, Tierce Sext, Nones, Vespers, Compline, and Nocturne, although the exact number and times of prayers might vary from monastery to monastery. To ensure that all brothers were familiar with the rule, it was also read aloud at various times throughout the year—usually during mealtimes—so that particular strictures and concerns would not be forgotten or neglected. Although Benedict envisioned a simple and somewhat spartan life for his monks, this proved difficult, as many monastic institutions became quite wealthy in spite of themselves through donations.

Although Benedict envisioned a simple and somewhat spartan life for his monks, this proved difficult, as many monastic institutions became quite wealthy in spite of themselves through donations.

Although Benedictine monasticism was the dominant form in the early medieval world, there were other types as well, particularly Irish monasticism, which developed independently of monastic traditions on the continent. Whereas continental monasticism was communal, Irish monasticism was more eremitic, with monks living in clusters of small individual huts or cells. Whereas Benedictine monasticism was hierarchical and stressed unity of belief among its various houses, Irish monasticism was much more varied and independent and was influenced by local traditions and leaders. The difference between the two Christian traditions came to a head with a fierce debate about the date of Easter. This dispute was settled in favor of the Roman Church at the Synod of Whitby in 664. Until the 12th century and the Cistercian reforms, Benedictine monasticism and Roman Christianity would dominate the religious landscape of the medieval world. ■

Suggested Reading

Jones, *Medieval Lives*.

Rosenwein, *A Short History of the Middle Ages*.

Questions to Consider

1. What types of people was monasticism able to encompass within its embrace? How open was it to people of different classes, ideals, and genders?

2. In what ways did early monasticism adhere to, depart from, or revise/enhance traditional religious practices and beliefs of the Western church?

Early Monasticism
Lecture 5—Transcript

Welcome back. In our last lecture we discussed how many of the cultures in the early medieval world displayed an intertwining of Roman, Germanic, and Christian elements in their artistic expressions. Today we're going to talk about an expression of Christian faith that would become a hugely significant element of the medieval world: monasticism.

I'm sure most of us today have some idea of what "monastic" means—this term can refer to the way of life of monks or nuns: men and women who have opted to devote their lives to prayer and service to God, vowing in most cases to live a life of poverty, obedience, and chastity in a communal setting, either a monastery—or, in the case of nuns, an abbey or convent, or sometimes the word "nunnery" is used. Today I'm going to talk about the origins and early development of monasticism in the European West, and we're going to explore what the daily life of a monk or a nun might have been like.

The word "monk" comes from the Greek *monos*, meaning alone, and we see two forms of early monasticism. The first is what we might call eremitical monasticism, which comes from the greek word for desert, *eremos*, and from which the modern English word "hermit" is derived, and this is a type of monasticism that is truly about singular aloneness. The tradition here goes back to those first spiritual athletes for God—a group of men often called the Desert Fathers, people like Simeon the Stylite who lived on top of a pillar for 47 years and occupied his time with doing things like bowing continuously as a form of prayer.

The second form of monasticism is called cenobitic monasticism and comes from the Greek word meaning "common," or "community." It is this type of monasticism that we'll be focusing on today. As you might suppose, cenobism is characterized by communal living—where the community prays, works, and lives together. I'm often asked by students how this type of lifestyle became popular and why so many people joined monastic orders in the Middle Ages. There are a couple of answers to this question. The first is that there were many devout believers in Christianity who wanted more of a challenge for their faith. Once Christianity became the dominant religion of the Roman Empire and then of the societies that developed out of the empire, some found the practice of their faith too easy. They longed for a spiritual challenge, and monasticism was it. I should note here that in early medieval Europe, monks were people who renounced everything about their former lives, including property and marriage. At this time, bishops and parish priests could still own property and have families. The injunction against priests marrying would come some time later. So, monasticism was a form of piety above even that of priests or bishops, in many instances.

The second answer as to why so many people joined monasteries and convents in the medieval world would seem, in some ways, to contradict my first answer, and that's because monasteries and convents were places where the younger sons or daughters of noble families, or widowed queens, for example, might go to live. There, they could be assured of care and comfort. Although the monastery was supposed to be a place where, ideally, all connections and status that a person had enjoyed in the outside world were forgotten, and everyone within the monastic community were equals, in practice this was not often the case. Although there were some people of the peasant class who became monks or nuns—for the most part, the members of the monastic community were members of the noble classes. We have several scandalized reports from visitors to various monastic institutions who reported that the denizens of this religious community carried on as if they were still out in the secular world—feasting, socializing, and behaving in ways generally deemed unbecoming to a member of a religious order. Over the decades and centuries, various reforms would be brought to bear on monastic communities. In several instances, new orders were founded in response to perception that existing orders had fallen into sin and away from the Opus Dei, the work of God, that they were supposed to be performing.

Although the existence of Christian monasteries and religious hermits is recorded in the 3rd century or even earlier, the man who should be considered the father of Western monasticism is a man called Benedict of Nursia. Saint Benedict was born in the late 5th century, and while a young man studying in Rome, he decided to forego his education, and he retreated to the countryside of Campagna, where he began to live as a religious hermit. Benedict's reputation for holiness spread, and he was soon invited to become head of a monastic community. He accepted this offer, but his zeal for reform soon upset the monks he was overseeing, and they reportedly tried to poison him. He left this monastery and founded a new monastery at a place called Monte Cassino. He also founded other monasteries and a convent for his sister, Scholastica.

These houses were governed by a rule, the Rule of Saint Benedict—or, as many refer to it, the RSB. Almost everything we know of Benedict's life comes from a text known as the *Dialogues of Pope Gregory the Great*, and Gregory takes care to point out that Benedict was one of many holy men who lived in Italy in the 5th and 6th centuries, but what distinguished him from others was that he had written directions for organizing monastic life. His rule is a remarkable piece that successfully synthesizes the asceticism that dominated the Eastern monastic tradition, or the more eremitical tradition, with the Roman virtues of stability, order, and moderation. Benedict laid out his monastery like a roman villa, and he intended for all monastic communities to be self-sustaining—thus, manual labor was an important component of the life in his community. To Benedict's mind, the monastery should be run by the abbot, or head of the community, as a kind of paternal autocracy. The abbot was supposed to consult elders of the community for advice, but ultimately all decisions affecting the community were his. It is not surprising, then, that Benedict considered obedience to be the most important principle of monastic life.

He also did not see the monastery as a retreat away from the world—the monastery was a place where the monks were, in fact, engaged in saving the world through the work of prayer. It was commonly thought that after death, many people—because of various sins they had committed—would necessarily spend some time in purgatory. People still living on earth, however, could lessen that time in purgatory by praying for the soul of the recently departed—and the more people praying, the quicker the time in purgatory would pass. In fact, a little later in the medieval period we find royals and nobles founding monasteries with the idea that doing so would mean that the monks or nuns of said institution would certainly pray for them—and thus, their sins would be expiated more quickly. For example, William the Conqueror, whom we'll discuss at length in a later lecture, founded religious houses at the site of the Battle of Hastings, in Essex, and in Yorkshire. This may be, in no small measure, due to the fact that after the Battle of Hastings, the church told the men who fought there that they needed to do 120 days of penance for each man killed. Founding religious houses and donating land and money to other religious houses already in existence was sort of a shortcut to the cleansing of the soul.

But to return to Saint Benedict and his rule—the rule itself consists of 73 chapters plus a prologue. The first seven chapters are essentially a treatise on the ascetic life, and the rest of the rule provides practical guidelines for the daily life of the monastery. He provides details on which prayers should be said when, how the day should be divided between work and prayer, what kind of man the abbot should be, and he even addresses sleeping arrangements. Here he says: "Let each one sleep in a separate bed … if possible let all sleep in one place; but if the number does not allow this, let them take their rest by tens and twenties with the seniors who have charge of them." He goes on to add that a candle should be kept burning in the dormitory at all times, and that the monks should sleep in their habits—so that upon arising they are immediately ready to go to their prayers or work without delay. He gives instruction for the preparation of food as well—stating that for the main meal of the day, there should be two different cooked dishes from which the monks can eat, that fruit and vegetables should be added if available, and that each monk should also be allotted a pound of bread per day. At the same time, Benedict's rule provides for some flexibility, as he notes that the abbot may increase the allotted food if he feels the labor of the monks has been particularly heavy that day. Benedict also makes exceptions for those monks who are ill or aged.

Benedict indicates that all monks except those who are ill should abstain from eating meat, and he also urges moderation when it comes to drink—limiting the amount of wine each monk shall drink each day. He lists what kinds of clothing each monk should have, what bedding should consist of—again, allowing the abbot to make exceptions due to weather. He quite specifically forbids the owning of any personal property, going so far as to suggest that a monk's bed should be regularly inspected to ensure that he is not keeping some piece of personal property hidden.

Benedict's rule envisioned monastic life as revolving around prayer and manual labor, and one thing that you could be sure of if you became a Benedictine monk was that you were unlikely to ever get a good night's sleep again. The prayer schedule was very rigorous, and although the specific prayer times varied by monastery, the first prayer of the day—known as Matins—usually occurred in what was essentially the middle of the night, sometime between 2 AM and 4 AM. The monks' dormitory, in fact, was often directly above the chapel in many monasteries so that the brothers could rise and go to prayer quite quickly and easily. After Matins, most of the monks would go back to sleep for a little bit until the next prayer service—known as Lauds, which usually occurred at first light. Then came Prime sometime around mid-morning, then Tierce, Sext, and Nones—eventually these prayer services were combined into one, as you can imagine that any labor the monks were engaged in was being continually interrupted—and plowing, gardening, etc., needed to be accomplished. The prayer service known as Vespers usually occurred at dusk. Compline took place at sundown, and then came Nocturne, and after that—Vigils. So that's about 10 occasions for prayer throughout the day.

Making all of this run smoothly were the various monastic officials who oversaw the day-to-day running of the monastery. At the head of this hierarchy was the abbot—or in the case of a convent, an abbess. The prior was second in command after the abbot. There might be a few men who occupied the office of dean of the order. The person who held this office made sure that the monks attended all the services they were supposed to, and these men also had the task of making sure everyone stayed awake during services when one might be prone to nap—such as during the services of Matins or Lauds. This was usually effected by shining a lantern on the sleeping brother and/or poking him with a staff reserved for just this purpose.

There were several other offices, including that of cellarer, who was in charge of food and drink; and the hostillar, who maintained the guest house—an important role because Benedict had stressed in his rule that the monastery should be a place of welcome and refuge for all travelers. He said in his rule: "Let all guests who come to the monastery be entertained like Christ Himself, because he will say 'I was a stranger and you took me in.'"

Benedict made the frequent re-reading of his rule within the monastery one of its requirements—and it, along with other appropriate spiritual material, was to be read aloud in the refectory during mealtimes. The monks were to listen in silence—indeed, Benedict decreed that they should spend most of their time in silence, speaking only when absolutely necessary. As a result, a rather complex sign language eventually developed in many monasteries, which allowed monks to do everything from asking someone to pass the salt to indicating that they needed a new pair of socks.

Although Benedict had envisioned a somewhat simple and Spartan life for monks following his rule, plenty of evidence suggests that the ideal of pious asceticism was not always followed. Indeed, recent archaeological discoveries suggest that at some monasteries, the daily food intake of many monks exceeded 6,000 calories, and examination of the bones of some monks that have been excavated reveal evidence of extreme obesity. Obviously, as time went on many Benedictine monasteries were being less than exact when it came to following the Rule of Saint Benedict, and as we'll see in a later lecture, this led to the development of new orders like the Cistercians, Domenicans, Franciscans, and others.

Part of the problem for the Benedictines and for other orders lay in the fact that although they embraced the ideal of poverty, in practice it was very difficult for them to remain poor. When property or money was given to the church, it tended to stay with the church—and remember, offerings to the church were common, and expected, and sometimes quite large, as in the case of William the Conqueror. Since monks did not marry, could not legally own anything, and officially had no heirs, none of the gifts given to a monastery ever left it as the inheritance of an eldest son or the dowry of a daughter. Add to this the frugality—at least, in theory—of those living the monkish life, and you can see how quickly wealth might accumulate.

In the early Middle Ages, Benedictine monasticism was the dominant mode of cloistered life, but there were other forms. The most important of these is Irish monasticism. What we have to remember here is that Ireland had never been a part of the Roman Empire, so the structure of its society had never had much in the way of *romanitas* about it. Early Ireland was agrarian. It was a tribal society, where kin relationships structured everything, and there was nothing approaching a major city like those that had existed in the empire. Ireland was supposedly and quite famously converted to Christianity by Saint Patrick, but he remains a figure lost in legend, and we know very little about him. There are a lot of stories about Patrick. You might have heard that he drove the snakes out of Ireland, that he ran his sister over with a chariot three times because she was unchaste, and that he explained the Holy Trinity by means of a three-leafed shamrock as an example. None of these stories, as far as we can tell, are true. What we do know for certain is that Patrick lived in the 5th century and came from a well-established Romano- British Christian family. At some point in his life, he was kidnapped by Irish pirates and forced into a life of slavery in Ireland. He escaped, made it home, but later said he was called in a vision to go back to Ireland and spread the message of Jesus Christ—and so he returned. He says he converted thousands, although we can't be sure of that, but we can be fairly certain that he established churches and monasteries.

Irish monasticism, however, was different from Roman or Benedictine monasticism. The Irish way of life was much more conducive to eremitical, rather than cenobitic or communal, monasticism. Whereas bishops were the most important religious leaders on the Continent—meaning an abbot of a monastery would regard himself as being subject to a bishop's orders—in Ireland, by contrast, it was the abbots themselves who were most important, and this was in part because the abbots maintained close relationships with secular tribal leaders. The layout of Irish monasteries was also significantly different than those of Benedictine monasteries. Irish monasteries tended to be like great walled cities. Within the city walls, each monk had his own individual cell or hut. They might come together for meals and prayer, but the unity of action that the Rule of Saint Benedict made essentially compulsory was missing from Irish monasticism. Whereas Roman monasticism was very hierarchical and stressed a unity among religious houses, Irish monasticism was more decentralized and individualistic. This individualist spirit produced some of the most important and interesting figures and centers of learning to be found in early Christianity. Indeed, if it were not for Irish monasteries and their dedication to copying and preserving manuscripts, as well as the lucky happenstance that they were on the far edge of the European world and so not subject to as much in the way of invasion or war as their fellows on the Continent, many of the most important texts in the Western tradition would be lost for all time—as Thomas Cahill has persuasively argued in his book, *How the Irish Saved Civilization.*

One of the Irish religious houses discussed in Cahill's book is the monastery of Iona, founded by Saint Columba. Columba was a prince of one of Ireland's ruling clans, and after he founded his monastery on the island of Iona—sometime around the year 565—he and his monks used that site as a jumping-off point to launch missionary expeditions to the Anglo-Saxons, who had settled in northern Britain. Almost a century later, it would be monks from Iona who would found the famous monastery of Lindisfarne on a tidal island off the northeast coast of Britain. If you remember from one of our previous lectures, Augustine of Canterbury had been sent from Rome on a similar mission in 597 at the express command of Pope Gregory the Great. So what happens is that we have two monastic traditions in early medieval England: We have the Celtic Church, and we have the Roman Church. While these two churches obviously shared much in the way of doctrine, rituals, and theology, there were some significant and problematic differences. One of the most significant issues had to do with the date of Easter.

At first this might seem a surprising issue for debate, but the Easter debate of the 7th century was so significant that a special synod was called to try and resolve it. Here's the problem: As many people are aware, in a given year Easter can occur anytime from March 22 to April 25. This is because the date of Easter is calculated based on a lunar calendar. At the Council of Nicea in 325, it was decided that Easter should fall on the first Sunday after the first full moon on or occurring after the vernal equinox. Everybody got that? The basic problem was trying to fit a lunar calendar of months totaling 29 and a half days each into a calendar year of 365 days, and that was based on the changing of the seasons.

This problem was extremely serious because Easter, the day of Christ's resurrection, was considered the most important day of the year, and the celebration of any number of other religious feasts was dependent upon the date of Easter. While in modern times Christmas—the celebration of the birth of Christ—is viewed by many as the major holiday, in the Middle Ages Easter was the really important date. Still, Christmas was considered such an important day that many people took it for granted that December

25 should mark the start of a new year. But if one counted backward nine months to March 25, one came to the Feast of the Annunciation, otherwise known as Lady Day, which marked the first moment of Christ's presence on earth, when he descended into the womb of the Virgin Mary. Well beyond the Middle Ages, many people took March 25 as the first day of the new year. As you can imagine, this leads to some confusion, especially for scholars who study the period. For example, when a medieval chronicle says that something occurred in 1185, if that event occurred in January, February, or early March, that usually—but not always—means that it actually occurred in 1186 by our modern reckoning.

The dating of Easter posed such a thorny problem for early medieval people that some of the earliest manuscripts we have are texts called Easter Tables, in which some monk has laboriously calculated on which date Easter would fall for a large number of years. In many cases, these texts looked ahead more than a century, and they were cherished and consulted often by the monasteries and churches who possessed them. In fact, some early chronicles probably started life as Easter Tables. In the margins, alongside the entry for each year as it passed, someone might make a comment like: "This was the year the plague came," or "This was the year of the great famine," or "In this year, the danes laid waste to the countryside."

To put it simply, the Celtic Church tended to calculate Easter one way, while the Roman Church calculated it another. This was a problem—especially in royal houses where the king and queen, as was often the case, came from different communities and traditions. It was primarily a problem in England, where we tend to find both Celtic and Roman traditions side by side, although there were some successful Irish missions to the Continent— most notably that of the Irish monk Columbanus, who has a similar name to Saint Columba, but who is a different man altogether. After establishing a monastery in Bangor, Wales, Columbanus launched a successful mission to Burgundy—in what is today modern France—sometime in the late 6th and early 7th centuries, and from there he crossed the Alps and moved into Italy, bringing Celtic monasticism with him wherever he went.

Our friend the Venerable Bede discusses the conflict between the Celtic and Roman churches at some length in his *Ecclesiastical History*; being

English, it was obviously of some interest to him. He notes that "such was the confusion in those days [here he means the 7th century] that Easter was sometimes kept twice in one year, so that when the king had ended Lent and was keeping Easter, the queen and her attendants were still fasting and keeping Palm Sunday." King Oswy of Northumbria wanted the matter settled once and for all—and in 664, he called for an ecclesiastical synod at the monastery of Whitby. What is interesting about this is that although high-ranking ecclesiastical representatives of both the Roman and Celtic churches were present and offered their arguments, it was Oswy who called the synod, and he was the one who pronounced the final judgment. Also of interest is that the monastery of Whitby was what is called a double monastery— meaning that it included a monastery of monks and a convent of nuns—and in charge of all of this was a woman, the Abbess Hild. She was a grand-niece of King Edwin of Northumbria, demonstrating the point I made earlier about the presence of nobles in these religious houses, and she figures prominently in Bede's *Ecclesiastical History*—not only in his discussion of the Synod of Whitby, but also in one of his miracle stories. This is the miracle of a man named Cædmon, a low-ranking man in charge of taking care of the cattle on a large estate, who is—in a miraculous visitation by an angel—given the gift of composing religious verse. After his encounter with the angel, he is brought before the Abbess Hild, who pronounces his poetic gift as sent from God, and he is then brought into the fold of the monastery, where he lives out his life in great holiness. His example underscores both the fact that it was possible for peasants to become monks, and also that it might be unusual for such a thing to happen.

The result of the Synod of Whitby was that King Oswy decided in favor of Rome, and by his decree those churches and monasteries following the Celtic tradition were brought into the ecclesiastical fold. Although Hild had favored the Celtic tradition, she obeyed King Oswy's decree.

Medieval monasteries were, in many respects, kingdoms unto themselves, ruled over by an abbot—often producing their food, clothing, and other necessities; engaging in trade, both with nearby towns and locales far distant. But at the same time, the monastic life was far removed—in most respects—from the secular world beyond its walls, and that world could be dangerous and violent, as local lords jockeyed with one another for power and lands. One of the most important dynasties to emerge from the violence of the early medieval period was that of the Merovingians, a people whose kingdom would eventually evolve into Francia—arguably the single most important political entity ever to exist in the medieval world, and that will be the subject of our next lecture.

From Merovingian Gaul to Carolingian France
Lecture 6

Perhaps more than any other culture that rose out of the remains of the Roman Empire, Frankish society managed to preserve the best of what the empire had had in place in terms of government and infrastructure, while also adapting and innovating. ... The Franks were the catalysts of Western culture.

In the 8th century, the Merovingian Franks controlled most of what is modern-day France, Belgium, Luxembourg, the Netherlands, and parts of Germany. Their culture would serve as a model for European social and political organization for most of the next 1,000 years. Merovingian society was structured along two axes: the comitatus, or band of loyal warriors, and the family. While family was very important in Frankish society, the Merovingians practiced polygamy, coupled with inheritance rules that equally divided wealth among all heirs, which meant that power often quickly dissipated. The comitatus and the family often clashed violently, as the example of King Clovis and his four sons demonstrates.

Radegund's experience helps to illuminate the somewhat contradictory position of women in Germanic society.

The Merovingians sought to conquer the neighboring Thuringians. Examining the details of this episode can help us better understand this society and societies that emerged from it. The Thuringians were a loose confederation of tribes who lived along the Czech border in what is now Germany. In the early 6th century, they broke a truce with the Merovingians when a Thuringian leader murdered several Frankish women and children. In 531, the Merovingians retaliated, all but wiping out the Thuringians. Two Thuringian survivors were six-year-old Princess Radegund and her brother. The Frankish leader Clothar claimed Radegund as one of his wives as a means of cementing his claim to Thuringian territory.

Radegund's experience helps to illuminate the somewhat contradictory position of women in Germanic society. Although critically important as a means of forging peace between peoples (through marriage) and responsible for the running of the household and education of the children, Germanic women were often treated as objects to be traded or exchanged. A poem entitled "The Thuringian War," most likely composed by Radegund herself, points up these contradictory aspects of the life of a woman in this society and suggests a high level of education for its author. In 550, Clothar killed Radegund's brother, which was the last straw for this Frankish queen. She fled to her villa at Saix, which was her own personal property through the Germanic custom of *morgengabe*, or "morning gift," traditionally bestowed on a bride the morning after a marriage was consummated. She browbeat the local bishop into consecrating her as a nun, something that was quite dangerous, given that Clothar was still alive. She took control of the abbey at Poitiers, acting as both abbess and queen, procuring for the abbey several important religious relics.

Pepin the Short, the first Carolingian king of the Franks, secured his throne through military victory and an alliance with the pope.

Around 600, the power of the Merovingians started to wane, and a new dynasty, the Carolingians, rose up to replace them. Because of the practice of dividing property equally among all sons, the Merovingian world was divided into several small kingdoms, none with any significant power. One of the most powerful positions in the Frankish bureaucracy was the office of mayor of the palace, the right-hand man to the Frankish king. Starting in 687, a mayor of the palace named Pepin of Heristal and his son, Charles Martel (known as The Hammer), were able to lead their personal comites to victories over neighboring communities, establishing a significant power base in the Frankish world. Charles Martel cleverly worked with the church, coming to Pope Gregory III's assistance when the papal territories were threatened by the Lombards. In 751, Pope Zacharius declared that whoever exercised the power of a king should also occupy the throne. This led directly to the deposition of the last Merovingian king and the crowning of Charles's son Pepin the Short. In return for this support, the Pepin ceded the lands that have become known as the Papal States to the church.

This new dynasty of Frankish rulers became known as the Carolingian dynasty, a nod to its greatest ruler, Charles the Great, or more commonly, Charlemagne. Charlemagne was said to cut an impressive figure, standing seven feet tall. An examination of his bones reveals that this is only a slight exaggeration; he seems to have stood 6'7"—truly remarkable in the medieval period. Charlemagne set out to make his mark on the medieval world in four distinct areas: First and foremost, he was a conqueror. Every year, his army was on the move, and he rarely suffered defeat. Secondly, he set in place the apparatus of managing a large state, blending a central cultural idea of Frankishness with a fair degree of local autonomy. He was a huge supporter of the church, commissioning model sermons that could be disseminated throughout the kingdom and instituting the practice of tithing. Finally, he was a patron of the arts. ■

Suggested Reading

Collins, *Charlemagne*.

McKitterick, *Carolingian Culture*.

Questions to Consider

1. What does Radegund's particular situation suggest about the status of women in Merovingian society? How does her position seem to differ (or not) from women in other early medieval communities?

2. Which of Charlemagne's achievements seems most deserving of the fame and reputation he enjoys to this day? Or is it the combination of campaigns and activities that is most significant, as opposed to any single area of achievement?

From Merovingian Gaul to Carolingian France
Lecture 6—Transcript

Welcome back. In our last lecture we discussed the development of the monastic life in early medieval Europe, and how monasticism and its ideals had a far-reaching impact throughout the medieval world. Vowing to live a life of chastity, poverty, and prayer, monks and nuns worked to perfect their own souls and to save those of their fellow Christians living in the secular world by engaging in acts of prayer, devotion, and labor. Given the violence to be found in the world beyond the cloister, it is not surprising that many people turned to the monastic life as a refuge. Such is the case with one of the people we'll be discussing today—the Thuringian Princess Radegund, who sought sanctuary in a convent in order to escape her husband, one of the more ruthless leaders of a Frankish people known as the Merovingians.

The most important society to emerge in the early medieval world of Western Europe was that of the Franks, a people that we met briefly in an earlier lecture when we discussed Gregory of Tours's account of the conversion of King Clovis. Today we will visit Francia, the most dominant of the cultures to arise from the former Roman Empire and examine the dynasty that shaped its origins, the Merovingians.

If we look at a map of Europe in the 8th century, we'd see Anglo- Saxon England to the west—and we'd see that, although dominant, the Anglo-Saxons had not attained clear control of the British Isles, where a strong Celtic presence remained, particularly in the west and north of Britain and in what is today Ireland. In the southeast of the European Continent, we'd see that what is today Italy was subdivided into several very small states. Modern Spain was under mostly Islamic rule, something we'll spend considerable time discussing in a later lecture. Dwarfing all of these societies was the kingdom of Francia, which controlled what are the countries of modern-day France, Belgium, Luxembourg, the Netherlands, and a great portion of Germany. Perhaps more than any other culture that rose out of the remains of the Roman Empire, Frankish society managed to preserve the best of what the empire had had in place in terms of government and infrastructure, while also adapting and innovating. I do not think it is overstating matters to say that the Franks were the catalysts of Western culture. Their society became the model for European social and political organization for over 1,000 years.

In order to understand how this came to be, we need to begin at the beginning—and the beginning for the Franks is with the rise to power of the Merovingians, one of those barbarian peoples whose origins lie outside the bounds of the Roman Empire, in Germania. The Merovingians have also been called the long-haired kings. You see, they believed that much of their power lay in their uncut hair, and in this respect they were quite different from the Romans, who favored shorter hair styles and shaven faces.

The organization of Frankish politics and society occurred along two axes— the military band, also called the comitatus, which is the same basic idea of loyal retainership that we've already encountered in our discussion of the Anglo-Saxons—and the family. Family could be quite a complicated issue— as the Merovingians were polygamous, and many kings had more than one wife, and some had both wives and concubines. The first and most important of the Merovingians is Clovis, a name that would eventually evolve into the French name Louis, and this Clovis lived in the late 5th/early 6th century, and his conversion to Christianity—significantly rewritten by Gregory of Tours in his history, which we discussed in our third lecture—played such an important role in the Christianization of medieval Europe.

The Merovingians were quite accomplished and brutal warriors, and it is through warfare that they gained power. A good leader in the Frankish tradition rewarded his loyal retinue with land and treasure—again, something we've already seen in our discussion of Anglo-Saxon England. So, in contrast with the tradition of the Roman Empire, where patriotism and loyalty to the State was arguably the most important bond that united people, Merovingian society was held together primarily by bonds of personal loyalty—although the early Merovingian leaders made clever use of Roman administrative apparatuses, like appointing a series of *comes* (or counts) and delegating to them local administrative tasks, like tax collecting. This was very like the Roman system, but in this case, the taxes went straight to the king and not to the State.

The major problem for the Merovingians, however, was that their system of succession tended to dilute the power of the dynasty. All property was divided equally among any and all surviving sons. Clovis had four surviving sons, and the partition of land was made without considering ethnic, geographic, or administrative divisions. The only real matter of concern was that the portions be of equal value. The boundaries of each region were poorly defined, and their capitals were all centered in the area known as the Paris Basin. The eldest brother, Theodoric, had Reims as his base. Clodomir used Orleans. Childebert took Paris as his base of operations, and Clothar claimed Soissons as his capital. Although this sort of inheritance system obviously looked likely to provoke violent dynastic struggles and civil war, the Merovingians in the early going tended to enjoy a strange kind of luck— whereby all the brothers might die without heirs, so that the lands would be reconsolidated into one Frankish kingdom. This is what happened in the case of Clovis's sons—the youngest, Clothar, survived all his brothers, and so the partitions of the kingdom were reconsolidated. Unfortunately or fortunately, depending on your point of view, Clothar had four sons, and upon his death in 561, the kingdom was once again divided up.

In addition to the in-fighting, the Merovingians were always looking to extend their territory—as I said, they were warriors—and I'd like to focus for a moment on one of Clothar's campaigns against a people known as the Thuringians, because this rather lengthy episode allows us a way of getting a sense of many aspects of the world of early medieval Frankish society— particularly in terms of the status of women and the conventions of war. The Frankish/Thuringian War will also rather indirectly lead us to one of the oddest moments in the monastic tradition and allow us to deepen our understanding of that way of life, which was the subject of our last lecture.

The Thuringians were a loose confederation of tribes that lived in what is modern-day Germany along the border with the Czech Republic. They were often at war with the Merovingians, who sought to expand their territories in the 6th century. There had been a truce between the Franks and the Thuringians, but the Thuringian leader broke it in a most spectacular way— murdering several Frankish women and children. In response, the Franks, in 531, sought revenge. This attack was led by Clothar, the youngest son of Clovis. According to Gregory of Tours, the slaughter was so immense that the river was choked with the bodies of the Franks, and the Franks used the bodies of their fallen comrades as a bridge by which they could cross the river and continue their attack on the Thuringians. Clothar and his brothers killed the entire Thuringian ruling family, except for 6-year-old princess Radegund and her brother, whom they took as war booty—something that was quite a common practice. Clothar's intent was to raise Radegund and then marry her when she came of age, something that would be seen as cementing his claims to former Thuringian territory.

Radegund and her brother had already had a bit of a difficult time, in that their father, King Bertechar, had been murdered by his brother, Hermanfred. After killing his brother, Hermanfred had then taken his niece and nephew into his own household to raise. So we can clearly get a sense of the brutality of this world and also of the contradictory nature of the position of women like Radegund. Women are extremely important in the way that they represent their families—and thus, can serve to cement bonds between tribes or claims over territory. Something very similar occurs in Anglo-Saxon society, which we should remember is also a Germanic culture—so the fact that we find similar practices and institutions, like the comitatus, in both societies shouldn't be surprising. The Anglo-Saxons actually had a word for this practice of marrying a woman of one tribe into another in order to effect a truce or consolidate claims to territory—the word is *freothewebbe*, which means "peace weaving"—and although the establishment of peace is its intent, as we can see from Radegund's examples and the experiences of others, peace was rarely the ultimate result.

We see a very moving account of Radegund's experience in a poem called *The Thuringian War*, which is told from Radegund's point of view. Many scholars believe it was actually composed by her. This poem is interesting not only for its eloquent mourning of what has been lost and the family and friends that were killed, but also in its numerous allusions to the classical world. She compares the destruction of Thuringia with that of Troy, for example, and at other moments alludes to Alexander the Great and the world of Byzantium, far to the east, where some of her relatives had fled to safety. The poem thus demonstrates a certain level of worldliness and education on her part, and it suggests also that the Thuringians were still polytheistic pagans. The poem reads in part:

Not Troy alone must mourn her ruins/The thuringian land suffered equal slaughter. The matron was rapt away, with streaming hair, bound fast, without even a sad farewell to the household gods. ... A wife's naked feet trod in her husband's blood, and the tender sister stepped over the fallen brother. ... Anguish is private and public both to me. Fate was kind to those whom the enemy struck down. I, the sole survivor, must weep for them all.

When she took up residence in Clothar's household, Radegund was converted to Christianity—but although a Christian in name, Clothar rarely behaved as one, and I think by almost anyone's standards, he could be considered—at the very least—a colossal jerk. He had several wives, Radegund being just one of many—and when one of his brothers died, he married the widow and then put all of her children to death, so that there would be no one to claim that brother's portion of the Frankish kingdom and those lands would then revert to him. He was ruthless and cruel. For example, in 560 he put his own son, Chram, to death along with Chram's entire family because his son had rebelled against the father.

In 550, Clothar killed Radegund's only surviving brother, which—as you might imagine—was really the last straw for her. Radegund had converted to Christianity at an early age and—according to contemporary chroniclers—had long expressed a desire to live a religious life. After the murder of her brother, Radegund fled to her villa at Saix, which was her own property because of the Frankish custom of the *morgengabe*. This term, morgengabe, means literally "morning gift," and this refers to the practice of bestowing on one's wife a gift of property on the morning after the consummation of a marriage. This property was fully and legally hers to do with as she saw fit. Radegund's morgengabe had been the villa at Saix, and she retired there after the murder of her brother. Although we have evidence that in 558 Clothar made overtures to try and win her back, actions that seem to have caused her to flee from Saix to Poitiers, Radegund herself seems to suggest that Clothar came to accept her desire to live a religious life. It seems that on his deathbed, Clothar may have made arrangements to endow the convent at Poitiers, where Radegund would live out her life. Clothar was Clothar to the end, however, and it is also reported that as he lay dying, wracked by fever, he demanded—and no one's sure here if this question was asked in outrage or admiration—"What manner of God would bring great rulers to their deaths in such a fashion?"

In Radegund, then, we can see the contradictory nature of the position of Frankish queens, in that many enjoyed great power and were comfortable wielding it—while in many respects these same women were, at least at times, helpless pawns in the conflicts between men. Although so much of what happened to Radegund was beyond her control, she also demonstrated an impressive will and determination—taking charge of her own destiny. When she fled from Clothar, she apparently browbeat the local bishop into consecrating her as a nun, which was a dangerous thing to do while her husband was still alive. Although she did become a nun and an abbess, she never really relinquished her position as queen—she acted, effectively, as queen of the convent and used her connections for things like obtaining a relic of the True Cross. Having this relic in its position enhanced the status of the abbey at Poitiers, ensuring that pilgrims were certain to travel there, and that donations to the community would increase. She also maintained some semblance of order and normalcy when the abbey at Poitiers was burned and looted as sort of collateral damage during some Merovingian dynastic infighting. Far from renouncing the outside world, Radegund worked hard at maintaining relationships with important people outside the monastery in order to protect her community of sisters.

Nothing makes the power of Radegund's personality clearer than the events that occurred at her abbey after her death. These events make plain that a great deal of strife was kept in check by Radegund's force of will and commanding way of running the abbey. An internal dispute arose over how the abbey was being run, and two women who were members of the Merovingian royal family actually led a revolt against the new abbess who had taken up Radegund's position. Around 40 nuns or so joined the revolt and ended up leaving the convent. Some of them tried to reform and reestablish their community at the Church of Saint Hilary, but Gregory of Tours ordered them to disperse because they had no way to sufficiently provide for themselves through the winter. Some of the nuns got pregnant. Some renounced their vows and married, and some others hired mercenaries who attempted to break into their old convent and kidnap the abbess. It is an episode, as one of my students once remarked, that is essentially nuns gone wild.

So by focusing on the experiences of Radegund, we get a bit of a feel for the nature of the Merovingian world. That world began to change significantly around the year 600. At this time, the ruling family of the Franks was increasingly land poor—a result of bestowing large parcels of land on retainers to ensure their loyalty, and also the practice of dividing land equally among all surviving sons. By 600, we have several very small kingdoms—the most important of which were Austrasia, Neustria, and Burgundy. We also have a landed aristocracy that has more wealth and power than the kings themselves. The Merovingian star begins to wane, and in its place we have a new dynasty—the Carolingians.

The Carolingians come to power through the Frankish office known as the mayor of the palace. Although this position was originally subservient to the position of king, over time the Mayor of the Palace became the real power in Frankish government, while the king was increasingly ineffectual, weak, and more of a figurehead. The Carolingians were wealthy in terms of land holdings, and they practiced the Germanic tradition of building a loyal comitatus by generously gifting wealth, and land, and other goods to several warriors—effectively creating their own army. They had managed to make the position of Mayor of the Palace hereditary—so their power was passed down generation to generation, and thus was more easily increased.

In 687, a Mayor of the Palace named Pepin of Heristal managed to lead his *comitatus* to victory against the Neustrians, and he was also able to dominate Burgundy—meaning that for the first time, essentially, since Clovis, there is one Frankish leader dominating major territory. Pepin's son was Charles Martel, also known as the Hammer. He continued his father's consolidation of power and expansion of territory, and he was successful for four reasons. The first was his personality. He was as ruthless and ambitious as any Frankish leader we have met thus far. He knew what he wanted, and he would stop at almost nothing to get it. The second factor in his success was the fact that he made sure he had no rivals—killing potential challengers to his power within his own and other aristocratic families. Third, he was a skilled soldier—and most significantly, he managed to turn the cavalry into a highly effective military unit that was able to dominate the units of foot soldiers. Finally and perhaps most importantly, he worked with the church. I cannot stress enough how much the support of the papacy meant to his success. Pope Gregory III was so impressed by Charles Martel's success in battle that when the papal territories in central Italy were threatened by Lombards, he called on the Hammer for help.

Charles Martel had two sons named Carloman and Pepin the Short. While the usual practice would have been to divide power, land, and wealth equally among them, Carloman seems to have been persuaded to become a monk—something that probably saved his life—and he retired to the Benedictine Abbey of Monte Cassino in Italy in 747, leaving Pepin to rule alone, a fact that resulted in relative peace and unity in the Frankish lands. Pepin felt that enough was enough—he was king in all but name, and it was time he had the name, too. At the urging of Pepin, Pope Zacharius declared that an individual who exercised the power of a king ought to have the title. In 751, the Merovingian era of Frankish history came to an end when King Childeric III, the last of the long-haired kings, had his hair cut off—an act that symbolized his lack of power and was probably carried out by an agent of the Carolingians. Weakened and ashamed, Childeric was exiled to a monastery. In return for this support, Pepin gave Frankish-controlled lands in Italy to the pope—effectively creating what we've come to know as the Papal States. The Merovingian rule of the Franks was over, and the Carolingian dynasty had officially supplanted it.

This exchange between Pepin and Pope Zacharias is hugely significant, as it represents one of the first instances when the right to rule is decreed by ecclesiastical sanction. Although Gregory of Tours had earlier stated quite plainly that he saw the Merovingian kings as playing a providential role in history, meaning that their reign was ordained by God to ultimately promote the power of the church on earth, there was no really formal union between the church and Frankish kings. So this becomes an issue with Pepin, but it will be an even more pressing issue during the reign of his son, Charlemagne. If ever there was an historical figure who fit the description "larger than life," Charlemagne is that figure. Even the name by which we call him today registers this. His name was actually simply Charles, the French form being *Charles*, and it was not long before he was being described as Charles the Great—*Charles le magne*—which has became Charlemagne in most of the English-speaking world. At first, it didn't look as if the power accumulated by Pepin would continue to grow during the reign of his successor, for, you see, Charlemagne had a brother, Carloman—popular name in the family—and so, in keeping with the tradition of Frankish inheritance, the land, wealth, and power of Pepin was initially split between the two brothers. According to Charlemagne's biographer, Einhard, who wrote his account of the king's life at the behest of Charlemagne's son, Louis the Pious, there was bad blood between Pepin's two sons. But fortunately, he says Carloman died within two years, and Charlemagne became the undisputed king of the Franks.

According to Einhard, Charlemagne cut an impressive figure. Many people have understood him to be described as seven feet tall, but actually what Einhard said was that Charlemagne's height was more than seven times the length of his foot. So by today's standards, he was not seven feet tall, yet measurements taken of his skeleton suggest that he was around six feet, four inches tall. Even if these measurements are not exact, we can rest assured that Charlemagne certainly stood out from the majority of the population in terms of height—although I should point out here that the idea that medieval people were significantly smaller than modern people is a misperception. Recent archaeological studies of medieval skeletons from Britain suggest that average height for a man in the Middle Ages was around five feet, seven inches. Today's average is five feet, nine. Women in the Middle Ages averaged five feet, two inches, while today's average is around five foot, four. There was some variation in terms of class—peasants were on average shorter than nobles because of their poorer diet and harder lifestyles, but if we're talking about today or the late 8th century—six foot, four, is tall.

Einhard went on to note of Charlemagne's appearance that "the upper part of his head was round, his eyes very large and animated, nose a little long, hair fair, and face laughing and merry. Thus his appearance was always stately and dignified, whether he was standing or sitting; although his neck was thick and somewhat short, and his belly rather prominent; but the symmetry of the rest of his body concealed these defects. His gait was firm, his whole carriage manly, and his voice clear, but not so strong as his size led one to expect."

The tall man with the round head and prominent belly conceived of the audacious plan to re-create the culture, prestige, and power of the Roman Empire—to make a new empire modeled on Rome. He worked toward this goal by taking significant action in four different areas. We see

Charlemagne's significance first and foremost as a conqueror. He was nearly invincible in wars of aggression that consolidated or expanded Frankish territory. Essentially, every spring his army was on the march against various enemies—both internal and external. He was victorious against the Saxons, for example, in 772, 775, 776, 780, 782, 784, and 785. He defeated the Lombards in 774, convincing their king that it might be a good idea if he retire to a monastery. He defeated peoples known as the Beneventans and the Avars on numerous occasions. In fact, the only campaign of his that was not a success happened in 778, when he fought against the Muslims in Spain. The narrative of this defeat is the basis for the great French poem, the *Chanson de Roland*.

In addition to being a true conqueror, Charlemagne was also, significantly, a State builder—and by this I mean he had recognized that part of the fundamental problem of being ruler of the Franks was that one had to figure out how to govern a vast geographic territory that included people who spoke many different languages, who had differing laws and customs, and who wouldn't necessarily identify themselves first as Frankish. They might be Frankish subjects, but in terms of cultural identity, these people might very well consider themselves to be something else. Charlemagne strengthened his central government and established a bureaucracy, but at the same time he allowed a fair amount of local autonomy. He often appointed native members of the landed aristocracy in a particular region as his representatives. The third area in which we can see the significance of Charlemagne's actions is in terms of the church. He considered it his duty to reform spiritual life in the kingdom—so he instituted some changes and requirements. For example, he wanted all parish clergy to give competent and useful sermons, so he commissioned some model sermons to be written by a man named Paul the Deacon, and these were disseminated where he thought they were most needed. He set up the custom of tithing—whereby 10 percent of any harvest would be given to the church, as one way to support monasteries. He also supported missionary efforts, particularly those of a British man named Boniface, who made a mission to the Frisians, who lived in what is today the Netherlands. Believing that worship should be regularized throughout the land, he made the Roman Liturgy, or public prayers of the church, the standard of Frankish Christianity. To help with these efforts, he had liturgical manuals produced for every church and monastery. Through these actions, he brought Frankish lands and Frankish Christianity firmly in line with the Roman Church, a process that we've already seen occur once with the Synod of Whitby.

The fourth—and, to my mind, most interesting—aspect of Charlemagne's reign is his status as a patron of the arts. It is his commitment to learning, education, art, architecture, music, and literature that produces a glorious flourishing known as the Carolingian Renaissance, and it is this that will be the focus of our next lecture.

Charlemagne and the Carolingian Renaissance
Lecture 7

The word "Renaissance" means literally "rebirth," and ... when applied to the early modern period seems to suggest that after the long, dark, obscure, and ignorant days of the Middle Ages, there was finally a rediscovery, a rebirth, of the humanistic tradition we so often associate with the Roman Empire. Charlemagne, however, got there first.

A flowering of art, architecture, literature, music, and education occurred under the rule of Charlemagne. By the year 800, Charlemagne's kingdom was the largest realm ruled over by a single individual since the Roman Empire. Charlemagne thus thought it proper to act like an emperor and made significant achievements as a conqueror, state builder, and supporter of the church. But perhaps his most important legacy was in the arts and education. Charlemagne created a vibrant center of scholarship we call the Palace School at Aachen, attracting the greatest minds of the age. One of Charlemagne's major goals was to collect, preserve, and copy the era's most important manuscripts. Today, in many instances, we know of particular texts only because of a copy made at Charlemagne's behest.

In his quest to make these great works accessible to as many as possible, Charlemagne fostered the creation of new, more legible style of writing, known as Carolingian miniscule. Almost all of the important manuscripts of the age were written in Latin, so Charlemagne set up programs to ensure that future generations would be able to read the language. The center of the Carolingian Renaissance was the Palace School at Aachen, a former Roman military camp. Its center was the marble Palatine Chapel, whose columns were imported—in some instances stolen—from Italy. The chapel had three levels: the top, representing the heavens; the bottom, the place of worship; and the middle, where Charlemagne placed his throne, a clear suggestion that he was an intermediary between the people and God. Charlemagne instituted numerous reforms to make the experience of the Mass more pleasant. Perhaps the most famous is the use of Gregorian chant, a singing style attributed to Pope Gregory the Great but popularized by Charlemagne.

While Charlemagne was building his empire, a debate raged between the churches in the former western and eastern halves of the Roman Empire. After the fall of the West, the emperor in Constantinople declared that he was now the de facto emperor, and he and his people were working toward the moment when the empire would be restored and reunited once more. The eastern emperors thus felt that they had authority over the pope, an idea known as caesaropapism. At Christmas in the year 800, Charlemagne attended services in Rome. There, in a move Charlemagne claimed was a surprise, Pope Leo III placed a crown on his head and proclaimed him Holy Roman Emperor. While this move was primarily an end run around any claims of the Byzantine emperor, it gave rise to an at-times vicious debate about secular versus religious authority.

While Charlemagne was building his empire, a debate raged between the churches in the former western and eastern halves of the Roman Empire.

Although at its height Charlemagne's empire was one of the greatest entities the medieval world would see, within 60 years of his death all of its power had dissipated. The idea of a Holy Roman Empire, however, would continue to be a potent one for the next 1,000 years. ■

Suggested Reading

Collins, *Charlemagne*.

McKitterick, *Carolingian Culture*.

Riché, *Daily Life in the World of Charlemagne*.

Questions to Consider

1. How does Charlemagne's interaction with the Western church reflect or embody medieval concerns about the relationship between secular and religious leaders?

2. What was it about the idea of a Holy Roman Empire that made it such a potent concept in the medieval world? What is the legacy (if any) of this idea today?

Charlemagne and the Carolingian Renaissance
Lecture 7—Transcript

Welcome back. In our previous lecture we focused on the kingdom of the Franks, the most powerful and largest realm to emerge from the former Roman Empire. While it was under the rule of the Merovingian family that the Franks rose to power, the real power lay behind the throne, in the office of Mayor of the Palace. In the 8th century, the Mayor of the Palace, Pepin the Short, demanded that his title match his office and function, and with the support of the pope, a new dynasty, the Carolingians, supplanted the Merovingians. Last time we talked also at considerable length about the greatest scion of that family—the Frankish leader, Charles the Great, or Charlemagne—and we explored how he consolidated and expanded his power through key actions in four areas: first, as conqueror; second as a state builder; third as defender and promoter of the church; and fourth as a patron of the arts. By the year 800, Charlemagne's realm stretched more than 800 miles from east to west. His territory extended south into Italy, north into Saxony, and he had several of what seem to be buffer zones that effectively made his realm the largest under a single lord since the Roman Empire.

Historian Barbara Rosenwein suggests that as this territory under Charlemagne's rule looked like the closest thing to an empire that the Western world had seen since the 5th century, Charlemagne also thought it fitting that he begin to act like an emperor. He borrowed ideas of Roman bureaucracy and administration in order to facilitate the running of his empire. He imposed uniformity and consistency on religious practices. As a promoter of art, architecture, and education, he established what scholars have come to call the Palace School at Aachen, and it's his activities here and as a patron of the arts that produced the first true Renaissance in the medieval world.

The word "Renaissance" means literally "rebirth," and very often you will hear people use it to refer to what is more often called the early modern period, which began sometime in the 16th century. The word "Renaissance" when applied to the early modern period seems to suggest that after the long, dark, obscure, and ignorant days of the Middle Ages, there was finally a re-discovery, a rebirth, of the humanistic tradition we so often associate with the Roman Empire. Charlemagne, however, got there first. In the 8th

century, he sought—as far as was possible—to re-create and preserve the best and most glorious elements of what had been the Roman Empire. All modern scholars owe him a debt of gratitude for the learning he preserved for later generations. The establishment of the Palace School at Aachen was an astoundingly ambitious undertaking, and it effectively shifted the center of learning in early medieval Europe away from the British Isles, the monasteries of which had become famed for their collections of manuscripts. Charlemagne relocated the center of learning and culture to the Continent. He recruited the leading scholars of the day away from their homes in places as far away as England, Italy, and Spain and sought to establish a learned community and intellectual center at Aachen. One of those scholars he lured to the Continent was a man named Alcuin of York, considered one of the greatest minds of the early medieval period, and it was he who really served as Charlemagne's architect of cultural reform. Einhard, another learned man who joined the community at Aachen, would go on to write a biography of Charlemagne—and, significantly, he used as his model a 2nd-century classical work called *The Lives of the Caesars*, a fact that underscores that many people thought of Charlemagne as a new Roman emperor.

It is an interesting fact that although the occupations of warrior and patron of the arts might seem to be mutually exclusive, Charlemagne funded almost all of his programs of educational and cultural renewal with the booty he had won in his many war campaigns, and he spared no expense. He wanted to gather and preserve knowledge—and to that end, he sent couriers throughout Europe to acquire important manuscripts. He was especially interested in classical works—those of Virgil, Horace, and Tacitus. He didn't just want to possess these manuscripts for himself—he wanted the knowledge they contained to be disseminated, so once the manuscripts were acquired, they were copied by scribes working in Charlemagne's court. In fact, most of our editions of the works of these classical authors are based on 8th- and 9th-century copies made at Charlemagne's behest. In several instances, the original version from which his scribes made their copies has been lost. We can tell which manuscripts come from Charlemagne's court in part because of the hand in which they are written.

A brief comment about medieval handwriting is in order here. As many of you already know and as I mentioned in my first lecture, all texts in the

Middle Ages had to be written by hand. Just to get an animal hide into a condition in which it would be suitable for writing was a laborious and painstaking process—and, perhaps not coincidentally, the act of writing itself was similarly time-consuming and difficult. A scribe would usually sit before a table that looked like an angled lectern. He would have, most usually, a quill that would need to be dipped repeatedly in an inkwell, perhaps more than once, just for the formation of one letter. The animal hide before him, although it had been stretched and treated, had a tendency to want to spring back into the shape of the animal from which it had come—so the scribe often used his knife, which was necessary to have on hand for periodic sharpening of the quill, or another similar object as a kind of pointer to hold the parchment or vellum in place.

Because it was so difficult and time-consuming to prepare a piece of animal hide for writing, scribes tended not to want to waste any space—so words were often run together, and abbreviations were quite common. There is little or no punctuation to be found in early medieval manuscripts, and the letter forms themselves look like alien symbols or glyphs to our modern eyes. There is a whole field known as paleography that is devoted to the study of early hand-writing.

One thing that is of major interest to paleographers are the different styles, or hands, to be found in medieval manuscripts. By understanding conventions of style, particular variations in letter forms, and occasionally unusual spelling, paleographers—those who study the writing of the past—can usually locate a manuscript in both time and place—say, 12th-century England—and sometimes they can even identify the particular monastery and even the specific scribe who copied a text, even if there is no signature.

Medieval texts were thus very difficult to read, and Charlemagne wanted to make the process of acquiring knowledge easier and more accessible, so he promoted a new hand that was simpler and easier to read called Carolingian miniscule, and he decreed that this is the hand that should be used consistently throughout the kingdom. This hand was better than those that had preceded it because it was more legible—there were spaces between words, and there was more punctuation. Charlemagne also added a hierarchy of font styles—for example, titles should be written in all capitals, subtitles a mix of capitals and lowercase letters, and the main text should be all in lowercase. This made navigating a manuscript much easier than had been the case in the past—as in many instances there was little to distinguish titles, subtitles, and even marginal commentary or notes from the main text.

Interestingly, although he could read—and could read Latin, which was the language of education and learning in the Middle Ages and the language in which virtually all texts were written—Charlemagne himself could not write. According to his biographer, Einhard, Charlemagne used to keep slates or a wax tablet with a stylus near him, and when he had a moment, he would practice forming letters, but he concluded ultimately that he had come to the study of writing too late in life to be successful at it.

This aspect of Charlemagne's life reveals something fundamentally different about literacy in the Middle Ages compared to literacy today. Most of us today learn to read and write at about the same time—in other words, we practice using a pencil and writing words around the same time we're learning how to identify them on the page and read them aloud. In the Middle Ages, there were several varieties or levels of literacy. We must remember that when we speak of medieval literacy we are talking about a very small percentage of the population. Reading and writing were considered two separate skills, and reading and writing in a particular language further distinguished the level of one man's literacy from another. Truly literate men would be able to read and write Latin, while others might be able to read in only their native language, what we call a vernacular—like French, or English, or German—in order to distinguish it from Latin, the language of learning and culture.

Although it was not terribly common, there seem to have been a few instances in which we find a scribe who is trained in the copying of letters, but he might be functionally illiterate—meaning he wouldn't be able to read and understand the text he was copying.

Knowledge of Latin was key in medieval society, as it was a kind of lingua franca that made travel, trade, and communication easier. For example, an English speaker and a French speaker might not know one another's native languages, but if they both knew Latin, they could communicate with one another quite easily. Of course, Latin was the language of the Roman Empire, so it is no surprise that in his quest for the preservation of knowledge, Charlemagne emphasized those texts that were written in Latin—and rather than a program of translation, he favored making copies of the texts in their original language. He then instituted various educational programs—for example, funding schools at the great monasteries of Fulda and Saint Gall with the intention of providing an education for clerics and laymen alike. He also made sure that every church and monastery had a copy of the Vulgate Bible, and that those copies had been carefully checked for errors. Errors in medieval manuscripts were a huge source of concern—for once an error had been made, it was likely to be repeated in subsequent copies of a text. While this might not have been a big deal in some instances, one can imagine that a scribal error in an important theological text—or even worse, the Bible—was particularly frightening because of the potential of people being accidentally led into sinful behavior. Many medieval manuscripts have corrections in the margins. Usually these would be in the case of larger errors—say, when a monk, tired from a long day of copying, might actually do an eye-skip and omit a word or an entire line by accident, as is the case in a medieval manuscript of Saint Augustine. A later reader has corrected the scribe's error by drawing a little picture of Augustine himself in the margin.

Augustine is standing beside the missing line and pointing to where it is supposed to go. In the case of a simple error recognized at the time of its making, the knife that the medieval scribe used to hold the page flat came in handy—as pages made of animal hide are so thick that one can literally scrape the word off the page, and the vellum or parchment would still be sufficient for him to be able to write the correct word where it belonged. There was even a story in the Middle Ages about a demon named Titivillus, whose sole purpose was keeping track of errors scribes made in copying manuscripts. At the end of a monk's life, Titivillus would weigh the good work a monk had done in copying manuscripts against the errors he had made. One version of this story says that a particular monk, when his errors and good works were weighed against one another, made it into heaven on the balance of just a single letter.

So, Charlemagne made sure that Latin learning was revived and expanded, that texts from the classical tradition were collected and copied, and that religious texts especially had been checked and corrected for errors. What we might call his base of operations, Aachen, was an old Roman military camp. Charlemagne modeled the palace there on old Roman palaces and even graced it with a statue of the Emperor Theodoric—which he stole, by the way, in order to emphasize his link with the classical world. His compound there included a church that he modeled on the Basilica of San Vitale in Ravenna, Italy, and he went to great pains to import Roman columns and Italian marble. He called the church the Palatine Chapel—Palatine because of the clear connection to Rome; the Palatine Hill is one of the seven hills of Rome. He called this structure a chapel because one of the Saint's relics that was housed there was a piece of the cloak that Saint Martin had famously given to a beggar, and the word *capella*, which means "chapel" in Latin, can also mean "cloak." So, in its very name, his church advertises both its Christian holiness and its links with the Roman Empire. In its layout, the church also quite specifically emphasized Charlemagne's royal position and piety. The church was designed to have three levels—the top represented the heavens, and the ground floor was the place where the clergy and the people met to worship. Between these two levels was a gallery that connected the church to the Royal Palace. Charlemagne placed his throne on this level in direct alignment with the altar, so that as the people looked up at the emperor, they were reminded that Charlemagne mediated between them and God.

As we've seen, Charlemagne wanted very much to regularize Christian worship in his realm, but he also wanted to make attending church a pleasurable experience, so that people would enjoy themselves during the service. He decreed that the prayers of the divine office should be sung by monks in a style known as Gregorian chant. This style of religious music is named for Pope Gregory the Great, who is credited by many as its originator, but there are some scholars who feel that while its roots may be a Roman style of chant, it is Charlemagne who really was the impetus behind its creation and development, and he only named Gregory as its creator to lend this style of liturgical music prestige and help its popularity. Gregorian chant is also known as plainchant, and it is a type of monophonic vocal performance—meaning that what we have is many voices who all sing the same notes for the same duration at the same time. If you remember our lecture on monasticism, you'll recall that most of a monk's day was taken up with prayers that were usually sung; given this, Gregorian chant was one of the major soundtracks in the medieval world. If you're wondering what it sounded like, here's a sample: [PLAYS MUSIC]

So clearly, Charlemagne felt strongly when it came to religion, and his own contemporaries recognized the important role he played as a champion of Christianity—to the point that he was frequently called a second Constantine, or a new Constantine. The Emperor Constantine, as you'll remember, famously converted to Christianity in the early 4th century, helping make that religion go from being the most persecuted in the Roman Empire to the official religion of the empire in the space of just a century. Constantine also significantly acted as the head of the church council of Nicea, an act that established a precedent for the idea that church leaders were more or less subject to the secular ruler. This precedent gained additional support with the Synod of Whitby, which was called to help settle the date of Easter, as you'll recall from an earlier lecture. Although a meeting that drew religious leaders from throughout the British Isles and the Continent, the head of the Synod of Whitby was King Oswy of Northumbria, rather than an ecclesiastical official, and he was the one who decided that the Roman—rather than Celtic—means of calculating the date of Easter should be observed.

We're going to talk much more about Byzantium, or what had once been the eastern half of the empire, in our next lecture, but for now it is important that you know that once the western half of the Roman Empire had effectively collapsed after 480, the Byzantine leadership, based in Constantinople, claimed that the empire had technically been reunited—with the Emperor of Byzantium controlling both East and West. For a couple of centuries prior to Charlemagne's rise to power, Byzantine emperors had tried to control the pope in Rome according to a principle called caesesaropapism, which is really just a fancy way of saying that the Byzantines believed that church leaders were subject to the emperor.

In the year 800, Charlemagne traveled to Rome at the invitation of Pope Leo III, where he celebrated Christ's nativity. Historians do not agree about what was planned or what actually happened in terms of the sequence of events during church services on December 25th of that year, but the story goes that without any foreknowledge on the part of Charlemagne and completely unexpectedly, Pope Leo—in the middle of the service—placed a crown on

Charlemagne's head and declared him the Holy Roman Emperor. Centuries later, the French writer Voltaire would famously remark that the realm over which Charlemagne ruled was neither Holy, nor Roman, nor an Empire. While there is certainly a great deal of truth to this statement, as any casual observer can see, at the very least the idea of a Holy Roman Empire lasted for over 1,000 years and came to be one of the most important forces in medieval politics.

Pope Leo's imperial coronation of Charlemagne was significant for a number of reasons. For the papacy, it was effectively an attempt to move out from under Byzantine domination—suggesting that if any power might have the right to direct the church, it would be a Western, rather than Eastern, power. It meant that the Carolingian kings could now claim a line of imperial descent from the Emperor Augustus, strengthening their connection to Rome. It is interesting, however, that Charlemagne did not adopt this title right away, preferring to be called rex or "king" instead. He eventually did use the title of emperor, and his successors certainly did—especially when attempting to establish or maintain their right to hold power.

Perhaps because of the uncertainty surrounding how the events of the coronation played out exactly, the moment when Leo placed the crown on Charlemagne's head has given rise to a debate surrounding interpretation of the coronation known as the Royalist versus Romanist Debate. The Romanist position would hold that the pope holds all power from God, but while he oversees the church, he bestows or grants his secular power of rule to the leader of the Holy Roman Empire. In other words, Romanists hold that the church has the right and the power to decide who will be emperor. As you might suppose, the Royalists have a different position. They would argue that it was Charlemagne who restored the Roman Empire, and his coronation was simply an acknowledgment of what he had already accomplished on his own. The implication here is that the church is part of the Holy Roman Empire—and not the other way around. This is not the same as saying that the ruler had any specific religious or priestly functions, but he did have extensive control over the church and was seen as a kind of partner allied with the office of the pope.

This is perhaps the greatest legacy of the Carolingian period—the fact that with the creation of the Holy Roman Empire we have a Christian realm whose supreme leader is in a position parallel to that of the supreme spiritual leader, the pope. But as I said earlier, although the Holy Roman Empire would continue to exist for 1,000 years, it would have no real power for much of that time—except as an idea. When Charlemagne died in 814, only one of his sons, Louis the Pious, was still alive, which meant that the Carolingian Empire continued to be a unified realm. It seemed clear to Louis that the Frankish custom of dividing wealth, property, and power among all surviving sons was not in the best interests of the empire, so he tried to set up an inheritance system among his own sons that looked more like primogeniture—a system in which the first-born son inherits most, if not all, of the assets. Early in his reign he named his firstborn son, Lothar, as his co-ruler, and he had his other two sons, Pepin and Louis, agree to rule as sub-kings under their older brother after Louis the Pious died. This arrangement seemed prudent and reasonable, but after the death of his first wife, Louis married again, and by his second wife he had another son, who came to be called Charles the Bald, and this new arrival threw the earlier plan into disarray, as did the death of Pepin in 838. Louis the Pious died in 840, and his three surviving sons engaged in a bitter dynastic struggle for the right to rule the Carolingian Empire. Lothar attacked Charles the Bald, who in turn went and made an alliance with Louis, and these two brothers together defeated Lothar in 841. Fighting continued until 843 when the Treaty of Verdun divided the Frankish realm into three parts—divided roughly into a western, middle, and eastern Frankish kingdom. Charles the Bald took the west, which comprised most of what is modern-day France. The east, which would eventually become Germany, went to Louis, who became known as Louis the German. The middle kingdom ran from what is today the Netherlands in the North down through modern-day Switzerland and into Italy, and this went to Lothar, Louis the Pious's eldest son. The three brothers went on to have sons themselves, and the kingdoms were further subdivided. The result was that within 60 years after Charlemagne's death, the unity of his empire had completely disappeared. Those differences that existed throughout the various regions of the Carolingian Empire that Charlemagne had worked so hard and successfully at overcoming—differences of language, and custom, and ethnic identity—proved to be too much for his successors. Without a stable, centralized power to hold it together, the various kingdoms splintered into smaller and smaller pieces—and eventually, the Carolingian dynasty was supplanted by the Ottonians.

In 911, the last Carolingian king of Germany, Louis the Child, died. The local military leaders in the German duchies crowned one of their own as king. Around this same time, the German states were suffering attacks from the Hungarian Magyars. In 919, the German military leaders gave the right to rule to the most powerful man among all of them—Henry, duke of Saxony. His son Otto I brought stability and order to the various German territories, unifying them and then adding to his territory by conquering part of Italy. He borrowed a page from Charlemagne and made excellent use of the church in promoting his rule. With the Ottonians we have the beginning of the idea of a German Holy Roman Empire, and it and Francia—once united under the rule of Charlemagne—would remain two distinctly different societies from that point until the modern period.

So, in what we might think of as the homeland of the medieval world, the Carolingian Empire—both in the physical extent of its borders and the ideals that it embraced and promoted—would dominate Western Europe for several hundred years to come. Beyond the traditional borders of the medieval world, however, events were taking place that would have a profound impact on the Europe of the Middle Ages. The former eastern half of the Roman Empire, Byzantium, was a facing a new series of challenges, in part due to the rise of a new and powerful belief system—Islam.

Although the West, the Byzantine Empire, and the Muslim world were strikingly different and would clash on several occasions, it is important that we understand the many cultural, political, and religious aspects that they shared—for in the words of historian Barbara Rosenwein, all three of these entities are sibling cultures of Rome, and as we'll see in our next lecture, the influence and legacy of the Roman Empire affected all three in significant and important ways.

Byzantium, Islam, and the West

Lecture 8

> What is interesting about Byzantium in the late 5th and 6th centuries is that its emperor and its citizens, for the most part, still considered themselves to be Roman. ... Yet ... when the Goths sacked Rome itself, there was no help forthcoming from Constantinople. Essentially, the inhabitants of the eastern half of the empire hunkered down and consolidated their power.

The societies of the Middle Ages were shaped in important ways by entities beyond the borders of the former Western Empire. The West, the Byzantine Empire, and the Islamic world all affected each other significantly and should be thought of as sibling cultures of Rome. The Byzantine Empire, or the eastern half of the former Roman Empire, is often described as becoming Hellenized in the 5th and 6th centuries, while the West became barbarized. The Byzantine Empire was more stable than the West in part because of its more stable tax base. They also had lower defense costs, a more urban economy (which was less susceptible to vagaries than the West's primarily agricultural system), and a capital ideally situated as a trading center. Emperor Justinian further encouraged growth and stability by issuing a series of law codes, reforming Christianity, and reclaiming portions of the former Roman Empire through military conquest.

Justinian, Roman emperor of the East in the 7th century, commissioned the great church of Hagia Sophia in part as a sign of Rome's, and Christianity's, enduring power.

In the 7th century, however, the Byzantine Empire found its borders under threat by the Persian Empire, whose attacks resulted in ruralization of the empire and sparked a rise in Christian piety, including an iconoclastic movement. The eastern and western halves of the empire continued to drift further and further apart, which would have significant repercussions later in the medieval period. This movement away from one another was accelerated by the rise of Islam.

Islam had a more profound impact on the former eastern half of the Roman Empire due to the close proximity of the Byzantine Empire and the Islamic world. Islam originated on the Arabian Peninsula in the 7th century in a society that was organized primarily by tribal affiliation. Islam has much in common with Christianity and Judaism, all of which spring from a common root culture. The prophet Muhammad received a series of visions from the angel Gabriel in the year 610, which led him to found Islam. The messages from the angel continued throughout his life; when written down, they became the holy book of Islam, called the Qur'an. Muhammad came to power by allying himself with various nomadic leaders and defeating many political leaders from Mecca in battle. In this way he established the *ummah*, the community of the faithful, and the important precedent of blending religion and politics in the Arab world.

[Muhammad] established the *ummah*, the community of the faithful, and the important precedent of blending religion and politics in the Arab world.

In the West, the changes happening in the Byzantine and Islamic worlds would have significant effects, even though some of them would not be felt for many years. In 711, Spain was conquered by North African Muslims and would remain Islamic for more than 300 years, until a Crusade was launched to retake Spain for the Christians. The Arab world became a society of education and scientific advancement. Many ancient texts would be lost to us today had they not been preserved in Arabic copies, and most of the medical and scientific advances of the late medieval world came about due to contact with Arab learning. For all its advances, the Islamic world suffered its own share of difficulties after the death of Muhammad, as various factions claimed the right to lead the *ummah*. Eventually, these groups began to war with one another. ■

Suggested Reading

Berkey, *The Formation of Islam.*

Mango, *The Oxford History of Byzantium.*

Whittow, *The Making of Byzantium, 600–1025.*

Questions to Consider

1. In what ways did the Byzantine Empire demonstrate a continuity with the ideals of Roman Empire that differed from that found in the world of the medieval West?

2. In what areas was the Muslim world more advanced than that of the European West? How did it contribute to the development of medieval culture?

Byzantium, Islam, and the West
Lecture 8—Transcript

Welcome back. For the last several lectures, we have been focusing on the legacy of the Roman Empire in Western Europe, and it is true that when one speaks of the medieval world or the Middle Ages, most often it is understood that these terms are specific to the West. However, the eastern half of the former Roman Empire is extremely important in the development of medieval culture, as are those regions in the Middle East and north Africa, where the religion of Islam originated and to which it spread. Much of these areas had once been Roman territories as well, and historian Barbara Rosenwein has suggested that we should think of Western Europe, the Byzantine Empire, and the Islamic world as sibling cultures of Rome. Today we're going to discuss both Byzantium and the rise and spread of Islam, situating these cultures in relationship to the West so that we can more clearly see the important differences and distinctions among them, as well as some of the similarities and continuities.

We'll start with what we've come to call the Byzantine Empire. As you may recall from a previous lecture, one of the responses to the Crisis of the Third Century in the Roman Empire by the Emperor Diocletian was to divide the empire into a western and an eastern half—with an emperor and an emperor-in-training, a caesar, for each. Diocletian himself took the eastern half, an indication that the East was the richer, more stable portion of the empire. This was due to a number of factors, including the fact that the borders of the eastern part of the empire were less frequently attacked than those of the West, the East had a more stable economy, and it had a thriving urban life. By comparison, the West was less stable, prone to more frequent attacks, and its economy was primarily agrarian—meaning that the difference between good health and starvation was often only a harvest or two. As we discussed in a previous lecture, the differences between the two halves of the former empire are often characterized by a kind of shorthand terminology. As we head into the 6th century, these two formerly united regions are going in opposite directions—the West toward barbarization, becoming more like the so-called barbarian peoples who had once lived beyond its borders, and the East toward Hellenization, or becoming more influenced by Greece and Greek culture. The center of that culture was the city of Constantinople, which had once been known as Byzantium, but which had been renamed by the Emperor Constantine. The terms "Byzantium" and "Byzantine" eventually came to refer to the whole of the eastern half of the former Roman Empire.

The location of Constantinople was a huge factor in its prosperity, as it was strategically located on the Bosporus Strait, a waterway connecting the Black Sea to the Mediterranean—and so it was a center for commerce and trade, and it was a very cosmopolitan city from its earliest days, as people from all different cultures, speaking many different languages, passed through it.

What is interesting about Byzantium in the late 5th and 6th centuries is that its emperor and its citizens, for the most part, still considered themselves to be Roman, and they called the language that they spoke Romaic, although it was actually Greek. Yet, even though they thought of themselves as Roman, when the Goths sacked Rome itself, there was no help forthcoming from Constantinople. Essentially, the inhabitants of the eastern half of the empire hunkered down and consolidated their power, and this happened in a few key ways. First, in order to shore up their support, Byzantine rulers reduced taxes—always a popular move in any century. At the same time, however, they maintained a fairly steady income from taxes, as the East was not losing a significant portion of its tax base as the West was. The more territory the West lost to invaders, the smaller its revenue from taxes—which meant it was more difficult to maintain the military, which meant the West was more susceptible to invasion, which meant it was more likely to lose significant territory, which would in turn decrease its tax base, and I think you get the picture that what we have in the West is a kind of downward spiral.

In the East, not only did the tax base remain fairly stable, but the wealth of the empire was greatly increased due to the fact that Constantinople was a major center of trade between East and West. As I discussed in a previous lecture—after 476, when there was no longer an emperor in the West, the emperors in the East claimed that essentially the Roman Empire had been reconstituted as a single whole rather than two halves, and the only thing that hindered making this a reality was the need to drive out the invaders from the West. Many emperors asserted that they were simply awaiting the time when they would have sufficient resources to bring the West back under imperial Roman control. When the pope crowned Charlemagne as Holy

Roman Emperor in the year 800, he was essentially doing an end run around the Eastern emperors, who had consistently acted as if they had the right to oversee the office of the papacy, even though it was based in Rome.

One of the most important things that happened in Byzantium during the 5th and 6th centuries was that the emperors issued sets of laws. The first substantial set of these is called the Theodosian Code, after the Emperor Theodosius II, and it appeared in the first half of the 5th century. In the 6th century, the Emperor Justinian issued his own set of laws—the *Corpus Juris Civilis*, also called the Justinian Code. Above all else, this Code emphasized the absolute right of the emperor. To quote from the Code: "The emperor alone can make laws ... it should also be the province of the imperial dignity alone to interpret them."

Justinian also made other significant moves that defined and refined the Byzantine Empire, and he arguably is the greatest force in terms of the development of the Byzantine Empire before the 10th century. He was an educated man, a religious man, and he had an eye for beauty. The most famous church of Constantinople, Hagia Sophia, had burned to the ground during a riot in 532, and Justinian ordered it rebuilt—employing a reported 10,000 workers and lavishly decorating it with real silver and gold. He also commissioned the Church of San Vitale, in Ravenna, the church that so influenced the Emperor Charlemagne. In each of these structures were breathtaking mosaics that clearly depicted the emperor as God's earthly representative.

This he definitely believed, as we can see in his conflict over the religious doctrine known as Monophysism. We've talked a little bit already about Christian heresies that were popular in the West—such as Arianism, which held that Christ or God the Son could not be as divine or co-equal with God the Father; and Pelagianism, which was the belief that one could earn one's way into heaven through doing good works. The Western Church had established as doctrine that Christ had two natures—one human, one divine—but many Egyptian and Syrian Christians subscribed to the belief that Christ had had only one nature—hence the name, Monophysism: mono meaning "one" or "alone," and physism meaning "form." Most Monophysites believed that although Christ had both a human and divine nature, the human had been fully absorbed into the divine, ultimately leaving the Son of God with only one nature—the divine one. Justinian launched a persecution against the Monophysites, in part because he wished for papal support for his claim to rule as emperor of both the East and the West. His emphatic position regarding Monophysism, however, alienated some of the most important regions of the Eastern Empire, which would have huge significance later on.

Most importantly, perhaps, Justinian moved to try and make good on the claim of the Eastern rulers that they now ruled over all of what had once been the Roman Empire. His armies reclaimed portions of north Africa, Spain, and Italy—but in the end, this insistence on reclaiming the Western, or Latin, half of the former Roman Empire would hurt Byzantium, as would his persecution of Monophysities. So focused was Justinian on reclaiming Rome that he increased taxes to fund increasingly long and difficult campaigns. In particular, his fight against the Goths, who had taken Rome in 410, lasted more than three decades—seriously draining the resources of the empire and earning him much dislike and enmity. Add to this that his focus on Rome led him to neglect enemies on the Byzantine border, such as the Persians who were a constant threat, and this meant that after his death, Byzantium contracted bit by bit as the Persians as well as groups such as the Slavs, Avars, and Bulgars encroached on its territories. Soon, it had lost all the territories that Justinian had won in north Africa and Spain, but the idea of empire was preserved in the capital of Constantinople, which was protected by thick, well-nigh impenetrable walls—some of which had been built by Emperor Theodosius in response to the sack of Rome by the Goths in 410. Constantinople survived because these walls surrounded not only the urban center, but a significant amount of farmland—so starvation was not an issue for the city when it was under siege.

Still, the threats on multiple fronts needed to be addressed realistically, and one of Justinian's successors, the Emperor Heraclius—who came to the throne in the year 610—realized that he would have to choose which enemy he was going to fight, and which he was going to accommodate. He allowed various Slavic groups, as well as the Bulgars, to settle in the portion of Europe we call the Balkans today. He agreed to have only limited authority over them, a decision that allowed him to turn his attention to the more serious and pressing threat—the Sassanid Empire of Persia. One of this kingdom's most important leaders, King Chosroes II, had dreams of reestablishing the ancient Persian Empire ruled over by Xerxes and Darius. In the early 7th century, he managed to conquer significant portions of Byzantine territory, including the cites of Damascus, Jerusalem—and then, all of Egypt. Heraclius eventually defeated him, however, taking back into the Byzantine embrace those regions that had briefly been wrested away. As historian Barbara Rosenwein says: "On a map it would seem that nothing much had happened; in fact the cities fought over were depopulated and ruined, and both Sassanid and Byzantine troops and revenues were exhausted." One consequence of this fighting is the decline of urban centers in the East and a rise in what we would call ruralism. Concomitantly with this, we have an increase in religious fervor—most likely a response to the devastation that had been wreaked on so much of the Byzantine Empire. People were looking for answers—and has been the case throughout history, one of their responses was an increase in piety. One of the manifestations of this new spiritual feeling was iconoclasm, a word that means "the breaking of icons." Icons were a singularly Byzantine aspect of Christianity. Simply put, they were artistic representations of Christ, the Virgin Mary, various saints, etc., etc. Many Christians in the East treated their icons with reverence and, indeed, worship—believing them and the figures they represented to have intercessory powers with God. In the 7th and 8th centuries, Byzantine emperors passed laws banning adoration of icons and ordering their destruction. Icons became a hot-button issue, with feelings running strong on both sides, and this religious matter would further undermine any unity the Byzantine Empire had enjoyed.

By this point, the western and eastern halves of the former Roman Empire had moved even farther away from each other. Although the memory of their shared heritage would be an important factor throughout the Middle Ages and beyond, the East and West would continue to drift apart—a movement that was accelerated with the rise of Islam.

Islam began on the Arabian Peninsula in the early 7th century. The communities living in Arabia were primarily organized in terms of tribal affiliations and included nomadic groups, such as camel- and goat-herders, farmers—especially in the southwest, where there was more rainfall than elsewhere on the peninsula—included also traders and craftspeople, many of whom lived in communities focused around oases. The religious beliefs of pre-Islamic Arabia were a mix.

Most people living there appeared to be polytheistic, worshipping a variety of gods and goddesses who were revered as particular protectors of this tribe or that. In the city of Mecca, for example, the holy shrine known as the Ka'ba was surrounded by more than 300 idols representing these various deities. There was also, however, the concept of a supreme god, Allah, who was above all others. There were a few monotheistic communities of Christians and Jews living in Arabia as well, and it is important to remember that Judaism, Christianity, and Islam all spring from the same root—Christianity, as we have already discussed was long considered a branch or sect of Judaism in its early days. In Jewish tradition, the figure of Abraham is considered the father of the Israelites through his son, Isaac, whom God famously asked him to sacrifice as a test of faith—sending an angel to stay his hand at the last moment. As Christianity developed out of Judaism, Abraham and Isaac are also centrally important to this faith—and, indeed, the story of the sacrifice of Isaac has provided the source for some of the most beautiful and brilliant works of Christian art in the Middle Ages and beyond. Isaac was Abraham's son by his wife, Sarah. Abraham had another son by his wife's handmaid, Hagar, named Ishmael. According to tradition, Abraham was compelled by his wife to cast Ishmael and Hagar out into the desert, but God assured him that a great nation would be born from Ishmael's seed, and it is Ishmael who is regarded as an ancestor of the Arab people and, indeed, as the direct ancestor of Muhammad himself, Islam's prophet. Yet, although the greatest of Allah's prophets, Muhammad is not the only one—according to Islamic teaching, there were many prophets who paved the way for Muhammad. One of these is Jesus Christ, but in the Islamic tradition, obviously, he is not part of a Holy Trinity as it is understood in Christianity.

Muhammad was born in the area around Mecca in the second half of the 6th century, sometime around 570. He was orphaned while quite young, and he was taken in and raised by an uncle who was an important leader of one of the most important tribes in Mecca—the Quraysh. He seems to have had a relatively normal, happy, and comfortable early life—becoming a trader, marrying, and having children. At the same time, however, it seems clear that he had a longing for something more, and in his adult life, he often retired to a cave on a mountain—where he would meditate, reflect, and pray. It was here, sometime around the year 610, that the angel Gabriel spoke to Muhammad—giving him messages that he then passed along to others of his community. By far the most important of these was that there was only one God—Allah—and that he alone should be worshipped. These messages continued throughout Muhammad's life, and when written down they became the Qur'an—the Holy Book of Islam.

The Qur'an covers almost all of human experience, delineating codes of behavior and codifying moral and legal issues. The Qur'an was transformative for Arabian society—especially in terms of the position of women, in that it emphasized the nuclear family as the foundation of a community, rather than the tribe. Infanticide was banned; inheritance rights for women were spelled out, and although polygamy was approved, the Qur'an limited a man's wives to no more than four and stated that they should all be treated equally.

While polygamy may not seem at first to be a positive arrangement for women, the impulse for allowing a man to have multiple wives and specifying how he should treat them rose from a perceived need to protect women—to offer as many women as possible the safety and security that came from living under the roof of one's husband. It solved the problem of what to do with unmarried women, who often had little in the way of a safety net in this society.

As many historians have observed, what is interesting about Islam's emphasis on the immediate family is that a similar sort of shift in focus is occurring in the Byzantine Empire at roughly the same time. As I mentioned earlier, with the faltering of Byzantium and the decline of its cities, there was a new kind of emphasis on agriculture, and local powers for most citizens became more important than the centralized power that had once been located in Constantinople. With this shift away from urbanism and centralization came a renewed focus on family ties as a support in difficult or uncertain times.

Family ties would also be incredibly important in the early days and later development of Islam. In the first stages of the development of the Muslim faith, tribal leaders around Mecca found this new religion threatening, especially in its insistence that pagan practices—many of them centered around the Ka'ba—be abandoned. The pressure came from Meccan tribal leaders, and it became so intense that in 622, Muhammad made the Hejira—fleeing from Mecca to the city of Medina, where he had many followers and where he was soon established as both a religious and secular leader.

The importance of the precedent Muhammad established in Medina—that of blending politics with religion—cannot be overstated, as it will be one of the defining aspects of Islam down through the centuries. Its importance is underscored by the fact that the date of the Hejira became the year one in the Muslim calendar. Muhammad rose to power by dominating and ousting the Jewish presence in Medina, allying himself with various nomadic groups and engaging in a series of successful battles against leaders in Mecca—some of whom were his own relatives. In this way, he formed the *ummah* or the "community of the faithful." This community, after Muhammad's death, believed its most important directive was to defeat the enemies of God—in other words, they felt called upon to expand the Islamic world—although interestingly, when they did enlarge their territory, forced conversions of non- Muslims were relatively rare. Enlarge it they did—in the 7th century they took over much of Persia and then conquered the once-great cities of the Byzantine Empire, including Alexandria, Antioch, Carthage, and Damascus. In the 8th and 9th centuries, many cities on the Mediterranean that had once been strongly Christian converted to Islam. Although communities of Christians and Jews, as well as other faiths, remain in the regions of north Africa and the Middle East to this day, it is also clear that the conversion of these regions was lasting and profound—as those same areas are considered the center of the Islamic world today.

Perhaps the most interesting Islamic conquest in terms of our focus in this course is that of Spain in the year 711. After the conquest of Rome by the Visigoths in 410, they had spread out—pushing west into the Iberian Peninsula and north into France. They were pushed back down south by the Franks and entrenched themselves there, and what is modern-day Spain became a Visigothic kingdom. The unity of this kingdom was only ever fragile at best, with struggles over succession often resulting in wholesale slaughter of entire branches of noble families. So fractured were the Visigoths that the whole kingdom was essentially brought to its knees by the killing of the Visigothic king in the early 8th century. Most of Spain was quickly conquered by Muslim leaders, and the Iberian Peninsula would remain predominantly Muslim until the 12th century. Although populations of Christians and Jews continued to live there, an important piece of evidence of Islamic tolerance of other monotheistic traditions, Spain is considered by some scholars to not really be part of Europe until the later Middle Ages. "All of Europe, throughout the Middle Ages, is Christian," I once heard a professor say. "What about Spain?" a student asked. "Spain doesn't count," the professor answered, "it's really north Africa and not part of Europe at all." However, contact between the European and Islamic worlds would be a huge factor in the development of medieval society, and the presence of an Islamic community in Western Europe would play a significant role in that development.

Yet although Spain was ruled by Muslims, these rulers—called emirs— comprised a minority of the population. Their armies consisted mostly of non-Arab speakers—and, in fact, the raid into Spain that had resulted in the death of the last Visigothic king had not really been an Arab raid; rather, Muslim leaders had used a band of mostly north African berbers—some of which had converted to Islam, but some of which had not—to effect their coup. Populations of Christians and Jews were allowed to remain in part because they provided a large tax income—essentially they had to pay for not being Muslim. There was inter-marriage between Christians and Muslims, and there was also a blending of artistic traditions. The best-known example of this perhaps is the Great Mosque of Cordova. It borrowed its overall design from the Roman aquedact at Merida, the shape of its arches from Visigothic traditions, and its decorative aspects—in this case alternating white and black stones—from the Great Mosque of Damascas in the Middle East.

While Islamic Spain itself is fascinating as a contact point between disparate cultures, in terms of contact with the rest of Europe, its impact was fairly negligible throughout the early Middle Ages. It is only in the High Middle Ages, starting about the 11th century, that the rest of Europe really begins to notice and appreciate Spain as a center of learning and culture.

Indeed, much of what we know about the Middle Ages in the West comes from sources that were preserved in Arab texts, and many advances in the West came about as a result of contact between European and Islamic society.

After their numerous conquests, by the mid-8th century, Muslim communities began to flourish—particularly in the areas of education, literature, medicine, science, and mathematics. There's a reason that we refer to the numbers we use as Arabic. The branch of mathematics known as Algebra, for example, preserves in its very name traces of the people who first made significant advances in it. The works of the great Greek philosopher Aristotle were, until the 12th century, almost completely unknown in Western Europe. By contrast, in the 8th century in Syria all of his works were translated into Arabic, making them accessible to Islamic scholars and philosophers. The Islamic world in the early Middle Ages was wealthy and cosmopolitan, rich in both agricultural resources and trade. Its cities were grand and impressive and famed as centers of learning. By comparison, Western Europe looked like a provincial backwater.

Still, all was not well in the Islamic world, despite its many successes. Muhammad was succeeded by leaders known as caliphs—who, significantly, did not necessarily come from the most powerful tribes, but rather, were drawn from Muhammad's closest circle of friends and confidantes. The first two caliphs after Muhammad were both his fathers-in-law, and there was little trouble here. But soon, the young faith would be divided between leaders of two rival factions—and again, family was involved, particularly in-laws. The third caliph after Muhammad's death was his son-in-law Uthman, who had married two of Muhammad's daughters. He was not well liked, and those who opposed him favored another of Muhammad's sons-in-law as caliph. This son-in-law, Ali, had married the Prophet's daughter Fatima, and supporters of this branch of Islam came to be called Fatimids, after Fatimah, or Shiite Muslims.

Uthman's faction were known as the Ummayads, and in a later incarnation, elements of the Ummayads became known as Sunni Muslims. In the struggle over the position of caliph, both Uthman and Ali were killed. The Ummayads pushed west, and it is they who conquered Spain—properly called at this time by its Arabic name, Al-Andalus, and properly it's called Al-Andalus from about the 8th to the 12th centuries. In the East, the Ummayads were ousted by an order known as the Abbassids in the middle of the 8th century. This group moved the center of the Islamic world to Iraq and founded the city of Baghdad. This, more than anything else, helped the Islamic world to flourish. Like Constantinople, Baghdad was a link between the East and West, and burgeoning trade made it a wealthy city. In the 10th century, however, conflicts between the Fatimids and other groups that were rising to power in the Islamic world undermined and eventually decimated the rich cultures that had risen in tandem with the spread of the new religion. The Fatimids, who were mostly in north Africa, began to push back into the East—leaving Spain to the Ummayads, while Iraq itself was attacked by a group known as the Carmathians, with the result being the destruction of the region's agricultural system—long one of its greatest sources of wealth. Without this, the caliphs could not pay their troops, but troops were exactly what they needed.

As we head into the High Middle Ages, the period between roughly 1000 and 1300, both Byzantine and Islamic culture have a new emphasis on the importance of military strength above all else—something that would come to be hugely significant in terms of the medieval world as a whole. Back in the West, on the opposite end of what had once been the Roman Empire, a very different kind of violence from that which was taking place in the Byzantine and Islamic communities had thrown the medieval world into an uproar. This was the marauding, looting, and pillaging activities of the Scandinavian peoples we have come to call Vikings. What sparked their raiding activities has long been a matter of debate, but there is no debate about the profound impact these activities had on the peoples and communities who encountered these fearsome seawarriors. That impact will be the subject of our next lecture.

The Viking Invasions
Lecture 9

> Those Scandinavian seafarers who landed at Lindisfarne on June 8,
> 793, were not interested in books or Christianity. ... To them, there was
> no sacrilege in attacking a religious institution; to them, monasteries
> were simply large treasure houses that housed a population of men
> unable or unwilling to properly defend it.

The Vikings began to spread across Europe and beyond in the late
8th century, gaining a fearsome reputation for looting and pillaging.
Their expansion was swift, violent, and far-reaching: They made it to
Ireland, Italy, Russia, and North America. This lecture examines the impact
of their raiding practices on various European societies—particularly the
Franks—and discusses the unique aspects of their culture as represented in
the Norse Sagas and other accounts.

In June 793, a group of Scandinavian raiders attacked the monastery of
Lindisfarne off the northeast coast of Britain. While this may not be the first
event of the Viking Age, it is certainly the most memorable, and it has come
to characterize this period in the medieval world. The Scandinavian seafarers
we think of as Vikings would not have considered themselves part of a unified
group; their loyalties lay with a particular leader or lord. But their activities
over the next 200 or so years eventually gave rise to the national identities
of Norway, Denmark, and Sweden. While most Vikings were Scandinavian,
not all (or even many) Scandinavians were Vikings; most were farmers or
craftspeople. Scholars are unsure why these seafarers turned outward from
Scandinavia in the 8th century, but all agree that the Viking diaspora was
remarkable for its swiftness and spread.

Several elements contributed to the Vikings' success as seafarers and raiders;
these, in combination with the location and situation of Lindisfarne, produced
a perfect storm that made the sacking of the monastery almost inevitable.
Perhaps the most important element of Viking success was their skill as
ship builders and seafarers. Longboats were remarkably strong, fast, and
maneuverable. Lindisfarne was situated in close proximity to the Vikings'

usual maritime territory on a tidal island with plenty of beaches for easy landing. It was known to be filled with treasure, and it was inhabited by men who either could not or would not fight.

In the 9th century, Viking raiders traveled throughout the known world and beyond, sometimes simply raiding, at other times settling down. Swedes, Norse, and Danes each focused their attention on a different part of the medieval world. The Swedes penetrated deep into the Continent, all the way to Russia; some of them joined the elite protective unit of the Byzantine Empire, the feared Varangian Guard. The Norse looked west; some 500 years before Columbus "discovered" the New World, they established settlements in Newfoundland, Greenland, and Iceland. The Danes focused on England and the Carolingian Empire; their raids became so frequent and so violent, desperate peoples took to paying a bribe called the Danegeld (literally, "Dane gold") to persuade the Danes to leave their communities unmolested.

Scholars are unsure why these seafarers turned outward from Scandinavia in the 8th century, but all agree that the Viking diaspora was remarkable for its swiftness and spread.

By the end of the 10th century, the days of Viking marauding were mostly over, and many of these fierce warriors had settled down into new, stable, agricultural communities. One of these settlements was in the area of France now called Normandy, taking its name from these "northmen." The Norman leader, Rollo, was made a count; his heirs, over the next few generations, rose to the status of dukes. One of the scions of the House of Rollo, William of Normandy, would later conquer England, reshaping that nation's social, cultural, and linguistic institutions in dramatic ways. ∎

Suggested Reading

Rosenwein, *A Short History of the Middle Ages*.

Sawyer, *The Oxford Illustrated History of the Vikings*.

1. What are some common misconceptions people today hold about the Vikings and their activities in the 8th–10th centuries?

2. How does the story of the settlement and society of Iceland flesh out our thinking about the medieval world and its various societies?

The Viking Invasions
Lecture 9—Transcript

Welcome back. In our previous lecture, we discussed the rise of the religion of Islam and the development of Muslim communities, as well as the significant changes—in terms of social structure, militarism, and religious expression—occurring in the Byzantine Empire. Although these societies obviously differed in significant ways, we discussed the importance of recognizing the legacy of Rome in the formation and development of Byzantium, Islam, and the West—and the importance also of thinking of these three entities as sibling cultures of Rome. As we head into the High Middle Ages, both Byzantine and Islamic culture placed a new emphasis on the importance of military strength above all else. Back in the West, on the opposite end of what had once been the Roman Empire, a very different kind of violence from that which was taking place in the Byzantine and Islamic communities had thrown the medieval world into an uproar. This was the marauding, looting, and pillaging activities of the Scandinavian peoples we have come to call Vikings. What sparked their raiding activities has long been a matter of debate, but there is no debating the profound impact these activities had on the people and communities who encountered these fearsome sea warriors.

On a day in early June in 793, a raiding party of Scandinavian seafarers attacked the monastery of Lindisfarne. A remote piece of land off the northeast coast of England, which became an Island twice a day at high tide, Lindisfarne Abbey had been established by the Irish Saint Aidan in the early 7th century, some time around the year 635, and had become a justly famous center of learning and a repository of great wealth—both in terms of the monetary value of many of the precious objects it housed—and in religious terms, in that it was the resting place of Saint Cuthbert, who had also been its bishop at one point. Artistically speaking, it is perhaps most famous for the so-called Lindisfarne Gospels, an illuminated manuscript of breathtaking skill and beauty executed at the monastery. Originally written in Latin in the early 700s, a later hand added a gloss or translation of the text in Old English in the margins, making this the oldest surviving version of the Gospels in English.

Those Scandinavian seafarers who landed at Lindisfarne on June 8, 793, were not interested in books or Christianity. They were pagans—non-Christians—who were after treasure, mainly easily portable objects of gold and especially silver, and to them there was no sacrilege in attacking a religious institution—to them, monasteries were simply large treasure houses that housed a population of men unable or unwilling to properly defend it. The sack of Lindisfarne was a particularly violent episode in which monks, priests, and livestock were slaughtered, sacred relics were smashed, and the survivors were taken as slaves. Alcuin, the British monk whom Charlemagne had brought to his Palace School at Aachen as part of his agenda to make the Carolinigian Empire a center of learning and education in the medieval world, wrote in response to the Viking attack:

> Never before has such terror appeared in Britain as we have now suffered from a pagan race, nor was it thought that such an inroad from the sea could be made. Behold, the church of St. Cuthbert spattered with the blood of the priests of God, despoiled of all its ornaments; a place more venerable than all in Britain is given as a prey to pagan peoples.

For a long time, the sack of Lindisfarne was considered by many to be the start of what has come to be called the Viking Age. More recently, evidence has been unearthed that shows peoples from Scandinavia were setting out from their homelands to explore, trade—and in a few cases, mostly likely to raid, starting much earlier, around the first decade of the 8th century. Whether or not one considers outward movement from Scandinavia of any kind to mark the start of what we might call the Viking Age, or whether one considers raiding and plundering specifically to be the hallmark of what it means to go "a-Viking" as the term was, we can all agree that the sack of Lindisfarne is an important event in this history. If it didn't mark the beginning of the Viking Age, then—at the very least—it most certainly defined it in a way that any earlier ventures had not.

The attack on Lindisfarne incorporated all of the major elements that would come to be associated with what one thinks of when one considers Vikings in the modern popular imagination. We will use the events at Lindisfarne as a way to explore those qualities often conceived of as Viking in greater detail. But in order to understand what we mean when we refer to Vikings or the Viking Age, we need to back up a little and define some of our terms. The people we refer to as Vikings were almost without exception Scandinavian— Norse, Swedish, and Danish—but not all Scandinavians were Vikings. In fact, most Scandinavians in the 8th century were farmers and fishermen. The term "Viking" first shows up in of all places an Old English document known as the *Anglo-Saxon Chronicle*, and here it seems to refer to raiders who came by sea who were of Scandinavian origin. It seems unlikely that there was any sort of pan-Viking identity as such, and it also seems unlikely that in the 8th century these raiders would have even gone so far as to think of themselves as having a national identity—like Danish, or Swedish, or Norse. They most likely would have had local loyalties and allegiance to a particular chieftain or leader—but it is during what has come to be known as the Viking period that these national identities began to form and consolidate, and so it remains a crucial period for understanding the development of the entities we think of today as Norway, Denmark, Sweden, etc.

So if they did not share a common sense of identity, what did these raiders share? The sack of Lindisfarne gives us a good idea about the elements that were essential parts of Viking culture. Perhaps the first and most important component of the Viking identity is the amazing sea craft they used to launch their raids. Archaelogical evidence going back to the 4th century A.D. shows that the peoples living in the area of the North and Baltic seas were master shipbuilders—and by the 8th century and the beginning of what we might call the Viking Diaspora, they had raised this craft to an art form. Viking longships were generally narrow—built of thin, overlapping oak planks, and their design was such that they could flex and bend in a way that many modern boats—which simply absorb the impact of waves—could not. They sliced through the water with a team of strong rowers propelling them along, and when sails were added to their design, it is calculated that they could move at a rate of 10 knots. They also had a very shallow draft; it seems that a depth of three feet of water was all that most Viking ships—even those carrying as many as 50 men—needed in order to move through the water. The shallow draft, flexibility, and speed meant that the Vikings almost always had the element of surprise in their favor, as they could seem to appear from nowhere.

This appears to be what happened at Lindisfarne. When you examine the particulars of Lindisfarne's geographical location and the wealth it was known to house, it's amazing the Vikings waited as long as they did to attack. This tidal island has several beaches perfect for landing a boat, is easily visible from a great distance at sea, and was close enough to the usual realm of Scandinavian seafaring activity to make it an almost irresistible target. The Vikings who attacked Lindisfarne in 793 probably made great use of the element of surprise, probably taking down their sail and resorting to rowing as they drew closer—a move that, in combination with a Viking ship's generally low profile in the water, would mean the monks wouldn't have seen them until they were just moments away from attack.

After Lindisfarne, Viking exploration and raiding exploded throughout the medieval world of Western Europe and beyond. No one is quite sure why there was this sudden outward expansion from Scandinavia, although most feel it is likely that some sort of overpopulation drove the Vikings to seek out new lands to settle and new ways of generating income. England and the coast of continental Europe—particularly the Carolingian Empire—were mostly plagued by Danes. In fact, no matter their origins, all Viking raiders in England were usually referred to collectively as Danes, as we will be reminded when we discuss Alfred the Great's establishment of peace with the Vikings in the 10th century by ceding to them a portion of Britain that became known as the Danelaw—or, in other words, the part of the island where the laws of the Danes, the Vikings, were in effect. Vikings established settlements at York and made Dublin a center of Viking trade in the 9th century—and trade included not only goods, but slaves as well.

It was mostly Swedes who penetrated deep into the European continent, traveling all the way to Russia and the Orient. Contemporary accounts, including one by the Arab traveler and writer Ibn Fadhlan, describe a people known as the Rus who traded furs, practiced ritual sacrifice, and were such renowned fighters that they were recruited as members of the Emperor of Constantinople's elite protective force, the Varangian Guard. It seems likely that these Rus as they were called—who were clearly expert navigators of the river systems of modern Russia, such as the Don, the Dniepper—were the ones who gave this part of the world the name "Russia," a fact that for many years was hotly contested in Soviet and Russian intellectual circles, as the leaders there preferred to think of their origins as being from Slavic—rather than Scandinavian—warriors.

The Norse tended to look to the West, and it seems indisputable now that 500 years or more before Columbus set out to discover the socalled New World, the seafaring Norse had already established a settlement there. Archaeological evidence at a site in Newfoundland known as L'anse aux Meadows clearly indicates a Scandinavian settlement, and most scholars agree that the size and nature of the settlement suggest that it was settled by a leader who was most likely the famous Leifr Ericson—commonly called Leif Ericson.

According to the Norse sagas, around the year 1000, Leifr Ericson sets off in search of lands rumored to be west of Greenland, and he encounters territories that he names Helluland, Markland, and Vinland. Some evidence suggests that the Viking settlers engaged in trade with the native North Americans, but within a short time the North American settlement was abandoned—carefully and deliberately, it seems, as there was very little left behind. It appears that the Scandinavian settlers felt that there was little benefit to remaining in Newfoundland, and they returned to more familiar locales.

It is a similar story with Greenland. According to tradition, Greenland was discovered by Eric the Red—Leifr Ericsson's father—around 981. He persuaded a group of about 300 settlers to return there with him. About half of them made it, and there was a more or less continuous presence there until about the middle of the 14th century, when the settlements there were abandoned—and not in the orderly fashion one can see in North America at L'anse aux Meadows. The failure of the Viking communities here seems to be in part because the settlers were unable to adapt to changing climatic conditions and refused to adopt the survival techniques that the native Greenlanders—Inuits, closely related to North American Eskimos—used to survive. They also seem to have had some armed confrontations with the native Greenlanders. Whatever the reason, the abandonment of the Greenland Viking settlements marks the end of the Scandinavian push to the West.

One of the more interesting chapters of the Viking story is the settlement of Iceland, a portion of the Viking narrative that often gets lost in the broader story of their amazing seamanship, pillaging and plundering, ferocious warrior skills, and wide-ranging trade activities—which, as we've seen, included practically the whole known world, and also parts that were still considered unknown by those living in Western Europe. In the late 9th century, a Norseman by the name of Ingolfr Arnarsson was exiled from Norway because of his participation in a blood feud. According to legend, Arnarsson tossed a wooden beam over the side of his ship and then followed it until it washed ashore in Iceland—in the spot that is supposedly modern-day Reykjavik. Although some accounts say there were a few Irish-Christian hermits living in Iceland at the time, it was—for all intents and purposes—completely unpopulated. Iceland is a geneticist's and a genealogist's dream, as there is really only one initial wave of colonization—and after that, while people may leave, very few new groups of peoples choose to immigrate to Iceland in the Middle Ages. Modern DNA analysis proves what was long suspected, which is that on the way to settling in Iceland, many Vikings stopped by the British Isles—probably Dublin or York, which were Viking settlements and centers of slave trade—and there they picked up some women, willingly or not. Modern DNA analysis suggests of the early settlers in Iceland, 75 percent of the men were of Scandinavian extraction, but only 35 percent of the women were, and that it is likely that most of the women who settled Iceland in the early days were of Irish or Scottish descent.

After the Viking men collected these wives, they continued on to their new home—which, even at the best of times, was not terribly hospitable. Farming of grains or vegetables was not really possible given the short growing season so far north. Within a few generations or less, it seems clear that whatever timber had been growing in Iceland had been cut down so that the landscape was almost completely denuded. Animal husbandry—particularly in the form of horses, sheep, and cows—and the sea provided most of the Icelanders' sustenance. It is an indication of the realities of life in this place that a traditional delicacy, known as *hakkarl*, is shark that has been buried for six months so that it has putrefied sufficiently so that it's edible.

Inhabited by people eminently practical and resourceful, not to mention strong in both body and will, Iceland is interesting in terms of the medieval world mainly for two reasons: its politics and its literature. The terrain of Iceland—volcanic here, glacial there, high desert-like in other places—meant that the early settlers were spread out over a great distance and clustered mainly along the coastlines.

At first disputes between households were often settled by raids, but in the year 930, the medieval world saw what could be called its very first parliamentary meeting. Once a year, almost all of Iceland—but especially the most powerful men of their particular communities, known as *Gothar*—would come to the open plain at Thingvellir, where they would convene to settle disputes, make laws, and pass sentence on those who had been found guilty. Thingvellir has the distinction of being one of the few places in the world where you can actually see plate tectonics in action—the European and North American plates are pulling away from each other at the rate of about two millimeters a year, creating a rift that also conveniently enough serves as a path from the Visitors Center down toward the plain of Thingvellir itself.

The most important spot within Thingvellir was something called the *Lögberg*, or "Law Rock," and one of the most important figures was the *lögsogumathur*, or "Law Speaker," who every year would recite the laws from atop the Law Rock. This was an illiterate society, so it was important that someone had this information committed to memory, and important also that the laws be recited in the hearing of all, so that no one could claim ignorance of the law as an excuse for committing a crime.

Given the amount of darkness during the winter months—on some days it's said the sun doesn't even really come up over the horizon; all you get is a hint of light, what they call the gleam—it should be no surprise that the early Icelanders spent that time committing their very colorful history to memory, and that they would create a body of literature the likes of which is truly rare among the stories that emerge from the medieval world. Frequently, the one became part of the other, and it is hard to tell where history stops and fiction begins in the Icelandic sagas. Even to this day, when Iceland is a thoroughly modernized and Christianized country—and before the recent economic collapse they were known as the happiest country in the world—there are holdovers from its unique settlement and history. For example, when engineers lay a road, they check with those who are familiar with such things to make sure that the path they've plotted in no way disturbs the "hidden folk," what we might think of as elves or trolls, as belief in such creatures seems to be standard and accepted.

The story of Iceland and its transformation into supposedly or recently (relatively recently) the happiest nation in the modern world could be considered a triumph of all the greatest strengths of Viking culture—hardiness, skilled seamanship, a curiosity and zest for exploration, and a particular kind of internal fortitude. As much as Viking culture has been glorified in recent years—particularly with festivals celebrating the Viking world in places like York and Dublin, where one can buy items like Eric the Red bottle openers—we would do well to remember the less romantic and noble qualities of those who went a-Viking. These were fierce warriors and merciless fighters who burned, looted, pillaged, and raped their way through much of the British Isles, the Carolingian Empire, and beyond. Late in their history, they found a way of continuing to enrich themselves without bothering to strike a blow—by demanding that communities threatened by them pay a bribe in order to be spared an attack. So frequently were these payments demanded by Viking raiders that the English and Carolingians had a special name for it—the Danegeld, or literally Dane gold—the money you would pay to the Danes in order to get them to go away. Depending on your point of view, this strategy was either one of great cleverness or a mark that those who bore the sobriquet "Viking" were getting a little lazy. A great example of the typical Viking approach to raiding, especially in the later period, is given in the late 10th-century Old English poem called *The Battle of Maldon*, which we've already discussed a little in a previous lecture. This poem recounts the events of a day in the year 991, when a Viking army showed up at Maldon in what is today the region of Essex in England. The Vikings established a base on an island at the mouth of a tidal river, today known as the Blackwater. At low tide, this island, Northey Isle, is connected to the mainland by a very narrow causeway that disappears under water at high tide. This was a typical Viking strategy—to set up a base of operations at a location that was easily defensible, like an island, and as I said, by this point in their raiding and plundering activities, they were so feared that very often they didn't even need to strike a blow. They would show up, demand a payoff from the locals, and go away. The problem with this, obviously, was that just because one community paid them off and that community was safe didn't mean that they wouldn't just sail up the river a little further and attack someone else. This problem is at the heart of a major debate about what happened at Maldon.

An English nobleman named Byrthnoth had gathered an army of nobles and peasants to oppose the Viking invaders, and they were waiting on the shore across from Northey Isle. Because the causeway is so narrow—you can really only walk three abreast—the English had an advantage, as they would just be able to pick the Vikings off as they came across the causeway. According to the poem, the Viking leader called across the water to Byrthnoth, urging him to send treasure in the form of rings as a bribe to the enemy army.

Famously, Byrthnoth replies: "Gehyrst thus, sælida hwæt this folc segeth? hi willath eow to gafole garas syllan!" or "Do you hear, seafarer, what these people say? They wish to give you spears as tribute!" He goes on to tell the Viking leader that he feels it would be a shame for the Vikings to have come all this way and not get the fight they were looking for. Then, the poet tells us Byrthnoth makes a decision because of something called *ofermod*, which translates roughly as something like "too much pride" or "excessive selfassurance"—and his decision is to allow the Vikings to come across the causeway without being attacked and then form ranks, so that a proper battle may begin. In that battle, the English suffer a devastating defeat, in which their numbers are decimated and some of the English nobles actually flee the battle in fear. The poet takes special care to note that it was a noble named Godric and his brothers who essentially turn the tide in favor of the Vikings by fleeing the conflict and undermining the confidence of those English who remained. The poet takes care also, when discussing a different Godric, to note that this man is not at all the same Godric who committed such a shameful and cowardly act.

For a long time there was a general scholarly consensus that Byrthnoth had made a foolish decision in allowing the Vikings to come ashore, and that the poem was condemning him for this action. At the same time, however, the poem is unusual as a whole in that it is a celebration in large measure of a defeat—but what is being celebrated is the fact that although it was common practice to pay off the Vikings, one group of English took a stand against them and refused to shame themselves by buying off the enemy. The other point—and this is a very important consideration when we're talking about

Vikings—is that Byrthnoth had an army gathered at Maldon. If he refused the Vikings' request to come safely ashore to line up for the battle, all the Vikings would have had to do would be to get in their famously navigable boats and sail a little further up the river to a town that did not have an army ready and waiting to defend it.

Viewed in this light, Byrthnoth did the only brave and honorable thing possible when confronted with opponents who were known to have names such as Eric Bloodaxe and Thorfinn Skullsplitter. In time, the Vikings transformed from fierce marauders who traveled by water—plundering, looting, and pillaging—to people in settled communities who turned their attention back toward more domestic pursuits, like farming. But even at their most bloodthirsty, surprisingly, they seem to have been fastidious when it came to certain aspects of personal hygiene. Several excavated Viking graves, for example, have yielded up devices known as earspoons—used for cleaning the wax out of one's ears. Untrimmed fingernails also seem to have provoked particular horror. Loki—one of the Norse gods and not the nicest fellow—famously travels around in a ship that is made out of the untrimmed fingernails of dead men.

One place in which the transformation of Vikings from marauders to citizens happened, and which will be very important in our later lecture on the Norman Conquest of England, was in the part of France that is today known as Normandy. As one might guess from the name, Normandy is the region that was ceded to the "northmen," who were led by a man named Hrolfe. The Carolingians, unable to pronounce his name, called him Rollo. In 911, the Carolingians were able to strike a deal with him—they would allow him to keep control of Normandy as long as he agreed to rule over it in the name of the Carolingian Empire. They made him a count, he changed his name to Robert, and he converted to Christianity. Then, something even more interesting happened: Over the course of the next 150 years, the Northmen living in Normandy ceased to be culturally Norse and became more culturally French. Although they remembered and treasured their connections with the other Royal Houses of the Germanic world—particularly the English Royal House, with which the Dukes of Normandy would intermarry—they were, in essence, no longer Vikings, no longer Norse, no longer Scandinavian in many important respects, a fact that would have profound repercussions when William the Conqueror, scion of the House of Rollo, would invade England in 1066.

But long before that, the Vikings would temporarily meet their match in England when confronted with the shrewd cunning of King Alfred of Wessex, a man never expected to sit on the throne and whose achievements would earn him the epithet "the Great," the only English monarch to be so styled. We turn next to this fascinating man and the world he created.

Alfred the Great
Lecture 10

> Yet while [the Vikings] penetrated throughout the medieval world and beyond ... in Britain an unlikely king put a stop to their activities and achieved peace—albeit, only temporarily—with the Viking invaders. That king was named Alfred.

The only English monarch to be given the epithet "the Great," Alfred, king of the West Saxons, seemed unlikely to ever come to the throne at the time of his birth. Under his rule, the Viking threat was resolved; the remaining Anglo-Saxon kingdoms were consolidated; and an ambitious program of learning, education, and the arts flourished. In many respects, Alfred was similar to Charlemagne in his vision for his kingdom. In his account of Alfred's life, Einhard emphasized stories of Alfred's youth that foretoken his later love of learning, his ascent to the throne of Wessex, and the skill and cunning with which he defeated the Vikings.

As the youngest of five sons, there was no early indication that Alfred of Wessex would ever become king of his father's realm. When Alfred was born in 848, there were four Anglo-Saxon kingdoms: Northumbria, Mercia, East Anglia, and Wessex. Although Anglo-Saxon rulers were not strict adherents to primogeniture, they did not believe in dividing wealth and property among all heirs. Any aetheling, or prince, might be deemed successor to the throne; usually one was chosen either by his father or by consensus of the family or immediate community. Alfred inherited the

Alfred the Great overcame remarkable odds to defeat the Vikings and unite the Anglo-Saxon kingdoms into one nation—England.

throne in 871 after the death of his father and brothers—most of whom met their ends fighting against Viking invaders. Although he was never expected to inherit, his official biographer, a monk named Asser, composed an account of Alfred's life that suggested he was destined for greatness from a very young age.

Alfred's reign was remarkable for several reasons. The Vikings were a huge problem in 9th-century England, one that a number of English rulers had tried to address with little success. Alfred himself had several false starts at making peace with them. Part of Alfred's eventual peace with the Vikings involved ceding much of what had been the northern portion of Anglo-Saxon England to them, creating a true kingdom of the Anglo-Saxons and a territory known as the Danelaw. Ever the pragmatist, Alfred created a system of fortified towns, roughly equidistant from one another, known as the Burghal Hidage. Skilled seamanship made the Vikings such a significant threat, Alfred also commissioned a fleet of ships to augment the land defenses, an act that has given him the title "father of the English navy."

> **Once the threat of the Vikings was diminished, Alfred sought to bring greater stability to English society.**

Once the threat of the Vikings was diminished, Alfred sought to bring greater stability to English society. One way he did this was through the compilation, simplification, and codification of earlier laws. Alfred was very similar to Charlemagne—whom he consciously imitated on several occasions—in his desire and actions to preserve learning and create a system of education in England. Alfred felt strongly that the Viking attacks were punishment from God. Thus he also actively promoted the church, having many monasteries and churches devastated by the Viking attacks rebuilt. As part and parcel of his other reforms, Alfred sought to make his court a place of culture and learning. He thus tried to attract the greatest minds of the age to his court, ushering in a flowering of arts and letters that came to be known as the Alfredian Renaissance. Alfred's reforms set the stage for formation of the England we know today. ■

Questions to Consider

1. In what ways did Alfredian England mirror the policies, programs, and achievements of the Carolingian Empire under Charlemagne? In what important ways did the Alfredian Renaissance differ from the Carolingian?

2. What role did religious belief play in Alfred the Great's successful negotiation of peace with the Vikings? How did Alfred connect learning, books, and the religious tradition of England in his own words?

Alfred the Great
Lecture 10—Transcript

Welcome back. In our previous lecture, we discussed the awesome and terrifying threat posed by those Scandinavian seafarers known as the Vikings. Marauders and pillagers, sometimes little more than pirates, they were also great and occasionally hygienically fastidious explorers—journeying into parts of what is modern-day Russia, establishing and settling Iceland, and traveling to North America almost 500 years before Christopher Columbus "discovered" the New World. Yet while they penetrated throughout the medieval world and beyond, much of their activity occurred in the medieval West—particularly in parts of the Carolingian Empire and the British Isles. In Britain an unlikely king put a stop to their activities and achieved peace—albeit, only temporarily—with the Viking invaders. That king was named Alfred.

King Alfred of the Anglo-Saxon kingdom of Wessex is the only English monarch to be given the moniker "the Great," and as we will see there is good reason for this. But as we will also see, the fact that he not only became king, but also arguably became the greatest king of the English, was not at all to be expected given his family circumstances, the specific situation of Wessex in relationship to the other Anglo-Saxon kingdoms, and the serious threats posed by the Vikings.

Alfred was born into the Royal House of Wessex in the year 848. At this time, there were four main Anglo-Saxon kingdoms. North of the River Humber and south of what is today Scotland was the kingdom of Northumbria. Directly south of that was Mercia, and to the east of Mercia was the realm of East Anglia. In the south of the British Isles was the kingdom of Wessex, which had—at the time of Alfred's death—expanded beyond its traditional borders to the east to encompass the regions of Surrey, Sussex, Berkshire, Kent, and Essex—while to the west it had brought the largely Celtic region of Cornwall under its control. Wales, to the north and west of the West Saxon kingdom, remained strongly Celtic.

At his birth, no one could have predicted that Alfred would sit on the throne. He was the youngest of King Aethelwulf's five sons. The Anglo-Saxons managed to avoid the problems that the Merovingians and Carolingians constantly encountered in that they did not divide power, wealth, and property among all surviving sons. One son tended to inherit everything, although the Anglo-Saxons did not practice a strict form of primogeniture—any prince, or aetheling, had the potential to ascend to the throne, and occasionally we see second or third sons coming to rule—something that might happen if such a son had proved himself to be a particularly effective warrior, or an elder son had a disability of some sort. But more often than not, it is eldest sons that inherit everything in Anglo-Saxon England. So, as the youngest of five, the possibility of Alfred coming to the throne seemed slim at best. But not one of his brothers lived past the age of 30—most of them were killed fighting the Vikings—and so in 871, the last scion of the House of Wessex became king of the West Saxons—and what a king he was!

The legacy of Alfred's rule can be seen mainly in seven areas, which we will talk about in greater detail in a moment. These are, first: his defeat of the Vikings; second, his systematic fortification of Anglo-Saxon England to protect it from invasion; third, his creation of a naval fleet; fourth, his codification of English law; fifth, his promotion of education; sixth, his support of the church—and last, but certainly not least, his position as a patron of the arts, which produced something scholars call the Alfredian Renaissance.

Even if his family tree and the circumstances that propelled Alfred onto the throne did not presage the amazing feats he would achieve during his reign, his biography—written by one of his bishops, a Welshman named Asser— suggests that from an early age, Alfred of Wessex was destined for greatness. Asser tells several stories of Alfred's youth that would seem to foretoken those virtues that have long been associated with this hero of the English. For example, he relates the story of Alfred's mother, who showed to all her sons a beautiful book of poems. She told them that whoever read or learnt it first could have it. According to the story, Alfred, the youngest brother, took it to his tutor, learned it, and then proved to his mother that he was the first to have completed the challenge she had assigned them. We're not sure exactly what this means—did he learn the poems by heart, or did he simply learn how to read them? In part, this difficulty in determining the true meaning of the story is due to the fact that the surviving copies of Asser's biography of the king are in a rough, unfinished Latin that also at times is overwhelmingly verbose. The other issue with this story is that it may not be true—given the fact that we are also told that the young Alfred made two lengthy trips to Rome, and based on the date of his mother's death, the event with the book would have had to have taken place around the time Alfred was six years old. If it is true, he was a truly precocious child. At the very least, we can be sure that Asser included this story, true or not, because it helped to demonstrate that Alfred's concern with literacy and education was born very early in his life.

Another story Asser tells is of Alfred's first pilgrimage to Rome, an event also recorded in the *Anglo-Saxon Chronicle*, which was one of Asser's main sources, and which really existed only because of Alfred's desire that there be such an historical record. We are told that in the year 853, when Alfred was four or five, he was sent to Rome by his father—where Pope Leo IV consecrated him as king.

Again, although it appears that Alfred really did go to Rome, it seems unlikely that whatever happened with the pope was, in fact, a royal consecration. It might, in fact, have been a confirmation in the Christian faith. Alfred had older brothers aplenty, and although it would not be impossible for him to be designated heir to the throne, as Anglo-Saxon succession customs allowed for any prince or aetheling to inherit, Alfred's father was nearing the end of his life—and constant warfare would make it seem likely that that life might not run a natural course anyway. It would have been foolish to pass the throne to a five-year-old when there were older, more experienced and martially skilled sons who were obviously fit to rule. But Asser's story serves the purpose of making it seem as if Alfred's eventual reign as king and all the marvelous things he did as ruler of the West Saxons—and, eventually, all the Anglo-Saxons—were in some sense foreordained.

So, Alfred came to the throne of Wessex in 871 after the death of his brother, King Aethelred. He managed to secure a peace with the Viking invaders, but it lasted only 4 years. In 875, the Danes—as the Vikings were called by the Anglo-Saxons—renewed their attacks. As I mentioned earlier, Alfred was a supporter of the church and of education, and he saw the Viking attacks as being connected with the decay of religious practice and learning in the Anglo-Saxon world.

Interestingly, however, he did not think—as one might expect—that constant harassment of the English on the part of the Danes had caused religion and learning to decline, but rather, he thought of it the other way around—the decline of religion and learning had ultimately made the Viking attacks possible. He was a deeply pious man, who supposedly asked God, from a very early age, that he be sent a variety of physical ailments that would help him control his carnal lust. One such affliction sent by God was hemorrhoids, but as this interfered with his fighting ability, he asked that this affliction be removed and another be given—a prayer that God apparently granted, according to his biographer Asser.

For all his piety, however, he was pragmatic. The Vikings were not Christian, and Alfred recognized that getting their leaders to swear oaths of peace on bibles or Christian relics, such as saints' bones, was not going to have any binding effect. He tried to defeat the Vikings using their own logic—after one battle in 876 he had their leader swear on a ring holy to the Vikings— supposedly it was Thor's ring—and he had them swear on this ring that they would maintain a peace. To further ensure the continuance of a truce, both sides on this occasion exchanged hostages. This was a common practice in the medieval period, especially in Anglo-Saxon England—the idea was that you sent, say, 5 or 10 of your high-ranking men into the keeping of your enemy, and he sent the same number to you. The fact that these hostages could be killed at any provocation or perceived breaking of the treaty was supposed to keep everyone honest. But, as clever as Alfred's strategy seemed to be on this occasion, it failed—the Vikings killed their hostages, fled from Alfred's realm, and before the king was aware of what had happened, they had taken Exeter and fortified it against Alfred and his army.

Eventually Alfred was victorious in this conflict, but just a couple of years later, he was almost killed when a Viking raid took him completely by surprise. In haste, he fled into the Athelney Marshes in the region of Britain known as Somerset, and there he lived in hiding as he tried to come up with a strategy to defeat his enemy.

This is perhaps the most famous story concerning Alfred and is akin in the English tradition to the story in the United States of young George Washington chopping down a cherry tree. The story goes that while on the run from the Vikings in the fens of Athelney, Alfred took refuge in the hut of a swineherd and his wife, keeping his identity a secret from them. One morning, the wife asked Alfred to keep watch over some cakes that she was cooking while she left the house. Alfred was so preoccupied with his military strategy against the Danes that he allowed the cakes to burn, for which the housewife scolded him severely. Supposedly, Alfred bore her scolding meekly, and in return for his Job-like patience he was rewarded with divine assistance that eventually allowed him to defeat the Viking army. In fact, if you ask English schoolchildren today what they know about King Alfred, the response you are most likely to get is something like: "He drove the Danes out of Wessex, and he burnt some cakes." Another story has Alfred generously offering to share part of his meal with a stranger he encounters during his period of hiding. The stranger turns out to be Saint Cuthbert, who in turn, of course, later comes to Alfred's aid and gives him crucial information to help him defeat the Viking army.

Yet another story has Alfred disguising himself as a traveling entertainer—a juggler, or minstrel—and strolling into the Viking camp, where, in between entertaining the Vikings for several days, he learned their plans and war strategy—and thus, was able to come up with a plan of his own to defeat them.

Of course, defeat them he did. He did more than that, however. He in effect laid the foundation for England as we know it today. After defeating the Viking leader Guthrum in 878 at the Battle of Eddington, he made one of the conditions of the peace be that Guthrum accept Christian baptism—which the Viking leader did, with Alfred standing as his godfather. Alfred recognized that, like it or not, the Vikings were in England to stay, and so he proposed a division of land—essentially ceding the eastern portion of the kingdom of Mercia to the Vikings. This portion of Britain became known as the Danelaw, a term which signified that it was in this area that the laws of the Danes—rather than those of the English—were in effect, and which we've discussed briefly in a previous lecture.

Alfred also recognized, however, that the Viking threat continued to be a real one, and he took steps to further protect his people. One of these was the creation of a series of fortified towns, or burhs, scattered throughout his realm. These fortified spaces, the burhs, spelled b-u-r-h-s, is the source of our modern word "burg," or "bury," and it's often attached to place names—Pittsburg, Canterbury, and other cities too numerous to mention. If you look at a map, you can see that Alfred's fortifications are roughly equidistant from one another, and thus provided a remarkable system of safe havens to which people could retreat during times of conflict. This system of fortifications is known as the Burghal Hidage—a hide was an Anglo-Saxon measurement of land, usually thought to comprise about 120 acres, the amount of farmland that could support a single family.

As we've already discussed, the Vikings posed such a substantial threat in part because of their amazing seamanship. Viking vessels were easily maneuverable with a shallow draft, which meant they could quickly navigate up narrow rivers, taking rich communities there by surprise. Recognizing that he would have to deal with the threat from the water, Alfred also commissioned a fleet of ships to augment his other defenses, and thus he has become known as the father of the English navy.

Law was another area in which Alfred had a lasting impact on Anglo-Saxon society. He clarified and codified early Anglo-Saxon law codes, compiling them all in his *Book of Dooms*. "Doom" is an Old English word that means simply "judgment" or "law," so the *Book of Dooms* is not as frightening a text as it might sound at first. Alfred's law code provides a fascinating look at certain aspects of Anglo-Saxon society. For example, he builds on an earlier law code to standardize penalties known as *wergeld* and *bot*. Wergeld means simply "man-gold" or "man-price," and the institution of wergeld arose in Anglo-Saxon England as a strategy for ending the practice of blood-feud, whereby if a member of a particular family was killed, his kin might take revenge by killing one member of the killer's family, who might in turn take revenge by killing a member of the family of the man originally killed—and, well, you get the picture.

Wergeld codes established a price for every life, and bot was similar in that it established the cost of specific injuries—so that instead of families killing each other, one would be required to pay the other, and the matter would be considered settled. The lists of wergeld prices tell us something about the makeup of Anglo-Saxon society, as well as where many of their values lay. The penalties for various injuries make fascinating reading—for example, the law code originally instituted by King Aethelbert of Kent states that "if any one strike another with his fist on the nose, three shillings." If someone causes a bruise to another person, the cost was a shilling, but if the bruise was black and was on a part of the body not covered by clothing, additional payment needed to be made. To cut off someone's ear would cost 12 shillings, but causing someone to lose hearing in one ear would cost you more than twice that. The hierarchical nature of Anglo-Saxon society was quite clearly reinforced in the codes—for example, a nobleman's life was worth 1,200 shillings, but that of a peasant 200. Women who were of childbearing age had a higher wergeld than that of young girls or women past childbearing. The killing of a slave usually did not require a payment, but paying a small fee was considered the polite thing to do. Alfred himself showed concern for slaves by decreeing in his laws that on the Wednesday four weeks before Easter, slaves should be excused from performing any labor.

A word is in order here concerning slavery in Anglo-Saxon England. The word "slavery" conjures up, for most Americans, the tradition of race-based, lifelong slavery, as we know it from our own history. It was somewhat different in Anglo-Saxon England. While the fact that one of the early English words for slave is *Weallas*, from which comes the word "Welsh," tells us that certain groups were targeted as slaves in early medieval England. Anglo-Saxons themselves could also be slaves—either as a result of a military defeat, which happened when various Anglo-Saxon factions fought against one another from time to time—or one could be made a slave sometimes as punishment for a crime. For certain offenses, a person might be put into bondage—sometimes for a specified period of time, sometimes for life. Unlike in the United States, slavery in Anglo- Saxon England was a fluid, rather than static, position. One might be born a slave but achieve freedom through various means. One might be a slave for a short period due to some crime committed.

Occasionally, one might offer oneself up as a slave as a strategy for survival. This was frequently the case during periods of famine or other disasters.

People might approach the local lord or lady—and in a ceremony that solemnified the transaction would kneel before the nobleman or woman, who would place his or her hands on the supplicant's head. In the will of an Anglo-Saxon noblewoman from the 10th century, we see evidence of this, in that the lady decrees that she has freed from servitude "Ecceard the blacksmith and Aelfstan and his wife and all their offspring, born or unborn, and Arcil and Cole and Ecgferth [and] Ealdhun's daughter—all those people whose heads she took for their food in those evil days."

Alfred himself certainly believed that his society had fallen on evil times, and one of the signs of the decay of Saxon society to him was a sorry state of learning in his kingdom. As you may have gathered, there are many similarities between Alfred and Charlemagne, whose rule predated the Anglo-Saxon king's by about a century. Indeed, in composing his biography of Alfred, Asser used Einhard's biography of Charlemagne as a model—and in a few instances seems to have lifted entire passages from the account of the life of the Carolingian ruler and imported them into his own account of the West Saxon ruler's life. As much as this would seem to be egregious plagiarism, to a certain degree it makes sense, since these two figures had such similar concerns for their realms. One of the areas in which they are most similar is in their desire to create a system of education—but while Charlemagne focused on collecting and copying some of the greatest works to be found in the Latin tradition, Alfred was remarkable in that he wished to gather such important manuscripts and then translate them into West Saxon, making them accessible to a greater portion of the population. He himself translated several texts out of Latin into Anglo Saxon—including Boethius's *Consolation of Philosophy*, Bede's *Ecclesiastical History of the English People*, the *Pastoral Care* written by Pope Gregory as a guide for religious leaders, and the *Dialogues of Pope Gregory the Great*, among others. In his preface to *The Pastoral Care*, Alfred explains why he has undertaken this program—noting that once upon a time, England had been a great center for learning, and people had come from all over to learn and study there. Once upon a time:

> Before they were all ravaged and burnt, I had seen how the churches throughout England stood filled with treasures and books, and there was also a multitude of God's servants. They had very little benefit

from those books, because they could not understand anything of them because they were not written in their own language. It is as if they had said, our forefathers who formerly held these places loved knowledge, and through it they acquired wealth and left it to us. One can see their footprints here still, but we cannot follow after them. And therefore, we have lost both the wealth and the knowledge because we would not set our minds to the course.

In this preface, Alfred goes on to propose that certain books considered critically important should be translated into English, and that all free men be provided with the opportunity to learn to read these texts in their native Anglo-Saxon—particularly promising students could then go on to the study of Latin. In addition, Alfred established the *Anglo-Saxon Chronicle*, which exists today in seven different versions. These chronicles are fascinating in the way that they are all in agreement with the first series of events set down in them. They demonstrate a clear West Saxon bias—giving a significant amount of space to the rules of Alfred, his father, and grandfather. Up until the year 890 or so, they are roughly the same. At a certain point, however, they were deliberately dispersed throughout England to various monasteries—each of which added events as they occurred, and each of which displayed a local bias toward its particular region.

Part of Alfred's education program involved promotion of the church, and in this effort he ordered monasteries to be rebuilt—many of which had been ravaged by Viking invaders, who, as pagans, viewed them as treasure houses ripe for the picking inhabited by men who were not often able to mount any sort of effective defense. Much as Charlemagne had recruited learned scholars from across the Channel, particularly the Briton Alcuin of York, Alfred also sought to attract the greatest minds of his age—bringing in the most learned men to be found within Britain and on the Continent to help implement his program of education.

He also, like Charlemagne, wished to make his court a place of culture and learning, and his promotion of art and literature, his ambitious plan to educate all free-born men, his program of translation and his importing to the greatest scholarly minds of the day led to what has been termed the Afredian Renaissance—smaller in scale than the Carolingian Renaissance, but a flowering of culture the likes of which had not been seen in Britain for quite some time. With all of these programs, and most importantly, with his peace that he established through the creation of the Danelaw, Alfred ceases to be king of the West Saxons and becomes king of the Anglo-Saxons. Alfred's successes in battle against the Vikings and this division of land would set the stage for his grandson, Aethelstan the Glorious, to become the first real king of England.

Those Danes who had settled in the region known as the Danelaw fairly quickly became assimilated into English society. As I noted in our last lecture, "Viking" is not really a term that refers to any ethnic group; rather, it denotes an occupation—that of a sea raider, a kind of pirate, who is of Scandinavian heritage. When ceded the territory in the Danelaw, the Vikings essentially ceased to be Vikings—they became farmers, and crofters, and craftsmen. One interesting effect of this new, peaceful interaction between former enemies was the simplification of the English language. English is a Germanic language, and Old English was in many respects quite different from the language I'm speaking today. Old English nouns had three genders—masculine, feminine, and neuter—and it was also a heavily inflected language, meaning that the form of a word often revealed its function in a sentence, rather than word order conveying this, as is more the case today. One example that emphatically serves to demonstrate the difference between Old and Modern English: In Old English there were 18 different ways to say "the." The Vikings also spoke a Germanic language—probably something very close to Norse—and the languages were similar enough that a Dane and an Englishman could probably communicate fairly easily. Once these groups became neighbors, however, Old English lost much of its more complex inflections and forms, as the sort of rubbing together of the two languages resulted in a necessary simplification of both so that communication could be easier.

This first true incarnation of England, however, would be relatively fragile and short-lived. Viking attacks continued in the 10th century, and those people whose ancestors just a couple of generations earlier had found themselves the attackers, now found themselves on the receiving end of attacks by other groups of Danes. In this case, the word "Dane" is actually correct and is not just a catch-all word that might refer to sea raiders of any Scandinavian ethnic group. In the year 1013, Swein Forkbeard of Denmark declared himself king of England and Denmark—his hold on the throne was short-lived, however. But in 1016, Swein's son Cnut did become king of England, and his rule would usher in a period of struggle over the throne of England that would eventually culminate in the event we call the Norman Invasion, in 1066.

The 200 years right after Alfred's reign would bring huge changes to that island nation known as England—and huge changes as well for the rest of Europe and the communities on its borders. We've spent this lecture focusing on a particular region on the edge of the medieval world. In our next lecture, we're going to shift our attention back to the center and pull back a bit— so we can get a sort of bigpicture idea as to how particular religious ideas, invasions, and immigrations changed the shape of the medieval world in dramatic ways as we move from the early to the High Middle Ages.

The Rearrangement of the Medieval World
Lecture 11

> The watchword from about 900 to 1050 in Western Europe is "fragmentation," as formerly large realms divided themselves into smaller political entities—a process that was moved along by external as well as internal pressures. Then, as we move firmly into the High Middle Ages, particularly from 1100 on... medieval society begins to assume the forms that most of us ... tend to think of as quintessentially medieval.

Around the year 900, Western Europe began to rearrange itself. New leaders, their power based in military might, came to the fore, in the West as in the Byzantine and Islamic worlds, spurred on by Viking, Magyar, and Muslim invasions. Entering the High Middle Ages, Europe underwent further dramatic changes, including a population explosion, economic changes, technological advances, and the development of devout Christian piety among all classes.

These changes would lead to significant expansionist moves, including the Saxon push to the east, the Reconquista of Spain, the movement of Normans throughout Europe, and the crusading impulse. The religious fervor associated with the advent of the Crusades would also be felt in other areas of European society and would lead to the final break between the Byzantine and Roman churches.

El Cid captured Valencia from its Muslim rulers in 1094, a significant Christian victory during the centuries-long Reconquista.

© 2009 Jupiterimages Corporation, a Getty Images company.

Starting around the year 900, Western Europe began to rearrange itself in several different ways. One of the most profound was in terms of religion. In the Christian and Islamic worlds, almost all peoples that had previously practiced some form of polytheistic religion converted to one of the three major monotheistic religions. Latin, or Western, Christianity, would develop into what we know today as Roman Catholicism, while Byzantine Christianity gave rise to the Eastern Orthodox Church. The two churches began to go in different directions in the 8th century over iconoclasm and sharply different attitudes about the blending of secular and religious official duties.

Starting in the 10th century, the medieval world, due to external and internal pressure, began to fragment and rearrange itself roughly into the cultural and political entities we recognize today. Externally, Western Europe was pressured by various peoples on the move, including Muslims, Magyars (Hungarians), and Vikings. Internally, various peoples put additional pressure on the social and political structures of the medieval world, including expanding groups of Normans and Saxons. A revival of religious sentiment led Christian leaders to call for the Reconquista—a reconquest of Muslim Spain by Christian forces. The calling of the First Crusade set many groups of people on the move across Europe toward the Middle East.

> **By the 10th and 11th centuries, Christianity had fully trickled down into all classes, so that true religious faith was a powerful motivator in all social classes.**

Two fundamental changes in medieval society were at the root of most of this movement and expansion. The upper classes had become militarized, and greater emphasis was placed on patriarchy and primogeniture. Thus there were many younger sons denied inheritances but who nevertheless had military skills with which they could carve out a living. By the 10th and 11th centuries, Christianity had fully trickled down into all classes, so that true religious faith was a powerful motivator in all social classes.

In addition to the increased emphasis placed on military prowess and religious belief, several demographic changes played into Europe's rearrangement. From 1000 to 1300, the population of Europe roughly doubled, from approximately 38 million to 74 million. By 1300, most external invasions ceased. Slavery virtually disappeared. It was replaced by the more humane—and less expensive—system known as serfdom, improving quality of life for many. Advances in farming produced greater crop yields, and a warmer climate—known as the Little Warm Age or Little Optimum—helped produce still greater yields and made life easier for people at all social levels.

The major expansive moves of the 10th–12th centuries laid the foundation for many social developments that would occur in the later Middle Ages. The Normans, perhaps more than any other group, demonstrated successful social advancement as a result of military skill. They effectively "Normanized" much of Western Europe, claiming much of the British Isles and Sicily as their own. The Reconquista was a success (from a Christian point of view) primarily because of infighting within the Caliphate of Cordova. It also led directly to the formation of the new kingdoms of Castile, Aragon, and Portugal. Christian zeal led to a positive response to Pope Urban II's 1095 call to retake the Holy Land and Jerusalem. The Saxon *Drang nach Osten* (push to the east) was unique among these movements in that it was a push to secure more land for a growing population and was effected primarily through the resettlement of peasants onto lands that Saxon lords wished to claim. The various political entities of Europe had become more powerful and assertive—and more aware of the world beyond Europe's borders than previously. A new identity boundary—Christian versus non-Christian—would unify otherwise discrete and disparate European societies. ∎

Suggested Reading

Linehan and Nelson, *The Medieval World*.

Rosenwein, *A Short History of the Middle Ages*.

Questions to Consider

1. What role did religious belief and conversion play in the reshaping of Europe's borders in the 10th and 11th centuries?

2. How did medieval methods of self-identification—political, cultural, religious, and social—differ markedly from the ways in which modern people tend to identify themselves? Where can we see continuities of self-identification from the medieval to the modern period?

The Rearrangement of the Medieval World
Lecture 11—Transcript

Welcome back. In our last lecture, we talked about the only English monarch to be known as "the Great": Alfred of Wessex. We explored how this man, a fifth son and thus in the running for the title of "least likely to be king" came to the throne of the West Saxons and ultimately achieved peace with the marauding Vikings—dramatically reshaping the boundaries of the traditional Anglo-Saxon kingdoms in the process and setting the stage for a single unified English nation, over which his grandson, Aethelstan, would eventually rule. In the 200 years after Alfred's rule, England went through a dramatic period of dramatic transformation, culminating with the Norman Invasion led by William the Conqueror in 1066. England was not the only place in the medieval world that was undergoing some serious upheaval at this time, and in this lecture we're going to pull our focus back and look at the changes that were occurring throughout the medieval world during this period.

Starting around the year 900, Western Europe began to rearrange itself. New groups came to power, particularly as the might of the Carolingian dynasty began to wane. New political entities became dominant, and most often these entities were in some way connected with military strength. A similar shift occurred in the Byzantine and Islamic worlds, as we discussed in a previous lecture. In terms of religion, this is the period that I like to call "everyone pick a monotheism!" as essentially everyone in the European, Byzantine, and Middle Eastern worlds who had held polytheistic beliefs converted to either one of the two main forms of Christianity—Roman or Byzantine—to Islam or to Judaism.

In the beginning, there was little difference between the Christianity practiced in what we would call the Latin medieval church, also called the Western Church, and the one that would eventually develop into Roman Catholicism—and that practiced in Byzantium, which eventually became what we call Eastern Orthodox Christianity today. However, in the Middle Ages, Byzantine Christianity was much more markedly a Christianity in which secular and religious roles were often blurred together. With the iconoclastic controversy of the 8th century, a divide between the two forms of Christianity began to grow, as the Latin Church saw iconoclasm as threatening not only to its rituals and many popular expressions of religion, but also threatening to the office of the papacy. It would be a divide that would never truly heal.

This division within Christianity—in conjunction with other religious shifts—would be just one of the factors that would produce a remarkable change in how the medieval world looked. The watchword from about 900 to 1050 in Western Europe is "fragmentation," as formerly large realms divided themselves into smaller political entities—a process that was moved along by external as well as internal pressures. Then, as we move firmly into the High Middle Ages, particularly from 1100 on, Europe begins to expand its borders out from what we might call its heartland, the Carolingian Empire— and medieval society begins to assume the forms that most of us who know a little something about the period tend to think of as quintessentially medieval.

If we look at what we might call external pressures, we have three sets of invasions that reshape the medieval world during this period. In the area around the Mediterranean, we see conflicts with Muslim military forces. In Eastern Europe, the Hungarians (or Magyars) proved a formidable raiding force. To the north and west, the Vikings, whom we have already talked about at some length, began to shift from seasonal raids focused on looting and pillaging to more permanent moves involving the immigration and settlement of families.

Spain—properly called Al-Andalus—had become a Muslim territory in the 8th century, as we've previously discussed. The larger Muslim world itself was undergoing some significant changes and reorganization at this time, with new groups—such as the Samnids, Buyids, Fatimids, and Zirids— coming to power and jockeying for position. The Umayyads in Spain made some raids into southern France and Italy. In the early 10th century, they captured the island of Sicily and brought it under Muslim rule. Dissent within Muslim Spain itself led to Al-Andalus being divided into smaller realms—called *taifas*—in the 11th century. Obviously, in a practical sense, much of the division within the Islamic world directly affected communities on the Arabian Peninsula in the Middle East, and in north Africa. But at the same time it would be a mistake to think that understanding what's happening in the Muslim world isn't critical to understanding developments in the medieval world—and not just in Spain. Throughout the European Middle Ages, contact with the Islamic world would precipitate important developments—especially in the areas of science, math, and medicine. In some instances, conflict with the Muslim world would shape politics and religion in hugely significant fashion, particularly when it comes to those events known as the Crusades, which we will discuss in two later lectures.

Going back to the 10th century, however, Western Europe was significantly impacted by the Hungarians or Magyars. These were a nomadic people who came from the area around the Black Sea. Renowned for their ferocity in battle, they were hired as mercenaries by the king of the East Franks, but later decided to stay in the region—conquering the Danube River Basin, and from there continuing to raid into parts of what is today Germany, Italy, and southern France. Their raiding activity stopped under King Otto I of Germany, a powerful lord who not only managed to bring the German duchies under control, but who also marched into Italy and proclaimed himself king there in 951. These moves eventually earned him the imperial crown, and it is in this period that the idea of the Holy Roman Empire becomes more focused on what is today Germany—rather than the area we know as modern France, which had been the case when Charlemagne held the crown. For the rest of its existence, the Holy Roman Empire would continue to be torn between its German and Roman identities, a tension that would lead ultimately to the weakening of its power and influence.

So Francia, the Carolingian Empire of Charlemagne, had become divided and weakened; 60 years after Charlemagne's death, the unity of his empire had completely disappeared. Similarly, Alfredian England—which had become the unified kingdom of the Anglo-Saxons under his rule—was, after a brief period of peace, experiencing additional Viking raids. Alfred's successors had adopted a policy of appeasement—often paying off the Vikings whenever they appeared ready to make a raid, and as we discussed in an earlier lecture. But this policy rankled many Anglo-Saxon nobles—many of whom, although Christian, still held admiration for the ideals of the warrior band, the comitatus, and sacrificial devotion to one's lord. The Vikings' power increased, and the defensive measures put in place by Alfred proved to have been ill-maintained and woefully inadequate to counter their threat. For reasons too complicated to go into here, the end result of the English-Danish struggle would be the conquest of England by the Normans in 1066, which is the subject of our next lecture.

The Normans did much more than simply conquer England, however, and during this period they are everywhere—in the medieval world, from the Scandinavian North down into the Mediterranean. The movement of the Normans throughout Western Europe is just one of four major expansions of European borders that we have beginning in the 11th century. The Normans represent one of these expansive moves that we might identify as an internal pressure on the structure of medieval society. The other three are what we call the Spanish Reconquista, the Saxon expansion to the east known as the *Drang nach Osten*, and the Crusades. In order to understand how and why these shifts happen we need to understand some basic facts about how the medieval world was changing. There are two fundamental societal changes at the root of this expansion. The first is the increasingly military nature of the upper classes of society, and the second is the progressive Christianization of almost all social classes and groups in the medieval world.

First, the militarization of the upper classes: In the early Middle Ages, society was dominated by a rural aristocracy that adhered to what some historians—rightly, I believe—have called a "cult of violence." As we move toward the end of the first millennium, we begin to see the real development of a warrior aristocracy, and one of the most significant aspects of this was the fact that more and more, the horse became an important part of military strategy. In the early Middle Ages, before stirrups came into common use, you would ride your horse to the battle, dismount, fight, and if you survived, you would re-mount your horse and ride back home after the battle was over. We'll talk much more about military equipment and tactics in a later lecture, but for our present purposes, the important thing to understand is that by the time we get to the 11th century, the horse had become an important element in medieval warfare. Being a warrior was expensive. You had to be able to afford and maintain armor, sword, shield, and especially a horse—and thus, it was really only available to wealthier members of the upper class.

At the same time, we see a shift in the way aristocratic families are structured. Patriarchy, or the importance of the father's family, began to play a much more important role in family identification—whereas prior to this, the mother's family or heritage might be viewed as equally important in determining someone's social status. Family surnames come into usage around this time, and in a patriarchal system, it will almost always be the father's family name that is given to all heirs. In addition, we start to see more uniform practice of the system known as primogeniture, which is a system under which the eldest son inherits almost all the wealth, property, and—arguably most importantly—titles that are available to be passed down. This created a situation in which you have younger aristocratic sons who were denied inheritances, but who still had military skills. Although many younger aristocratic males entered the church, others had the ability to try and carve out a living and wealth for themselves by means of battle and conquest—a fact that fueled the impulse to expand the borders of the medieval European world.

By the 10th and 11th centuries, Christianity, which for much of the period immediately preceding the High Middle Ages had been largely confined to the upper classes of society, had effectively trickled down to all social strata. We can never discount how strong a motivator real religious faith was in the medieval world. Although many who participated in religiously oriented activities—such as the Reconquista of Muslim Spain or the Crusades to the Holy Land—certainly did so out of greed or ambition with an eye toward what earthly benefits they might accrue, it seems clear that the majority of those who participated did so with a sincere belief in the rightness of what they were doing.

Some demographic shifts during the High Middle Ages also fueled the rearrangement and expansion of the medieval world. Although we can never be exactly sure about the numbers, it seems probable to most historians that between 1000 and 1300, the population of Europe almost doubled—going from about 38 million to 74 million people. There are a few reasons for this. One is that those invasions of the 10th century—the Vikings, the Magyars, etc.—had essentially ceased. Also, around the year 1000, slavery—meaning true bondage, in which people were treated as chattels, as property—was replaced with a slightly less restrictive system known as serfdom. There are several reasons for this shift, but the simplest explanation is that under slavery, although the person who "owned" the people could demand any and all labor of them, he also had to feed, clothe, and house them—something that became expensive. Serfdom changed the rules a bit. Serfs might be bound to a lord and usually held lands from him that they farmed for themselves, giving the lord a percentage of the harvest, and they also owed the lord a certain number of days of labor on his own lands. There was also a complicated system of taxes that serfs might owe their lords, and any number of other inconveniences, but in return the serfs could expect protection from the lord in times of difficulty—no small matter when it came to the medieval world and its sometimes-rampant violence. Serfs thus enjoyed a quality of life much better than slaves, and under these more advantageous circumstances, their population increased.

The population explosion was also a result of some other factors, among them technological advances when it came to farming, which led to greater crop yields. This period was also marked by a slightly—but significantly—warmer climate, and, in fact, some scientists have labeled this time the Little Warm Age, or Little Optimum. The common use of cast iron cooking pots meant that people were getting more iron—from this source and from increased consumption of meat—and this helped to prolong life expectancy and general health. The added iron in the medieval diet had, from a reproductive standpoint, the benefit of allowing adolescents to reach puberty earlier than had previously been the case. Some scientists estimate that medieval people, on average, entered puberty sometime between 16 and 18. With increased iron in the diet, the onset of puberty moved to sometime between the ages of 14 and 16 on average, which meant that people could reproduce sooner.

So we have more people, and we need a place to put them all. An examination of the major expansive moves of the 10th through the 12th century helps us to see more clearly how these social and demographic changes were manifested in Western Europe, and how they laid the foundation for many of the social developments that would occur in the later Middle Ages and which we'll be talking about in several lectures to come.

The Normans, whom we've already talked about some this time and whom we'll discuss at even greater length in our next lecture, are the prime example of successful social advancement as a result of military prowess. Descendents of Viking raiders, in the 10th century, they settled in that portion of France that is called Normandy—a name that literally means "home of the north men." The French king, being no dummy, realized that it would be much better to have such fantastic warriors fighting with him than against him, so he made their leader Hrolfe, or Rollo, a duke; officially ceded him Normandy; and the rest, as they say, is history. From this base, the Normans spread throughout Europe so pervasively that many scholars actually refer to the Normanization of Europe, a process that gently—or, in some instances, not so gently—caused cultures and societies that had been vastly different to become, to at least some degree, more alike, resulting in a certain amount of cultural uniformity in the medieval world that had not previously existed. Both by conquest and by grafting themselves onto established noble families, the Normans moved into positions of power and influenced economic infrastructure in places where they conquered and/or settled—making Western Europeans more similar to one another in many respects than they had been prior to this.

A very different sort of expansion occurred on the Iberian Peninsula in the form of the Spanish Reconquista, or reconquest of Spain from Muslim rule. As you'll remember from a previous lecture, most of what we think of today as Spain had been Muslim from the year 711, although a few Christian principalities remained on the peninsula. The increase in Christian belief through all levels of society in combination with the militarization of the nobility as we head into the High Middle Ages meant that there was a large body of armed men willing to fight to "free" Spain from its Muslim rulers. Properly speaking, the Reconquista had been happening almost since the moment Muslim leaders had claimed portions of Spain for themselves in the 8th century, and there had been several moves to take back Spain for Christianity. Charlemagne himself had made forays into Spain in the late 8th century. But although ruled by Muslim leaders for over two centuries, Al-Andalus—which again, is the proper name for Spain during the period from the early 8th to the late 11th centuries—was not a wholly Islamic community. Plenty of Christians lived side by side with Muslims—holding official jobs, speaking Arabic, and occasionally intermarrying with them. These Christians were called Mozarabs or "would-be Arabs," and they and the Muslim and Jewish inhabitants of Al-Andalus enjoyed a life that was flourishing in terms of culture and the arts.

But in the year 1002, the caliphate of Córdoba broke up, and the various Muslim communities began warring amongst themselves—soon dividing themselves up into those taifas I mentioned earlier, small communities that were ruled by local strongmen. This meant that the Spanish Christian rulers to the north of Al-Andalus suddenly had a real opportunity to conquer the regions to the south that were now fractured and divided against themselves—and that is exactly what happened. In 1085, King Alfonso VI of Léon and Castile conquered the Muslim stronghold of Toledo. In 1094, one of Alfonso's subjects, one Rodrigo Diaz de Vivar, who came to be known as El Cid and who is the subject of the famous *Poem of the Cid*, took Valencia. At the same time, another kind of reconquest, a religious reconquest, was happening—as Cluniac monks and others began moving into Spain in the 11th century to found, reform, and conquer Spanish monasteries and other religious institutions. The religious and military fervor bubbling through Europe accelerated what we might call the Europeanization of Spain. In 1212, Pope Innocent the III officially declared a Crusade against Muslims in Spain—and in 1236, Córdoba itself fell to Castile. By the late 13th century, the only Muslim stronghold left was in Granada. The crusading zeal of the High Middle Ages rearranged most of Spain into the three kingdoms of Castile, Aragon, and Portugal.

This Crusading ideal that had transformed Al-Andalus into Spain was just an offshoot of a much larger movement that had as its aim the Christianization of the Holy Land in the Middle East—and which officially began in 1095 when Pope Urban II, at the Council of Clermont, called for the First Crusade. We will devote two later lectures to the issue of the Crusades, but it is important for our purposes here to note that huge numbers of men—young and old, but very often young, and junior members of noble families as well—found in the Levant opportunities that would have been unavailable to them in the medieval world of Europe. While it is certain that true, sincere, religious feeling provoked many of them to join the Crusading movement, it is also true that many of them who went East did not return home—instead remaining there and establishing themselves more comfortably than could have ever been possible in the West—with some of them becoming lords, dukes, and even kings in a land that became known as Outremer, or "across the sea."

So, we have the Normans spreading throughout the medieval world from north to south and especially west into England, Christian forces moving into Spain, European incursions into the Middle East, and then the fourth example of expansion I'd like to discuss: the Saxon *Drang nach Osten*, which means literally "push to the east," and which is unique among the expansion movements we've explored today in that it was not a product of royal or papal policy, or one man's ambition to conquer a particular territory. Rather this movement was spearheaded by the Dukes of Saxony, and its original motivation had nothing to do with military conquest and everything to do with relocating a burgeoning population.

Interestingly, the main group that participated in this movement into central Europe were not aristocrats, but rather members of the peasant classes. What had happened is that many of the German lords had claimed new territories in central Europe, but they had no real means of overseeing those territories and controlling them from their original home bases in Saxony. Starting in the 1060s, peasants and skilled laborers were actively recruited by a class of men known as *locatores* who served as middlemen between commoners and a lord who wished to develop the territories he had claimed in central Europe. In exchange for having the peasants do the heavy labor of settling and working what was—in some cases—virgin land, as well as recruiting other settlers, those who traveled east were given a substantial grant of land to call their own with hereditary privileges.

One of their number would usually also be named to act as *schulze*, or the local magistrate, of the new territory. What we have to remember is that medieval society in the High Middle Ages was very static, especially when it came to upward mobility. Movement between classes was practically unheard of, and those peasants who lived on the manor of a lord were probably descendents of peasants who had served the ancestor of that lord, and the descendents of those peasants would most likely serve the descendent of the lord, and so on, and so on. The *Drang nach Osten* was largely unprecedented in that it was not just an aristocratic migration, but that commoners were relocating—and further, it was unusual in that it provided unique opportunities for farmers to actually own their own property, instead of simply holding it from a lord in exchange for labor and a percentage of the harvest. It was unique also in that it offered the opportunity for advancement up the social scale into political office, albeit to a relatively minor post. The *Drang nach Osten* also made these new opportunities hereditary, dramatically affecting the futures of the families who participated.

As a result of the *Drang nach Osten*, central Europe became Germanized and Christianized—with peoples such as the Poles, Bohemians, and Magyars or Hungarians now looking toward Germany and Rome as models of civilization. Paganism, which had retained a hold in central Europe, was put on the defensive—and the Baltic lands of Prussia, Lithuania, and Latvia had given up pagan or polytheistic beliefs by the 14th century.

The result of these expansive moves is the beginning of what we might call European hegemony. Although there was no central European authority, the various political entities of Europe had become more powerful, more assertive, and more alike. More aware of the world beyond Europe's borders than previously, a new identity boundary—Christian versus non-Christian—would unify otherwise discrete and disparate European societies. This European hegemony would arguably last until the beginning of the 20th century and the First World War.

As we discussed in today's lecture, the Normans were one of the most important groups moving through the medieval world at this time. Perhaps the most significant and far-reaching example of Norman Expansion occurred in 1066, when William of Normandy staked a claim to the throne of England after the last Anglo-Saxon king, Edward the Confessor, died without an heir. As we will see, William was cousin to the members of the English Royal House, and thus he may have had a legitimate claim. The English, understandably, didn't see it that way and fought bitterly to keep the invader at bay. They almost succeeded. If they had defeated William and his army, the history of England—and, indeed, the whole medieval world—would have been vastly different. Until 1066, England, on the far west fringes and across the Channel from the Continent, had been more Scandinavian than continental European.

With one fell swoop, William's conquest literally reoriented the medieval world, bringing England within the embrace of continental Europe and dramatically re-shifting the power structures that were in place. How and why this happened is the subject of our next lecture.

The Norman Conquest and the Bayeux Tapestry
Lecture 12

> Harold stands between two reliquaries that most likely held the bones
> of saints—and with a hand on each, swears to support William's claim
> to the throne. ... Soon after [Harold's] return to England, Edward the
> Confessor dies, and Harold—violating his oath to William—becomes
> king of England. The occasion of his coronation, according to the
> tapestry, is marked by a meteor or comet in the sky—an omen of ill
> fortune for the English.

The Norman Conquest of England was in effect a family dispute. The
life of one woman in particular, Emma of Normandy, helps illustrate
the interconnectedness of the ruling families. Emma was the daughter
Richard I, Duke of Normandy. To maintain peace between the Normans and
the Anglo-Saxons, Emma was married to King Aethelred II of England.
When Aethelred died, Emma was promptly taken as a wife by the Danish
king, Cnut, who claimed to be ruler of Denmark, Norway, and England;
England at this time was more part of the Scandinavian than the Continental
world. Emma became mother and stepmother to four other English rulers. First
came her stepsons by Aethelred, Edmund Ironside and Harold; then her son by
Cnut, Harthacnut; then finally her son by Aethelred, Edward the Confessor,
returned from exile to take the throne.

The major and immediate situation that led to the Norman Conquest was the
fact that Edward the Confessor had no heirs. He had spent much of his life
living in exile in Normandy and had supposedly developed a fondness for
his Norman cousins. One of these, William, was the grandson of Edward's
uncle (his mother's brother). William claimed Edward had named him as
heir. While there may be some truth to this, it seems clear that near the end of
his life, Edward had a change of heart and named his brother-in-law, Harold
Godwinson, as the heir to the throne.

Although many chronicle accounts tell the story of the Norman Conquest,
one of the most fascinating accounts is pictorial: the piece of embroidery
known as the Bayeux Tapestry. The tapestry is 231 feet long and tells the

The Tower of London was the first Norman castle in England, built under the direction of William the Conqueror.

story of the Norman Conquest in colorful embroidery, most likely executed at Canterbury by English hands. According to the tapestry, near the end of his life Edward sent Harold across the channel to confirm that William would inherit the English throne. It shows William rescuing Harold from a precarious situation in Normandy and the two cementing their friendship by engaging in various military campaigns. Harold is depicted as swearing to uphold William's claim to the throne. On his return to England, however, Harold is shown to renege on his oath and assume the English throne on Edward's death.

Here the tapestry skips over some of the key events that contributed to William's conquest of England, the most important of which was the surprise invasion by King Harold Hardrada of Norway. While William and his assembled fleet waited for good weather to cross the English Channel, Harold Hardrada invaded the North of England. In a stunning military victory, Harold Godwinson and his army defeated Hardrada at the Battle of Stamford Bridge on September 25, 1066. Two days later, William and his army set sail and landed at Pevensey. Bolstered by his victory at Stamford

Bridge, Harold moved his army south in a forced march to meet William's army on October 14, 1066.

According to the tapestry, the battle that raged was a fierce one, and it looked for a time as if Harold would prevail. William's army held the disadvantageous downhill position. The crush of bodies in the battle was so thick that according to some accounts—and graphically depicted by the tapestry—there was not even room for the dead to fall. At one point a rumor swept the battlefield that William had been killed or had fled. He removed his helmet to show his troops that he was still alive and in the thick of the battle. The tide was firmly turned in favor of the Normans when Harold was killed by an arrow through the eye.

> **The crush of bodies in the battle was so thick that according to some accounts—and graphically depicted by the tapestry—there was not even room for the dead to fall.**

The Norman Conquest is a rare historical instance where, almost overnight, everything about a culture was transformed. Within just a few years, 99 percent of the Anglo-Saxon aristocracy had either been killed or displaced. The wealth and lands of some 4,000 English were redistributed among just 200 or so of William's barons. The language of the ruling class switched from English to a type of French we call Anglo-Norman. Other changes—from hunting laws to the use of stone for building and the introduction of the fireplace—were also attendant on William's conquest of England. By far the greatest effect was that from this point on, England would be more a part of the continental European world than of the Scandinavian world. ■

Suggested Reading

Bloch, *A Needle in the Right Hand of God*.

Chibnall, *Debate on the Norman Conquest*.

Lewis, *The Rhetoric of Power in the Bayeux Tapestry*.

1. How might later medieval history been different if England had remained part of the Scandinavian rather than continental European world?

2. What kind of value does a historical witness such as the Bayeux Tapestry have in comparison to more typical documentary evidence from the medieval world?

The Norman Conquest and the Bayeux Tapestry
Lecture 12—Transcript

Welcome back. In our previous lecture, we discussed the major reorganization of the medieval world from about 900 to 1100, examining how religious belief contributed to activities such as the Spanish Reconquista and the Crusades, and how the desire for land led aristocrats from Saxony to resettle peasants in territories in central Europe—a move known as the *Drang nach Osten*. One group that spread throughout Europe were the Normans—originally a Germanic people with cultural ties to both the Vikings and the Anglo-Saxon Royal Houses. Today we're going to talk about the Norman Conquest of England in 1066, but we're going to examine it from the perspective of a family conflict, and also engage it in terms of one of the earliest accounts of that event—which is not a text, but a famous piece of embroidery known as the Bayeux Tapestry.

In order to understand how William of Normandy came to conquer England, we need to remember some background—primarily, that the Vikings and Anglo-Saxons are culturally related. Both are Germanic groups. In the case of the struggle over the English throne in the 10th and 11th centuries, what we have is really a family feud of sorts. Those Danes and English who fought one another for control of England were cousins, and at the center of this maelstrom of ambition is a woman named Emma of Normandy. The family relationships are complicated, but it is worth trying to sort through them so that we can understand what happened at the Battle of Hastings in 1066, and why. By using Emma as a focal point, we can begin to make a kind of sense out of the complicated family relationships that eventually brought England under Norman control.

Emma was the daughter of Richard I, duke of Normandy, who ruled until the late 10th century in that area of what is today part of France. As we've discussed in a previous lecture, the word "Norman" simply means "northman," and that was who had settled Normandy—Northmen, or Vikings. After they did this, something very interesting happened—they essentially became domesticated. Within just a century or so, they gave up most of their distinctly Germanic cultural identity, including their language, and became French—adopting the language, social conventions, and cultural ideals of the people they had defeated.

In order to help maintain a truce between the Normans and the English, Emma, daughter of Richard, duke of Normandy, married King Aethelred II of England, during whose reign attacks by Danes became increasingly violent and frequent. Aethelred had made a policy of paying Danegeld—literally, "Dane gold"—to buy off the Danes and persuade them to cease their raiding activities, but their activities were continuing to increase—and his hold over his kingdom had essentially collapsed when he died in 1016. It was he who was king during the infamous Battle of Maldon, which occurred in 991. As we've already discussed a bit, Anglo-Saxon monarchs in the later 10th century had adopted a policy of paying off the Vikings.

Essentially, when a boatload of raiders showed up, they offered the community they were about to plunder a choice—pay us off and we'll go away peacefully, or suffer the consequences. King Aethelred II, called *Æthelred the Unraed* in Old English, which translates as "Ethelred the Ill-Advised," but is often rendered in modern English as "Ethelred the Unready," had long had a policy of paying off the Vikings. As we've already discussed, on this occasion, Lord Byrtnoth famously told the Viking leader that instead of gold, he would send him spears for tribute, and then Byrtnoth allowed the enemy army to cross the tidal river Pante—today called the Blackwater—from the island on which they were waiting, form ranks, and commence a battle in which the English forces were decimated.

Aethelred's widow, Emma, had spent much of this dangerous period during the Viking raids in exile back home in Normandy, where she had fled for her safety along with her children by Aethelred—two boys and a girl, one of whom would grow up to become the English King Edward the Confessor. When King Aethelred died, Emma was promptly taken as a wife by the Danish King Cnut who claimed the kingships of England, Denmark, and Norway. By him, she had two children—one of whom, Harthacnut, would also be king of England for a time. We know very little about what Emma thought and felt about this situation, but taking a moment to grasp the realities of her situation helps drive home how interconnected the English,

Danes, and Normans were at this time—and it helps us understand as well how the Norman Invasion came to happen.

So, to sum up the situation of Emma—she is daughter of the Royal House of Normandy; she is married to two Kings of England—the Anglo-Saxon Aethelred II and the Danish King Cnut. In each of her marriages, she was the second wife her husband had taken, and in an odd coincidence, the names of both kings' first wives were Aelfgifu—which means "elf gift." So, she is queen of England twice. She is also stepmother to two kings of England. Aethelred's son by his first wife, Edmund Ironside, was king of England just briefly in 1016. Upon his death—perhaps from natural causes, perhaps from an assassination by poison—the Danish King Cnut took the throne and Emma as his wife. After Cnut's death, another of Emma's stepsons, Harold, Cnut's son by his first wife, came to the throne. Upon Harold's death, Emma's son by Cnut, Harthacnut, became king of England. Emma's son with Aethelred, Edward, was invited back to England from Normandy in 1041 by members of the Anglo-Saxon nobility. When Harthacnut died, Edward became king in 1042. You thought your family tree was complicated.

The problem was Edward the Confessor had no heirs. There has been much speculation about the reasons for this, and there are some who feel that his deep religious piety—hence the moniker "the Confessor"—had led him to live a chaste life, even though he was married to Edith, daughter of Earl Godwine of Wessex. Because he had spent a great part of his life living in exile in Normandy among his mother's family, he had supposedly developed a fondness and closeness with this branch of his family—and according to his cousin, William, Edward had named him as his heir. William's grandfather was the brother of Edward the Confessor's mother, Emma, so he did have some sort of legitimate claim to the throne. Toward the end of his life, so the story goes, Edward had a change of heart and named as his successor his brother-in-law Harold, the head of the most powerful family in England at the time, the Godwinesons.

The story of what happened next is mentioned in a few written accounts, but none tell it as compellingly as one of the most remarkable pieces of art to survive from the medieval period: an embroidered textile known as the Bayeux Tapestry—231 feet long, it tells the story of the Norman Conquest of

England in images stitched in colorful thread. For a time it was believed that this piece had been commissioned and perhaps sewn in part by Mathilda, William's wife. More recently, scholars have tended to think that Bishop Odo of Bayeux, the Conqueror's half-brother, commissioned the piece to be displayed in the Cathedral at Bayeux—although there has been some fierce debate about this as well. The style and a few of the images suggest fairly convincingly that, although the *Tapestry* tells the story of the defeat of the English, it was, in fact, sewn in England at Canterbury. Indeed, a few of the curious animal figures in the margins of the Bayeux Tapestry seem to have been copied directly from designs found in Canterbury Cathedral.

The *Tapestry* seems to be missing a few panels, but it is amazing that we have as much of it as we do. After being mentioned in an inventory at the Cathedral of Bayeux in 1476, it largely disappears from the record until the French Revolution, when it was being used as a wagon cover. Rescued then from what was sure to be its certain death, it probably survived into the modern period because it was largely forgotten—it was wound around a large spool in the basement of the Louvre while World War II raged over and around it.

The *Tapestry* as we have it opens with a scene in which Edward the Confessor is deciding to whom he should leave his kingdom. After deciding on his cousin, William, across the Channel, the *Tapestry* indicates that he sends his brother-in-law, Harold Godwineson, to Normandy to inform William that he has been named heir to the English throne. Harold's party is depicted as setting off accompanied by hunting dogs and birds, symbolizing that this is a peaceful mission. Harold and his party are also depicted with moustaches, while the Normans are represented as having the backs of their heads shaved throughout the *Tapestry*—an easy way to distinguish the enemy fighters from one another.

Although this is a story of war, the *Tapestry* includes some delightfully whimsical moments—the vibrant colors of these ships and their sails suggest cartoons of the modern age. Little details, such as the men hiking up their tunics to keep them dry as they wade out to board their ships, speak to the input of an eyewitness, or at least an experienced warrior and seafarer—and to the sense of humor and delight in detail present in the hands that stitched these scenes.

According to the *Tapestry*, Harold Godwineson's arrival in Normandy does not go well, as he is taken captive almost immediately by one of Duke William's vassals. William ransoms Harold, and they return to William's palace. Next occurs one of the great mysteries of the Bayeux Tapestry. Standing between two pillars is a woman whose name—Aelfgyva—is stitched above her. Stretching his hand out so that he can touch or strike her face is a male figure who is clearly a monk. More shocking, however, is what is embroidered in the lower margin, which up until this point has depicted what we might think of as simple decorative flourishes—various animals, plants, crosses—some of which are so crudely rendered that a few scholars have suggested that children were allowed to help with the *Tapestry*. But below Aelfgyva and the monk is stitched a naked man, squatting so that his genitalia are on full display. No one today knows who Aeflgyva was—it was a commonenough name—and why a monk might be touching her face while a naked man is represented below. The general consensus is that it must have been a reference to some sexual scandal that was so wellknown there was no need to offer more explanation than that that was already given in the *Tapestry* itself. Nor do we know what this might have to do with William's eventual conquest of England. It is a mystery that we can only hope scholars might be able to solve one day.

After this moment in the *Tapestry*, we see William and Harold engaging in some campaigns together—culminating in the key moment in the narrative and the linchpin in William's claim to be king and his right to invade. Harold stands between two reliquaries that most likely held the bones of saints—and with a hand on each, swears to support William's claim to the throne. The fact that this oath is made on two such sacred objects is hugely important— as such an oath is inviolable, even if it is made under duress. For medieval Christians, oaths that were compelled could be rendered null, but an oath made on the bones of a saint could never be undone or withdrawn—no matter the circumstances that led to its being sworn.

Soon after his return to England, Edward the Confessor dies, and Harold— violating his oath to William—becomes king of England. The occasion of his coronation, according to the *Tapestry*, is marked by a meteor or comet in the sky—an omen of ill fortune for the English. William across the Channel then begins to plan for an invasion of England to take what is rightfully his, as the narrative of the *Tapestry* suggests, and he orders the building of boats.

Here, the *Tapestry* largely elides or skips over some of the most important events that led to William's eventual victory over the English. If we think back to Emma of Normandy and the family tree of the English, Norman, and Danish royal families, you'll remember how much England was really at this time a part of the medieval Scandinavian world, rather than the world of continental Europe that had been so dominated for a time by the Carolingian Empire. Once he had his fleet assembled, William was hindered by bad weather and contrary winds, and he had to delay his intended Channel crossing by some weeks. While William waited on the weather and Harold waited for William, the new king of England was stunned to receive the news that the ambitious Harold Hardrada, king of Norway, had invaded the north of England. It was in response to this crisis that Harold Godwineson would receive the nickname that would stay with him down through the ages—Harold Harefoot, meaning quickfooted, speedy like a hare or rabbit. He marched north more quickly than anyone would have thought possible, taking Hardrada by surprise and defeating and killing him at the famous Battle of Stamford Bridge on September 25th, 1066.

As stunning and impressive as this battle was, the timing could not have been worse for Harold Godwineson. Two days after Stamford Bridge, the winds changed and William set sail for the south of Britain—landing at Pevensey, where he and his troops found little or no opposition. The next scenes of the Bayeux Tapestry are fascinating for their detail and their domesticity, as they show the daily life of a war camp—foraging through the countryside to secure food and other supplies; setting up kitchens, and cook fires, and dining tables; and then what would become the hallmark of the Norman presence in England and the means by which William would ultimately consolidate his power—the building of a castle.

When we hear the word "castle" today most people bring to mind an image that somewhat resembles Sleeping Beauty's castle at Disneyland, which itself was modeled on a real structure—Germany's Neuschwanstein Castle.

But this castle was not built until the 19th century, and it reflects an overly idealized and sanitized image of what a medieval castle should look like. In reality, medieval castles were built first for advantage of position and defense, and only incidentally—if ever—with comfort or luxury in mind. The quickest and most effective sort of castle and the type favored by William, at least initially, was something called the motte-and-bailey castle. Usually these were constructed by digging a circular trench. The earth from the trench was piled in the center of the circle—forming a mound, or the motte. On top of this motte would be the defensive structure—usually built of wood, occasionally built of stone. Sometimes wooden structures would be replaced by stone once a firm command of an area had been established. Below the motte and also encircled by a ditch would be the area known as the bailey, which is essentially where the day-today living and working of all the people associated with the castle took place. The stronghold, the castle itself, was a place where all those people could retreat at a time when they might need protection.

After landing in England, William quickly built motte-and-bailey castles at Pevensey and Hastings to shore up his position. William's men, who had chafed at the long wait while they sat across the Channel waiting for the wind to change, were in no mood for another delay. William encouraged them to loot and pillage, hoping to provoke Harold Godwineson into battle sooner rather than later. It would have been smarter for Harold to take his time heading south, as supplies for William's troops and their patience was likely to run out. But bolstered by his triumph over Harold Hardrada at Stamford Bridge, Harold Godwineson felt that it would be best to strike at William hard and soon. Harold and his troops made it back to London on October 6th. After a rest of only a few days, he sent his men on a forced march to Hastings, covering approximately 65 miles in just three days.

On the 14th of October, the two sides met in battle. Harold's troops had the high ground, and therefore should have had an advantage, but they were exhausted. As William's forces fought their way up the hill toward the English, they found their ranks turned back again and again by the English shield wall. It seemed likely that the English would be victorious against the invader.

Among William's ranks were a number of Breton warriors, as well as a minstrel or two. We need to remember who the Bretons were—they were the descendents of those native Britons who fled across the Channel in the 5th century in the face of the Anglo-Saxon Invasion. They settled in the part of modern France that is today called Brittany, which just means "Little Britain." Their language belonged to the Celtic branch of the Indo-European language family—so it was closer to Welsh than it was the English of the Anglo-Saxons or the Old French of the Normans. They had joined forces with William in part because they viewed his invasion of England as an opportunity for them to right an old wrong—to wrest power away from those invaders who had caused their own ancestors to flee. But it was the Bretons who threatened to cause the tide to turn decisively in favor of Harold and the English. In some of the most eye-popping of the panels of the Bayeux Tapestry, the conflict of the battle is depicted. The fighting was so close, according to both eye-witness accounts and the *Tapestry* itself, that there was no room for the dead to fall, and they remained standing—packed in with the living and others who were dead or dying. In the margins of the *Tapestry*, all manner of body parts and animal parts are shown strewn about the battlefield. It must have been a gory, bloody, fraught battle, indeed.

In the face of the fighting, the Bretons—who were attacking the left flank—panicked. They broke ranks, and they ran—pursued by a contingent of Saxons. A rumor quickly spread among William's troops that the Conqueror himself had been killed. In order to quell this rumor, William did something almost no medieval warrior would ever do—as the Bayeux Tapestry depicts, he removed his helmet so that his troops could recognize his face and see that he was still alive. If you've ever seen a medieval battle scene in a Hollywood movie, no matter how carefully researched the details are, no matter how accurate the portrayal, there is almost always at least one significant inaccuracy—the actors playing the lead roles usually are portrayed as going into battle with their heads uncovered. In reality, this would obviously be an incredibly foolish thing to do, as it exposes one of your most vulnerable body parts to significant danger—but for the sake of Hollywood, this is done so the audience can follow who is doing what to whom. Thus, it is hugely significant that William is depicted as removing his helmet—exposing himself to great danger in order to reassure his men that he is still alive and fighting.

It turned out to be a wise decision. Many of those in the Norman contingent who had turned and fled, now turned back and faced their pursuers—bringing many of them down. In fact, this then became part of William's strategy for success on that day—on several occasions various of his warriors pretended to retreat, a temptation the Saxons could not resist, often breaking ranks to pursue and cut down the Normans—who would then turn and catch the English by surprise, turning the hunted into the hunters.

As the day progressed, William finally ordered his archers to shoot high, so that their arrows would sail over the English shield wall and land on those of Harold's troops positioned behind the main primary defense. Here, as the Bayeux Tapestry depicts, Harold Godwineson met his end when an arrow pierced him through the eye. By late afternoon on October 14th, 1066, William of Normandy had become essentially king of England, even though it would not be until Christmas of that year that the crown would be officially placed upon his head.

Most scholars dislike relying overly much on dates as a way of structuring our understanding of the past, particularly in terms of boundaries between historical epochs. It is very rarely that one can say that things were one way in say, 1484, but completely different in 1485. For example, for the sake of convenience, most scholars think of the Middle Ages lasting approximately 1,000 years—from about 500 to 1500. Yet certainly, many ideas and institutions that we might consider medieval have their origins long before the 6th century—and similarly, certain medieval concepts and values continued to be socially significant well beyond the year 1500. But with the conquest of England in 1066, we get as close as we're ever going to get to a dividing line that truly separates one culture and way of life from another that is radically different.

Within just a few years, all of the Anglo-Saxon aristocracy were either dead or displaced, their lands and titles given to William's followers from Normandy. It is estimated that the wealth and property of some 4,000 Anglo-Saxons was parceled out to around 200 or so Normans. The language of the ruling elite was now a type of French that we tend to call Anglo-Norman, but it was certainly more French than it was Saxon. Granted, the elite made up a relatively small portion of the society of Norman England, but even though the peasants continued on much as before, they, too, were affected in serious ways by the changes. One of the most interesting, I think, was a new law that would have an impact on their very survival. Prior to the conquest, any Anglo-Saxon could go out into the forest and hunt game that he could bring home to feed his family.

William brought with him the Norman law that all forestland was the domain of the king, and only he had the right to hunt there. He also brought with him some changes in architecture and building, most of which were welcome. It was under his direction that the White Tower, the oldest portion of the Tower of London, was erected. Most of the stone itself was imported from William's native Normandy. He also brought with him a newfangled invention known as the fireplace. Up until this point, even the wealthiest nobleman's home was most likely timber, with a hearth in the middle of the room and a hole in the roof to let out the smoke—not the most pleasant of living situations.

In terms of the larger medieval world, the repercussions of William's conquest of England would be felt for some time. Perhaps the most significant effect of William's conquest was that England—once on the fringes of the medieval world, and until this point more a part of Scandinavia than anything else—would be brought firmly into the embrace of continental Europe. Indeed, William and his nobles all spent a great deal of time shuttling back and forth between their lands in England and in Normandy. In a few generations, this situation would create significant friction between the thrones of England and France and require that many nobles would have to choose to forsake one holding or title in favor of another.

Many of those Bretons who had followed William across the Channel with the idea of reclaiming some ancient patrimony had, contemporary accounts tell us, been accompanied by minstrels who sang songs of that greatest Celtic leader, Arthur of Britain, who had fought against the invading Anglo-Saxons and held them off for a time. Some of William's Breton companions had hoped to finish the work that Arthur had been unable to complete, ousting the interloper Saxons from the shores of Britain. The mythic figure who inspired them is the subject of our next lecture.

King Arthur—The Power of the Legend
Lecture 13

The story of King Arthur was both popular and useful politically—and as we'll see, a variety of groups and people used the Arthurian story to promote often-conflicting agendas. The story of King Arthur has been popular for centuries, and his legend has been and continues to be so compelling because it is, at its foundation, a story about what is best in human nature.

Perhaps no other legend has been as enduringly popular as the story of King Arthur. Claimed as ancestral tales by various groups from the Middle Ages to the present, the story of Arthur's reign and the exploits of his knights have been used to entertain, persuade, and promote a political agenda in almost every time and place in Western Europe and beyond. Achieving international fame with the appearance of Geoffrey of Monmouth's *History of the Kings of Britain* in the 12th century, the Arthurian story was quickly translated into several languages and became one of the most popular bodies of literature ever known.

The story of King Arthur has been used by a variety of peoples over the past 1,000 years to entertain, to inspire, and even to promote a political agenda—not surprising, as the Arthurian legend at its core is about what is best in human nature, restoring order out of chaos, and making the world a better place. The reality on which the legend is based, however, was quite different from that depicted in medieval romances. To understand the legend's enduring power, we need to examine its origins.

The Celtic peoples immigrated to the British Isles in about 500 B.C. In the 1st century A.D., parts of Britain—roughly the area of modern-day England—were incorporated into the Roman Empire. With the fall of Rome, the legions withdrew and the Romanized Celts were left to the depredations of various invaders from present-day Ireland, present-day Scotland, and the Continent. One man, whose name was Arthur or something like it, was able to stem the tide of invasion for a time and restore some peace and stability to Celtic Britain. Although most scholars agree that the legendary Arthur is likely based on a real person, there is much dispute about exactly who he was, as there is very little concrete evidence from 5th- and 6th-century Britain. The Arthur-type figure quickly became larger-than-life, and many oral and written legends sprang up concerning him.

Archaeological evidence seems to confirm his association with certain places in Britain, particularly Tintagel, Glastonbury, and Cadbury Hill. At Tintagel in Cornwall, long held to be the birthplace of King Arthur, evidence shows the settlement of a very powerful leader here in the 5th or 6th century. In 1998, archaeologists uncovered a 5th-century stone inscription there bearing a name that looks very much like "Arthur." Glastonbury Tor is usually associated with the Isle of Avalon, to which Arthur was carried after his final battle to be healed or to die, depending on the version of the legend; nearby Glastonbury Abbey was long reputed to be the final resting place of Arthur and Guenevere. In 1190, a grave attributed to them was discovered at the abbey, though it may have been a hoax. The Iron Age hill fort of Cadbury Hill has long been associated with the legendary Camelot, Arthur's court, due to the age and

Tintagel Castle, Cornwall, is the legendary birthplace of King Arthur. Recent archeological evidence seems to support this legend.

scale of an early medieval refortification at the site. Scholars estimate that it would take a minimum of 800 men—eight times the size of a typical war band—to man and defend it.

In addition to archaeological evidence, textual and literary evidence suggests that there was indeed an Arthur-type figure active in the late 5th and early 6th centuries. Fifty years after Arthur's supposed death, the name starts to appear in the royal genealogies of Britain, when it was previously completely unattested. He also shows up in a very early poem from about the year 600 called the *Goddoddin*, in which another character is described as being a great warrior, yet "he was no Arthur."

In addition to archaeological evidence, textual and literary evidence suggests that there was indeed an Arthur-type figure active in the late 5th and early 6th centuries.

While the core of the legend may be based on reality, many of the more popular aspects of it seem to have no basis in fact. Arthur was most likely never called king—it is more probable he was referred to as a war leader of some kind. The name "Camelot" is not attested until the 12th century. Merlin, the wizard-advisor, is not associated with Arthur until Geoffrey of Monmouth links them in his largely fictitious 12th-century *History of the Kings of Britain*. The Round Table and its famous knights, considered by many a central element of the legend, is also not attested until the 12th century. Additionally, many of the knights—in particular Lancelot—appear to be creations of French authors who wished to embellish Arthur's story with their own flourishes. Every age and culture has tended to create a version of Arthur that embodies the very best ideals from their own society. The broad appeal and fascination with Arthur continues to this day. ∎

Suggested Reading

Lacy et al., *The Arthurian Encyclopedia.*

Snyder, *The World of King Arthur.*

1. What is it about the legend of King Arthur that makes it one of the most enduringly popular stories to this day?

2. How was the development of the legend shaped by specific nationalist and political agendas? How has the legend of Arthur been appropriated and manipulated over the past 1,500 years?

King Arthur—The Power of the Legend
Lecture 13—Transcript

Welcome back. Last time we talked about the Norman conquest of Anglo-Saxon England and its depiction in one of the most famous textile pieces to survive from the medieval period—the *Bayeux Tapestry*. Among its many scenes depicting the events leading up to and including the actual invasion, there is one panel that shows William the Conqueror's troops on their way to Britain in ships. Included there is the image of a minstrel, who presumably was brought along for entertainment. There are some accounts that suggest that the Breton minstrels had in their repertoire of songs a version of the story of King Arthur, which they sang in the spirit of thinking that the Normans would right the ancient wrong committed by the Saxons when they invaded and conquered Arthur's Britain in the 5th century. We need to remember that Bretons—spelled B-r-e-to- n—were those Britons who fled from the island of Britain in the face of the Anglo-Saxon Invasion in the 5th century. After the Bretons settled in what is today Brittany, they maintained some contact with their former homeland, and it is by this means that some of the Arthurian tradition is thought to have made its way to France. So it is not entirely out of the realm of possibility that information about Arthur would have been preserved in the oral tradition of Breton singers.

This fact demonstrates that the story of King Arthur was both popular and useful politically—and as we'll see, a variety of groups and people used the Arthurian story to promote often-conflicting agendas. The story of King Arthur has been popular for centuries, and his legend has been and continues to be so compelling because it is, at its foundation, a story about what is best in human nature. No matter the time, place, or language in which his tale is told, the core of the story of King Arthur is the account of how one man made a difference. In a bleak and difficult time, one person attempted to push back the darkness, to restore order to chaos, and to make the world a better place. It is a fascinating tale at least in part because it was obviously as compelling and engaging a story in the Middle Ages as it is today.

People have been fascinated with Arthur's story for well over 1,000 years because its central truth is easily adapted and appropriated to reflect the values and ideals of whatever group or individual is retelling his story. He has been a hero to the medieval Welsh, English, and French—groups often at odds or, indeed, war with one another. His story appears in German, Polish, Spanish, Italian, Japanese, and numerous other languages. The narrative of his reign functions whether his story is set in medieval Britain, the European battlefields of World War II, or outer space in some distant future. So who was this man who has inspired some of the greatest literature ever written? In order to answer this question, we have to go back to one of the earliest lectures of this course and return our focus to the Roman Empire and its presence in Britain.

We know very little about the earliest peoples living in Britain because they had no written language, and they were absorbed by the various waves of invaders/immigrants who later came to Britain from the Continent. Thus, the people who built such fantastic monuments as Stonehenge are largely a mystery to us. The first group in Britain that we can really identify in terms of language and culture are the Celts, who came from the Continent and were settled in the British Isles by about 500 B.C.

Although the Celts did not have a written language at this time, we know quite a bit about them from that group of people who were famously skilled at keeping written records—the Romans. In 55 B.C., the Romans tried to extend the reach of their empire to the British Isles, drawn there by its natural resources—particularly tin. Repelled on their first attempt to bring Britain into the embrace of the empire, they were more successful in A.D. 43, and fairly quickly they brought most of what is today England under their control—although they were never able to Romanize those regions that today we call Ireland, Scotland, and Wales. The Romans did in Britain what they did everywhere they went, which is to try and re-create Roman culture and infrastructure—what we have called *romanitas*, or "Romanness." So when they got to Britain, they got right down to the business of building roads, establishing cities, minting coins, erecting public baths, and constructing Roman-style villas.

Those Celtic peoples whose territories were subsumed into the Roman Empire adapted to the idea of Romanitas or Romanness relatively quickly—although not without some initial resistance. We call these people the

Romano-British to indicate their status as citizens of the Roman Empire who still in many cases retained some sense of a Celtic identity.

For almost 400 years, these Britons living at the edge of the empire considered themselves Roman subjects and enjoyed the privileges and style of living that went with such status. All that changed dramatically in the late 4th and early 5th century, of course, when Rome found itself under siege from various barbarian hordes. To protect its borders, Rome started to call its legions home. In 410, the unthinkable happened, and Rome itself was sacked by the Gothic leader Alaric.

As the Roman forces began to withdraw from Britain, peoples who had been kept at bay by their presence began making incursions into Romano-British territory. These people include the Scots, the Picts, and various other non-Romanized, non-Christian peoples—including the Anglo-Saxons from the Continent. In response to these attacks, the Romano-British sent to the Roman consul across the Channel in Gaul, but the response that came back was not what the Britons had hoped for—essentially, the message was: "You're on your own." Try to imagine what this must have been like for the Britons. For almost 400 years, they had considered themselves citizens of Rome—with all the rights, privileges, and protections that accompany that status—and then suddenly, they are cut off, abandoned, with their infrastructure and urban centers perilously close to collapse. They were Christians, and they found themselves under attack from non–Christian peoples and unable to defend themselves. When you consider that the United States has only been in existence for a little more than 200 years, you can get a sense of the kind of disorientation that must have surrounded the Britons after 400 years under Roman rule.

What happened next is chronicled in the histories of two monks—Gildas, who wrote in the 6th century; and the Venerable Bede, who wrote in the 8th and whose work we've already discussed at some length in this course. Both Gildas and Bede chronicle the story of how the British leader King Vortigern decided to hire mercenaries to fight for the Britons, essentially to take the place of the now-departed Roman military. Sometime in the mid-5th century—tradition usually puts the date as 449—three boatloads of mercenaries, led by two brothers named Hengist and Horsa, landed on the shores of Britain. The mercenaries were skilled fighters and did a good job of pushing back the Picts and the Scots, but then they looked around, and they liked what they saw. They sent word back to the Continent, to their families and friends, and the result was what we call the Anglo- Saxon Invasion.

Although their victory in Britain seemed decisive, there was some native resistance to the Anglo-Saxons, and here is where the figure of King Arthur enters our story. To tell that story requires exploring three different kinds of evidence—archeological, literary, and genealogical. Although plenty of Britons moved away in advance of the Saxon incursion—most significantly perhaps, many crossed the Channel and established the realm of Brittany, or "Little Britain," in what is today France. Someone in the late 5th century was able to rally the British against the invaders, and this someone won a decisive battle against the Saxons at Mount Badon around the year 500. No one knows where Mount Badon is or was, but most historians agree that it is a real place—even though its location is lost to us—and they agree also that this battle most likely did happen.

The archeological evidence shows that right around this time, the Anglo-Saxon encroachment into Britain stopped and may have even reversed itself somewhat—sending some of the invaders back to the Continent. One way we know this is due to the fact that the Anglo- Saxons had unique burial practices—which makes their cemeteries, and thus their nearby settlements, quite easy for archaeologists to identify. If you plot these settlements on a map, there's a very clear line about halfway across Britain, beyond which the Anglo-Saxons are held at bay for a considerable period of time. The area right on the border of this Anglo-Saxon line is also, not coincidentally, the area of Britain most associated with Arthur's legend for hundreds of years. The archeological record indicates that starting around the year 500, we have almost 50 years of relative peace and prosperity—towns grew, crops were brought in, and burning and pillaging were kept to a minimum. It was not to last, however, and eventually the Anglo-Saxons won out over the Romano-Celtic population, and the land of the Britons became Angleland, or England.

That is the historical milieu in which the figure who was the inspiration for King Arthur, as so many people today imagine him, is situated. Actually, it would be more accurate for me to say "figures," as there are several candidates for the historical Arthur. Some are real people, some are purely the stuff of legend, and some are a combination of the two. Some scholars believe that Arthur is actually the 5th-century British leader Ambrosius Aurelianus, who is cited in Gildas's *History of Britain* as a figure who resisted the Anglo-Saxon Invasion. Gildas describes him as being of Roman descent, the son of parents who had "worn the purple," suggesting that he came ultimately from a high-ranking Roman family.

Other scholars believe that Arthur was a 5th-century leader of purely Celtic—not Roman—descent, but who was Romanized and rallied the population left behind when the Romans withdrew from Britain. Still, others think that Arthur was the leader referred to only by a title—Riothamus, which is a Latinized form of the British *Rigotamos*, which meant something like "supreme king," and this figure fought several battles on the Continent. Several scholars have also proposed various Welsh leaders as candidates for Arthur, such as Arthroos ap Meurig and Owen Dantgooyne, who were active at about the right period.

On the fringes of Arthur scholarship we have those who think that Arthur was never a real person at all, but was a wholly mythic figure whose legend extends back in some cases almost 3,000 years. Perhaps the best known of these is the theory that the Arthurian tales are based on Sarmatian folklore and were brought to Britain when the Sarmatians—a nomadic people living in the Caucasus region of Europe—were conscripted into the Roman army. These conscripts served under the Roman leader Lucius Artorious Castus in the 2nd century. This Castus had a descendent with the same or similar name in the 5th century, and very often he is identified as the leader whose name gets mixed up with Sarmatian mythology. This is the theory that in part was the basis for the 2005 movie *King Arthur*.

My own belief—and one I think is more or less accepted among most scholars working on the Arthur question today—is that there was, indeed, a real person with a name like Arthur, perhaps of mixed Roman/Celtic descent, who fought against the Anglo-Saxon incursion and achieved some success in stemming the tide of invaders around the year 500. Esteemed Arthur scholars Geoffrey Ashe and Leslie Alcock have been quoted as saying this person was what we might call an Arthur-type figure, and I think that's the best way to think of him.

So, what was this Arthur-type figure like, and how do we know about him? In this time and place, which scholars refer to as sub- Roman Britain or the Brittonic Age, we have very little to go on in the way of written texts and histories. As I've already noted, most medieval scholars very much dislike the term "Dark Ages" to refer to anything concerning the medieval period. But if there ever was a time that we could truly call a Dark Age, Arthur's time is it.

With the Romans pulling out of Britain, we lose all those wonderful records that the Roman bureaucracy would have kept. Once the Roman civil infrastructure vanishes, so, too, do the record-keepers and their records—and monks, who did most of the copying of texts, were more concerned with staying alive than recording the events that were taking place around them. The invaders—Picts, Scots, and the Anglo-Saxons—were at this time preliterate. They had, of course, an ample body of stories, tales, and histories, but these are only preserved and passed down orally—so we can't look to them for accurate accounts of what is happening.

When we take the archeological record and combine that with what we can glean from later written accounts that may be recording facts and stories that were part of an oral tradition, or that were copied from earlier texts that are now lost, we start to get a picture of who this Arthur-type figure was—and the evidence is fairly convincing that he did, indeed, exist. There are a number of locales—clustered in the south and west of Britain—that have names that either reference Arthur or reference places that are cited in various accounts of the legend. Three of these important places are Tintagel, Glastonbury, and Cadbury Hill.

Tintagel, which is on the west coast of Britain in Cornwall, is the reputed birth site of Arthur according to several legends—and Arthurian pilgrims have long journeyed here, to a place that literally seems to be on the edge of the world to pay their respects to the once and future king. Arthurian enthusiasts just about lost their minds in the summer of 1998 when an excavation team at Tintagel found a stone that had inscribed on it in early

Britishized Latin something like "Artogunou, father of a descendent of Coll, has had this made." Specialists are fairly certain this comes from the right time, the sub- Roman or Brittonic period, and the hubbub at conferences and on email newsgroups and Web chat rooms was over the name Artogonou, which in its non-Latin, British form would be something like Arthnou—which, obviously, is similar to the name "Arthur." There's also a cross on the stone, suggesting this figure was a Christian, which the historical Arthur-type figure most certainly was. Previous excavations at Tintagel have revealed that it was a bustling community in the sub-Roman period, and that even during the incursions from Picts, Scots, and Saxons, this outpost was maintaining a healthy trade with the Continent. So, someone of obvious power, influence, and wealth oversaw this community. It would be the right setting into which someone who would grow up to be like Arthur might be born.

Glastonbury has often been associated with the Island of Avalon, to which Arthur is famously carried off to be healed at the conclusion of some of the legends. This site is also associated with the Holy Grail and is cited as the last resting place of Arthur and Guinevere. One problem with Glastonbury Hill—or the Tor, as its called—being associated with Avalon is that it is, quite obviously, not an island. Impressive, imposing, standing out from the countryside for miles around—yes; island—no. However, archeologists have determined that during what we can call the Arthurian period, the hill was surrounded by marshy, swampy land that in effect made it an island. Below the Tor is Glastonbury Abbey—and in the late 12th century, around 1190 to be exact, King Henry II claimed that he had learned this was the last resting place of King Arthur, and that he had learned this information from a Breton storyteller—just like one of those who reportedly accompanied the Normans during their victorious conquest of Britain.

On Henry's information, the monks at Glastonbury dug where he said to dig and unearthed a coffin containing the bones of a large man and a woman. Above the coffin was the lead cross that said: "Here lies the famous King Arthur in the Isle of Avalon and his second wife, Guinevere." On the face of it, there are a few problems with the authenticity of this discovery. One is that Henry II was an Arthurian enthusiast and perhaps a bit biased. Another is that there had been a fire at the abbey in 1184, and the monks were in need of funds in order to rebuild and perhaps saw an opportunity to capitalize on interest in the Arthurian legend. A third problem is that the bones and lead cross have disappeared, leaving us no way to prove or disprove their authenticity. But, at the same time, we don't have any evidence that the monks exploited this find for money, and an excavation in 1958 showed that the monks had dug where they said they did, and they found a burial where they said they had. The bones were lost—as were so many, including those of Thomas à Becket, for example—during the vandalism that occurred after Henry VIII broke up the monasteries and ushered the Reformation into England. Whosever bones they were, they did exist, and they occupied a space on the altar at Glastonbury until the 16th century, as many accounts attest. A copy of one side of the lead cross was made by one William Camden. While many people think it was a forgery or that it never existed at all, what's interesting about Camden's facsimile is that the form of Arthur's name given is "Arturius," which is a very early form of the name "Arthur"—we have it attested in the 7th century—but it's not the preferred form of 12th-century writers. That form would have been something like "Artus," and that form would have been much more likely to have been used by a 12thcentury forger. Also, the letter forms themselves seem to indicate a very early date—so it is possible that the account of the monks contains some truth.

If the evidence of Tintagel and Glastonbury's association with the Arthurian legend is suggestive, if very circumstantial, the case of Cadbury Hill is a little more solid. The hill is one of many Iron-Age hillforts that were in existence in Britain before the arrival of the Romans, but this one has several things that lend it to association with Arthur. At exactly the right time for Arthur, someone came along and refortified this hillfort on a massive scale. Excavations have unearthed a great hall at the top of the hill. Earthen ramparts and terracing provided a level of security against hostile attacks. The upper bank of the hillfort is a 16-foot thick stone wall that runs along the perimeter of the flat top of the hill. It is built in Celtic, rather than Roman, fashion and must have taken an enormous amount of labor.

Experts judge that it would have taken at minimum 800 people to man and defend this site, and this is at a time when the size of the average warband in Britain is estimated to be around 100 men. At the time the main archeological excavations took place—from 1966 to 70—it was thought that other excavations on other hillforts would reveal a similar pattern of refortification of older sites at around the same time this occurred at Cadbury. So far, this has not been the case. As far as we know, this is the only site in Britain where anything like this refortification occurred, a fact which suggests that at this chaotic time—the late 5th/early 6th century—a single strong, commanding leader emerged from the disarray left by the Roman withdrawal and the Pictish, Scottish, and Saxon invasions. This leader is most likely the same man who led his people to a rout of the Anglo-Saxons at Mount Badon, and thus ushered in a new era of peace for the Britons.

Some 50 years after the supposed date of this battle, the name "Arthur" or "Artorius" suddenly appears in the genealogical record—we have at least four sons born into British Royal Houses who are given this name. Prior to this, we haven't seen much evidence of this name being used—so its sudden appearance and its being given to people of such high rank suggests that certainly this Arthur figure for whom they are named is a man of extremely important status and reputation. Around the year 600, we have the first mention of Arthur in a piece of literature. What is interesting is that this mention is almost an offhand comment, suggesting that Arthur and his story were so well known there was no need to fully explain who he was or what he did. The text is known as the *Gododdin*, a series of laments—and one stanza mentions a warrior named Gwawrddur who, we are told, was pretty fantastic, but "he was not Arthur."

There are other bits and pieces of evidence, but these are the most significant for our attempts to try and get at who this historical figure was. Obviously, his story is in many respects quite different from the popular conception of the legend—which includes, as I mentioned at the opening of this lecture, the fact that he was king, who established the Round Table at his court, which was at Camelot; that he had an advisor named Merlin; a queen named Guinevere; and a great knight named Lancelot. For one thing, this Arthur-type figure was most likely never called king. The earliest texts give him Roman titles like *Comes Britanniarum* or *Dux Bellorum*, which means "leader of battles." Unless he is, indeed, the High King Riothamus, neither he nor his followers thought of him as a king.

Likewise, the name "Camelot" isn't attested until the 12th century, and then it's by a French writer. Arthur's stronghold itself, whatever its name, bears very little resemblance to the large stone castle conjured up in most people's imaginations. It's the Romans who build in stone, and once they leave Britain, the population reverts mostly to building in wood. Arthur's stronghold at the top of Cadbury Hill may have been impressive by 5th-century British standards, but to us today it might have seemed nothing more than a rather small, smoky, dark, wooden building. The character of Merlin, while most likely based on a real-life Welsh bard named Myrddin, had absolutely nothing to do with Arthur's story, as far as we know, until the writer Geoffrey of Monmouth links them together in the 12th century. Geoffrey's account of Arthur's story was a bestseller in its day, and the popularity of his version is really what sent the Arthurian legend through the roof.

Guinevere shows up in early Welsh accounts of the legend, but unfortunately the manuscripts that contain these accounts date from the 13th century—although the material they contain is most certainly much older and probably copied from earlier texts now lost. I think it is possible and probably even likely that Guinevere is a part of the legend from its beginning, but Sir Lancelot is most certainly a later creation—appearing fully formed in the work of French writer Chretien de Troyes in the 12th century. It is possible that Chretien was working with an older Celtic source, but the love affair between Arthur's queen and his greatest knight is probably completely made up.

It's a similar story with the Round Table and its Knights. The first mention of the Round Table comes in the 12th century in the account of the French writer Wace. While the historical Arthur surely had a band of men or retainers whom he commanded, the concept of knighthood and chivalry as we generally associate them with the Arthurian legend would have been utterly foreign to the Brittonic Dux Bellorum who fought off the Anglo-Saxon invaders. Indeed, knighthood as an institution can't properly be said to exist before the 12th century—no shining armor, no fighting on horseback. While chain mail might have been worn, the plate armor we associate with knights is a much later invention. It's far more likely that Arthur's men wore boiled leather for protection, and they would have ridden their horses to a battle site, dismounted, and fought on foot. Stirrups, necessary for fighting on horseback, aren't attested in Europe until the 8th century, at the earliest.

What really caused the Arthurian story to take off was the work of a 12th-century cleric named Geoffrey of Monmouth, whose *History of the Kings of Britain*—finished sometime in 1136 or 1138—included a long section on Arthur. His work became the equivalent of a medieval bestseller, especially on the Continent. Over 200 manuscript copies survive, a huge number for the period—and it was his work that really fired the imaginations of later medieval writers who turned Arthur into the mythical figure he's become today. So who was Arthur? My belief is that he was a minor Romano-Celtic leader who rose to power in the chaos surrounding the Roman withdrawal and the Anglo-Saxon Invasion. He would have to have been a skilled fighter and a charismatic leader, but the elements of chivalry so intrinsic to the Arthurian legend—romantic love, service to ladies, noble ideals of might for right—were most likely not part of his experience. He certainly had followers, but these were not Knights of the Round Table; they would have been men unconcerned with chivalry and most preoccupied with survival—who gathered around their leader in the timber building, behind earthen defenses, that served as Arthur's base of operations. He might have had advisors, but there was no magical Merlin to guide him as he fought back the invaders. It is a dark, grim picture lacking magic or romance—hardly the stuff out of which such a legend, as we know it, is likely to spring.

How did we get from that figure to the King Arthur who exists in the popular imagination today? The turning back of the Anglo-Saxons was an incredible feat, and because it occurred in late 5th-/early 6thcentury Britain, which was such a Dark Age, there was fertile ground for the legend to really take root and grow. Stories about this Arthur figure grew more fantastic as they circulated orally. Because what he had done was so remarkable, and because it had provided hope to so many, various peoples wished to claim him as one of their own—and when they did so, they imbued him with all the behaviors and trappings that they themselves found admirable and worthy.

Every age has claimed him and made him the embodiment of what an ideal king should be. In the 15th-century *Morte d'Arthur* by Sir Thomas Malory, Arthur is a 15th-century king who rules according to 15th-century values. In the 1960s musical *Camelot* by contrast, Arthur's beliefs and values are downright modern and democratic—anyone can become a knight, and knights should fight only for good—might for right. It is this malleability—

this adaptability—that has made the Arthurian legend so enduringly popular. Because the main story of Arthur is one of overcoming adversity, of triumphing against tremendous odds, we can be certain that his legend will continue to hold sway over the popular imagination for many years to come.

The Three Orders of Medieval Society
Lecture 14

It was believed that in order for society to function successfully, members of each order needed to fulfill their destinies. A peasant should be the best peasant he could be; the knight should be the best knight he could be; and the priest should be the best priest he could be—and none of them should attempt to fill the offices of the other.

As we move into the High Middle Ages—starting around the year 1000, the medieval world began to organize itself in terms of the hierarchical social structures we most often associate with it. This social structure is usually known as the three estates or the three orders. At the top of the hierarchy were the nobles—those who fought. The next tier was made up of members of the church—those who prayed. In many respects, this estate overlapped with the nobility, and the two often vied for prestige and power. At the bottom of the order was the largest group, the peasants—those who worked. They comprised 90–95 percent of the population. There was very little opportunity for advancement out of the lowest estate for most of the medieval period.

Perhaps the best means of understanding the three-estates model can be found in an examination of the general prologue to Geoffrey Chaucer's *Canterbury Tales*. Chaucer wrote at the end of the 14th century, a time when the model held powerful sway over the medieval imagination but its long-static divisions were beginning to collapse. He was not the first to write in this literary genre, known as estates satire, but he is arguably the writer who did it best. He makes use of the stereotypes in new and interesting ways and included representatives of the rising merchant class.

A quick examination of just a few of the characters helps us to understand the model and see how it was shifting at the end of the 14th century. Chaucer moves in order through the estates, at least initially. The knight represents the militaristic aspect of the noble classes, the original source of their power and status. He is a warrior who is distinguished in his description by the number of campaigns in which he has fought. The squire, the knight's son, represents aspects of noble identity that had come to be just as important, if not more so, by Chaucer's day. While still a fighter, the squire is identified primarily by his devotion and service to ladies.

His next descriptions are of members of the clergy. Both the prioress and the monk play to stereotyped ideas about how the clergy often fell short of the ideals they were supposed to embody. It has been said that there is not an honest miller in all medieval English literature, and Chaucer plays true to that stereotype with his representation of the miller as a coarse, drunken, base fellow who regularly cheats his customers. The plowman, on the other hand, represents the ideal of the third estate—honest, hard-working, and utterly anonymous. Several pilgrims in the general prologue do not fit neatly into the three-estates model. Perhaps no figure displays this better than the Wife of Bath, whose status as a widow and a merchant contradicts traditional medieval ideas of both gender and class. ■

It has been said that there is not an honest miller in all medieval English literature, and Chaucer plays true to that stereotype.

Suggested Reading

Ganshof, *Feudalism.*

Reynolds, *Fiefs and Vassals.*

Questions to Consider

1. What caused the ideal of the three orders of medieval society to maintain its potency long after it had ceased to function successfully in reality?

2. How does the work of Geoffrey Chaucer variously support and undermine the social division into those who fight, those who pray, and those who work?

The Three Orders of Medieval Society
Lecture 14—Transcript

Welcome back. In our last lecture, we discussed the legendary figure of King Arthur, exploring the origins of the stories surrounding this most famous of heroes from their likely historical origins in the 5th century through to much later incarnations of his story that reflected the values of the various societies that produced them. We saw how the story of Arthur changed over time, and how Arthur was eventually transformed from a Celtic warlord waging a desperate and defensive war against invading Anglo-Saxons into an incredibly powerful and civilized king—whose court was renowned throughout the world for honor, courtesy, and chivalry. As the Middle Ages progressed, the Arthurian story had grafted onto it a number of traditional tales and new characters—such as the figures of the magician Merlin and the knight Sir Lancelot—and its appeal, to this day, appears unlimited and unbounded.

Part of what makes the Arthurian story so compelling is the power of the idea at its center—the idea of a single man being able to unite disparate groups and peoples and make his world a better place. The subject of our lecture today might not seem at first to have much in common with King Arthur, but throughout most of the Middle Ages ideas about the proper order of things, about how society should be structured, about what kinds of relationships people should have with those above and below and alongside them in the social hierarchy, were incredibly powerful. This can be a hard concept for those of us living in 21st-century America to wrap our minds around, the idea that once you were born into a particular social class—that was your destiny. Upward mobility, making a success of yourself through hard work or ingenuity—these ideas were practically unheard of and, indeed, almost impossible to conceive of in the medieval world, although there are some notable exceptions.

But in general, the predominant view in the Middle Ages, and one that became entrenched as we entered the High Middle Ages, was that society was divided into three estates, or orders, and that these three orders were more or less divinely ordained. These three social strata consisted of the nobles—those who fought; the clergy—those who prayed; and the peasants, or everyone else—those who worked. Further, it was believed that in order for society to function successfully, members of each order needed to fulfill their destinies. A peasant should be the best peasant he could be; the knight should be the best knight he could be; and the priest should be the best priest he could be—and none of them should attempt to fill the offices of the other. This is a point that is driven home in the medieval dreamvision poem known as *Piers Plowman*, written and revised and rewritten—some might say obsessively (I would)—by a man known as William Langland in England in the late 14th century. In one scene, a community bands together to try and stave off the allegorical character of hunger, and a knight eagerly offers to learn how to work the plow so that he can help out. Piers the Plowman's response is significant, in that he refuses the knight's offer of help with the plowing, saying: "I shal swynke and swete · and sowe for vs boþe" or "I will work and sweat and sow for us both," provided, he goes on, that the knight does his job, which is to protect and defend the church and laborers like Piers.

So, at the top of this social order known as the three estates were the nobles, and this included those who held hereditary titles—from kings, to dukes and earls, and down to knights, who occupied the lowest rung of the noble ladder. In the early Middle Ages, the equation was simple: Those who were powerful and won battles ruled. In the High Middle Ages, we start to see more and more that those who conquered understandably wished to pass their power and status on to their offspring. We have the development of a hereditary nobility—in which people came to power more because of their bloodlines and less because of any battles won, although military prowess as an ideal would continue to be hugely important throughout the Middle Ages and beyond, and certainly status attained through conquest was not an uncommon occurrence.

To be a successful lord, one needed essentially two things—and those are castles and vassals. The 10th and 11th centuries were a significant period of what's called encastellation throughout the medieval world, but these are not castles in the way that most of us might imagine them, as we've already discussed a bit. Early castles were usually rather small, sometimes tall, and often made out of wood rather than stone. Such castles had nothing luxurious about them and usually were only able to house the lord's family on a regular basis. During a siege, those who were beholden to a lord—his vassals—and the peasants who worked the lord's land, usually referred to as a manor, might retreat here for protection. Such being the case, these castles needed to be defensible, and the most common castle plan was something known as the motte-and-bailey structure, which we discussed in our lecture on William the Conqueror and the Norman conquest. As you'll remember, the motte was a raised mound surrounded by a ditch, and the bailey was an area below this where, in fact, most of the day-to-day life of the nobleman's immediate community occurred. Having a castle was important if one was a lord, because it meant that one had means of protecting oneself when would-be conquerors set their sights on a particular piece of territory. So if you had claimed a particular region or inherited it, the surest way to hang onto it and maintain your power was to build a castle that could withstand attacks from enemies.

It is not a coincidence that one of the first things William the Conqueror did after winning the Battle of Hastings was to begin a massive program of castle-building. Some estimates are that there was a castle about every 10 miles, and William and his heirs built approximately 500 castles in the space of 50 years. This kind of significant encastellation even merits a mention in the document known as the *Peterborough Chronicle*—a continuation of the *Anglo- Saxon Chronicle*—portions of which are believed to be the only surviving history of England written in English after the Norman Conquest and between that time and the later Middle Ages. For the entry of the year 1137, the anonymous chronicler bemoans the fact that many nobles resisted the king at the time—Stephen—by building their own strongholds and filling the land full of castles that they could defend against the king's forces, a strategy that is described as *suencten suyðe*, an Old English phrase that translates to something like "seriously or viciously oppressing or burdening." In this case, the people who were viciously burdened or seriously oppressed were the local populace living in the region where such castle-building occurred.

In addition to castles, a lord needed vassals to support his cause and interests. Simply put, a vassal was a man who had sworn homage and fealty to a lord. In exchange for the lord's protection, and support, and the *enfeoffment*—or granting of lands to the vassal, the vassal swore to fight on the lord's behalf and render him a certain number of days of service a year. The system of vassalage in the medieval world worked much like a pyramid—the king was at the top, and the upper echelons of the nobility would swear fealty to him as his vassals. In turn, these lords would have homage done to them by nobles further down the food chain, who would become their vassals, and so on, and so on all the way down. In other words, almost everyone in medieval society was both above and below someone else in the hierarchical structure.

Below the nobles were the clergy, those who prayed. In many respects, this stratum of society overlapped with the noble estate, as members of the clergy very often came from the noble classes. Especially with the increased use of the system of primogeniture, by which only the eldest male heir inherited—thereby keeping estates and titles intact, we find many younger sons of noble families entering religious life. Evidence from the medieval world suggests that while there certainly were many sincerely and devoutly religious members of the clergy, there were others who continued to maintain the sort of lifestyle to which they had become accustomed in their secular lives as members of the noble classes. In fact, although required to take vows that usually included poverty, chastity, and sometimes stability of place, many members of religious orders owned goods and property and had wives and children—a situation that was widespread enough that church councils from the 12th to the 13th centuries repeatedly addressed this issue, forbidding it in the strongest language possible, which suggests that many carried on with this behavior despite the ideals of celibacy and poverty considered to be so fundamental to religious life.

It is perhaps because of the preponderance of members of noble families within the ranks of the clergy that there are so many conflicts between religious and secular leaders throughout the medieval world—even though, as we have noted before, there is really no concept of anything like the separation of church and state in the Middle Ages. Many kings and nobles argued that as they protected the clergy—who were forbidden to take up arms—they were, in fact, above them in status. The clergy—especially at the highest level, the papacy—contended that as their power came from God they, in fact, were in the superior position. It was a debate that we have discussed earlier in this lecture series when we examined the coronation of the Emperor Charlemagne by Pope Leo III in the year 800. As you'll recall, that debate is often described as a Royalist versus Romanist debate—the

Royalists holding that Charlemagne had earned the title of Holy Roman Emperor through conquest, and the pope's act was simply a recognition of what was already the case. The Romanist position was that Charlemagne did not become emperor until the pope, the representative of God on earth, crowned him as such.

While the orders of the nobility and clergy were almost side-by-side at the top of the social order, at the bottom were the peasants. Although medieval society was ideally separated into the three estates, the divisions were by no means equal. Some historians estimate that the nobility and clergy made up between 5 to 10 percent of the population, while the peasants—the everyone else—might have comprised as much as 95 percent of the people living in the medieval world. For much of the Middle Ages, there was no real way out of this estate. If you were a peasant, you were most likely born on the manor of a lord and were bound to him as a serf, meaning that the land you lived on and farmed technically belonged to the lord. In exchange for a place to live and the means to grow your own food, as well as protection in times of difficulty—famine, war, etc.—you would provide the lord with a percentage of your harvest. You would also be required to work a certain number of days on the lord's personal fields—usually one to two days per week, with additional days required at harvest time. Serfdom also meant that you might be subject to a number of taxes, and that many things we consider basic individual rights today—for example, getting married—would be subject to your lord's approval. If he did agree to your marriage, one usually had to pay a marriage tax—often called a *merchet*, which often took the form of grain or livestock. A similar tax, called the *heriot*, was exacted from a serf's family usually on the occasion of a death of the head of the household—the logic being that the lord would no longer have the benefit of the labor of this serf, so he needed some sort of compensation.

In many respects, serfdom sounds somewhat like slavery, as technically serfs were unfree—bound to the manor on which they lived and worked, and bound also to the lord of the manor. There was a small proportion of the population who were known as freeholders—peasants who owned and worked their own lands, or who paid a nominal rent to a lord, but did not otherwise owe him service. If you were to ask almost anyone living in 21st-century America today if they would prefer to be free or unfree, the answer would be clear: free, of course. But if you were to ask a peasant living in the medieval world that same question, the response you might get would be: "Well, how much land do I get?" Given the choice of being a free man with little or no land, or a serf with lots of land under one's control, the medieval peasant is going to pick unfree with land almost every time. Even without the promise of substantial land, serfdom provided many benefits to those of the peasant class in the form of guaranteed protection, food, and clothing in times of difficulty—it was a safety net that made the situation of being technically unfree quite desirable in many instances.

As we move toward the later Middle Ages, we start to see the breakdown of the idea of the three orders, even though at its height its divisions were never wholly impermeable, and it never functioned as ideally as many might have believed or hoped. Starting in the 14th century, for a number of reasons, one of which is the occurrence of the Black Death, which killed up to a half of the population of the medieval world and to which we'll devote an entire lecture later on, we start to see some real upward mobility in the third estate. As we head into the late medieval period, urban and merchant life becomes vital in a way it had not been since the fall of the Roman Empire. There is a sea change in the social order—as many commoners, particularly among the merchant classes, achieved levels of wealth that had previously been only possible for members of the nobility. At the same time and for some of the same reasons, many of the members of the nobility found themselves rich in titles but poor in cash, leading to intermarriage between members of different strata of the three estates.

A great example of this new upward mobility can be found in the person of Geoffrey Chaucer, a poet and sometime government official who lived in the 14th century, and who has been called the father of English poetry. Chaucer was the son of a vintner, someone who imported wine, and the relative wealth of his family meant that he was able to receive an excellent education, which would be the foundation of his later success. The Teaching Company has a wonderful series of lectures devoted to Chaucer and his work, so I won't go into too much detail here concerning his life. Still, it is worth mentioning that Chaucer found employment in the house of John of Gaunt, son of King Edward III of England and the wealthiest man in the land. In response to the death of John of Gaunt's first wife, Chaucer wrote one of his most important works, *The Book of the Duchess*. It was his skill and inventiveness as a writer—combined with a shrewd mind and entrepreneurial spirit—that raised his social status and that of his family, so that two generations later his granddaughter was able to marry the duke of Suffolk.

Not coincidentally, perhaps the best means of understanding the three-estates model's ideal structure and its weaknesses or faults can be found in an examination of Chaucer's general prologue to his masterful and unfinished *Canterbury Tales*. This work participates in a genre of writing known as estates satire, wherein it was traditional to represent sort of stock characters or stereotypes—such as a dishonest miller, a lascivious friar, a scheming pardoner, and a virtuous knight. While Chaucer was certainly not the first writer to work with estates satire, he is arguably the one who did it best—elevating his characters beyond mere stereotypes and including figures not typically found in estates satire. In particular, the roster of characters in *The Canterbury Tales* includes a significant number of figures representative of the rising merchant class of Chaucer's day.

The premise of *The Canterbury Tales* is that a disparate group of people have come together at an inn known as the Tabard. From all walks of life, what these people have in common is that they are all engaged in a pilgrimage to Canterbury Cathedral and the shrine of Thomas Becket—some 70 miles away. The innkeeper decides to make things interesting and keep everyone entertained by suggesting that every pilgrim tell two stories on the way to Canterbury and two on the way back; the pilgrim judged to have told the best story will win a free dinner. Chaucer then offers us various tales told from the mouths of his various characters, a strategy that allows him to share with the reader or listener tales both religious and ribald, moral and mocking—something to please everyone.

Before the storytelling begins, however, Chaucer gives us portraits of each of the travelers, and an examination of just a few of these will help us understand the ideals and flaws of the three-estates model. Chaucer begins his character description with a knight, who with his son is the only representative of the noble estate on this particular pilgrimage. As such, it is fitting that we start with the knight, and following the ideal of the social hierarchy, the knight is also the first pilgrim invited to tell a tale. His description is almost entirely focused on the numerous military campaigns he has fought. He represents the warlike, militaristic aspect of the noble classes—the original source of their power and status.

By contrast, the knight's son, the squire, represents aspects of noble identity that had come to be just as important, if not more so, as elements of noble identity by Chaucer's day. While still a fighter, the squire, the knight's son, is identified primarily by his devotion to and service to ladies—as Chaucer tells us that he was "a lovyere and a lusty bachelor," "a lover and a lusty young knight," who is talented at singing, dancing, writing poetry, and playing the flute, and who has quite the fashion sense. "So hoote he loved that by nyghtertale/he sleep namoore than dooth a nyghtyngale"—in other words, so passionately did he love at night that he slept no more than did a nightingale. While Chaucer takes pains to tell us that the young squire has spent significant time on military campaigns, it is clear that what is most important about this character are his social graces, his courtly and chivalric attributes.

At first, Chaucer moves in order through the three estates—so he proceeds from the nobility to the clergy, several members of which are also on this pilgrimage. The character of the prioress, a kind of nun, is next described, but instead of a description highlighting her faith and devotion, Chaucer's narrator—an avatar of Chaucer the narrator named Geoffrey—describes the prioress's singing, her ability to speak French, her exquisite table manners, and her love of small animals—qualities that would be more fittingly found in a noblewoman who was head of a secular household. Indeed, nuns in the medieval world were generally not supposed to go on pilgrimage outside the cloister. It was considered that within the convent walls, they were on a figurative pilgrimage that would arguably bring even greater spiritual rewards than any voyage taken through the physical world. Yet, we know that religious women often went on pilgrimages throughout the Middle Ages, and we know this because almost every year, various church officials would issue sternly worded injunctions forbidding nuns from leaving the convent to pursue such activities. The fact that this activity was constantly forbidden to nuns meant that they must constantly have been engaging in it. Why would they do such a thing? Although many pilgrimages were physically rigorous, they could also be social events. We'll talk at much greater length about medieval pilgrimage in our next lecture, but the basic fact on which Chaucer is commenting here is that a pilgrimage could be good for the soul and good for the social life, and not everyone went on pilgrimages primarily for the spiritual benefits they might bring. Indeed, as I noted in the first lecture of this course, the opening lines of *The Canterbury Tales*—perhaps the most famous lines in all English poetry—suggest as much, when Chaucer tells us that "Whan that Aprill with his shoures soote the droghte of March hath perced to the roote ... thanne longen folk to goon on pilgrimages" or to translate roughly—"When winter is over and the dryness of March has been tempered by sweet April rain showers, that's when people decide they'd like to go on a pilgrimage." In other words, "Let's wait until the weather gets a little better before we set off to save our souls and honor God."

Next in Chaucer's catalogue is the monk, and like the prioress, his description hardly seems befitting a man of religion who has sworn an oath of poverty and who is supposed to be living within the walls of the monastery. Chaucer tells us how the monk has many wonderful horses that he loves to take out hunting, and how this man—who ideally should demonstrate restraint in all areas of his life—is rather rotund, as he loves a good feast.

Chaucer continues his skewering with his depiction of the miller, long a favorite figure for satire in the Middle Ages. It has been said that there is not a single honest miller in all of medieval literature, and Chaucer's miller fits the tradition perfectly as a coarse, drunken oaf who regularly cheats his customers. The miller in a medieval community performed an essential function, as it was to him that people had to bring their grain to be ground. As payment, the miller usually took a portion of the grain that he ground. This portion was known as the soke—s-o-k-e—and it is from this word that we get the phrase "to get soaked"—meaning "to get taken advantage of," as millers notoriously always took a little extra grain here and there.

On the other hand, Chaucer does offer some positive representatives of the three estates: The knight is the ideal representing the nobility; the character of the parson is held up as a good and virtuous representative of his class; and the peasantry have as their role model the plowman. Interestingly and perhaps not coincidentally, these three characters—and the stories told by those of them who manage to get around to it—are incredibly boring. Much more interesting are the characters and tales of the scandalous pardoner, the crotchety reeve, and the unpleasant summoner.

One of the most fascinating aspects of Chaucer's version of estates satire is that he includes several pilgrims in the general prologue who do not fit neatly into the three-estates model, an indication of how that ideal was no longer an accurate reflection of the social structure of the medieval world. The doctor, the shipman, the cook, to name just three—none of these are really a part of the tradition of estates satire. Perhaps no one figure best displays this than the larger-than-life Wife of Bath, whose status as a widow and a merchant contradicts traditional medieval ideas of both gender and class—demonstrating how at this period the social structure was changing. Five times married, the wife gives a scandalous account of her sex life that is riddled with euphemisms for female genitalia—such as "queynte," "sely instrument," and "bele chose." She is perhaps the most entertaining pilgrim of the bunch, wearing a 10-pound headdress and red stockings.

She, like so many others among this group, seems to regard pilgrimage as a kind of social activity—kind of like an early version of going on a cruise—as she has been to all the major pilgrimage sites of the medieval world: Jerusalem, Rome, Bologne, Santiago de Compostella, Cologne. She had visited some of these sites more than once. Such travel throughout the medieval world suggests a remarkable freedom of movement and access to wealth that was unusual, but still common enough to confound and complicate the ideal of the three estates. Where does a wealthy, lusty widow involved in the cloth trade fit, exactly? What about the religious figures clearly not adhering to the ideals of their class—and characters such as the miller who seem to be out only for themselves, with little interest in the greater social good? In his *Canterbury Tales*, Chaucer offers us a few model representatives of each of the three estates, but the preponderance of his characters display traits that are hardly in keeping with—and are often at odds with—the ideals of the three estates.

Chaucer cleverly used the idea of pilgrimage as an organizing principle for his collection of tales, and as we will see in our next lecture, pilgrimages to religious sites were an important feature of medieval religious life for members of all social classes. Although Chaucer's pilgrims seem more interested in socializing than spirituality, thousands of medieval people felt compelled to make journeys to places as far away as Jerusalem and as close as the next village in search of forgiveness, to seek healing, to give thanks, to atone for sins, to demonstrate their faith. Next time, we will talk about the phenomenon of medieval pilgrimage and explore the saints, events, and objects that made the destinations at the end of these journeys holy.

Pilgrimage and Sainthood
Lecture 15

At the center of most medieval *mappae mundi* is the city of Jerusalem, a fact that reflects its centrality in the consciousness of medieval Christians. It was the center of the world, and although the journey could be long and dangerous—usually lasting some months or more—a pilgrimage to Jerusalem was one of the greatest expressions of religious faith available to medieval Christians.

For medieval Christians, Jerusalem was the holiest city in the world, and a journey there—a pilgrimage—could be a way of seeking forgiveness for sins and of healing afflictions. Closer to home, people might undertake numerous pilgrimages to holy places near and far throughout their lifetimes for a variety of reasons. Usually a site was considered holy because of its association with a particular saint, but the process by which a person achieved sainthood was far from regularized, and many figures long venerated were later declared not to be saints by the medieval church. The surviving accounts of these would-be saints and the pilgrims who flocked to their shrines provide a fascinating glimpse of popular religious expression in the Middle Ages.

The activity of pilgrimage is not unique to Christianity; many religions that predate Christian hegemony in the West include pilgrimage as part of their practices or rituals. As early as the 4th century, Christians were making journeys to sites they viewed as imbued with certain holy or spiritual aspects for a variety of reasons. Medieval people might have several different motives to undertake the rigors and expense—which were sometimes substantial—of a pilgrimage.

In the earliest days of pilgrimage, one of the major motivations would be to seek healing. Many ill and ailing people essentially took up residence in these locations, and the monks and nuns often cared for them in what would become a de facto hospital. People also made pilgrimages to seek forgiveness for their sins. Pilgrims might be self-motivated or sent by a confessor. The desire to prove that one had completed a pilgrimage led indirectly to the creation of pilgrim badges, a kind of early souvenir keychain. The third major reason people tended to go on pilgrimages was to offer thanks for an instance of good fortune. A fourth reason, one that Geoffrey Chaucer hints at, is that pilgrimages, for reasons of safety and economy, tended to be undertaken in groups, so it was in many respects a social activity—kind of like the early version of a luxury cruise.

What made a site holy and thus worthy of a visit was usually its association with a particular saint or being the repository of saintly relics. Prior to the 12th century, there was little in the way of a formal process for declaring someone a saint. A process known as canonization was put in to place—and still exists to this day—to assist the church in determining whether or not a person in question had been a saint or not. It is important to understand that the church did and does not "make" saints; it only affirms the status that God has conferred on the person in question. This process could not always counteract popular sentiment, as demonstrated by the example of Saint Guinefort—a greyhound revered in the 13th century.

Once a person had achieved sainthood, that person's bones and personal effects—clothing, hair, even fingernails—were often considered to be imbued with holy and healing powers. One of the key factors in determining whether someone was a saint was the test of incorruptibility, whereby the lack of decomposition of a person's corpse was regarded as a sign from God that this person was a saint. It is rather ironic, then, that many saints' remains were broken up and dispersed among several religious sites. The possession of a saintly relic could be a benefit to a religious house, as it would encourage more pilgrims to visit, many of whom would make donations.

> **The possession of a saintly relic could be a benefit to a religious house, as it would encourage more pilgrims to visit, many of whom would make donations.**

With the Protestant Reformation, many holy shrines were dismantled, and in some cases the bones and other relics of saints were destroyed. The activity of pilgrimage continued, however, and it remains an important aspect of religious life for Christians—both Catholic and Protestant—today. ∎

Suggested Reading

Sumption, *The Age of Pilgrimage*.

Webb, *Pilgrims and Pilgrimage in the Medieval West*.

Questions to Consider

1. In what ways did medieval pilgrimage both strengthen and undermine the position and status of the institution of the Western Church?

2. What qualified one to be a saint? How did different criteria for holiness or sainthood reflect particularly medieval concerns and ideals?

Pilgrimage and Sainthood
Lecture 15—Transcript

Welcome back. In our last lecture, we discussed the structure of medieval society and the ideal of the three orders, or three estates, that held sway over the imagination of the population of the medieval world for centuries. According to this view, society was divided into three groups of people: the nobles—those who fought; the clergy—those who prayed; and the peasants (or everyone else)—those who worked. If society was to function properly, then the members of each order had to fulfill their particular duties and obligations—the nobles to take up arms in defense and protection of the other two orders; the clergy to engage in spiritual labor, in prayer, to help save the souls of the rest of society; and the peasants to work the land and provide food and other necessities for the nobles and clergy. We concluded our last lecture with a brief look at some of the representatives of the three orders depicted in 14[th]century English writer Geoffrey Chaucer's masterpiece, *The Canterbury Tales*. In this text, perhaps the most famous work of medieval literature, Chaucer uses the device of a pilgrimage as a means of assembling representatives of all three estates in one group.

While Chaucer may have been stretching things a bit—nobles rarely associated with peasants and most often would go on pilgrimage only with other nobles—his depiction of the activity rings true in that people from all levels of society took part in the activity of pilgrimage throughout the medieval world. Some pilgrimages were relatively short—perhaps just a journey to the next town, where there might be a holy shrine—and some were long—perhaps to Rome or even Jerusalem—and others were in between: The *Canterbury Tales* pilgrims are described as journeying from London to Canterbury, a distance of about 70 miles.

In today's lecture, we are going to discuss the phenomenon of pilgrimage in the medieval world and the ways in which certain sites came to be deemed holy, which usually occurred through association with a particular saint. In order to do this, however, we need to literally re-orient ourselves in terms of how we imagine the geography of the medieval world. If one looks at medieval world maps—called *mappae mundi*—one notices a very curious thing: Most of these maps are oriented so that at the top is not north, as is the case with modern maps, but rather east is the direction at the top of the map. At the center of most medieval *mappae mundi* is the city of Jerusalem, a fact that reflects its centrality in the consciousness of medieval Christians. It was the center of the world, and although the journey could be long and dangerous—usually lasting some months or more—a pilgrimage to Jerusalem was one of the greatest expressions of religious faith available to medieval Christians, especially those who lived in the secular world.

Such a journey to Jersualem or other holy sites might be undertaken to give thanks, ask forgiveness for sins, to seek healing for afflictions, or to do penance at the order of one's confessor. Although we are talking about pilgrimage in a strictly medieval Christian context today, the activity of pilgrimage is not unique to Christianity. Many religions that predate Christian hegemony in the West include pilgrimage as part of their practices or rituals, and it is likely that the activity of pilgrimage was incorporated into Christianity from older traditions—rather than being something new that arose as a result of Christianity's rise in prominence. As early as the 4th century, it seems clear that Christians were making journeys to sites they viewed as being imbued with certain holy or spiritual aspects for a variety of reasons.

There were several different motives that might be a factor in persuading medieval people to undertake the rigors and expense—sometimes substantial—of participating in a pilgrimage. In the earliest days of pilgrimage, one of the major motivations would be to seek healing from some sickness or affliction. Visitors to the shrine of Saint Oswald, for example, would mix dust from near his gravesite in water and then drink it in hopes of a miraculous cure for whatever ailed them. Other sites, such as that of Saint Martin of Tours, also became renowned for cures. The result was that many ill and ailing people essentially took up residence in these locations, and the monks and nuns would often care for them in what would become a de facto hospital. Some holy places associated with healing also had to designate space for all the crutches and other mobility aids left behind by people who had been healed and no longer needed them. The display offered hope to all those who arrived at the shrine, as it was a striking visual testament to the number of successful healings that had taken place there.

People also made pilgrimages to seek forgiveness of a sin or sins. Sometimes this pilgrimage would be undertaken at the individual's own desire to make atonement for some past wrong, and sometimes such pilgrimages were given to individuals as penance by the sinner's confessor. Fulk III, Count of Anjou, was ordered to perform four pilgrimages to the Holy Land to atone for the murder of his wife after he supposedly caught her *in flagrante delicto* with a goat herder. Not only did Fulk make the required pilgrimage to the Holy Land, he did it in excessively spectacular repentant fashion—at one point having himself dragged through the streets and beaten with branches. While many pilgrims did not go to the lengths that Fulk did, plenty of pilgrims sought to make their journeys to religious sites more holy by, for example, making the trip without shoes, or maybe without a warm cloak, or perhaps fasting along the way—the idea being that the more the flesh suffered, the greater the purification of the soul.

The third major reason people tended to go on pilgrimages was to offer thanks for blessings that had occurred in their lives. Very often such pilgrims would leave offerings at the tomb of a saint or holy shrine, an obvious benefit and source of income to the religious community in charge of overseeing and maintaining such places. Pilgrims left more than offerings of cash or goods, however, at such shrines. In the early medieval period, shrines such as that of Saint Victor in Marseilles were often filled with objects such as the chains of former prisoners, who felt that they had been freed through the intercession of the saint, and they brought their shackles there as a form of offering and thanks. Other contemporary accounts tell of the crew of a fishing vessel who had prayed to Saint Edmund during a storm. In gratitude for their survival, they supposedly fashioned an anchor out of wax and brought it to Edmund's basilica. Such offerings came to pose a problem in some instances, however, in that often the offerings were so many that there was no place to store them all. One ingenious abbot, Geoffrey of Vézeley, used the chains left behind by grateful pilgrims who had been prisoners to fashion a new set of altar rails.

A fourth reason, and one that we've discussed in previous lectures, is the social or entertainment aspect of pilgrimage—which makes it a little like an early version of going on a cruise. As we've noted, people liked good weather for pilgrimages. Geoffrey Chaucer famously suggests this in the general prologue to his *Canterbury Tales*, which opens with a discussion of how people prefer to go on pilgrimages in spring. For reasons of safety and economy, medieval pilgrimages tended to be undertaken in groups—and as the example of Chaucer's pilgrims makes clear, these groups would be interested in finding some entertaining way to pass the time as they traveled. The storytelling contest in which *The Canterbury Tales* pilgrims engage is probably in many respects true to the spirit and nature of many medieval spiritual journeys.

The desire to prove that one had completed a pilgrimage led indirectly to the creation of pilgrim badges, a kind of early souvenir that one could stitch to one's cap or cloak and thereby alert all and sundry that one had been to Rome, or Santiago de Compostela, or any other number of places—all of which had their own identifying symbols. Pilgrims who made the journey to Rome, for example, would often bear the symbol of a pair of crossed keys—representative of the fact that Saint Peter held the keys to heaven. Those who had journeyed to Santiago de Compostela—the supposed shrine of James, one of Jesus's original disciples—would return home with the emblem of a scallop shell, as it was this symbol that is carved into the stone in front of the cathedral that houses the saint's remains. Stepping on the stone marks the end of a pilgrimage that, traditionally, is several hundred miles—usually beginning somewhere in France and ending in the northwest of what is modern-day Spain. For those who had been to Jerusalem, the badge most usually pinned to one's clothing as a mark of this accomplishment resembled crossed palm fronds. In his *Canterbury Tales*, Chaucer makes a reference to palmers, a word used to describe people who more-or-less spent their lives as professional pilgrims—traveling from shrine-to-shrine throughout the medieval world, often relying on the piety and generosity of those who regarded helping pilgrims on their way to these holy sites to be a form of prayer or pilgrimage itself.

Interestingly, the display of badges was not the only way that pilgrims distinguished themselves from the rest of the population. Often, those going on a pilgrimage would don distinctive clothing before setting off—thus identifying themselves to all and sundry as engaged in a spiritual endeavor. In some cases, this piece of clothing might be a particular style of hat or a particular color of clothing.

The late medieval Englishwoman Margery Kempe traveled throughout the medieval world dressed all in white—something that drew a great deal of attention to her and occasionally got her into trouble. Some pilgrims could also be identified by the staff they carried, which served both symbolic and practical functions in that it could advertise a pilgrim's status while serving to help them on their long journey on foot. Those who were engaged in a pilgrimage were also entitled to special dispensations and exemptions. A letter from Charlemagne to King Offa of the Anglo-Saxon kingdom of Mercia, written in 797, is evidence of abuse of this special status, as it contains the emperor's complaint that some English merchants were dressing up as pilgrims in order to avoid paying tolls as they moved throughout the Carolingian Empire.

Given that pilgrimage was supposed to be a solemn, spiritual undertaking, one might expect to find the atmosphere at the destination suitably hushed and reverent. This was usually not the case. Holy sites were often packed with people jostling one another for position—and in many places, the cries and moans of the sick, or injured, or those who were just plain emotional created a startling cacophony. In the early 12th century, Abbot Suger of Saint Denis in Paris offered this justification for rebuilding the Abbey Church:

> On feast-days ... the mass of struggling pilgrims spilt out of every door. A man could only stand like a marble statue, paralyzed, and free only to cry out aloud. Meanwhile, the women in the crowd were in ... intolerable pain ... they screamed as if they were in childbirth ... In the cloister outside, wounded pilgrims lay gasping their last breath ... the monks who were in charge of the reliquaries ... were often obliged to escape with the relics through the windows.

As the practice of making pilgrimages increased in popularity and frequency throughout the medieval period, all sorts of what we might call support industries rose up along the most popular routes. Pilgrims would need food and drink, a place to sleep—and in some unfortunate circumstances, a place to be cared for if sick, and a place to die. While some pilgrims embraced the activity in its purest sense—essentially throwing themselves on the mercy of the world—most were better prepared and set out with ample coin to see them through to journey's end.

Perhaps one of the most interesting medieval pilgrims is the latemedieval Englishwoman named Margery Kempe, whom I mentioned a moment ago. We know of Margery primarily because she dictated what may well be one of the earliest autobiographies in English, if not the earliest. A well-to-do member of the merchant class of the town of Lynn in Norfolk, she was a married woman and mother of 14 children who relatively late in her life began to have a series of spiritual experiences—many of which took the form of conversations with Jesus Christ, and others of which manifested themselves in the form of what Margery herself referred to as cryings or vocal outbursts that seemed, more than anything, to annoy those around her. Like *The Canterbury Tales* pilgrims, Margery often traveled as part of a group. On more than one occasion, her companions—to put it bluntly—tried to ditch her, so tired were they of what seems to be her constant hectoring concerning proper behavior, speech, and dress of good Christians. Margery made many pilgrimages to sites both far and near, and her journeys included visits to Rome and Jerusalem, as well as shorter trips to speak with religious figures—such as the Anchoress Julian of Norwich. An anchoress was sort of a super nun.

As mentioned in a previous lecture, anchoresses and their male counterparts, anchorites, often lived completely enclosed in small cells—with perhaps only a window onto the outside world. This spiritual athleticism and extremism gave many of them a holy—almost saintly—reputation while they were still living and drew many people seeking spiritual guidance to travel to their enclosures. But what made a site holy and thus worthy of a journey to visit it was usually its association with a particular saint, or if it was the repository of any saintly relics. A relic is any object directly associated with Jesus Christ or one of his saints, and it can be a body part, a piece of clothing, footwear—almost anything. Many such items are housed in containers known as reliquaries. Thus, those pilgrims who traveled to the Cathedral of Notre Dame in Paris might venerate a piece of the True Cross, a portion of the cross on which Christ was crucified, and this piece was housed in a magnificent gold and jeweled container. Although the piece of the cross itself is not readily visible, the large size of the container relative to the object within made veneration easier for those making the journey to see it.

In Bruges, Belgium, a vessel containing some of Christ's holy blood is still displayed before the faithful every Friday. In the Italian hill town of Assisi, one can see the tomb that holds the remains of Saint Francis in the basilica that is named for him. At the other end of the town, in the Chapel of Saint Clare, one can see the hair and sandals, among other things, of this friend and protégé of Saint Francis. In yet another Italian hill town, Siena, the head and thumb of Saint Catherine are on display for all who wish to venerate them.

Prior to the 12th century, there was little in the way of a formal process for declaring someone a saint. In 1173, Pope Alexander III reprimanded certain subordinates for venerating figures as saintly whom he considered ill-suited for sainthood. Partly in response to this situation, a process known as canonization was put into place—a process that still exists to this day—in order to assist the church in determining whether or not a person in question had been a saint or not. It is important to understand that the church does and did not "make" saints—the church only affirms the status that God has conferred on that person. Today, only the papacy may declare someone a saint—but in the medieval world, bishops and other more local religious leaders had the power to canonize, a fact that sometimes led to inconsistencies in the process of sainthood from place to place. In fact, no real formal means of canonization existed prior to the 11th century. In the early medieval period, saints were often "made" by popular acclaim, and local traditions as to what made someone eligible for sainthood varied so widely that one community's saint might be another one's average Joe, which resulted in some serious confusion in the roster of saints. Later, many figures who had been revered as saints for decades or even centuries were declared not to be saints at all. For example, after William the Conqueror claimed England, he installed his own bishop, a man named Lanfranc, as archbishop of Canterbury. Lanfranc set out to clean house—and after examining the Anglo-Saxon roster of saints, removed all but two of them from the official list of the canonized.

Generally speaking, candidates for sainthood needed to have lived an exemplary life, and there needed to be evidence of some sort of miracle or miracles associated with the saint after that person's death. Those martyred for their Christian faith usually got to take the fast track, as it were, to sainthood. Sainthood in the medieval world could happen quickly, or over a very long span of years. Thomas Becket, archbishop of Canterbury who was murdered in Canterbury Cathedral by four knights of King Henry II in the year 1170, was elevated to the status of saint within just three years, but even contemporaries felt a little uneasy about the speed with which he was canonized.

This process could not always counteract popular sentiment, as the example of Saint Guinefort—a greyhound revered as a saint beginning in the 13th century—demonstrates. The story of Saint Guinefort begins near the town of Lyon, in what is present-day France. According to the story, a faithful dog—named Guinefort—is left alone briefly with the child of a nobleman. A member of the family comes into the infant's room to find a chaotic scene—the cradle has been overturned, the child is nowhere to be seen, and the dog has blood all over its muzzle. Thinking the worst, the nobleman immediately kills the dog. Just after he does this, he hears crying coming from underneath the cradle—there's the baby, unharmed, with the body of a snake lying beside it. Guinefort had, in fact, protected the child from the snake. With great sorrow, the family buries the dog with great estate. Some accounts say they put the body in a well, which they then filled in with stones—and fairly quickly, locals come to revere Guinefort as a kind of patron saint for infants.

Many treat the dog's burial site as a shrine, and some locals even bring sick or injured infants there in hope of healing, actions that sometimes did more harm than good—as some people apparently would leave their children there at the base of the tree by the dog's grave for long periods of time, or hang them from the branches by their clothes, or even set the children down and light candles nearby. Babies and fire, anyone could tell you, really don't go together. Pretty quickly, church officials stepped in and said: "Look, you cannot have a dog be a saint, and we forbid any acts of worship at this animal's burial site—the church does not recognize that a greyhound could be given healing powers by God." Popular belief is hard to fight, however, and even though the church repeatedly issued injunctions against treating the site as a shrine, evidence suggests that it was a popular place for prayer and pilgrimage until at least the 1930s.

But to return to human saints: Once a person had achieved sainthood, that person's bones and personal effects—clothing, hair, even fingernails—were, as I've previously mentioned, considered to be imbued with holy and healing powers, and they became, properly speaking, relics. One of the key factors in determining whether someone was a saint was the test of incorruptibility, whereby the lack of decomposition of a person's corpse was regarded as a sign from God that this person was a saint. It is rather ironic, then, that once the process of canonization was complete, many saints' remains were broken up and dispersed among several religious sites—an eyeball here, a shinbone there—as it was recognized that the possession of a saintly relic could be a benefit to a religious house, as it would encourage more pilgrims to visit, many of whom would make donations to the institution that possessed these relics. Soon, there was a market in relics, with the leaders of religious houses and monarchs seeking to purchase the toe of this saint or the hand of that one—knowing that the presence of such relics could be a boon to one's community.

Not surprisingly, such a situation resulted in opportunists flooding the market with fake relics. It was a situation that became even more pronounced in 1204, when the companies who had set off on the Fourth Crusade—which we'll discuss at greater length in a later lecture—got sidetracked in the city of Constantinople. The city was filled with religious relics and the Crusaders viewing those, who followed the Eastern Orthodox Christian tradition as being unfit to be keepers of such sacred items, sacked the city, and looted its religious objects. Soon, a flood of relics, supposedly from Constantinople, began to flood into the Western medieval world—with no way for devout believers to tell the fake from the real. It was a forger's dream, and a nightmare for the religious leaders of the day.

In his *Canterbury Tales*, Chaucer includes the character of the pardoner, a man who roamed the countryside, hearing confessions, and granting pardon for sins—carrying religious objects with him that, for a fee, could be used in an attempt to effect cures for ailments, cleanse one of sins, and even help one's livestock and crops to thrive. As Chaucer tells us, the pardoner carries with him a piece of pillow case, which he tells gullible listeners is part of the veil that belonged to Jesus's mother, Mary. He passes off pigs' bones as the remains of a saint and claims that another piece of fabric he carries with him is a portion of the sail of Saint Peter. Chaucer goes on to say that "With this relikes, whan he that he fond/A povre person dwellynge upon lond, Upon a day he gat hym moore moneye/than that person gat in monthes tweye," or, in modern English, "With these fake relics the pardoner is able to convince even a poor person to part with some cash, so that in one day the pardoner is able to make as much money as another man might earn in two months from honest labor."

Although fiction, Chaucer's pardoner reflects real late medieval concerns with the abuse of relics and sacraments, such as confession, a situation that contributed in no small measure to the Protestant Reformation in the 16th century, during which many holy shrines were dismantled—and, in some cases, the bones and other relics of saints were destroyed. The driving force behind such activity was the idea that what had come to be called the cult of the saints bordered on idolatry—those who prayed to particular saints, it was believed, should more properly be praying directly to Jesus or to God the Father. Although the activity of pilgrimage abated somewhat, it continued and remains an important aspect of religious life for Christians—both Catholic and Protestant—today.

Religious pilgrimage was a form of expressing piety in the medieval world, and those who engaged in this activity were not only participants in medieval spirituality, but through their actions they also actually helped create and shape medieval religiosity. In the secular world, a preoccupation similar in the intensity of its pervasiveness and expression, but radically different in its nature, could be found. This was the interest with matters of chivalry and genealogy that became a major concern—one might say, a kind of religion—for members of the noble classes from about the beginning of the High Middle Ages onward. In our next lecture, we will discuss the fascination members of the first estate of the medieval world had with bloodlines and noble lineage—focusing in particular on the science of heraldry, or coats of arms. We will explore how what began as a practical means of identifying friend and foe on the battlefield evolved into a rigid and rule-governed system that in some instances led to conflicts—both physical and legal.

Knighthood and Heraldry
Lecture 16

> At the same time that pilgrimage was increasing in frequency and popularity, in the secular realm interest in genealogy and bloodlines was becoming almost a religion unto itself among the nobility. One of the most fascinating aspects of this almost obsessive interest with the science of heraldry,

In the High Middle Ages, a new class of person was added to the lowest rung of the ladder of nobility: the knight. Although in its earliest stages the position was open to anyone who could afford the necessary equipment—sword, armor, horse, and shield. As knights came to be considered members of the nobility, there arose a desire to limit and define the ranks of knighthood and to make the office a hereditary one. By the 13th century knighthood had become hereditary and had developed a complex system of rituals, identity practices, and public displays that were increasingly distant from its original, practical function of military skill and defense. Over the course of the High and late Middle Ages, the function of a knight began to shift, moving away from the practical activity of warfare and toward ideals of gentility, courtliness, and what we call chivalry—the combination of martial prowess with romantic behavior toward ladies.

One of the most interesting ways that knights and other nobles sought to define their individual identities—and that of their families—was through the practice of heraldry. The practice of painting one's shield with a particular image or color arose for practical reasons: On the battlefield, one fully armed and helmeted knight looks very much like another. Over time, these images came to be associated with a particular family and came to be referred to as coats of arms

The science of heraldry came to be quite rigorously defined, with only certain colors or textures allowed, and then in only certain patterns or orders. The elements of a coat of arms were basically three—colors, metals, or furs. Any of these materials could be used to represent a particular animal or symbol, but there was a strict process of interpretation. A heraldic device was "read" from background, or "field," to foreground. Also, a color could never be placed on a color, nor a metal on a metal, nor a fur on a fur. The eldest male member of a household bore the family's coat of arms in its pure, or original, form, whereas sons of the main branch or members of related branches might bear coats of arms that differentiated themselves in some way—by changing the color of the background, reversing the main symbol, or adding a border or band over the top. Such differentiations are known as marks of cadency, or brisures, words that simply mean "difference" in Old French. An entire language to describe and explain these heraldic devices, with a specialized vocabulary and syntax, was quite developed by the end of the Middle Ages.

Coats of arms came to be regarded as the exclusive property of a particular family. On occasions when members of two different families discovered that they were each bearing similar or identical coats of arms, a court case to decide the legitimate bearer of the arms might ensue.

An entire language to describe and explain these heraldic devices, with a specialized vocabulary and syntax, was quite developed by the end of the Middle Ages.

As advances in weaponry made the mounted knight almost obsolete, the ideal of the knight as a champion of justice, righter of wrongs, and devoted rescuer of ladies became enshrined in the popular literature, especially that dealing with King Arthur. Geoffrey of Monmouth was arguably the first writer to link excellence in combat with romantic love in *The History of the Kings of Britain*. Writers in 12th- and 13th-century France took the ideal of the chivalric knight to new extremes, particularly in stories of Sir Lancelot. At the end of the Middle Ages, an Englishman named Sir Thomas Malory glorified knighthood and knightly activity in his *Morte d'Arthur* at precisely the same moment when knighthood had become more of a blight than a boon to society, as the Wars of the Roses in England would demonstrate resoundingly. The ideals of knighthood and chivalry would continue to hold sway over the popular imagination well into the early modern period, when writers such as Spenser, Sidney, and even Milton would look back toward the medieval world with a kind of nostalgia. ■

Suggested Reading

Fox-Davies, *A Complete Guide to Heraldry*.

Keen, *Chivalry*.

Questions to Consider

1. How did the philosophy of chivalry transform from one of practical function to one concerned with abstract concepts like love, honor, and loyalty?

2. How was the real world of medieval knighthood influenced by literary representations of it, and vice versa?

Knighthood and Heraldry
Lecture 16—Transcript

Welcome back. In our last lecture, we discussed the medieval practice of pilgrimage, and the saints to whose shrines people flocked throughout the Middle Ages. Medieval pilgrims made these journeys for a number of reasons—including to give thanks, to atone for sins, or to perhaps seek divine intervention with a particular problem, or healing for a particular ailment. Pilgrimage was perhaps one of the most potent expressions of religion in the medieval world. At the same time that pilgrimage was increasing in frequency and popularity, in the secular realm interest in genealogy and bloodlines was becoming almost a religion unto itself among the nobility. One of the most fascinating aspects of this almost obsessive interest with the science of heraldry, as it was called, or coats of arms, and the particular ideals and values of knighthood, all came to be grouped together under the term "chivalry." In our lecture today, we will explore the development of the knightly class in the medieval world and the traditions, beliefs, and practices that grew up around it.

In the High Middle Ages, a new class of person was added to the lowest rung of the ladder of the nobility—the knight. Initially, entry into the order of knighthood was contingent upon whether an individual could purchase and maintain the equipment necessary for the office: sword, armor—and, most importantly, a horse. As knights came to be considered members of the nobility, there soon arose a desire to limit and define the ranks of knighthood, and to make the office a hereditary one. We've seen this pattern repeatedly—once an individual accrues power, status, lands, wealth, or titles, there is a natural inclination to wish to pass these things on to the next generation—and to pass them on more or less intact, so that their potency does not become diluted by dividing a family's heritable wealth into smaller and smaller portions. As we've previously discussed, this impulse lent to the entrenchment of a system of primogeniture, or inheritance on the part of the eldest surviving son, more or less throughout the medieval world. Part of the development of this system would be an intense focus on identifying not only a particular family, but differentiating between senior and junior members of that family, or major and minor branches of a family, as we'll see in a moment.

Over the course of the High and late Middle Ages, the ideals and function of a knight began to shift, moving away from the practical activity of warfare and defense and moving toward ideals of gentility, courtliness, and what we would call chivalry—the combination of martial prowess with a romantic behavior toward ladies. We've already seen this shift depicted in Geoffrey Chaucer's *Canterbury Tales* in the difference between his characters of the knight—who is a no-nonsense military man—and the knight's son, the squire, who is skilled at such activities as singing, dancing, and wooing ladies. It is a shift that would have a number of significant implications.

One of the most interesting ways that knights and other nobles sought to define their individual identities—and those of their families—was through the practice of heraldry, or what we might think of as coats of arms. The practice of painting one's shield with a particular image or color arose for very practical reasons. On the battlefield, one fully armed and helmeted knight looks very much like another. By painting a particular image on one's shield, one's friends and foes could more easily identify a particular knight. Over time, these images or patterns came to be associated with a specific family and came to be referred to as a coat of arms, which followed particular rules of what is known as blazon.

Men wore their coats of arms on their shields or occasionally on the trappings of their horses. A woman might wear a lozenge-shaped medallion bearing the coat of arms of her father until such time as she was married, at which point she would adopt the coat of arms of her husband. In a few instances, a man might combine his own family's coat of arms with that of his wife's, particularly if she came from a more powerful or more-noble family than his own. The science of heraldry came to be quite rigorously defined, with only certain colors or textures allowed, and then in only certain patterns or orders. The vocabulary associated with the practice sometimes sounds like a completely foreign language, which is not surprising given that most of the terms were adopted from the French. I should pause here and note that although coats of arms were primarily used by the noble classes, in continental Europe, at least, any member of society could possess a coat of arms. The situation is somewhat different in England, where only members of the peerage—the nobility—were allowed to display and use heraldic blazons.

The elements that went into making up a shield or coats of arms were basically three—one could use colors, metals, or furs. Any of these materials could be used to represent a particular animal or symbol, but there was a strict process of interpretation. The shield was normally "read" in layers, starting from the bottom layer up—with the lowest, most basic level called the "field." A color could never be placed on a color, nor a metal on a metal, nor a fur on a fur. Thus, if a shield happened to have a red band on it, that red band could never be layered directly on top of a blue field—nor could any gold element be placed directly on top of a silver element; nor vair, a type of fur; layered directly on top of miniver, another kind of fur; and so on, and so on.

The eldest male member of a household bore the family's coat of arms in its pure or original form, whereas sons of the main branch or members of related branches of a family might bear coats of arms that differentiated themselves in some way—by changing the color of the background, or field, by reversing the main symbol or image, or by adding a border or band over the top of the whole thing. Such differentiations are known as marks of cadency or *brisures*—words that simply mean "difference," essentially.

An entire language to describe and explain these heraldic devices was quite developed by the end of the Middle Ages, with a specialized vocabulary and even syntax. So, for example, a knight bearing a coat of arms that, to our modern eyes, appears to depict a red stag walking with one leg raised on a yellow background would more properly be described in the language of heraldry as something like *Or a stag passant gules*. The first word, *Or*, the French word for "gold," refers to the field, or background, of the shield. The next three words, *a stag passant*, refers to the animal on top of the field and the position in which he is depicted—*passant* means an animal who is walking with one foreleg raised. If the stag were to be shown rearing up on his hind legs and pawing at the air, he would be described as *rampant*. If he were to be shown lying down, then he would be described as *couchant*. Finally, the last word *gules* is an older French word for the color red. To take another example—a shield with a white field and a red cross on top of it would be a shield *argent*, or silver, with a *cross gules*.

Heraldic devices, or coats of arms, came to be regarded as the exclusive property of a particular family. On those occasions when members of two different families discovered that they were each bearing similar or identical coats of arms—as could conceivably happen—a court case to decide the legitimate bearer of the arms might ensue, as in the famous Scrope-Grosvener dispute of the 14th century, at which the poet Geoffrey Chaucer himself testified as a witness. This incident began when King Richard II of England invaded Scotland in 1385. When his knights assembled to fight for their lord, two of them, Sir Richard Scrope and Sir Robert Grosvenor, discovered they each bore coats of arms that were nearly identical; they were both *Azure a Bend Or*—or in English, "a blue field with a gold band across it." Grosvenor had already had a conflict about these particular arms. On a 1360 expedition to France, Grosvenor had discovered that a knight from Cornwall, one Thomas Carminow, was bearing arms identical to his. Presumably, this case was brought before a military court, but the outcome of the trial does not survive—whatever the outcome was, it does not seem to have prevented either the Grosvenor or Carminow families from bearing the same arms. The later dispute between Scrope and Grosvenor is amply attested, and in this case, Carminow got involved again—charging that Scrope did not have the right to bear these arms. So we have three families, each claiming the right to bear a particular coat of arms. Supporters of each of the complainants were called to testify before the military court, primarily to give evidence as to how far back in time each of these families had borne these particular arms.

In the end, the court found that Carminow's family had been bearing these arms since "the time of King Arthur"—something patently impossible as the time of King Arthur, 5th-century Britain, preceded the age of heraldry by several hundred years. The judges were also persuaded that the Scrope family had borne their arms since the time of the Norman Conquest, another unlikely situation. In an initial ruling in 1389, the court found that Grosvenor could continue to bear the Azure a Bend Or arms as long as he differentiated it with a border around the shield. In 1390, the king himself revoked this decision, explaining that this difference was not a great enough distinction for two families who were not in some way related—adding a border was essentially a mark of cadency, a brisure, something a cousin might do. For whatever reason, the Scrope and Carminow famililes were both permitted to keep their identical coats of arms—and have done so since the late 14th century. Grosvenor, on the other hand, had to pick a new heraldic device. He chose *Azure a Garb Or*, or "a blue field with a gold wheatsheaf on it." Grosvenor's descendent, the duke of Westminster, has this heraldic device incorporated into his coat of arms even to this day.

As the Scrope-Grosvenor dispute might suggest, as we move from the High into the late Middle Ages those who held the office of knighthood were becoming somewhat less engaged with the practical, day-to-day concerns of military skill and defense, and more obsessed with the details and trappings of this position. Nothing demonstrates this more clearly than a change in the way that peculiarly upper-class entertainment, the tournament, was conducted. The tournament had its origins, like coats of arms, in practicality: When not fighting actual wars, knights needed to keep in fighting form, so tournaments served as a sort of means of practice and entertainment, as knights would joust against one another or compete in mock battles known as mêlées. By the late medieval period, however, these tournaments had become more about spectacle and less about training, as is evidenced in the fact that a knight might have two sets of completely different equipment— one that was used for tournament fighting, and one that was used for real fighting.

This development was not just due to shifts in attitudes about the rank of knight and its inclusion in the noble classes—although that was, indeed, part of it. As we move through the medieval period, advances in weaponry made the mounted knight on horseback almost unnecessary and obsolete. Whereas in the year 1000 the mounted cavalry might have been the most potent element of the medieval army, by the year 1500 archers, *trébuchets* (or catapults), cannon, gunpowder, and other similar developments meant that military strategy did not have much use for a heavily armored man brandishing a sword on the back of an animal that it was extremely costly to maintain and train.

We'll focus much more on how warfare and military tactics evolved throughout the Middle Ages in a later lecture, but for now it's important that we recognize how the ideal of the knight as a champion of justice, righter of wrongs, and devoted rescuer of ladies had become a popular belief, enshrined in the literature of the day. As with the case of the concept of the three orders of society, the knight as the epitome of all that was right with medieval society was a difficult idea to dispel once it had a hold on the popular imagination and a place in the fashionable fiction of the day. This was particularly the case in those stories dealing with the legendary King Arthur. As we've previously discussed, the 12th century Welsh cleric Geoffrey of Monmouth was arguably the writer whose treatment of King Arthur brought the legendary British monarch to the attention of the rest of the medieval world.

Geoffrey's *History of the Kings of Britain* was a bestseller in its day, being translated and circulated throughout Britain and on the Continent. As I noted in our lecture on King Arthur, this is evidenced in part by the number of copies of Geoffrey's manuscript that survive—we have over 200 extant copies of the *History of the Kings of Britain*. Compare that with some 80 surviving manuscripts of Chaucer's famous *Canterbury Tales*, and just one manuscript containing that masterpiece of late medieval romance, *Sir Gawain and the Green Knight*. Geoffrey of Monmouth's text is important for many reasons, but for our purposes today, what was most important was that he explicitly linked excellence in combat with romantic love in his *History*. Geoffrey tells us that in the court of King Arthur, women refused to grant their love to a knight until he had proven himself in combat three times. By this means, the knights increased in their martial prowess, and the modesty and chastity of the female population of the court was also greatly enhanced.

Twelfth- and 13th-century French writers took the ideal of the chivalric knight to new extremes, particularly in the stories concerning the great knight Sir Lancelot. It is always a crushing blow to my students, when I teach the Arthurian tradition, for them to discover that the legendary Sir Lancelot most likely never existed—that there seems to be no historical basis for his figure. He first appears in the works of a French writer of the 12th century named Chrétien de Troyes, and the creation of this knight and his explicit status as the greatest knight at the court of King Arthur most likely came about, at least in part, as a way for the French to get involved with the hottest literary phenomenon in town—the heroes of which were, for the most part, all English.

Lancelot du Lac, Frenchman and the greatest knight to wield a sword in all medieval literature, was famous in no small measure because of his love for Queen Guinevere. It is his devotion to the wife of the king at whose table he sits that is, in fact, responsible for most of his stellar reputation. Because of her—in Chrétien's tales and throughout the later Arthurian tradition in the medieval world—Lancelot repeatedly leaves the court, seeking out adventures in which he can prove himself, and thereby win her admiration and esteem. The potentially ridiculous extremes of the knightly ideal of devotion to a lady are also made clear in tales about this greatest knight of King Arthur, in that we see Lancelot willing to humiliate himself in order to please the queen. On one occasion, while fighting a duel beneath a tower from which the queen is watching, Lancelot engages in all sorts of ridiculous contortions so that he may keep his eyes on his beloved while he fights. He is gaining ground and pushing his opponent back when he suddenly realizes he is out of view of the queen. He then gives up the ground he has gained and moves backward so that he can see her again. When he and his opponent end up switching positions on the field of combat, Lancelot turns so that he is facing the tower while continuing to fight backward, with his arm behind him—all so he can keep looking at Guinevere.

Another story tells of how Lancelot enters a tournament while wearing a disguise. It's difficult to find someone to fight you when you're known as the best knight of the world, so Lancelot often has to resort to trickery such as this just so he can keep his skills sharp. Guinevere, suspecting that the knight in disguise might be Lancelot, sends one of her handmaidens to him. The maiden tells the mysterious knight that Queen Guinevere wishes him to "do his worst." The next day at the tournament, Lancelot performs abysmally—losing challenge after challenge and suffering the mockery of all those in attendance. Guinevere then sends her handmaiden to tell Lancelot to "do his best," after which, of course, he reverts to his splendid knightly self—winning the tournament resoundingly. Although this is fiction, it does suggest, at the very least, the extent to which the practical and useful nature of knighthood had been compromised over time—as the power of a lady's command could conceivably result in knights being injured or killed, and battles lost.

At the end of the Middle Ages, an Englishman named Sir Thomas Malory glorified knighthood and knightly activity in his *Morte d'Arthur* at precisely the same moment when knighthood had become more of a blight than a boon to society—as the Wars of the Roses in England, which we'll talk about at greater length in a later lecture, would demonstrate resoundingly. Malory was a minor nobleman, a knight, at a time and place—15th-century England—when the practical function of knighthood had become obsolete. No longer did monarchs rely on their noble vassals for a certain number of days of military service per year; that duty had largely been obviated by the ability of knights to pay a tax known as *scutage*—which meant that instead of committing to fight, say, 40 days out of the year in their lord's conflicts, knights could simply pay a fine and stay home. Their lord could then use that money to hire archers, gunners, and the like—a much more effective means of engaging in combat and a more prudent use of funds.

Although a knight, there is little about Sir Thomas Malory that resonated with the ideals of chivalry that continued to be such a popular element of romance literature of the day. To put it bluntly, Malory was something of a scoundrel. At various times he was charged with crimes that ranged from ambush, to cattle stealing, to assaulting an abbot, to rape. Some of these charges may have been trumped up—they may have been politically motivated. The dispute between the rival Royal Houses of York and Lancaster during Malory's lifetime meant that knights and other nobles were regularly switching sides, depending upon which claimant to the throne was in power, and many of these knights ended up in prison as a result. Although we can't be entirely sure of Malory's guilt, it seems pretty certain that he was no Lancelot—and he was one of those who ended up in prison.

During his captivity, he decided to do a rather curious thing, and something that no other medieval writer had done before him, and something that no other writer would do with any real success after him until the Modern period. He decided to write a book that glorified precisely those knightly behaviors and attributes so glaringly absent from 15th-century English society and the lack of which had most likely landed him in jail. In this book, he set out to tell the most coherent, comprehensive, and chronological story of King Arthur a single medieval author had ever composed. He began at the beginning and moved through the story of Arthur and his rule to the very end—to Arthur's death and beyond. Along the way, he incorporated the various adventures of many of Arthur's knights, such as Lancelot, Gawain, Gareth, and Tristan. Malory drew heavily on earlier French—and some English—sources for his tale, weaving together different elements of the story—the founding of the Round Table, the quest for the Holy Grail, the love of Lancelot and Guinevere—to produce a rich and varied whole. He also added one key element that was entirely his own, and this is a vow taken by Arthur's knights at the Feast of Pentecost. In this so-called Pentecostal Oath, Malory articulates both the values and ideals Knights of the Round Table should uphold, while simultaneously calling attention to many of the less-than-noble activities of other knights living in his time. According to Malory, the knights swear:

> Never to do outerage nothir mourthir, and allwayes to fle treson, and to gyff mercy unto hym that askith mercy, uppon payne of forfiture of their worship and lordship of kynge Arthure for evirmore; and allwayes to do ladyes, damesels, and jantilwomen and wydowes socour: strengthe hem in hir ryghtes, and never to enforce them, upon payne of dethe. Also, that no man take no batayles in a wrongefull quarell for no love ne for no worldis goodis.

In other words, noble knights should never commit outrage, or murder, or treason; they should always help women, and they should not rape them. Knights should not agree to fight a battle simply out of love for a lady, or for some payment of cash or goods. It is striking that so many things that Malory's knights swear to avoid are things that Malory himself was accused of.

Malory has his knights swear to uphold this oath early on in the text, and then he depicts Arthur's knights struggling to adhere to these ideals—some of which conflict directly with one another from time to time—as the narrative moves toward its inevitable conclusion: Arthur's death and the collapse of the society he founded. Malory's text is important for our understanding of medieval knighthood in that it seems to simultaneously promote specific chivalric ideals as a means of stabilizing society, while also depicting these ideals as almost impossible for knights to adhere to consistently and successfully. Malory's text is thus a product of his age, when knighthood was essentially broken. In his *Morte d'Arthur*, he both condemns and praises chivalry, suggesting that its ideals—while laudable and noble—ironically compromise the very social order they're meant to support in their contradictory nature and the vagueness of their articulation.

Yet, well beyond the medieval world—into what we might call the early modern period and even later than that—the ideals of knighthood and chivalry would continue to hold sway over the popular imagination. In England, in particular, writers such as Edmund Spenser, Sir Philip Sidney, and even John Milton would look back toward the medieval world with a kind of nostalgia and invoke the values of courtliness and knighthood in their literature. Spenser's epic *Faerie Queene*, for example, is an allegory that, at least in part, celebrates the reign of Queen Elizabeth I through the depiction of characters that at times seem drawn straight from the Arthurian legend. Similarly, Sir Philip Sidney's *Arcadia* draws on episodes and themes from the medieval romance tradition. Milton, perhaps most famous for his masterpiece *Paradise Lost*, first considered writing an epic poem on the subject of King Arthur. After some consideration, he abandoned that topic in favor of a religious one, but the fact that he seriously considered it at all points to the lingering power of medieval concepts of nobility, gentility, and military prowess.

Thus, in the literature of the medieval world, we find preserved extreme examples of the ideals that helped shape the self-concept of the noble classes. Heraldic devices also serve as testaments to the desire of those at the top of the social ladder to identify and define their bloodlines, and to maintain their position in the hierarchy of the medieval world. While interest in chivalry and heraldry became almost a religion for the noble classes during the High Middle Ages and beyond, true religious belief and devotion were leading medieval people to construct some of the most awesome edifices the world has ever seen—monuments to faith and piety. These were the great cathedrals of Europe, which will be the subject of our next lecture.

The Gothic Cathedral
Lecture 17

When Gothic architecture appeared on the scene in the early 12th century, the architectural elements it used were not necessarily new, but what Gothic did is borrow from different architectural traditions and combine these elements in an utterly new and original way that made it possible to construct houses of worship that seemed to soar—that were taller and lighter than any that had been seen before and thus, seemed a truly fitting place to try and become close to God.

In the year 1140 at the church of Saint-Denis outside Paris, France, a new form of building came into being that would dominate European architecture for several centuries to come: the Gothic. Prior to the 12th century, most religious structures were built in the Romanesque style, which was based on the Roman basilica with its rounded arches. The Gothic style, which first appeared in the 12th century, was not in itself radically new in terms of building techniques; what was original was the way it combined existing architectural techniques to create something new.

Perhaps the most distinctive feature of Gothic architecture is its pointed arches, a feature that had flexibility and many benefits compared with the rounded Romanesque arch. Another element that differentiated Gothic from Romanesque was the use of rib vaulting, which gave the interior of a building a much lighter feel than the rounded, Romanesque barrel vault. Instead of breaking up the interior space of a building with thick support columns, the Gothic style used the flying buttress—supports that were built outside

Notre Dame de Reims, a 13th-century cathedral in the French Gothic style.

the structure and were used to transfer much of the weight, or thrust, of the building into the ground.

Within two centuries, literally hundreds of Gothic cathedrals sprang up throughout much of the Continent and in England. The layout of a Gothic cathedral is fairly standard and follows a cruciform model. The building of a Gothic cathedral was a massive undertaking that involved hundreds of workers, from skilled architects and master craftsmen to laborers who transported the massive stone blocks and put them in place. Many Gothic structures were simply superimposed over existing buildings. In Canterbury Cathedral in England, the choir and nave were each rebuilt at different times, and when one descends into the crypt, the style is quite clearly Romanesque.

By the 14th century, Gothic had become strongly localized. In France, the emphasis was on large round windows and a substyle called flamboyant. Spanish and Portuguese treatments of Gothic architecture tended to focus on decorative flourishes, many of which may seem bizarre to the modern eye. German and central European styles played with a wild and wide variety of vaulting patterns. In England, styles diverged into two main trends: decorated and perpendicular.

The carvings at Chartres also deliberately juxtapose religious subjects with secular ones, an attempt to link the rulers of France with the power of God.

Two examples—Chartres Cathedral in France and Salisbury Cathedral in England—can help us see how the Gothic style became so localized that each structure was unique. Chartres Cathedral was constructed and added to over many centuries, so we can see a number of different substyles of Gothic in its edifice. There is a deliberate lack of symmetry in its facade. One spire is much higher than the other, and each is executed in a different style. The carvings at Chartres also deliberately juxtapose religious subjects with secular ones, an attempt to link the rulers of France with the power of God. In contrast with Chartres, the major construction of Salisbury Cathedral took place in nearly record time— just 38 years for the construction of the main portion—but like Chartres, significant additions and changes were made over the years. Perhaps its most famous element is the spire, the tallest such on a medieval cathedral that still stands today. However, mistakes were made in its construction, and its massive weight is causing the stone piers inside the cathedral to twist and bend. Salisbury also has a cathedral school, one whose origins can be traced back to the 11th century. Coincidentally, it was most likely the place where John of Salisbury, one of the greatest philosophers and academic minds of the medieval world, received his initial education before traveling to Chartres to continue his studies. ■

Suggested Reading

Sumption, *The Age of Pilgrimage.*

Wilson, *The Gothic Cathedral.*

Questions to Consider

1. How did advances in technology and architectural engineering make possible the construction of Gothic cathedrals, and/or how did the desire to build these structural marvels contribute to improvements and innovations in building techniques?

2. How do the two examples of Chartres and Salisbury demonstrate consistencies in Gothic architecture while underscoring the possibility for localized differences?

The Gothic Cathedral
Lecture 17—Transcript

Welcome back. In our last lecture, we discussed the chivalric tradition in medieval society and its literature—examining how a concern with chivalric values and the system of heraldry, or coats of arms, became a nearly religious obsession with members of the noble estate. Today we're going to shift our focus back to religion proper and explore how faith and piety led to the construction of some of the most awesome and awe-inspiring structures the world has ever seen: These are the Gothic cathedrals that sprang up throughout the medieval world, starting in the 12th century.

On July 14th, in the year 1140 at the Church of Saint-Denis near Paris, a new form of architecture came into being that would dominate European architecture—especially religious architecture—for the rest of the Middle Ages. That style is known today as gothic—a misnomer since it has absolutely nothing to do with those people called the Goths whose interactions with the late Roman Empire helped to bring about its transformation into the medieval world, and about whom we talked in one of our earliest lectures. The term "gothic" was retroactively applied much later and may have come from the idea that when the Goths overran the Roman Empire, they brought to an end building in the classical Greek and Roman style. Whatever its source, "gothic" is the term all scholars of the Middle Ages use to discuss this architectural phenomenon—which began in the 12th century, and which had its fullest expression in the cathedrals found mostly in France and England, which are true marvels of architecture, engineering, and artistry, and still inspire awe in visitors to this day.

In order to understand the significance of this new style and its origins, we have to go back in time to the Christianization of the Roman Empire. As we discussed in an earlier lecture, once persecutions of Christians had ceased, Christianity solidified its position within the empire by borrowing from the secular and bureaucratic institutions of Rome. One way it did this was to model the early churches after the shape of many Roman public halls. This shape was the basilica—which was essentially a long, rectangular building with one end built in the shape of a semicircle. This end was called the apse, and it usually had a high vaulted ceiling, and it was where the altar was situated when this building style was borrowed by Roman Christians.

By about the year 1000, most European churches were built in what we today call Romanesque style. As you might guess from its name, this style was also ultimately modeled on Roman architecture and is distinguished by several key features. Perhaps the best known and most easily identifiable of these is the shape of the arch that is used for windows, for doors, and as part of the supporting structure inside the church—the Romanesque arch is a simple round arch. As builders wanted to construct larger and more impressive edifices around the turn of the first millennium, they strengthened these churches and cathedrals with massive stone walls. In order to support the structure, the inside of the church would be broken up by several thick stone columns that were classical in style—very often having capitals, as you might see on classical Greek and Roman columns. These columns worked to support the heavy stone vaulted ceilings. The divisions made by these columns are known as bays, and this chopping up of the interior space of a Romanesque church is one of the hallmarks of this form of architecture.

When Gothic architecture appeared on the scene in the early 12th century, the architectural elements it used were not necessarily new, but what Gothic did is borrow from different architectural traditions and combine these elements in an utterly new and original way that made it possible to construct houses of worship that seemed to soar—that were taller and lighter than any that had been seen before, and thus, seemed a truly fitting place to try and become close to God.

Perhaps the most identifiable element of Gothic architecture is—as in the case with Romanesque architecture—the arch used for windows and door entrances. But whereas the Romanesque arch was a simple round arch, the Gothic arch was pointed at the top, which had several advantages from an architectural point of view. One of these was that it was possible to have arches of different widths all be the same height, a strategy that could be effective both from an aesthetic standpoint and from a practical standpoint—in that this was a new way to deal with the weight, or thrust, of all that stone that went into the construction of a church. The pointed arch was not the invention of Abbot Suger or his architects—rather, it had been in use for some time in Burgundy, and the abbot and his builders borrowed this style when they were rebuilding the choir of Saint-Denis. The truly innovative thing that they did is that they combined this pointed arch with a style of vaulting of making high ceilings out of stone that was known as rib vaulting, and which had been in use in Normandy.

We should remember that although they are part of what we think of as France today, in the 12th century, Normandy and Burgundy were essentially their own sovereign territories—and the Dukes of Normandy were, in fact, also Kings of England. The 12th-century entity known then as France was relatively weak compared to these two regions on its borders, despite the fact that the two French kings who were involved with the rebuilding of Saint-Denis—Louis VI and Louis VII—considered these regions to be properly part of France as a whole, as part of the patrimony of Charlemagne.

Indeed, it is significant that this architectural innovation took place at Saint-Denis, because this church was the burial place of many of the leaders of the Merovingian and Carolingian dynasties. The church was also dedicated to France's patron saint, Saint Dionysius, so the innovative work here was significant not only from an architectural standpoint, but from a political standpoint—as the re-glorification of Saint-Denis was felt to mark a turn in the fortunes of France and the French kings who, as I just noted, were weak in comparison to the rulers of Burgundy and Normandy.

So, Saint-Denis borrowed the pointed arch from the Burgundians, rib vaulting from the Normans, and there were a few other key innovations. Instead of using heavy, thick walls for support, Gothic architects throughout the period wanted to aim for a feeling of lightness, so much thinner stone walls were used than had traditionally been the case. Instead of supporting them from the inside, with massive columns that broke up the interior space, buttresses—often called flying buttresses—were used on the outside of the building as a means of transferring weight and thrust down into the ground. With new strategies for support, this allowed Gothic architects to try some new things when it came to apertures for light. Romanesque churches had tended to have very thick walls, occasionally broken up by small windows to let in a little bit of light. One of the hallmarks of the Gothic cathedral quickly came to be what is called stone tracery—a kind of light latticework of stone into which could be fitted panes of stained glass that would flood the interior of the church with colored light. Perhaps the best example of this is the Cathedral of Sainte-Chapelle in Paris, which has been described as a medieval light-box by some—instead of stone walls into which windows have been placed, the effect is one of colored glass from floor to ceiling, with the stone tracery that holds up all that glass almost invisible.

Once this style came into being, it caught on quite quickly, and between 1180 and 1270 around 80 cathedrals are built in France. From a very early moment, cathedrals become a way of broadcasting the power and prestige of France—with some scholars going so far as to say that the age of high cathedral building was just one expression of newly aggressive and expansionist French monarchic intentions. In the late 12th century, architects in England begin to adopt this style, and it becomes the predominant mode of religious building for the rest of the period—with very little real innovation occurring, except for attempts to build higher and to add more and more elaborate tracery and decorative flourishes to Gothic structures.

I should pause here to make a note about the word "cathedral." I've been using it as probably the man or woman on the street would—as a term to describe a large building where religious worship takes place. What makes a cathedral a cathedral, however, is not its size, or its style, or its location; what makes a cathedral a cathedral is the presence of the cathedra—that is, the bishop's seat. So usually, the bishop's seat will be in the largest church in his bishopric, which then becomes, by definition, a cathedral. But there are a few instances of glorious, grand churches that would seem to fit the description of cathedral—but are not because they happen not to be the bishop's seat. There are a few instances of relatively small churches, in fact, being called cathedrals because they have the bishop's cathedra. While I don't wish to belabor this point, it is something to be aware of—and a little bit of information with which you can amuse and amaze your friends.

The layout of a cathedral is fairly consistent. As opposed to the long, rectangular shape of the basilica, a cathedral is laid out as a cruciform—meaning that it has four arms, and in this it recalls the cross on which Jesus was crucified. The longest arm is the nave, and this is the part of the cathedral where worshippers would gather to hear Mass. One thing that always surprises Americans, especially those who might be visiting cathedrals in Europe for the first time, is the seating. Very often, in many cathedrals, there will be folding chairs set up for the service, and this seems to many to be a jarring anachronism. I often have students ask me: "Where are the pews?" and the answer is that originally, there were no pews—the congregation simply stood in the nave. When it was time to kneel, they knelt on the hard stone floor. Some well-to-do worshippers might bring along cushions specially made for just such a situation and to protect their knees from the cold and discomfort of the stone, while many felt that such discomfort was an important part of demonstrating one's faith.

The building of a cathedral was a massive undertaking that involved hundreds—if not thousands—of people, and that might last decades or even centuries in a few cases. This meant that the architect, the master builder, and others who were in on the ground floor, as it were, of the design and construction of a cathedral most certainly would not live to see it completed. In addition to requiring the most advanced in the way of architectural and technological skills, the head of such a project needed to have what we might call excellent management and people skills. He needed to be able to oversee a variety of craftsmen, masons, carvers—everyone from those hired to perform brute manual labor to those engaged in the finest, most delicate detail work, and everyone in between. One gets a sense of this if one looks at the record of men employed to work on the construction of Westminster Abbey in the year 1253. For the week of June 23rd that year, the records list 53 stone cutters, 49 monumental masons—these would most likely be responsible for carving letters or images into monuments that would go into the cathedral, 28 regular masons, 28 carpenters, 15 sanders, 17 smiths, 14 glassmakers, 4 roofers, and 220 laborers who would be employed to set all this stone in place. This doesn't even take into account the quarrymen who cut the large block of stone from the earth to begin with, and those who transported the stone from the quarry to the building site. Those who dressed and shaped the stone needed an accurate way to ensure that they were paid, so if you go to a cathedral today, you can often find small marks incised on many of the stones—and very visible if you just look closely. Every stonecutter had his own mark—sort of like a brand. It might be a geometric shape. It might occasionally be an initial, and this claiming of ownership of work was important not only so that the number of stones completed by an individual could be counted and he could be paid what he was owed—but also so that the overseers of the project could check the quality of the work of the individual stonecutters.

Another kind of mark that might be visible on the walls of cathedrals—if you look for it—are what are called position marks. A cathedral might have spaces designated for hundreds or thousands of statues, and it was important that workers know the correct location of each. In the great Cathedral of Notre-Dame in Paris, a series of statues representing the months of the year had actually originally been installed in the wrong order. It was not too long after this that the overseer of the Cathedral of Rheims found himself confronted with the need to correctly position more than 3,000 statues. He came up with a system of marks that told the laborers information about where a statue should go—the first mark indicated which side of the cathedral; the next mark which doorway beside which the statue was to stand; and then third, the exact position with regard to the doorway. This was a clever system that was far more efficient than having a unique symbol for each of the statues and then trying to match them to their locations, or having to carve out lengthy directions.

The construction of Gothic cathedrals often took place over or incorporated earlier structures. So, in many cases, if one starts at the bottom and moves up, one is also moving through time. For example, if one goes to Canterbury Cathedral in England today and starts at the bottom, underneath the nave, one finds oneself on the original site of the cathedral that was built here in 597 when Augustine of Canterbury, the first bishop in England, came to Christianize the Anglo-Saxons. Later, this portion of the church was extensively rebuilt in a Norman style, which was similar to Romanesque in its dependence upon massive stone columns for support. One can still see this Norman style in the 11th-century crypt beneath the cathedral today. In the 11th century, Archbishop Lanfranc had a cathedral constructed above the crypt that was Romanesque in style. We start to see a more obvious mishmash of styles in the late 12th century, after a fire destroyed the section of the cathedral known as the choir. If we go back to thinking of the shape of a cathedral as a cross with four arms, the choir is the short arm directly above where the nave meets the other two short arms that come out to the side. So if one is standing in the nave and looking straight ahead, one is looking directly toward the altar, and beyond this is the choir.

Canterbury's choir was destroyed by fire in 1174—and to rebuild it, a French architect named William of Sens, who was familiar with the groundbreaking work of Saint-Denis, was hired. The rebuilt choir of Canterbury would prove to be hugely influential, and many other choirs of English churches were built at this time using this style, which came to be known as early English gothic. Canterbury's nave, however, remained Romanesque until the 14th century, when many scholars believe that an architect named Henry Yevele, who was the master builder of the royal court, designed and constructed a new one. What is most impressive about this nave is the sense of verticality it imparts. The piers, or supports, are unusually slender, and the sense of height and of a single unified space is overwhelming—so much so that it is considered a prime example of a style that scholars have come to call English perpendicular gothic.

As you may gather from the use of phrases like "early English gothic" or "English perpendicular gothic," it was not long after the building of the choir at Saint-Denis before the basics of Gothic architecture spread throughout France and then throughout Europe to England, Spain, and Germany, and then became what we might call localized—that is, variations developed in particular places that were unique to that geographic location. Interestingly, with a few notable exceptions, Gothic never really caught on in Italy.

By the 14th century, the localization of Gothic architecture was fullblown. In France, the big deal was big, round windows and a style that has come to be called flamboyant. In Spain and Portugal, Gothic architecture was enhanced with excessive decorative flourishes—many of which seem somewhat bizarre today. In Germany and central Europe, Gothic distinguished itself by a sort of wild play on ideas of vaulting patterns. In England, styles diverged into decorated and perpendicular.

What is fascinating about Gothic architecture is that it is the dominant style of religious building in most of Western Europe for about 500 years—from the mid-12th century to the mid-17th century. For the first half of that period, Gothic building was full of new and exciting innovations; for the second half, the only thing that was new was the seemingly endless fascination with adding decorative flourishes—or making parts of the cathedral taller, longer, and bigger. Although there are many elements of Gothic architecture that would seem to be consistent from place to place, each church or cathedral is truly unique, and I'd like to talk about just two examples of Gothic architecture that demonstrate this uniqueness. The first is Chartres Cathedral in France, the birthplace of Gothic, and the other is Salisbury Cathedral in England, one of the most striking architectural examples in that country.

Chartres Cathedral is interesting for a number of reasons, and the first and most obvious reason is clear if you stand in front of it and look at the façade of the cathedral. The first thing you will notice is that there are two spires on either side of the entrance to the cathedral, but where one might expect symmetry, there is none. The one on the right, which is about 350 feet high, is quite simple, without overly elaborate decoration—and dates from about the 1140s. The one on the left, as you're standing outside and facing the front of the church, is almost 380 feet tall, and it is an ornate explosion of the Flamboyant style of Gothic architecture, and it was built in the 16th century. So before you even enter Chartres Cathedral, you have a reminder of how long the process of building a cathedral could be, and how styles and tastes might change over the centuries during which the cathedral was undergoing construction. Between these two towers is one of the most famous elements of Chartres, and that is one of its three so-called rose windows, which contain some of the most vivid medieval stained glass still in existence in the world today. During WWII and the occupation of France, the stained glass was actually taken out and hidden. The building itself became a German social club during the Occupation. After the war ended, the stained glass was taken out of hiding and restored to the cathedral, so this is a truly amazing story of historic preservation.

Like many cathedrals, the current site of Chartres had been the location of a church or cathedral for centuries before the present cathedral was built; most of these earlier structures were destroyed by fire. But no matter what kind of structure was there, the cathedral's importance as a focal point for the local community is instructive as we consider how other cathedrals functioned similarly. Arguably, the church was the center of the local economy, with sellers of various wares setting up shop just outside a particular church door.

At the northern end of the church, you could find sellers hawking textiles; at the southern end, one could find meat and vegetables. Wine merchants actually conducted business in the nave of the church, and this was also where laborers of various sorts might come if they were looking for work. For a time, the crypt of the church was used as a kind of hospital to care for sick pilgrims who came there seeking cures for various ailments. Chartres was a popular pilgrimage destination because it had a very powerful relic, the cloak of the Virgin Mary, and this made it one of the top choices of destination for people who were going on pilgrimage. When one of the various incarnations of the church burned down in 1145, it was at first thought that the relic had been lost in the fire; by a miracle, it survived, and this was taken to mean that the Virgin desired a more magnificent site to house her relic. A campaign to rebuild the cathedral on a truly magnificent scale thus began, and donations to the cause came in from all over Europe. The rebuilding itself was plagued by several fires that destroyed portions of the rebuilt cathedral. The main portion of the cathedral as we see it today was actually built fairly quickly—in about 30 years at the end of the 12th and beginning of the 13th century. It was dedicated in 1260 in the presence of King Louis IX, although the ambitious plans for the spires were never executed, which is why we have the façade as it exists today—with one tower a remnant from the 12th century that survived many of the catastrophes that befell the cathedral, and the other an attempt to complete the façade but in a much different style.

Like many cathedrals, Chartres is full of statues and carvings that tell various biblical and other stories. For example, on the west façade, there are various scenes from the life of Christ—and below these, what appear to be depictions of various kings and queens of France. This close juxtaposition is deliberate, as it would seem to suggest the divine right of French royalty to rule. Like many other cathedrals, Chartres also had a renowned cathedral school, and this was a direct result of Charlemagne's educational reforms enacted during that period called the Carolingian Renaissance. He decided to set up schools, and instead of building new structures, he made use of monasteries and cathedrals that already had the space, the texts—and in many cases, the greatest minds of the day—attached to them.

Chartres became an especially renowned cathedral school, so much so that the renowned philosopher John of Salisbury traveled there from England to study—eventually becoming the cathedral's bishop. This high academic reputation is reflected in sculptures of the seven Liberal Arts over one of the portals into the church. An understanding of the seven Liberal Arts was considered the foundation of a good education in the Middle Ages. The seven Arts were usually split into two groups known as the Trivium and the Quadrivium—what we might translate as "the three roads and the four roads." The Arts of the Quadrivium were arithmetic, geometry, astronomy, and music; and the Arts of the Trivium were grammar, rhetoric, and logic. It is this last Art for which Chartres became most famous.

In contrast to Chartres, which was built and added to over many centuries and thus displays a variety of Gothic styles, the Cathedral of Salisbury in England was built in what might be called record time. The foundation stone was laid in 1220—and by 1258, the main portion of the cathedral was complete. That's pretty quick for cathedral building. But, as is the case with so many Gothic cathedrals, this was not the end. Work has continued on Salisbury Cathedral up until the very end of the 20th century. In 1265, a bell tower was built. In the early 14th century, a more ambitious tower and a spire were added to the cathedral, and this has proven to be Salisbury's most fascinating feature. At over 400 feet tall, it is the tallest spire from pre-15th-century Europe still standing—but even as it is a masterstroke of medieval engineering, it is also a colossal blunder in many respects. The entire weight of the spire is supported by just four columns, or piers, of Purbeck marble, and under the weight of the spire, the stone piers themselves are twisting— which you can see if you go into the cathedral and look up the length of the piers from the bottom. Over the centuries, various strategies have been used to shore up the spire—from adding buttresses, to iron supports on the spire itself when it was found to be leaning out of true. In the year 2000, what one hopes is the final restoration effort on the spire and other parts of the cathedral was completed.

Like Chartres, Salisbury also had a cathedral school, which had existed in some form more or less from the year 1091, when the bishop's seat was nearby at Old Sarum. It most likely was an early place of study for John of Salisbury, whom I've already mentioned as one of the most famous of Chartres's cathedral school students, and one of the greatest philosophic minds of the medieval world. Cathedrals, thus, became important centers in the medieval world. They were places of learning; they became sites for trade and business—and, most importantly, they were centers for religious devotion. As such, the building of a cathedral came to be referred to as a Crusade in stone, so powerful was this structure in the way it served as a focal point for faith and piety—for those who designed it, for those who funded it, and for those who prayed in it. The phrase "Crusade in stone" is obviously an allusion to one of the other great manifestations of religious faith in the medieval world—the Crusading movement, which sought to reclaim the city of Jerusalem and the Holy Land in the Middle East for Christendom. In our next two lectures, we will explore the Crusading movement—examining the religious, political, and economic impulses behind it, and the way in which contact with the Muslim world—far to the East—would have significant ramifications for the medieval world in the West.

Piety, Politics, and Persecution
Lecture 18

The long-standing rift between East and West had been felt most strongly in the Great Schism of 1054, but for all that, the idea of a unified church—and even more, the idea of a re-unified Roman Empire—still held a great deal of appeal, and events on the borders of the Byzantine Empire seemed to present an opportunity to bridge the gulf between East and West.

In the year 1095 at the Council of Clermont, Pope Urban II called for Christian knights to embark on a venture that was part holy war, part pilgrimage, to try to wrest the Holy Land—and the city of Jerusalem in particular—away from the Turks. As an incentive, he offered papal dispensation for the sins of a lifetime to all those who participated. Throughout the rest of the Middle Ages, there would be numerous attempts to conquer and hold the territories of the Middle East, considered the inheritance of Christ, although only the First Crusade can truly be called a success, and many later Crusades—most notably the Fourth—never made it beyond the borders of the Byzantine Empire. Eyewitness accounts offer a fascinating and occasionally horrifying glimpse into the realities of life on a Crusade.

Although ruled by adherents of Islam, followers of all three monotheistic faiths were living generally peaceably side by side in Jerusalem in the 11th century, when Pope Urban II called the First Crusade, urging his Christian brethren wrest Jerusalem from Muslim control. Urban's call to "take up the cross" in 1095 proved the lasting potency of the idea of the Roman Empire, as one of his stated reasons for this venture was to assist the citizens of the former eastern half of the empire. Urban was also building on Pope Alexander II's earlier call for the Reconquista of Spain.

Although devout religious belief was certainly a major factor in the enthusiastic response to Urban's call, other factors helped create the climate for a military conquest of the Holy Land. The pope and the patriarch of the Byzantine Church had long squabbled over who was supreme head of the faith. In 1054, Pope Leo IX sent a delegation to Constantinople to address the issue. The debate led to each church excommunicating the other's members—a schism in effect to this day. A related issue was the Investiture Conflict, a debate over who had the power to appoint religious leaders: the head of the church or the head of the secular government.

Urban announced two primary goals for the First Crusade: to liberate Christians living in territories that had been overrun by Turks and to free Jerusalem from Muslim rule. The First Crusade was promoted as a kind of pilgrimage, but one that was new and unique: a military pilgrimage. Only men of fighting age were (supposedly) allowed to participate, and those Christians living near Muslim Spain were told to remain home and focus on reconquering that territory for Christianity. Although we use the words "Crusade" and "Crusaders" today, the word was not used in the 11th century; rather, those who participated were described as "taking the cross," a reference to the embroidered red cross they wore to indicate to the world their sacred mission.

Although those who took the cross were supposed to receive official sanction from the pope, other groups set off early for the Holy Land without papal approval. The most notable of these was the Peoples' Crusade (or the Peasants' Crusade). These Crusaders went overland through the Rhineland, home at that time to some of Western Europe's largest Jewish communities. According to several eyewitness accounts, they engaged in what amounted to wholesale slaughter of these communities, despite the vigorous efforts of many secular and religious leaders to stop them. The Crusaders made it as far as Anatolia, where most of them were sold into slavery or killed.

New orders of knighthood were created to protect European settlers in the Levant and pilgrims traveling to Jerusalem.

The legitimate Crusading forces did eventually reach the Holy Land, and as they went, they conquered. By the time they made it to Antioch, they were plagued by illness and starvation, and many formerly wealthy noblemen had lost almost all their possessions and money. But Antioch would mark the turning point in the First Crusade. After seven months, Antioch was finally betrayed to the Crusaders by one of its own citizens. On entering, the Crusaders slaughtered every Turk in the city. Hearing this news, the Fatimids, who were in control of Jerusalem, rejoiced, thinking the Crusaders would prove their allies. They were thus completely unprepared when, on July 15, 1099, the Crusaders showed up and conquered Jerusalem. The conquest of Jerusalem makes the First Crusade the only one that could really be called a success. The Crusaders established four main regions in the Holy Land: the county of Tripoli, the county of Edessa, the principality of Antioch, and the kingdom of Jerusalem. Together, these were known as Outremer, a French word meaning "across the sea," or "over the sea."

New orders of knighthood were created to protect European settlers in the Levant and pilgrims traveling to Jerusalem. Perhaps the most famous of the crusading orders was the Knights Templar, who took their name from their headquarters in the Temple Mount in Jerusalem. The Templars were an utterly new kind of knight in that they were also monks. They soon became incredibly wealthy through their banking system. Their wealth would inspire much jealousy and eventually lead to their downfall and dissolution. The Knights Hospitaller were established shortly after the Templars. Their main objective was

Saint Bernard of Clairvaux, a Cistercian monk, wrote the rule of the Knights Templar.

caring for sick and injured pilgrims once they arrived in the Holy Land. A third order, the Teutonic Knights, were established near the end of the 12th century for the express purpose of caring for injured or ill Crusaders.

The hold of Western forces over Middle Eastern lands was tenuous at best, and it was not long before much of Outremer was retaken. Western forces were further compromised by individuals fomenting conflict with local leaders, particularly Muslims, even though those in the upper echelons of the ruling elite sought practical solutions that would allow peoples of various faiths to live together in harmony. ■

Suggested Reading

Linehan and Nelson, *The Medieval World.*

Riley-Smith, *The Crusades.*

Questions to Consider

1. How did concerns over the status and power of the Western church lead to the calling of the First Crusade in 1095?

2. How many of those who participated in the Crusades seemed to do out of sincere belief and piety? How many seemed to do so for purely material gain? Were these two goals necessarily mutually exclusive?

Lecture 18: Piety, Politics, and Persecution

Piety, Politics, and Persecution
Lecture 18—Transcript

Welcome back. In our last lecture, we discussed one of the greatest expressions of faith known to the medieval world—the Gothic cathedral, the building of which was sometimes referred to as a Crusade in stone. In the next two lectures, we're going to discuss that phenomenon to which the phrase "Crusade in stone" alludes—the movement to reclaim the city of Jerusalem and the Holy Land in general for Christendom.

As we discussed in the lecture on pilgrimage, Jerusalem was the center of the world for medieval Christians—and for hundreds of years, Christians had been making pilgrimages there. But Christians were not the only visitors to Jerusalem. There was a sizeable Christian population in Jerusalem. By the end of the 11th century, Christians, Jews, and Muslims had been living in the area that we would call the Holy Land side-by-side and relatively peaceably for quite some time. But in 1095, Pope Urban II called for a new kind of pilgrimage, one that would take back the Holy Land from Muslim control—and in doing so, would help the Byzantine Empire, a plea that was cleverly designed to capitalize on the still-potent idea of the Roman Empire. Essentially, Urban was calling on the citizens of what had been the western half of the empire to come to the aid of the citizens of what had been the eastern half of the empire—the suggestion being that this might result in some sort of symbolic or literal reunification.

As is so often the case, there is much more here than meets the eye at first. At the end of the 11th century, several different factors came together in a sort of perfect storm of religion, politics, and power to precipitate Pope Urban's call for a military maneuver toward Jerusalem at the Council of Clermont in 1095. In today's lecture we're going to explore the causes behind—and the lasting effects of—the First Crusade.

For the last several lectures we've been focused primarily on Western Europe, but as we discussed near the beginning of the course, it is incredibly important that we always take care to situate the European medieval world in the larger context of both the Byzantine Empire and the Muslim world—what some scholars have identified as the three sibling cultures that emerged from the Roman Empire. In the events surrounding the First Crusade, we see these three sibling cultures interact and clash in dramatic fashion.

First, we need to remember that as the Muslim world expanded, its reach moved from the Middle East through North Africa and into Spain in the early 8th century. In the 11th century, Pope Alexander II called for a re-taking of these territories by Christian forces, a sort of mini-Crusade that anticipated the one Urban II called for in 1095. The first mini-Crusade was known as the Reconquista, or literally reconquest, of Muslim Spain. When Alexander II turned the attempt to re-Christianize Spain into a holy war, he was also attempting to affirm and expand the power and authority of the papacy, which had become a major issue in the 10th century. One of the central issues was the nature of the church as it existed in the West and in the Byzantine Empire. Remember that Byzantium, the eastern half of the former Roman Empire, had not declined in the way the West had. Its citizens considered themselves Romans long after the empire had effectively ceased to exist, and thus its emperor and the leader of its branch of Christianity—which we have come to call Eastern Orthodox Christianity, the supreme leader of which is known as the patriarch—had long considered themselves the true heirs of Rome in both the secular and religious arenas.

In the West, the popes, who initially had not been terribly powerful, began to make a claim for their power and supremacy in the 11th century, and this really began under Pope Leo IX, who became pope in 1049. What is interesting to keep in mind as we discuss the rise of the power of the papacy is that Leo was essentially appointed by the German ruler Henry III—so a secular ruler, the so-called Holy Roman Emperor, had chosen the leader of the church. But once Leo took office, he set about reforming the papacy and asserting the authority of the popes over secular leaders. In 1054, he sent a papal diplomat, the fabulously named Humbert of Silva Candida, to Constantinople. Once there, Humbert got into an argument with the patriarch over the status and power of the pope and the Western Church. The dispute became so heated that in an attempt to assert the supremacy of the Western Church, Humbert excommunicated the patriarch. In return, the patriarch excommunicated Humbert. This rift between these two major Christian churches, which has come to be known as the Great Schism, continues to this day—although several attempts at reconciliation have been made. In

1965, for example, Pope Paul VI and Patriarch Athenagoras issued a joint edict which rendered null those mutual excommunications of 1054—but as of today, the Western Catholic Church and Eastern Orthodox Church could not be called unified.

In addition to the Great Schism of the 11th century, we have another major conflict that is important for understanding the forces that led to the calling for the First Crusade, and this is something known as the Investiture Conflict. In a nutshell, this was a debate about who had the right to appoint religious leaders, and it began in 1075 when Emperor Henry III installed his own choice for archbishop of Milan into that position. The pope at the time, Gregory VII, had had his own candidate in mind and angrily rebuked Henry for not acknowledging the church's right and authority to appoint the archbishop. What followed is something that's probably starting to sound a little familiar—Henry told Gregory to resign, and Gregory excommunicated Henry. In the end, Henry submitted in spectacular fashion by standing barefoot in the snow for three days until Gregory lifted the excommunication, but the matter would not be definitively resolved until 1122—when the Concordat of Worms instituted a compromise that seemed to satisfy both sides.

So in the 11th century, we have the popes attempting to assert their authority over secular rulers in the West and over the church in the East, in the Byzantine Empire. The long-standing rift between East and West had been felt most strongly in the Great Schism of 1054, but for all that, the idea of a unified church—and even more, the idea of a re-unified Roman Empire—still held a great deal of appeal, and events on the borders of the Byzantine Empire seemed to present an opportunity to bridge the gulf between East and West. In the middle of the 11th century, the borders of Byzantium started to be overrun by Turks—many of whom had converted to Islam in the 10th century. Their raids into the Christian territories of Byzantium were less about religious issues and more about the acquisition of territory and wealth. But the fact that Christian territories were being lost—and, in what would seem to be the last straw, the Byzantine emperor himself was captured at the Battle of Manzikert—led to an appeal for help on the part of the Eastern leaders to their Christian brethren in the West, or so Urban II characterized it when he preached the First Crusade at Clermont in France in 1095.

So we can see how politics and events in the Muslim, Byzantine, and European worlds all came together at the end of the 11ᵗʰ century to produce a situation in which a combination of religious fervor, political idealism, and opportunism produced a willing body of warriors ready to travel to Jerusalem. When he called for the First Crusade, Urban announced two goals: The first was to liberate Christians who were residing in those territories that had been conquered by invading Turks; the second was to free Jerusalem, the holiest of cities, from Muslim rule. Because of this, the Crusade was, indeed, characterized as a kind of pilgrimage, but a pilgrimage unlike any other in that it was essentially a war. As such, only men who were of fighting age were officially allowed to go. Women, children, old men, priests, and monks—with a few exceptions, these people were not supposed to participate; although in any campaign of this sort, a support staff of cooks, laborers, servants, and smiths would be essential. Some women were given permission to accompany their husbands. It is estimated that the fighting force of the First Crusade numbered around 50,000, and there has been some debate about what exactly motivated many of those who took the cross. "Taking the cross" was the phrase used to describe the pledge to go on Crusade—in fact, the word "crusade" was not even used until much, much later. Crusaders were most frequently described as *croisiers*, from the French word for "cross," because as a sign of their pledge they would wear a tunic with a cross embroidered on it, announcing to all and sundry their goal. It is certain that for many who joined the First Crusade, a very real religious fervor was at the root of their decision to embark on this journey—but for a long time, many medieval scholars felt that this could not really be the case, and a very popular theory—known as the second son theory—held sway.

This was the idea that given the dominance of inheritance systems based on primogeniture in Europe—second, third, and especially fourth sons had very few options beyond perhaps going into the church. A campaign like the Crusade presented an opportunity for younger sons to acquire wealth, status, and property through that time-tested method of warfare and pillage that would otherwise be unavailable to them. It is the case that many young noblemen gained properties, and titles, and stature in what came to be called the Crusader states of the Middle East that they never could have attained if they had remained in Europe. But heading out on Crusade was also a very expensive, risk-filled undertaking, and so in the majority of circumstances a heart-felt religious devotion seems to have been the underlying motivation. When he preached the Crusade, Pope Urban also granted those who participated forgiveness for all their sins, including any they incurred while on Crusade and those that they had incurred in their lifetimes before setting out for the Middle East. For a citizen of the medieval world, to whom the dangers and pains of hell and purgatory loomed quite large, this was, indeed, an attractive incentive.

The depth of feeling that prodded many to go on Crusade is nowhere more visible than in the case of what has come to be called the Peasants' Crusade, which actually set off for Jerusalem earlier than any other group. Officially, instead of one giant military expedition, Crusading forces were a series of small armies—each commanded by a man who had been officially sanctioned by the pope as authorized to lead his unit on Crusade, and as these were all members of the warrior class, they were nobles. The Peasants' Crusade was an unofficial Crusade led by a man named Peter the Hermit, and it was made up of a group of commoners who headed overland across Europe toward the Middle East. We don't know much about Peter the Hermit, but he seems to have been inspired by the pope's call to liberate the Holy Land to give up a life of contemplation and solitude in order to gather together an army. The actions of Peter the Hermit's Crusaders also demonstrate that, while although the liberation of Jerusalem and the Christian communities in the Middle East and Asia Minor was the stated goal of the First Crusade, Crusading activity was happening throughout Europe. The Reconquista of Spain is just one example. Throughout the Crusading period, groups considered outside the mainstream of Western Christianity but living within the bonds of Europe became the victims of Crusading fervor—non-Christians in Scandinavia; heretics, such as the Cathars in France; and perhaps most significantly, the Jews.

Peter the Hermit's decision to march through the Rhineland on his way to the Holy Land was a deliberate one, and along the way his militia slaughtered huge numbers of Jews living in this area. Other groups of Crusaders engaged in similar behavior, and there are many chronicle accounts—most of them certainly based on eye-witness testimony—that relate in excruciating detail the vicious slaughter of entire Jewish communities, and how in several instances members of Jewish communities killed one another so that they would be spared the cruelty of death at the hands of the Crusaders. For example, Solomon Bar Simpson, a member of the Jewish community of Mainz, records that "Fathers fell upon their sons, being slaughtered upon one another, and they slew one another—each man his kin, his wife and children; bridegrooms slew their betrothed, and merciful women their only children." The chronicler Peter of Aachen relates a similar story, noting that the Jews of Mainz had asked for and received protection from the Christian bishop of that community, who took them into his household—but he also noted, then, that the Crusaders attacked the bishop's hall and killed over 700 of the Jews who had taken refuge there. Those that were not killed were forcibly baptized. It is not just at Mainz that this event, which we might call a holocaust, happened—the Jewish communities of Speyer, of Cologne, of Worms, and others all suffered similar terrible attacks.

Before the First Crusade, Jews were not systematically persecuted in the medieval world, but there were significant restrictions on trades or professions they could practice and places where they could live. As the medieval church and the office of the papacy became more centralized and powerful in the 10th and 11th centuries, religious fervor such as that harnessed for the First Crusade began to coalesce into what historian R. I. Moore has termed the "formation of a persecuting society." As we will see, such persecutions would only escalate as we move from the High to the late Middle Ages.

Peter the Hermit and his followers apparently made it as far as Anatolia, where most of his band were either slaughtered or sold into slavery. Other armed militias, however, made it all the way to the city of Jerusalem. From the point of view of Western Christendom, the First Crusade was a success. The number one reason for the success of this campaign was not because the Crusaders were particularly well organized or an efficient military force—but rather because of disunity in the Muslim world. As you'll recall from an earlier lecture, the Muslim world had begun to dissipate into factions—and by the year 1000, it was divided into many different groups. The biggest conflict was between the Abbasids, who were Muslims who were followers of the Prophet Muhammed's youngest uncle; and the Fatimids, who took their name from Muhammed's daughter, Fatima. The Fatimids were strong in Egypt and Syria in particular, but shortly before Urban's call for the

First Crusade, they—like the Byzantine Empire—had found themselves confronting a new enemy in the form of the Turks.

As the Crusaders—commonly referred to as Franks because so much of their ranks were made up of Frenchmen—made their way toward Jerusalem, they conquered whatever they could as they went. In 1098, after passing through Armenian lands that had been utterly laid waste by earlier conflicts between the local inhabitants and the Turks, one Crusading company reached Edessa—which they conquered and then effectively established as the first Latin settlement in the East. A short time later, another band of Crusaders arrived at Antioch. This group had encountered serious problems, not the least of which was that almost all the horses and pack animals they had started out with had died on the expedition. This was a serious blow to men whose very status was in so many ways tied to their position as a mounted knight on horseback. Many knights apparently were forced to appropriate donkeys as stand-ins for their horses, and others were reduced to fighting on foot—not the mark of a nobleman. They made camp outside the walls of Antioch with the intention of starving the citizens into submission, but contemporary accounts suggest that it is the Crusaders who were in constant danger of starvation. With provisions running low, and no such thing as a stable supply line, most of their time was spent not in attacking the city, but trying to find enough food to survive—and many of them appear to have become quite ill. Some noblemen who had started the Crusade as wealthy men found all their riches gone for necessities for survival, and many found themselves near destitute and were forced to become wage-earning servants of those Crusaders who still had the means to pay. The Crusading band had been reduced to a sorry state after seven and a half months of this—when finally, it seems, the city of Antioch was betrayed by one of its own citizens, who opened the gates and let the invading army in. When the Crusaders took Antioch, they killed every Turk in the city—something that the Fatimids, who had recently lost control of Jerusalem to the Turkish leader Atsiz, thought worked in their favor.

After the defeat of the Turks at Antioch, the Fatimids were able to retake Jerusalem from Atsiz, and it seems that they expected that the Crusaders would become their allies. So on July 15th, 1099, when the Crusading armies showed up and launched an attack on the city of Jerusalem, the Fatimids were completely unprepared and fairly quickly defeated. A week later, a man named Godfrey of Bouillon was elected the leader of this new settlement, and he quickly turned his attention to staving off an enemy army that was on its way up from Egypt. He managed this feat, and for a time, the Crusaders set up a new society—one that they called Outremer, which means something like "over the sea." It consisted of four Crusader states: the county of Tripoli and the county of Edessa, the principality of Antioch, and the kingdom of Jerusalem. All four of these were ruled over by Europeans—albeit tenuously at times—until 1291.

Trade flourished between East and West, and there was a surge in the number of pilgrims making their way to Jerusalem. Obviously, such a long journey—from the European West to the Middle East—required a significant outlay of expenses, and required also that pilgrims carry a significant amount of money with them. This, as you might guess, made them attractive targets for all manner of thieves and ruffians—and it is this situation that gave rise to the creation of an organization that has been the subject of much wildly imaginative discussion in books and movies in recent years, and these are the Knights Templar. A Templar was an utterly new kind of knight, in that he was also a monk. It was one thing for the pope to send secular fighting men to defend and protect the church through force of arms; it was quite another for him to sanction an order of monks who were given license to act like knights. The Knights Templar were initially founded by a man named Hugh of Payns, along with eight companions, around the year 1118—and their stated goal was to offer protection to pilgrims who were traveling to Jerusalem. They did this not only by serving as a kind of bodyguard for those pilgrims passing through Palestine, but also by cleverly coming up with a way to remove the need for pilgrims to carry money and other valuables with them. They came up with a very modern idea—which was, essentially, banking as we know it today. A pilgrim traveling to the Holy Land could deposit his money at one of the Templar strongholds to be found throughout the European West. The amount he had deposited was then inscribed in code on a piece of vellum or parchment, which could be decoded only by a member of the order on the other end, in Jerusalem. The pilgrim could then withdraw the amount of money he had deposited before his pilgrimage once he had arrived at his final destination in sort of the earliest form of ATM withdrawal.

As a further mark of their high and unusual status, the king of Jerusalem at the time—Baldwin II—gave the Templars as their headquarters part of the royal enclosure on the Temple Mount—hence, the name Templar. Perhaps even more importantly, one of the most important religious figures of the day, Bernard of Clairvaux—a Cistercian monk and abbot—further legitimized them by writing rules for their order, and the Templars adopted as a uniform the white robe of the Cistercians with a red cross emblazoned on the front. At the height of their existence, it is estimated that there were about 20,000 Templars roughly divided into three groups—the knights, responsible for overseeing the safety and security of pilgrims in the Holy Land; priests, who attended to the religious needs of the order; and commoners, who helped with the day-to-day running of the Templars' quite lucrative banking empire. They soon amassed wealth and power on a massive scale, something that worried many rulers, particularly the king of France. This, in turn, led to their persecution and the eventual dissolution of their order in the 14th century, a fact that meant that their property and money could be confiscated and enrich the coffers of others—particularly, in this case, the French monarchy.

The Templars were not the only new order of knights to be created as a direct result of the Crusades. Two others—the Knights Hospitaller and the Teutonic Knights—are worth mentioning. The Knights Hospitaller were formed around the same time and out of the same impulse as that which led to the founding of the Knights Templar—namely, a desire to offer assistance to pilgrims who had traveled to the Holy Land. While the Templars focused more on protecting pilgrims from theft or violence, the Hospitallers concentrated on caring for those who became ill while in Jerusalem.

As you can imagine, since the journey to Jerusalem was arduous and many people set out on pilgrimage for the express purpose of seeking relief from various ailments and afflictions, there was a significant need for medical assistance for many of those pilgrims who made it to Jerusalem. This order venerated poverty, subjecting themselves to the extremes of an impoverished life—but in contrast, they treated all of the sick in their hospitals, no matter their rank, as if they were great lords or noblemen. Of particular note are the lavish and rich diets all patients were fed. The Hospital of St. John was run on a staggering scale, with enough beds for 2,000 patients, and wards that divided the sick by gender and even by medical specialty—for example, one of the wards seems to have been devoted to obstetrics. Within 50 years of their founding, the Knights Hospitaller, like the Knights Templar, had become a military order of monk knights with a division of ranks—those who tended to the ill in the hospital, and those who fought on behalf of the order. While the Templars wore a white tunic with a red cross, the Knights Hospitaller were easily identified by their black tunics and white crosses.

The last of the new orders of knighthood to result from the Crusades were the Teutonic Knights. This order was established later than the Templars and the Hospitallers—closer to the end of the 12th century—but again, like the other two orders, the impetus for their existence came from a desire to help those in need. In this case, the Teutonic Knights set themselves the task of caring specifically for injured Crusaders. They are called the Teutonic Knights because most of the original members were nobles from the area of Europe that roughly corresponds to modern Germany and Austria—and thus, they are distinct from the mass of Crusaders who were usually referred to as Franks because their ranks were so dominated by the French. The Teutonic Knights wore white tunics with black crosses, and compared to the Templars and Hospitallers their order was rather small. Eventually, they moved the center of their attention away from Outremer into Eastern Europe, where they continued to participate in the Crusading fervor that had swept the medieval world by fighting against the Slavs—who at that point were non-Christians. Gradually, the Teutonic Knights conquered Prussia and converted any non-Christians living there to Christianity.

While all three of these orders suggest the strong European presence that existed in the Middle East during the height of Crusading, the hold of the Crusaders on the newly formed Crusader states was tenuous. It wasn't long before many of the Crusader states, starting with Edessa, were retaken by local forces, and new Crusades needed to be declared with the goal of re-taking, once again, these locations for Christendom. The inability of the Crusaders to hold onto these territories was not only due to hostility from Muslim forces, but also to many of the European warriors who rose to minor positions of power—and instead of seeking to live peacefully in Outremer with all its inhabitants, sought instead a policy of complete domination that led many of them to provoke attacks and foment violence. The Christian leaders of the Crusader states were very often in conflict with one another, and this weakened their position and made it difficult for any sort of consistent, peaceable situation to obtain—although there were some notable figures who sought to try and create a peaceful and harmonious community that included Christians, Jews, and Muslims.

In our next lecture, we're going to continue to explore the impact the Crusading movement had on the communities of the Levant—and the new influences, ideas, and learning that contact with the Muslim world transferred back to the medieval world of the West.

The Persistence of an Ideal
Lecture 19

> If we define Crusade as a military effort to bring portions of the Middle East—particularly Jerusalem—under Christian control, then we can identify roughly eight or nine within the medieval period, but each of these were actually a series of waves of invasions, so it's safest to say that pretty much from the 12th century until the end of the Middle Ages, someone, somewhere, was always mounting some kind of Crusading campaign or another.

After the somewhat surprising success of the First Crusade in 1099, Europeans set up four Crusader states in the Middle East, where they sought to recreate feudal society. But life in Outremer was different in significant ways from life in the West. European settlers discovered that accommodation with—rather than dominance over—Middle Eastern populations of Muslims, Jews, and others was the most successful way to negotiate life in the Levant. Although the Western presence in the Holy Land lasted less than 200 years, Crusading ideals would have a profound impact on the European world throughout the Middle Ages and beyond.

During the High Middle Ages, crusading fervor spread throughout the medieval world. In addition to Crusades to the Holy Land, campaigns were launched against Muslims in Spain (the Reconquista), Cathars (also called Albigensians) in southern France, and Jews and other non-Christians throughout Europe. The Second and Third Crusades to the Holy Land occurred in the 12th century and were launched to reclaim parts of Outremer that had been lost in the interim. Participants in these Crusades were a veritable Who's Who of European nobility: Emperor Frederick Barbarossa, King Richard the Lionheart, King Louis VII, and Emperor Conrad II, among others. While most Crusaders returned to Europe after the First Crusade, those who stayed behind quickly discovered that accommodation and friendship—rather than conquest and domination—with Muslims and other peoples was the only way any Crusader state could sustain itself.

The decline of the Crusader states began in 1144, when Edessa was recaptured by the Muslim leader Zengi, precipitating the call to the Second Crusade. By far the most formidable opponent facing the Crusaders was the Muslim leader Saladin, whose recapture of Jerusalem led to the calling of the Third Crusade in 1187. Saladin was a man of great intellect, generosity, and mercy as well as a brilliant military strategist, and his chivalric interactions with King Richard the Lionheart would pass into European folklore and myth.

> **By far the most formidable opponent facing the Crusaders was the Muslim leader Saladin … a man of great intellect, generosity, and mercy as well as a brilliant military strategist.**

After the Second and Third Crusades, the Holy Land was essentially given up as lost, although many other Crusades would be called throughout the Middle Ages and beyond. The Fourth Crusade in 1204 only made it as far as Constantinople, where the invading armies, arguing that the Byzantine Empire had strayed from the true faith, sacked the city and "liberated" much of its wealth and religious relics. From the sack of Constantinople, it was only a small step to turning crusading zeal on citizens of the West. In 1208, a Crusade led primarily by people from northern France engaged in almost wholesale slaughter of several heretical Cathar communities in the south, the result of a perfect storm of religious zeal and greediness for land and wealth. Similar horrors manifested in 1212, when two large groups of children—some estimates put the figures as high as 30,000—headed off on the Children's Crusade.

The idea of a Jerusalem ruled over by Christians remained a potent one, and attention once again turned toward sending military forces to retake the holiest of cities for Christendom. The Fifth Crusade, launched in 1218, focused most of its attention on Egypt—at that time the center of the Muslim world. This Crusade and those that followed were all dismal failures. In 1291, the Christian stronghold of Acre fell to the Muslims, and any Christian dominance in the Levant was ended. The Christian leaders still in Outremer retreated to the Isle of Cyprus, where they styled themselves as rulers in exile, always planning for a return to Jerusalem. The Crusading movement did not really exhaust itself until 1798, when the remnants of the Knights Hospitaller, then located on Malta, formally disbanded. ■

Suggested Reading

Riley-Smith, *The Crusades*.

Rosenwein, *A Short History of the Middle Ages*.

Questions to Consider

1. What were some unanticipated and unintended consequences of the crusading fervor that gripped the medieval world in the 11ᵗʰ–15ᵗʰ centuries?

2. Why did the idea of a Christian kingdom in the Middle East remain so potent long after any possibility of such an institution ceased to exist? How were crusading ideals expressed "at home" in Western Europe?

The Persistence of an Ideal
Lecture 19—Transcript

Welcome back. As we discussed in our last lecture, the Crusading impulse in Europe emerged from a sort of perfect storm of politics and religion in the West, and from pressures coming from both the Muslim world and the Byzantine world—those two cultures that, along with the medieval European world, could be considered to be, to some degree, heirs of Rome and its ideals.

We saw last time how the impulse to liberate Jerusalem and to free Christian communities in the Middle East and Asia Minor from dominance by Muslim rulers also resulted in violence on the European mainland itself—particularly in the Reconquista waged against Muslim Spain and the persecution and occasional full-scale slaughter of Jewish communities such as those at Mainz, and Cologne, and other places. As we move from the High to the late Middle Ages, this activity on the European mainland would continue and extend to non-Christians living in Scandinavia—and to Christian heretics, known as Cathars or Albigensians, living in southern France.

In our last lecture, we focused primarily on the causes behind, and the results of, the First Crusade—the only one that, from a Western point of view, could be considered any sort of success. The fact that we can refer to the First Crusade brings up the obvious question: How many Crusades were there? There's some debate about this, because defining the nature of a Crusade gets a little more difficult as we head toward the early modern period. For example, some Crusades, like the Fourth, never even made it to the Holy Land—and others, like that against the Cathars in France, never even intended to head toward Jerusalem. If we define Crusade as a military effort to bring portions of the Middle East—particularly Jerusalem—under Christian control, then we can identify roughly eight or nine within the medieval period, but each of these were actually a series of waves of invasions, so it's safest to say that pretty much from the 12th century until the end of the Middle Ages, someone, somewhere, was always mounting some kind of Crusading campaign or another.

As the Crusades continued, there was what we might call a rate of diminishing returns. The later Crusades had very little success—but for all that, the idea of a Christian Holy Land was an enduring idea whose appeal could be felt and stated all the way in England in the year 1485 when William Caxton, the first printer in that country, explained that he had chosen to print the story of Godefroy of Bouillon as a suitable text for his potential audience because "to th'ende that every Cristen man may be the better encoraged t'enterprise warre for the defense of Cristendom and to recover the sayd cyte of Jherusalem." In other words, at the end of the 15th century a member of the bourgeoisie in England thought it a worthwhile enterprise to try and reclaim the Holy Land for Christendom.

So, Crusading remained a potent idea, and we see this clearly in the period around the Second and Third Crusades, which attracted not only the usual group of nobles eager both to save their souls and/or enhance their coffers and improve their status with new titles and lands, but also these Crusades included such larger-than-life figures as King Louis VII of France, the Holy Roman Emperor Conrad III, King Richard the Lionhearted of England, King Phillip II of France, and Emperor Frederick Barbarossa. It's a veritable who's-who of powerful men in Europe in the 12th century, and while many of those who participated did so at least in part because it was a mark of honor and status, several found their positions and power diminished by their participation in Crusading—and a few even lost their lives. The Crusader states established after the conquest of Jerusalem in 1099—as you'll recall from our last lecture—were the counties of Edessa and Tripoli, the principality of Antioch, and the kingdom of Jerusalem. These entities existed at what we might call full strength for only a few decades, but in that time the Crusaders discovered that if they were going to manage to stay in the Middle East and support themselves, they were going to have to radically modify some of their plans and policies.

After the capture of Jerusalem, a good many Crusaders, their past sins expunged, returned to Europe—in fact, this is what the majority of Crusaders did. Those that remained did what any medieval occupying force did in order to maintain power—they set about building castles and strongholds, some of which, like the impressive fortress of Krak des Chevaliers in present-day Syria, remain to this day. Initially, they set about trying to fulfill their intended goal, which was to drive non-Christians out of territories considered holy and part of a new Latin Christendom. Unfortunately, what they discovered is that they had nowhere near the population necessary in order to make this a reality. Who was going to work the fields? From whom would they buy goods at the market if Jewish and Muslim trades people were forbidden in Christian territory? What the Crusaders discovered is that they were going to have to adopt a policy of accommodation if the settlement in Outremer—the word that means something like "over the sea"—was going to survive in any form at all. In fact, many of their policies were similar to those that had been in place when Jerusalem had been under the control of Muslim leaders.

As we discussed in a previous lecture, Muslims, Christians, and Jews had been living in the Holy Land relatively peaceably prior to the Crusades. Non-Muslims, however, were subject to a tax called a *dhimmi* and restrictions concerning clothing—to identify them as non-Muslims. As long as the non-Muslim citizens paid this tax, they were left in relative peace to go about their business. When Christian leaders came to power, they learned fairly quickly that this was the only really workable solution; they needed the labor and goods provided by the Muslims and Jews—and, in fact, as long as these groups remained unconverted, they could collect a significant amount of money by taxing them. Because there were, relatively speaking, so few Christians compared to peoples of other faiths, we have an odd situation in which we have lots of priests and bishops in Outremer who are at loose ends because they have very few worshippers.

Those Crusaders who did remain in the Holy Land and who started families there—often sending back to the European homeland for their wives—raised families with children who would have identified themselves as French or English, but whose everyday reality was far removed from what their counterparts in Europe were accustomed to. Although any significant European occupation in the Middle East was effectively over in 1291 when the last Crusader outpost of Acre fell, trade between East and West continued to grow and flourish because of the numbers of European settlers who had, even for such a relatively short time, called Outremer home.

The Crusading kingdoms began their decline in 1144, when an Arab leader named Zengi retook Edessa. The Second Crusade was specifically preached in order to retake Edessa, and one of its most vocal proponents was no less a personage than Bernard of Clairvaux, the Cistercian monk and abbot who had been such a supporter of the Knights Templar. The leaders of this expedition included both the king of France and the Holy Roman Emperor—and if their goal was to retake Edessa, they had a strange way of doing it. When their armies arrived in the Holy Land, the first place they headed was Damascus—which, if you look on a map, you can see is really nowhere near Edessa. The armies tried besieging the walls of Damascus, found that they weren't having any luck, and essentially turned around and headed home. After this, an Arab leader named Nurredin managed to unite Syria and take control of Egypt, a key strategic position for any force wishing to hold power in the Middle East. Nurredin was an ambitious man, and among his stated goals were not only to wage war against the Crusader states and drive out the Christians, but also to defeat other Muslim rulers and to reform the religion of Islam itself.

In his turn, Nurreddin was succeeded by one of the most remarkable figures in all medieval, if not world, history—and this is the great Muslim leader, Saladin. Saladin's background would give us no reason to suppose that he would become the scholar, leader, and warrior that he did. His uncle was one of Nurredin's lieutenants, but he was unusual in holding such a high-ranking position, because he was a Kurd. The Kurds were a minority, not in favor with most of the ranking Muslim leaders. But Saladin was not like other men. Incredibly well educated, intellectual as well as intelligent, he managed to consolidate his power and unite and rule over Egypt and Syria. He unified the previously fractious Muslim armies. In 1187, at perhaps the most famous and important battle since the siege of Jerusalem itself, the Battle of Hattin, Saladin defeated the Christian military forces at Jerusalem and managed to retake the city. But as brilliant a strategist and effective a warrior as he was, he also sought very often to avoid war and find a peaceful solution—showing great restraint on several occasions. One of the most problematic of the Crusader leaders was a man named Reynald of Chatillon, who constantly sought to foment discord with Muslim forces, much to the chagrin of many of the more prudent Christian leaders—particularly the young King Baldwin IV of Jerusalem, who tried heroically to achieve a lasting peace with his Muslim neighbors and foes. His efforts in this area seem all the more tragic because of the leprosy that would disfigure and eventually kill him at a very young age.

Reynald of Chatillon was famous for unprovoked attacks on unarmed Muslim pilgrims, among other things, so Saladin often found himself at war with him. Famously, once while besieging Reynald's Crusader fortress of Kerak, Saladin learned that a wedding had just occurred there that evening. He quite politely enquired as to which tower of the fortress was currently being occupied by the newlyweds, and then directed his artillery to aim away from that portion of the fortress. Even more famously, after his capture of the city of Jerusalem, Saladin mercifully spared most of the Christian inhabitants of the city at a time when it would be much more common to put them all to the sword, as the Crusaders had done to the Turks when they took Antioch on the First Crusade. Saladin allowed all those who could to buy their freedom—and then in a still greater act of generosity, he allowed thousands of others who could not afford to pay the ransom to be freed in a gesture that he characterized as a gift for one of his relatives.

It was Saladin's capture of Jerusalem and subsequent victory at the Battle of Hattin that reduced the Crusader states to just a few port cities and led directly to the calling of the Third Crusade, whose participants included King Phillip II of France, Emperor Frederick Barbarossa, and King Richard the Lionheart of England. This Crusade, which could be said to cover the years 1187 to 92, was beset by problems from the outset. The first blow was the loss of Emperor Barbarossa. Accounts differ, but most scholars agree that he had some medical emergency, such as a heart attack, while crossing a river in Anatolia. Eye-witnesses accounts report that he clutched his chest and fell from his horse into the river. Either the attack killed him, or he drowned—weighted down by his armor. The loss of the emperor meant that Richard the Lionheart and Phillip Augustus were now the two leaders of the expedition, and these two did not get along. After initially winning some battles, Phillip decided to return home to France, leaving Richard to continue the fight for Outremer.

This period passed into both European and Muslim folklore as a time of noble interactions between the two military leaders. Stories of the chivalrous behavior of Saladin and Richard were popular from Europe to the Middle East, and contemporary accounts relate the great respect that each man had for the other and his abilities. Although the two men never actually met face-to-face, their interactions via messenger fired the imaginations of medieval

Europeans and Muslims alike. For example, when Richard became ill, Saladin offered the use of his personal physician, should the English king have need. When Richard lost his horse, Saladin sent him two of his own. For his part, Richard proposed attempting to settle the conflict by marrying his sister to Saladin's brother, but nothing came of this proposal—although they did sign a tentative truce. The gains Richard had made were a setback for the Muslim cause, but Jerusalem, the jewel in the crown, had not been recovered—so it was only a matter of time before another Crusade was called.

From this point on, the activity of Crusading seems to lose much of its focus, you might say. The Fourth Crusade was called by Pope Innocent III in the early 13th century, with the goal of, once again, retaking the Holy Land—but this Crusade never even made it near Jerusalem. The stated goal was the conquest of Egypt. After the Third Crusade, those who returned to Europe had been in general agreement that it would be possible for Christian Crusader states to survive in the Holy Land, but only if the Crusaders could conquer and hold Egypt—which had been the strategic point from which so many of the opposing armies had organized and set out.

But this Crusade, the Fourth Crusade, only made it as far as Constantinople, and what happened there was fueled in part by the memory of the Roman Empire, which had once been a unified entity stretching from England in the West to Byzantium in the East. The events that took place there were also fueled by the Crusaders' claims that the citizens of Constantinople had betrayed the Roman ideals of unity, especially in the area of religion. What happened was this: The Crusading militias, as was usual, headed first for Italy, where they hoped to book passage on ships to the Middle East. Various city-states in Italy had become impressive maritime powers, and this had become the logical jumping-off place for a sea voyage to the Middle East. As dangerous as it could be, travel by sea was the quickest way to get anywhere in the medieval world. There is a famous formula—1:7:23. What these numbers mean, is that if it takes you 1 day to travel a certain distance by sea, it would take you 7 days to go that same distance overland on horseback, and it would take you 23 days to travel that distance on foot. Obviously, travel by sea was the quickest way to get where you needed to go—and had the added benefit of sparing your horses the long journey and getting you where you needed to go with much less necessary in the way of provisions. So those who had taken the cross for the Fourth Crusade headed to Italy, which was then a collection of city-states, and they went to Venice to try and hire ships. The Crusaders were long on zeal, but short on cash—but the Venetians, who had been having a conflict with the city of Zara in present-day Croatia, made them a deal: Sack the city of Zara for us, and we'll get you where you need to go. In 1202, this is exactly what the Crusaders did! The response from the pope was swift, and he excommunicated those who had participated.

Other bands of Crusaders made it to Constantinople, and in 1204, the Crusading camp, after having been stationed outside the city walls for some time, breached those walls, entered the city, and sacked it—pillaging over a period of three days. The justification for this on the part of some was that the Byzantine, or Eastern Orthodox, church was not the true church—remember, last time we discussed the Great Schism of 1054, when the patriarch of the Eastern Church and the papal representatives of the Western Church had excommunicated one another. That rift had obviously not healed, and in the eyes of many Crusaders, because the Eastern Christians did not recognize the authority and supremacy of the pope in the West they were not entitled to possess the numerous religious relics to be found within the city of Constantinople. So, in what many scholars have termed a kind of holy sacrilege, the Crusaders "liberated" these religious artifacts and brought them back to the West. Untold treasures—both of gold and silver and jewels, and treasures of literature, historical texts—many of these were utterly lost or destroyed in the sack of Constantinople. The relics that were taken included numerous bones of saints and a crown of thorns that was held to be the actual crown that Christ had borne on his head during the crucifixion. So, on the Fourth Crusade it was the Byzantines—those whose perceived need for assistance had, in fact, sparked the first Crusade—who were on the receiving end of the righteous militarism of Western Christendom. From there, it was just a small step to direct that righteousness toward other groups closer to home, which is exactly what happened in 1208—the year of the so-called Albigensian Crusade. For many years, a heresy—known most commonly as Catharism—had been growing in the area of what is today southwestern France. In fact, today if you drive through the area known as the Languedoc, it's become a source of pride and tourism for the local communities. As you drive through this portion of the south of France, you'll see signs along the highways proclaiming—in French, of course—"This is Cathar country." The Cathars were a group that believed in a kind of Neo-Manicheanism, or the idea that there were two forces at work in the world—one good, or God; and one evil, or the devil—and these two forces worked to keep the world in a kind of balance. You may recall that that most august member of early church fathers, Saint Augustine of Hippo, had been interested in Manicheanism before his conversion to Christianity. The Cathars, as far as possible, renounced everything having to do with the world—they were vegetarians who eschewed marriage. As you might imagine, the decision to forgo meat and wedlock was regarded as at least a little bit odd by most inhabitants of the medieval world. But the greatest fault of the Cathars in the eyes of the church was their belief that because all things of the flesh were evil, then Christ could not possibly have become incarnate.

They did consider themselves Christians, but a very strange sort of Christians in that they were vehemently opposed to attaching any sort of significance to the crucifixion or the cross that had become the symbol of Christianity. Many, in fact, denied that it had even happened. After a series of attempts to persuade local leaders to deal with the heresy, Pope Innocent III preached a Crusade against the Cathars, or Albigensians. In effect, this Crusade pitted the North against the South of France, and nobles from the North were particularly eager to participate, as the pope had decreed that the wealth and property of any Cathars was up for grabs. The fighting that followed for the next 20 years or so was horrifically violent and seemingly arbitrary in its direction, as many non-Cathars were caught up in the frenzy of Albigensian persecution and lost their property—and quite often their lives.

The horrors of the Albigensian Crusade were repeated in a different key in the year 1212, when spontaneously, it seems, two separate groups of children—one led by a 10-year-old boy named Nicholas from the Rhineland, and another led by a 12-year-old boy from the Loire River Valley named Stephen—rallied thousands of other children to their sides and set off to reclaim Jerusalem for Christendom. The sincerely held belief on the part of these children was that because they were innocents, they would have more success in retaking the Holy Land than would mature warriors, who had long lives of sinning behind them. While many of the participants of this endeavor were children, there has been some debate about how much of the company was made up of young boys and girls—with some scholars now believing that the number of children who participated has been largely exaggerated, and that a good portion of those participating were actually poor adults. The estimates range from a group of 7,000 to 30,000 heading off to liberate the Holy Land. It seems fairly clear that none of them actually made it. Most of them turned around and headed home early in the journey. Reportedly, some made it to Rome, where the pope released them from the vows they had sworn to take the cross—vows that were null and void anyway without papal sanction from the outset. But some accounts tell of shiploads of young Crusading pilgrims killed in wrecks, or of young girls being taken into brothels, and the boys sold into slavery by greedy merchants who had promised them passage across the Mediterranean.

No matter how much of the story of the Children's Crusade is true—and it is certain that a large portion of it is true, just as it is certain that a great deal was exaggerated—the prominent place that the Children's Crusade held in the consciousness of contemporary Europeans, when viewed alongside such campaigns as the Albigensian Crusade, speaks to deep religious and spiritual unrest throughout the Western Christian community.

Despite all these setbacks, the Crusading movement continued—with a Fifth Crusade getting underway in 1218, just a few years after the Children's Crusade. This Fifth Crusade focused its attention again on Egypt, as this was considered the heart of the Muslim world, but it was a dismal failure, as were the next three Crusades that followed in rather quick succession. The end of the Crusading presence in the Holy Land came in 1291, when the last true Crusader stronghold, the city of Acre, fell to the Muslims. The Christian leaders retreated to the island of Cyprus, where they continued to rule in what they at first saw as only a temporary exile. For a long while, the kings of Cyprus also styled themselves as kings of Jerusalem.

Crusading, in the words of scholar Jonathan Riley-Smith, died a lingering death. Although in the 14th century, the beginning of the Hundred Years' War between France and England—not to mention an outbreak of plague that would kill up to half the population of Europe—focused the attention of the medieval world elsewhere, as William Caxton's statement about why he chose to print the story of Godfrey of Bouillon near the end of the 15th century, Crusading still existed as an ideal. In fact, it is not until 1798 that we can really say Crusading exhausted itself, for it is in that year that an order of Knights Hospitaller on Malta—the last one still in existence—finally disbanded.

As the last two lectures have demonstrated, Crusading zeal sprang from multiple sources. While it is true that many Crusaders had material ambitions in mind when they set out for the Holy Land, it seems that most of the people who participated in the Crusading movement were inspired to do so by deep and sincere faith and piety. This new emphasis on religion and spirituality would be felt in many other places in the medieval world, particularly in the institutions of medieval Christianity—such as monastic orders and the papacy. In our next lecture, we will explore changes that occurred in the religious realm in the High and late Middle Ages.

Late Medieval Religious Institutions
Lecture 20

In the High and late Middle Ages, concerns over proper religious belief and practice were widespread and not confined only to official branches of the church. ... The Fourth Lateran Council ... sought to codify and clarify various aspects of religious belief and practice in a move that was unprecedented in its concern for the spiritual well-being of lay people.

Throughout the High and late Middle Ages, the religious institutions of the medieval world were transformed in dramatic and sometimes unexpected ways for a variety of reasons. Monasticism was subject to several reform movements, and new religious orders like the Franciscans and Dominicans came into being. The highest office of the church, the papacy, experienced a schism that at one point had three rival popes all claiming legitimacy. Heresy became a bigger problem, leading to Crusades against particular groups of Christian heretics. These struggles led to a variety of reforms and a more bureaucratic church. While many reforms were directed at members of the clergy, other reforms—especially those of the Fourth Lateran Council in 1215—more directly affected the lay population.

Saint Francis of Assisi founded his order of monks in 1209 on the principles of strict poverty and mendicant preaching.

Until the late 11th or early 12th century, the dominant form of monasticism was Benedictine, named for Saint Benedict of Nursia's monastic rule, a guide for all aspects of monastic life. Although all monks took a vow of poverty, in practice this ideal proved

267

difficult to adhere to, and many Benedictine monasteries were quite wealthy by the 11th century. One of the first attempts at reform of Benedictine life was the Cluniac movement, which began in the 10th century. An offshoot of the Cluniacs were the Cistercians, who wished to adhere to a stricter interpretation of the Benedictine rule, particularly with regard to living a life of poverty, but in time they too became excessively wealthy. The mendicant, meaning "wandering," orders came into existence in the 13th century. They include the Dominicans and the Franciscans.

Concerns over proper religious belief and practice were widespread and not confined only to branches of the church. In particular, the rise of certain popular heresies, such as Catharism, led to crackdowns—often violent ones. As part of the religious zeal that led to the First Crusade at the end of the 11th century, various local Crusades took place within Western Europe with the intent of rooting out heresy. Several inquisitions were held to question suspected heretics and to either punish or reform them. Although the idea of inquisition looms large in the modern imagination, most of the overly persecutorial acts we tend to associate with "The Inquisition" occurred during the early modern period.

Marriage, which until this point had been primarily a secular and economic institution, was officially made a sacrament.

In 1215, the Fourth Lateran Council, convened by Pope Innocent III and attended by religious leaders and clergy from throughout the medieval world, sought to codify and clarify various aspects of religious belief and practice in a move that was unprecedented in its concern for the spiritual well-being of lay people. Among other religious issues, the council clarified the dogma of the doctrine of the Trinity and the miracle of transubstantiation—the transformation of communion bread and wine into the actual body and blood of Christ. The necessity of priestly celibacy was affirmed, and standards of conduct for religious figures were articulated. Rules about frequency of confession and communion for lay people were clarified and codified. Marriage, which until this point had been primarily a secular and economic institution, was officially made a sacrament. The council also issued decrees concerning those who were outside the faith—like Jews—ordering that they wear some distinguishing clothes or mark to identify themselves as non-Christians.

Near the beginning of the late Middle Ages, the papacy found it was not immune to the disputes over proper behavior and concerns over relationships with the secular world, a situation that led to the Western Schism. From 1309 to 1377, the office of the papacy was not in Rome but in Avignon, France, as the seven popes who were elected at that time were all French. The last of these popes, Gregory XI, moved the papacy back to Rome. After his death, the College of Cardinals was under pressure to elect a Roman, which they did in the face of rioting mobs who feared the papacy would otherwise go back to Avignon. A group of dissenting cardinals disagreed with the election of a little-known Pisan to the church's highest office; they elected their own pope, whom they installed in Avignon. By the time the dispute was resolved by the Council of Constance in 1417, three men had all claimed simultaneously to be the true pope, and the crisis had embroiled all the major nations of Europe, who were forced to choose sides. The stature and reputation of the office of the pope had been seriously damaged, and it would be some time before it recovered. ■

Suggested Reading

Linehan and Nelson, *The Medieval World*.

Rosenwein, *A Short History of the Middle Ages*.

Questions to Consider

1. Why did monastic reform movements ultimately fail in their attempts to "perfect" Benedictine monasticism?

2. How did disputes over the office of the papacy affect and contribute to political and economic issues in medieval societies?

Late Medieval Religious Institutions
Lecture 20—Transcript

Welcome back. In our last two lectures, we've been discussing the phenomenon of the Crusades—the movement on the part of various groups from the medieval European world to try and reclaim Jerusalem and other Holy Cities in the Middle East. Crusading fervor was continuous essentially from the late 11th century until the early modern period, although only the First Crusade—which captured Jerusalem and established the Christian-controlled counties of Edessa and Tripoli and the principality of Antioch—could be considered a success. It is safe to say at almost any time in the medieval world from the end of the 11th century on, someone, somewhere, was planning, embarking on, or completing a Crusade. During this same period, the religious institutions of the medieval world—particularly monastic orders and the papacy—were undergoing some significant transformations, and the reasons for, and impact of, these changes on the wider medieval world is the subject of our lecture today.

Starting in about the 12th century, the perceived need for monastic change, disputes over the office of the papacy, and concerns about heresy, led to a variety of reforms and a more bureaucratic church. While many reforms were directed at members of the clergy—monks, priests, etc.—other reforms, especially those of the Fourth Lateran Council in 1215, more directly impacted the lay population of the medieval world.

As you'll remember from an earlier lecture, Benedictine monasticism was the dominant form of monasticism throughout the medieval world in the early period. Named for Saint Benedict of Nursia, who had composed his rule as a guide to monastic life in the 6th century, this form of monasticism emphasized prayer and physical labor. As you'll recall, becoming a Benedictine monk meant never getting a full night's sleep again, as the day and night were punctuated with calls to prayer. The first prayer of the day, Matins, might occur around two or three in the morning—and the last, Vigils, could occur near midnight. When not praying, Benedictine monks aimed to support their community through the labor of growing foodstuffs and producing other items necessary for life in the monastery.

Although one of the vows taken by all monks was a vow of poverty, in practice this ideal proved difficult to adhere to, and many Benedictine monasteries were quite wealthy by the 11th century. There were a couple of reasons for this. First, monasteries were often the recipients of large donations, as we've already discussed. The labor of prayer performed by the monks was believed by many to be efficacious in helping to move the souls of those who had passed on out of purgatory and into heaven more quickly. One often hears of donations being given to a church or monastery in order to pay for a certain number of masses to be said on behalf of someone's soul. So this was one way that monasteries accrued wealth. If you add that to the relatively Spartan life monks lived—although as we saw in some earlier lectures, many monks appeared to be living quite a comfortable life with an ample diet—you have a situation where more money is coming in to the monastery than is going out.

Because monks and other clergy technically could have no property—and also, technically, no children—none of the wealth that accrued was ever dissipated by being passed along as an inheritance. So many Benedictine monasteries, in spite of themselves, had become quite wealthy by the 11th and 12th century—with many monks living a lifestyle arguably more appropriate for a wealthy secular lord than a cloistered man of God.

One of the first attempts at reform of Benedictine life was known as the Cluniac movement, which began in the 10th century—but more important than this attempt at reform was an offshoot of the Cluniac movement: Cistercian monastic reform. The Cistercian movement had its origins in 1098 in a place called Cîteaux, from whence it takes its name. Led by a man named Robert of Molesme, a group of 21 Cluniac monks left their community to form a new monastic community at Cîteaux. Those who identified themselves as Cistercians wished to adhere to a stricter interpretation of the Benedictine Rule. With that in mind, they founded houses in remote locations, supported themselves primarily through agriculture, observed a strict diet, and often took vows of silence. In time they, too, came to be excessively wealthy—in part due to their great skill in farming and animal husbandry. Cistercians in England, in particular, became known for the fine quality of wool produced by their sheep—and although poverty had been their original goal, in time they became an important part of the commercial world. Just as had been the case with the Benedictines before them, the hard work and self-deprivation by which the Cistercians ordered their lives had unintentionally—and against their own original desires—made them wealthy.

There were many offshoots of both Benedictine and Cistercian monasticism, but starting around the 13th century, a different type of monastic order came into being. These were what have come to be called the mendicant orders—which means literally, "wandering"—and they include the Franciscans and the Dominicans. The Franciscan order was founded by and named for Saint Francis of Assisi, son of a wealthy cloth merchant from the hill town of Assisi in present-day Italy. Inspired by Christ's command to the apostles that they should go through the world without even shoes or a walking stick, Francis embraced a strict life of poverty and soon attracted followers. In 1209, he appealed to Pope Innocent III for permission to found a new religious order of wandering brothers who would preach Christian belief. After some persuading, the pope agreed, and hereafter Francis and his brothers became members of what came to be called the Order of the Friars Minor.

The extreme poverty embraced by the order became difficult to maintain once it became necessary to establish mother houses, or monastic lodgings that served as sort of anchor points for the brothers in their wanderings. This was a practical matter in part, as it was difficult to oversee an order that had no central base, and was also a response to a general medieval concern about people wandering about. If you were going to travel any great distance throughout the medieval world, you'd better have documentation proving that you were permitted to do so. For example, friars and other mendicant orders needed to be licensed by their mother house to move freely throughout the medieval world—as fake friars and pardoners—like the one Chaucer depicted—were a huge concern for the church. Groups of traveling actors needed to have their lord's authority to travel and would be expected both to make their living performing in various towns and at their lord's manor on feast days and the like. Margery Kempe, the religious woman we met in our lecture on pilgrimage, was constantly asked during her journeys if she, as a woman traveling alone, had either permission or an order from her confessor or other church official to be dressed in the white clothes she favored, and to be roaming about the countryside. On more than a few occasions, she came close to being burnt, and several times she was ordered to leave the vicinity of a particular parish or diocese.

Another mendicant order that caused the medieval world some anxiety, at least at first, was the Order of Saint Dominic—also known as the Order of Preachers, or simply the Dominicans. Founded in 1216, this order stressed learning and education. Dominic's feeling was that preaching was not going to be effective unless the person preaching was educated and persuasive. Conversion, in the eyes of the order, needed to be something that someone decided to do after hearing persuasive, compelling reasons for doing so. This order was heavily involved with the founding of the universities of Oxford and Cambridge.

A word is in order here about the rise of the university system in the medieval world. Starting around the 12th century, students began to cluster around various renowned scholars. By the end of the 13th century, these sort of ad hoc relationships had coalesced into the beginnings of the university system as we know it today. It's important to understand that when universities first came into being, they were essentially just groups of people, rather than physical places. Students might gather around the home of a famed scholar and philosopher in order to learn from him, and classes might take place in the home of the teacher—usually known as *magister*, or master. The contours of a formal curriculum began to be shaped over the course of the 12th and 13th centuries, and certain cities became known for the study of a particular field. For example, Paris was the place to go if you wanted to study theology; Bologna if you wanted to study law; Selarno, medicine. The associations of certain cities with particular fields of study had a kind of snowball effect— more scholars who worked in that particular field might move to a city that was known for education in that field, which in turn attracted more students, which in turn attracted other scholars, and so on, and so on.

Classes were conducted in Latin, and we have to remember how much medieval people had to rely on their memories—there were no notebooks or ballpoint pens for jotting down the important points of a professor's lecture. It would be expected that certain important books would be read by students— and in some cases, students might purchase the equipment or the services of a scribe in order to make their own copy of a particularly important text.

Whatever specialty students were interested in pursuing, their study usually made its way through the seven Liberal Arts—which were divided, as we discussed earlier, into the Quadrivium and the Trivium. The Quadrivium—or road of four—consisted of arithmetic, geometry, astronomy, and music. The Trivium—which, as you might guess, means something like the road of three—consisted of logic, grammar, and rhetoric.

By the time the Dominican order came into being, the universities of Oxford and Cambridge had already been established and had attracted clusters of renowned scholars from throughout England and the Continent. What the Dominicans and some other monastic orders did was establish houses for students so that they could have a place to live while they pursued their studies. Over time, these houses came to be tightly woven into the physical and intellectual life of the university, and the influence of these particular orders on courses of study was significant.

In the High and late Middle Ages, concerns over proper religious belief and practice were widespread and not confined only to official branches of the church. In particular, the rise of certain heresies, like Catharism, led to crackdowns—often violent—authorized by the church, but often executed by laypeople. Catharism—which we've discussed a little bit in our second lecture on the Crusades—is perhaps the best example of this, and it was the heresy of Catharism that was one of Saint Dominic's main concerns. As you'll recall from that earlier lecture, the Cathars—also known as Albigenisans—were a heretical sect based in the area of modern France known as the Languedoc. The Cathars believed in the idea that there were two forces at work in the world—one good, or God; and one evil, or the devil—and that these two forces needed to be kept in a kind of balance. As far as possible, Cathars renounced everything having to do with the world—for example, as I noted before, they were vegetarians, and many did not believe in marriage. But, of course, their greatest fault in the eyes of the church was their belief that Christ could not possibly have been divine because the flesh was evil. In 1208, Pope Innocent III preached a Crusade against this group—and as I noted earlier, it was essentially the North against the South of France. The nobles from the North were eager to participate, as the pope had decreed that the wealth and property of any of the Cathars was up for grabs. The fighting of the next 20 years was violent and seemingly arbitrary in its directions.

Many non- Cathars were caught up in the frenzy of Albigensian persecution, losing their property and very often their lives.

The Albigensian Crusade was just one offshoot of the religious zeal that had led to the calling of the First Crusade at the end of the 11th century—and was just one example of various local Crusades that took place within the bounds of Western Europe, with the intent of rooting out heresy. Concerns over heresy gave rise to several inquisitions designed to question those suspected of heresy, and to either punish or reform them. Although the idea of the inquisition looms large in the modern popular imagination, most of the overly persecutorial acts of this body that we tend to associate with the word "inquisition" occurred during the early modern period.

Much more important in the medieval world was the Fourth Lateran Council, which was convened by Pope Innocent III in 1215 and held in the Lateran Palace in Rome. Attended by church leaders and clergy from throughout the medieval world, this unprecedented gathering of religious leaders sought to codify and clarify various aspects of religious belief and practice in a move that was unprecedented in its concern for the spiritual well-being of lay people. Most of the work had been done ahead of time, as the pope and his closest representatives had prepared a series of canons, or laws, that were introduced at the Fourth Lateran Council and presented to those in attendance as doctrine.

Among other religious issues, the Council clarified the doctrine of the trinity and declared as dogma the fact of the transubstantiation of the bread and wine at the time of consecration for communion. What this doctrine said, in essence, was that at the moment the priest consecrated communion bread and wine, it, in fact, became the actual blood and body of Jesus Christ—even if it might continue to look like ordinary bread and wine. This move underscored the importance of the role of the priest in performing the Mass—as only an ordained priest had the ability, according to the doctrine, to consecrate the communion host and wine.

Not surprisingly, the Fourth Lateran Council also clarified rules pertaining to those who were members of the clergy. Among other things, the absolute necessity of priestly celibacy was affirmed, and clerical marriage—a surprisingly common occurrence prior to this—was explicitly forbidden. What is really interesting about the Fourth Lateran Council is that, not only did it clarify issues pertaining to religious doctrine and conduct of the clergy, but it also set out canons concerning matters pertaining to the laity in a way that just had not been explicitly done before this. For example, it established clear rules about frequency of confession and communion for lay people.

All Christians were required to confess and take communion at least once a year. Confession could occur at any time, but communion commonly occurred at Easter services. This once-a-year practice arose out of the practical matter of the difficulty of providing wine and bread to the entire congregation every Sunday—something that could get quite expensive. By more or less limiting communion to Easter Sunday, the church saved time and money. As a gesture for those who might wish to take communion more often, the elevation of the host or communion wafer at the moment of consecration allowed the faithful the opportunity to see the flesh of Christ and adore it, even if they were not going to consume it at that particular Mass on that particular Sunday. Some people in the medieval world confessed and took communion much more frequently than once a year. Margery Kempe—again, the Englishwoman we met in our lecture on pilgrimage—seemed addicted to confessing, seeking out clergy every place she went and practically browbeating them into hearing her confess her whole life again, and again, and again. Her frequent desire to take communion was a little more problematic, and she tells us on more than one occasion how she had to receive permission from a member of the clergy to take communion as frequently as she did.

In addition to clarifying rules about the sacraments of communion and confession, the Fourth Lateran Council also declared marriage to be a sacrament. It usually surprises my students when they discover that prior to the 13th century, marriage was predominantly a secular institution—negotiated and contracted between families and celebrated outside the church. Indeed, when a couple married, in those instances when they bothered to go to the local church at all, any ceremony or blessing would be performed outside the church—at the church door. This is why Chaucer's Wife of Bath tells us explicitly that "housbondes at chirche doore I have had five," or that she has had five husbands at the church door. Technically speaking, the only thing necessary to make a marriage valid was the consent of both parties, but the Fourth Lateran Council tried to crack down on secret marriages—those contracted between the parties themselves or, in some cases, those in which two parties met in secret and persuaded a priest or another witness to witness their marriage. This is a significant shift, because as we will discuss in our later lecture on marriage and the family, with the Fourth Lateran Council—marriage goes from being a primarily secular and economic matter to one that is ruled over by the church.

As you may remember from Lecture 11—in which we discussed the rearrangement of the medieval world—as we head into the High Middle Ages, factors such as the spread of the Normans throughout the medieval West meant that previously quite different societies were becoming more like one another. Whereas before, identity boundaries had tended to be between communities—you're French, I'm English; you're Saxon, I'm Burgundian; etc., etc.—the new boundary that came into being was the divide between Christian and non-Christian. The Fourth Lateran Council emphasized and solidified this new way of thinking, as it issued several decrees concerning Jews—who were an important element of the medieval world, as we have seen. Jews served several critical functions for the medieval Christian world, prime among them being their position as moneylenders. Because Christians were forbidden by church doctrine from making loans and charging interest, Jews provided a means for Christian merchants to get around this issue, as technically the charging of interest—or what Christian society thought of as the sin of usury—was not forbidden to Jews. Jews, thus, played a key role in the development of the medieval economy, which necessarily meant they grew in wealth. The Fourth Lateran Council was concerned about, among other things, intermarriage between Jews and Christians—and thus required that Jews wear some sort of identifying marker. In France and Spain, Jews were required to wear a badge—and in places like Vienna, they had to wear pointed hats. Initially, this decree was a moneymaker for many local lords, as they gladly allowed many Jewish citizens to purchase an exemption from wearing such distinctive markers—but eventually, pretty much all Jews had to distinguish themselves through dress, and usually they were required to live in particular parts of the city.

Thus, the Fourth Lateran Council in the early 13th century served as a way for the papacy to establish its authority and that of the church in general, as it claimed the right to have the last word in nearly every aspect of medieval life. Near the beginning of the late Middle Ages, however, this highest office of the church found its power and authority significantly undermined by internal conflict due to an event usually called the Western Schism by historians and church scholars. The problem began in 1309, when the man elected to the papacy in 1305, Pope Clement V, moved the papal office to the French city of Avignon. There was civil unrest in Rome at the time, meaning it wasn't the safest place to be, and Clement was French—so the move seemed at first to be a logical one. Between 1309 and 1377, the papal office remained in Avignon—as the next several popes who were elected were, for the most part, French.

The Schism began when the last of these popes, Gregory XI, moved the office of the papacy back to Rome near the end of his life. After his death, the College of Cardinals was under pressure to elect a Roman to the church's highest office, which they did in the face of rioting mobs who feared the election of another French pope would mean the papacy would go back to Avignon.

A group of dissenting cardinals disagreed with the election of a littleknown religious leader from Pisa to the church's highest office, and they elected their own pope, whom they installed in Avignon. So now there were two popes, both claiming to have been rightfully elected—and in a sense, both had been. Just to make things interesting, a third claimant to the papal seat, officially known as the antipope Alexander V, took up his position in Bologna in 1409. So now there were three men who all claimed simultaneously to be the true pope. The crisis had moved beyond a purely internal religious affair to one that embroiled all the major nations of Europe, who were forced to choose sides. The great secular governmental bodies found themselves in the position of determining who would be deemed the rightful pope, and the lines that were quickly drawn followed the patterns of alliance that already existed in the medieval world. Those who favored the pope in Avignon naturally included France and its allies—among them Scotland, the Italian city of Naples, and most of Spain. Those who supported the pope sitting in Rome included England, Germany, most of the Scandinavian countries, Poland, Portugal, and Hungary. As the dispute continued for several years, however, various countries from time to time switched sides—a fact that only complicated matters more.

The situation was more or less resolved by the Council of Constance, which was held from 1414 to 1418, and which was the largest gathering of church officials the medieval world had ever seen. More importantly, its proceedings were open to the public, and many nobles and state leaders attended. All the clergy who attended were allowed to vote, and in the end, this august body declared that all three claimants to the position of pope had to step down—and a new pope, Martin V, was elected. This effectively ended the dispute, although here and there an antipope would pop up from time to time—usually in Bologna.

The stature and reputation of the office of the pope had been seriously damaged, and it would be some time before it managed to recover. A new way of thinking about papal authority emerged from the Schism. This is known as the Conciliar movement, and proponents of it held that church authority rested more in a corporate body of ecclesiastical authority, rather than in the single person of the pope. Although this theory lost ground as the 15th century progressed and more authority was returned to the individual person of the pope, one result of the Schism was that individual nations were less inclined to want to answer directly to—or give monies to—the church in Rome. We begin to see what we might rightfully call the development of national—or even nationalist—churches, particularly in France and England. As we'll discuss in a later lecture, these two countries were engaged in the long, bitter, and expensive Hundred Years' War, and the last thing they wanted was for any of their desperately needed cash to be unnecessarily sent off to Rome when it was more urgently needed locally to support the military effort. Arguably, this would help set the stage for some of the activities of the Protestant Reformation, which was still a century or so away.

So as we can see, the medieval world in the High and late Middle Ages underwent significant changes in terms of the nature of certain religious institutions—particularly monastic orders and the papacy—and these changes would have an influence far beyond their immediate impact on those who belonged to the order of the clergy. Indeed, the Fourth Lateran Council in 1215, while it codified and clarified certain rules for clergy, also had a significant impact on the lives of lay people, or those who were not members of the second estate of medieval society, particularly when it came to their everyday religious practices.

Twelve-fifteen was a momentous year in the medieval world. Not only did the Fourth Lateran Council radically affect religious life, but 1215 was also perhaps the most important year in all of the Middle Ages in terms of basic human rights—for that was the year that King John of England was forced by 25 of his barons to sign the document known as the Magna Carta, which means in Latin "great charter." Although later on this document would come to be enshrined by many historians and scholars as marking a singular, unique, and momentous shift in thinking about the rights of individuals, at the time it was hardly regarded as such. As we'll see in our next lecture, the document now revered by jurists and human rights advocates everywhere almost never came to be—and early on was revoked, deliberately ignored, and almost completely forgotten. Next time, we'll explore how a document signed in a meadow at Runymede in a small corner of England came to exert a powerful influence over much of the imagination of the medieval world.

The Magna Carta
Lecture 21

"In 1215, England's wealthy barons refused to give King John the money he needed to wage war unless he signed the Magna Carta. The document codified that no man was above the law. Unfortunately for the peasant class, it did little to address how many were below it."

—Jon Stewart, *America (The Book)*

If you ask someone today, "What is the Magna Carta and why is it important?" you will most likely get answers like "It is the cornerstone of American justice system," "It is a triumph for the common man over the power of the monarchy," or "It is the foundation of the idea of human rights as we know them." While it is true that the Magna Carta has come to symbolize all of these principles, such concerns were not a major factor in its creation. When it was drafted by the rebellious English barons who met England's King John in a meadow at Runnymede on June 15, 1215, the clauses historians and reformers identify as most significant today were buried deep in the middle of the document and were not of primary concern to the barons who forced John to accept it.

Many people might be surprised by the events and issues that led to the signing of this document in a meadow at Runnymede by King John of England in 1215. The Magna Carta was drafted by nobles to benefit nobles. The heretofore almost unheard-of situation in which nobles were able to pressure a king into giving up many of his absolute powers had a number of causes. King John is perhaps best known from the Robin Hood legends, in which he is portrayed as doing a poor job while his brother, Richard the Lionhearted, was away on Crusade. The stories are not far off the mark. During his reign, England's once-mighty Angevin Empire shrank dramatically; he levied a series of outrageous taxes to pay for several largely unsuccessful military campaigns; and he increased the fees—known as "farms," the source of our modern word—that local sheriffs traditionally paid to keep their positions. Additionally, John placed England in a state of spiritual crisis by refusing to accept the pope's selection for archbishop of Canterbury. The pope placed all of England under interdict, meaning all manner of religious practice and comfort was denied to its citizens.

Fed up with this situation and John's abysmal leadership, 25 barons of the realm confronted John at Runnymede in 1215 and forced him to sign the Magna Carta, or Great Charter. An examination of the clauses of the original document gives us an idea of the abuses John had perpetrated on his subjects. Clause 2 established limits for death taxes, which John had been steadily increasing in an attempt to build up the monetary holdings of the Crown. Clauses 3 and 6 deal with wardship over minors in line to inherit substantial money and land. John had essentially been selling wardships to the highest bidder, often contravening the explicit wishes of the heir's families. Similarly, John had been arranging marriages between wealthy, widowed heiresses and those willing to pay the Crown a substantial kickback for the privilege. Clauses 7 and 8 stopped this practice. Clause 12 dealt with scutage, the fee nobles could pay rather than performing their military service. The levying of scutage had happened only eight times in the 38 years John's father had been on the throne; by contrast, John had demanded scutage 11 times in 17 years.

It would not have been surprising if the Magna Carta were forgotten after John's death.

After signing the document, John attempted to have it declared null and void and was plagued by a new series of troubles. Back in the pope's good graces after accepting the pontiff's choice for archbishop of Canterbury and agreeing to submit on other matters, the interdict was lifted and John got the pope to declare the charter invalid. Soon John became embroiled in a dispute with the pope's candidate for archbishop of Canterbury, Stephen Langton, leading to a series of rebellions throughout England. Disgusted with John's behavior, many nobles approached Prince Louis, son of King Philip Augustus of France, and offered him the throne of England. By the summer of 1216, two-thirds of English barons had recognized Louis as king. John went on the offensive but died suddenly of dysentery in 1216.

It would not have been surprising if the Magna Carta were forgotten after John's death, but one of his most loyal retainers, William the Marshall (or simply William Marshall) made sure the document was reissued and reratified, after making some amendments and revisions. William Marshall was the regent for John's son, the minor King Henry III, and his reissuing of the Magna Carta was a shrewd attempt to gain noble support for the young king. Marshall rewrote the document so that it had appeal for both loyalist and rebel barons. Henry III helped his own cause by affirming the charter of his own accord in 1225. It was not until the 17th century that the Magna Carta began to be cited as affirming the rights of a king's subjects by specifically defining and limiting the powers of the monarch. At this point, the Magna Carta began to enjoy the iconic status that it has today. Over time, shifting interpretations have made it a hallowed object in the history of human rights in England and around the world. ■

Suggested Reading

Breay, *The Magna Carta.*

Clanchy, *From Memory to Written Record.*

Questions to Consider

1. Why is the signing of the Magna Carta considered such a watershed moment in the development of human rights when, at the time, it was considered relatively insignificant for most of the English population?

2. What is the long-term effect of the intersection of secular and religious concerns that helped precipitate the signing of the Magna Carta?

The Magna Carta
Lecture 21—Transcript

Welcome back. In our last lecture, we discussed changes that were taking place in the various institutions and houses of medieval Christianity during the High and late Middle Ages. At the conclusion of that lecture, we saw how the papal schism—when multiple popes each claimed authority—and its aftermath would forever change the office of the papacy. An event with similarly far-reaching implications for the secular world occurred in 1215 in the meadow at Runnymede, England—the same year that the Fourth Lateran Council codified church doctrine and practices in the most comprehensive series of canons the medieval religious world had ever seen. The event that occurred that same year, and which is the focus of our lecture today, is the signing of the Magna Carta.

If you ask someone today, "What is the Magna Carta, and why is it important?" you will most likely get answers that include statements like: "It is the cornerstone of the American Justice System"; "It's the basis for English common law"; "It's a triumph for the common man over the power of the monarchy"; and "It's the foundation of the idea of 'human rights' as we know them today."

While it is true that Magna Carta has come to symbolize all of these principles, such concerns were not a major factor in its creation. It has been cited and revered over the centuries by visionaries and reformers who wished to establish rights for the common people, to fight against tyranny or set in motion the process of democracy. For example, the Founding Fathers of the U.S. made use of it as they were writing the Declaration of Independence. However, when it was originally drafted by the rebellious English barons who met with King John in a meadow at Runnymede on June 15th, 1215, the clauses historians and reformers have usually identified as most significant in terms of the iconic status of the Magna Carta were buried deep in the middle of the document—and seemed not to be of primary concern to the barons who forced King John to accept the document. These are Clauses 39 and 40; 39 reads:

No free man shall be seized or imprisoned, or stripped of his rights or possessions, or outlawed or exiled, or deprived of his standing in any other way, nor will we proceed with force against him, or send others to do so, except by the lawful judgment of his equals or by the law of the land.

Number 40 is: "To no one will we sell, to no one deny or delay right or justice."

Although these two clauses are among those that have ensured the enshrinement of the Magna Carta in the annals of the development of human rights, at the time it was signed, Magna Carta was really—in the words of scholar Claire Breay—simply "a practical solution to a political crisis." In fact, the Magna Carta—and all its clauses—had almost zero impact or significance in the years immediately after its signing. Perhaps the best assessment of the Magna Carta in terms of its original historical context and significance comes, from of all places, the recent publication entitled *America (The Book)*—which was composed by the writers of the popular comedy show, *The Daily Show with Jon Stewart*.

> Democracy had disappeared. The people needed a champion, and as is usually the case, the obscenely rich rode to the rescue. In 1215, England's wealthy barons refused to give King John the money he needed to wage war unless he signed the Magna Carta. The document codified that no man was above the law. Unfortunately, for the peasant class, it did little to address how many were below it. Startlingly ahead of its time, this extraordinary document had a profound effect on people [and here, the writers have a footnote] (Note—for purposes of the Magna Carta, "people" means "free adult males with property who signed the Magna Carta") [continuing on], and it continues to shape 21st-century views on topics as diverse as escheat, socage, burgage, novel disseisin, and the bailiwicks of Gerard of Athee. But even more importantly, the Magna Carta set a powerful precedent for our own Founding Fathers: there was no more powerful means of safeguarding individual liberty than a vaguely worded manifesto inked in inscrutable cursive on dilapidated parchment. The Magna Carta served as a wake-up call that Europe would be forced to answer … in about five

hundred years. For Lady Democracy, having lain dormant for more than a millennium, had risen from its slumber only to stretch its arms, reach for the clock, and groggily set the snooze bar for "The Enlightenment."

Tongue-in-cheek and perhaps a bit exaggerated as that assessment is—it, in fact, is not too far off the mark. Make no mistake: The document agreed to by England's King John and a company of rebel barons on June 15th, 1215, was a charter created by nobles to benefit nobles. The concerns of justice and rights for peasants—who made up approximately 90 percent of the population of England at this time—are only accidentally addressed by the Charter, if at all. Just 10 weeks after having John's official seal attached to the document, the Magna Carta was declared null and void by Pope Innocent III. Even its name—which means "great charter"—was not attached to it because those who drafted it and persuaded King John to accept it considered it to be a work of momentous historical significance—rather, it was called the Great Charter to distinguish it from another shorter charter that dealt with laws concerning England's forests. It would take several years before the document would be officially recognized as having some kind of power and authority. Its iconic status today has little to do with the events of 1215, and much to do with how the Charter was appropriated and used after the death of King John.

Today, we're going to talk about how the Magna Carta eventually came to be hailed as one of the most important documents in the advancement of human civilization toward liberty, democracy, and equality in the Western world. In order to understand how the Magna Carta came to be regarded as it is today, we need to examine the conditions of its creation. Simply put, it was created by a group of high-ranking nobles in protest of the behaviors of King John— during whose reign English subjects endured warfare on several fronts, high taxes, and a religious crisis. All of these events played a part in bringing John to Runnymede in 1215, but the primary motivation and concern on the part of the barons was financial.

King John is best known to Americans today through any number of Robin Hood stories and films that cast him as the evil usurper or regent of the throne belonging to his saintly brother, Richard the Lionheart, who was away on Crusade or being held hostage in foreign lands for much of his reign.

John was the fourth son of Eleanor of Aquitaine and King Henry II of England—and in his youth was given the name Lackland because it seemed so unlikely in a hereditary system that practiced primogeniture that anything would be left for him on the death of his father. Although through a series of accidents of early death and lack of heirs on the part of his brothers, John eventually ascended the throne in 1199—the early nickname would prove to be prophetic.

When John came to the throne, England was not just the England we know today, but had sizable holdings in France—territories that modern historians refer to as the Angevin Empire. The word "Angevin" comes from the region in France known as Anjou, which was the place from whence the Plantagenet rulers of England originally came. During the Middle Ages, however, the phrase "Angevin Empire" was not actually used—although as a descriptor it is convenient for modern historians who wish to convey the enormous size of English holdings in the 12th and 13th centuries. In part, these holdings included the patrimony of William the Conqueror, who in 1066 crossed the Channel from Normandy and conquered England—adding English lands to his Norman holdings. King John's father, Henry II, had added to these territories through military conquest and his marriage to Eleanor of Aquitaine, who brought with her extensive land holdings. Although threats to English lands on the Continent were constant, Richard, son of Eleanor and Henry II, was largely successful in defending Angevin lands during his reign. This was not the case with his brother John's reign.

John apparently was plagued by a combination of bad luck and abysmal military strategy. In a series of very expensive continental conflicts early in his reign, he lost almost all of the English lands across the Channel. At the same time that he was fighting in France, he was also waging wars in Ireland, Wales, and Scotland—so the royal treasury was stretched a bit thin, a situation that led him to levy increasingly burdensome taxes on the people of England. In fact, the loss of lands in France was a double-whammy, not only because of the cost of trying to defend those lands (from King Phillip Augustus of France), but also, when those lands were lost, the Crown also lost any revenue in the form of rents or other compensation that those lands had traditionally brought to the Crown. So, John tried to squeeze as much money out of official sources of royal revenue back home—particularly from royal office holders, from the justice system, and by abusing the system of feudal land tenure.

I should back up here and say a little about how the Crown received income in the Middle Ages. It used a system that is often called feudalism. Although the term is somewhat in disrepute these days, among scholars the idea that it embodies—a sense of loyalty and service that is hierarchical—is still the right way to think of relationships among king and subjects in the 13th century. As we discussed a little bit in our lecture on the three orders of medieval society, in the feudal system all land in the kingdom is theoretically held in fee from the king. He grants lands to the nobles just below him in rank, and these are his vassals, in return for their service. Usually this service takes the form of fighting in battles and the payment of annual rents. These nobles then divvy up and *enfeof*—or "grant"—their lands to sub-tenants, who in turn owe some combination of service—days of labor to help the lord bring in his crops, for example, and some type of rent, usually in the form of goods like livestock or a certain percentage of the sub-tenant's own harvested crops—and so on down the line, until you reach the peasants at the foot of the hierarchical pyramid. These people were really subsistence farmers who were considered unfree or serfs, meaning they were bound to the lands of the lord for whom they toiled. John angered the barons at the top of the pyramid by demanding increased fee payments, a cost that the barons would then have to pass on to their tenants, and so on, and so on.

John also leaned on sheriffs, who were officials appointed to oversee a large portion of the Crown's lands. Those appointed to this office were in a position to accrue substantial benefit for themselves—and thus they were expected to pay to the king an annual fee for the right to hold office, in addition to the rents they were in charge of collecting from tenants on the Crown's lands. The annual payment was known as a farm, and John upset the sheriffs by increasing the amount of the farm.

He worked the justice system as well—bribery was common here, as litigants often offered great sums of money to the court in hope of a favorable decision. John also worked the rules surrounding royal forests. Until 1066 and the Norman Invasion, any person living in England could go out into the forest and hunt for deer, or boar, or other animals to feed his family. With the arrival of William the Conqueror, all this changed, and those lands decreed royal forests were subject to all sorts of rules. Reserved for the king's hunt, there were serious fines for encroaching or poaching. John afforested more lands than were traditionally exclusive property of the Crown—and when the inevitable infringements took place, the Crown racked up a substantial amount of money in fines.

Added to the monetary woes was the fact that John placed England in a position of spiritual crisis, which really didn't help his popularity any. Remember, at this time England was Catholic. We are centuries before the Protestant Reformation would sweep through Europe, and King Henry VIII would split from the Catholic Church—so that he could put aside his first wife and marry Anne Boleyn. When John came to the throne in 1199, Innocent III had just been raised to the papacy. This pope would be both enemy and ally to John in the years ahead. Things got ugly in 1205, when the archbishop of Canterbury died. John quickly got into a conflict with the monks at Canterbury and the pope as to who had the final say on the appointment of the archbishop—a struggle over rights of the Crown versus rights of the church, which is probably starting to sound familiar to you by now. You might remember that there was some history here, in that John's father, Henry II, had appointed Thomas à Becket archbishop of Canterbury—and then, when he discovered that Becket was always going to put the interests of the church ahead of those of the Crown, complained so bitterly to all and sundry that four of his knights took it upon themselves to speed Becket to his heavenly reward in 1170, an act for which Henry was compelled to do public penance. During John's reign, the pope's choice was Cardinal Stephen Langton, and the monks confirmed him as archbishop in 1206; the pope consecrated him in 1207. In response, John refused to let Langton enter England and kicked all the monks out of Canterbury. The pope's answer to this was to put all of England under what was called interdict. From 1208 to 1213, church bells did not ring in England; Mass was not celebrated; people who died could not be buried in holy ground. As you might imagine, this was fairly upsetting for the majority of the English populace who were devout, practicing Christians.

In retaliation, John seized the lands and revenues of the Church in England for himself, which got him excommunicated by the pope.

So, to put it mildly, things were not going well for John. He had lost almost all of the Duchy of Normandy by 1204. In 1212, not only had he been excommunicated and his country put under interdict by the pope, but he was also facing the threat of an invasion of England by the French king, Philip Augustus. So, in 1213, John accepted Langton as archbishop and brought back and compensated the Canterbury clergy he had exiled. The most dramatic development to come out of this situation, however, was that in order to get back in the pope's good graces, John had to accept the pope's overlordship. In other words, he turned over Ireland and England to the papacy, but for an annual payment to Rome of 1,000 marks (which is approximately 666 pounds), he remained king. In essence, he became a feudal vassal of the pope. The immediate effect of this was that Philip Augustus rightly reconsidered his planned invasion of England. He didn't want to make an enemy of the pope, and the pope became one of John's biggest supporters—a relationship John exploited immediately after he was forced to accept the Magna Carta, as we will see.

In 1214, John lost even more of the English lands in France—so that by the end of that year, the Angevin Empire over which he had ruled was reduced to just Poitou and Gascony. His attempts to defend these lands had led to ever-greater increases in taxes and abuses of royal power, which provoked a group of barons to demand that John affirm the laws of the Anglo-Saxon king, Edward the Confessor, and reissue the charter of liberties that Henry I had issued at his coronation. John refused, and the barons petitioned the pope as feudal overlord of England, but he was slow to make any decisive move here. On May 5, 1215, after several attempts to arrange a meeting with John, a group of barons renounced their allegiance to the throne—in effect declaring civil war. There were some attempts to capture royal castles and heated negotiations between people like Stephen Langton, who was in favor of reform, and staunch Royalist supporter William Marshall, the First earl of Pembroke.

We can get a more specific idea as to what it was the barons were so upset about if we look at the Magna Carta itself. For example, Clause 2 establishes amounts that the regent was allowed to tax his subjects on specific occasions. John had been trying to up what is essentially a death tax. For example, he required nobleman Roger de Lacy to pay 4,500 pounds just to succeed to his father's lands—a huge sum of money. He demanded 6,666 pounds from Nicholas de Stuteville for his lands; de Stuteville had to lease some estates and surrender a couple to John as collateral for payment. Again, remember that these articles are of greatest impact to wealthy, landed nobles with estates and treasure. Clauses 3 to 6 deal with minor heirs. John was selling rights of wardship over young, orphaned heirs and heiresses to the highest bidder. The people who got these wardships often ruined the inheritance for the ward when he came of age—either by exploiting the estates for his own gain, failing to maintain them, or both. Also, the king had the right to give heirs in marriage—again, in this case, to the highest bidder, and often against the wishes of immediate family.

Clauses 7 to 8 deal with widows. John was also arranging marriages for widows who might have come into profitable estates. Very often, these arranged marriages went against the will of the widows. There were plenty of nobles eager to increase their lands and wealth by marrying these wealthy women, but it is safe to say that in many instances, the widows were perfectly happy to go on being widows, thank you very much. Pressure from the king—who received a payment from all those grateful men he married off—meant that many widows were essentially compelled to remarry when they did not wish to.

Clause 12 deals with the issue of scutage. This was the term for what feudal tenants owed the king instead of military service—instead of a certain number of days spent fighting, cash could be rendered, but there was no hard and fast rule about when such a tax could be levied. John levied 11 scutages in his 17 years on the throne; his father had levied 8 in 34 years. The Magna Carta established three situations in which the king could do this without baronial consent. So you see, the early clauses all reflect pertinent political problems that needed resolution, rather than stating grand ideas about human rights.

Finally, on June 10, 1215, the disgruntled barons met with John's representatives at Runnymede, where they held negotiations that resulted in a document called The Articles of the Barons. This contained 49 articles and was probably the rough draft of the Magna Carta. On June 15, 1215, John sealed the document we now call Magna Carta. This document contained 63 clauses—and on June 19th, the barons renewed their allegiance to him. Several copies were made of the Charter, and it was circulated throughout the land. Only four of the originals survive today—two in the British Library, one in Lincoln Cathedral, and one in Salisbury Cathedral.

It seems John never intended to adhere to the articles in the Charter, and on August 24, 1215, at a request from John, the pope declared the Magna Carta to be unlawful, unjust, base, and shameful. Within a few months of this, England became embroiled in a civil war much worse than the one the Magna Carta had been designed to try and avert. Archbishop Langton had the royal castle of Rochester in his keeping, and John demanded he surrender it. Langton refused, and it was handed over to the rebel barons. John beseiged the castle for seven weeks until it was recaptured, but there would be a series of rebellions throughout England in the months after this. Things got so bad that some of the rebel barons went to Louis—son of the French king, Philip Augustus—and they offered him the throne. Philip thought that this was not a good idea, but Louis went across the Channel—and by the summer of 1216, two-thirds of the barons had gone over to Louis's side, recognizing him as king. Shortly after this, however, disputes flared up between Louis's French company and the native English rebels—no surprise here—and the French cause lost most of its support. John went on the offensive, trying to quash various pockets of rebellion throughout the country, but the last few months of his reign were dismal. He contracted dysentery, and several cartloads of royal treasure were lost in the crossing of the marshy wetlands known as The Wash. John died suddenly of dysentery in mid-October, and at his request, he was buried in Worcester Cathedral; his father and brothers had been buried in Fontevrault, in France.

After his death, it would not have been at all surprising if the Magna Carta had simply been forgotten. John left behind a nine-year-old heir, Henry III, who was obviously too young to rule. William Marshall, one of John's most devoted and loyal nobles, was appointed regent. It is really because of William Marshall that the Magna Carta has come to reach the iconic status it has today. He reissued Magna Carta in late 1216 on behalf of the king, and again in 1217—both times with some shrewd revisions. He moderated the document to appeal both to rebel and loyalist barons, and so support for the young King Henry III increased. It was in 1217 that all the articles in Magna Carta that deal with forest issues were taken out and put in a separate Forest Charter. Thus, it was not until this date that Magna Carta received the moniker by which we know it today, as this was the first time it was referred to as the Great Charter, by way of distinguishing it from the shorter, Forest Charter.

In 1225, Henry III reissued the Charter under his own power as a response to a grant of taxation he had asked for and received. In 1297, Edward I, Henry III's son, had the Magna Carta copied into the first statute roll. It was read aloud twice yearly in county courts and cathedrals, and around this time it began to be read at the opening of each parliament. By 1341, members of parliament had to swear to uphold its strictures. In the mid-14th-century, the clause on "lawful judgment of equals" became "trial by equals," which evolved into "trial by jury." It was not until the 17th century, however, that English lawyers argued that Magna Carta stated fundamental issues of law—a reaction to Stuart kings, James I and Charles I, who believed that they ruled by divine right of kings, and thus had no need to acknowledge Magna Carta. Edward Coke, who was then the Lord Chief Justice, insisted the king was subject to the Magna Carta just like everyone else. In his use of the document, he was very selective—choosing only to focus on clauses that could be interpreted as declarations of individual freedoms, not rules made in the interests of 13th-century nobility.

In 1948, the United Nations adopted a Universal Declaration of Human Rights, in which you can hear echoes of the Magna Carta:

> ARTICLE 3: Everyone has the right to life, liberty, and the security of person. ARTICLE 9: No one shall be subjected to arbitrary arrest, detention, or exile. ARTICLE 10: Everyone is entitled in full equality to a fair and public hearing … in the determination of his rights and obligations and of any criminal charge against him. ARTICLE 17: No one shall be arbitrarily deprived of his property.

Today, only three clauses of the original Magna Carta remain law. These are the clauses dealing with the freedom of the church, the privileges of London and other cities—and most famously, Clause 39 that states in part that: "No free man shall be seized, imprisoned, stripped of rights or possessions ... or deprived of his standing in any other way."

Although in origin the Magna Carta was a practical document that sought to protect the interests of—in the words of *America (The Book)*—"obscenely rich noble landowners," embedded within these seemingly selfish clauses is the germ of the idea of fundamental rights for all. At its most basic, the Magna Carta sought to control and limit the power of one person—the king—over others, his subjects. It is the skillful interpretation and use of this document over the broad span of time that has brought it to its revered, iconic status.

In our next lecture, we're going to explore—at a little bit greater length—the lives of those noble landowners who pressured King John into signing the Magna Carta. When we come back, we'll examine in depth what life was like in a noble household in the medieval world.

Daily Life in a Noble Household
Lecture 22

Whether peasants were free or bound, worked the land, or practiced a trade or craft in a village or town, it is a fact of most medieval communities that they were in some way attached to—or associated with—the household of a particular lord.

Anoble household in the Middle Ages was a world unto itself. Cooks, scribes, teachers, butlers, reeves, pantlers, and other servants all worked together in a complex unit designed to cater to the needs, desires, and ambitions of the noble family, who in turn were beholden to all whom they held in their employ, providing shelter and protection. This arrangement was reciprocal; all those who worked for the noble family were under their protection and were supplied with food and shelter in recompense for their labor. This relationship often extended to the peasants who worked the manor's fields. In return for protection and the right to sow and harvest their own crops, peasant farmers gave their lord a portion of their harvest and a certain number of days of labor per week, season, or year.

In the modern imagination, the castle is most often associated with the idea of the noble household, but most medieval castles were far from the luxurious structures familiar from film and popular culture. Until almost the early modern period, castles were built first and foremost with defense and protection in mind. The most basic castle was the motte and bailey, in which the keep, or stronghold, was erected on top of an enditched hill, motte; the life of the household took place in the enclosed courtyard below, the bailey. Contrary to popular belief, many castles were originally built out of wood and later replaced with stone structures.

The center of any noble household was the great hall, where many of the household staff—as well as the lord and lady—might sleep. Sometimes lord and lady occupied a small room above the great hall called a solar. Even in the late Middle Ages, when a lord and lady had quarters separate from the main hall, they might sleep in a curtained, four-poster bed while servants slept nearby, often on a cot by the fire. Privacy is a relatively modern concept. Other buildings usually radiated outward from the great hall, and construction might happen over years or even centuries as storage rooms, kitchens, chapels, guest chambers, servants' quarters, stables, and other buildings were added to the main structure.

The day in the noble household began at daybreak and was typically busy. In most noble households, hearing Mass was the first order of the day, after which a light meal was eaten. From here the lord and lady usually went about their separate pursuits—he administrating and hunting, she running the household and embroidering. By far the most important event of the day was dining, and there were more or less elaborate processes for the preparation and serving of food depending on whether it was a feast day or holiday, whether there were guests staying in the household, and the rank of those guests. The main meal of the day, dinner, took place between 10 am and noon and might involve several courses. Menus varied according to the seasons and were prepared by a team of kitchen workers; the kitchen itself was some distance from the main hall because of concerns about fire. The character of Geoffrey Chaucer's Franklin provides us with a glimpse of what a high-ranking member of society might consume and in what style he might consume it, as do numerous images from the famous *Luttrell Psalter*, one of the richest witnesses of daily life in the medieval period.

The character of Geoffrey Chaucer's Franklin provides us with a glimpse of what a high-ranking member of society might consume and in what style he might consume it, as do numerous images from the famous *Luttrell Psalter*.

One of the greatest responsibilities—and potentially lucrative activities—of a nobleman was to oversee the peasants who lived on his manor and who were under his protection. Lords had the right to demand a complex range of rents, ranging from the modern equivalent of death and marriage taxes to a certain number of days of labor per year to a percentage of the tenants' harvest. The entrenched hierarchical structure of medieval society and the stranglehold the lords held over their peasants changed dramatically in the middle of the 14th century, when the Black Death wiped out at least a third of the population. Lords were now desperate for labor, giving peasants bargaining power. Although there were attempts to hold on to the preplague social structure, the three-estates model would continue to hold force as an ideal, rather than a practical reality. ■

Suggested Reading

Ganshof, *Feudalism*.

Gies and Gies, *Daily Life in Medieval Times*.

Linehan and Nelson, *The Medieval World*.

Questions to Consider

1. In what ways was the medieval nobleman both above the majority of the population and inextricably connected to—and responsible for—it?

2. How did the Black Death affect the social model of the three estates, particularly the noble classes?

Daily Life in a Noble Household
Lecture 22—Transcript

Welcome back. In our last lecture we discussed one of the most revered documents in the annals of human rights, the Magna Carta. As we discovered last time, although long cherished as promoting the rights of the common man—in fact this document came into existence because of the anger of some of the wealthiest and most elite members of medieval English society. In 1215, 25 of King John of England's barons, upset with the many failures of his reign and the excessive taxes he was levying on the noble classes, forced him to sign the Magna Carta—which essentially limited the rights of the monarch in relationship to his subjects. Although at that specific moment it was only really the noble subjects of the monarch whose circumstances were changed by this event, eventually the values enshrined in the document would be viewed as pertaining to all people.

Today, however, we're going to talk mainly about that wealthy minority who were perched at the top of the societies in the medieval world—the first estate or order of medieval society: the nobles, those who fought. We're going to take a look at what their daily lives were like. Our information comes from a variety of sources—from the literature of the period that depicts the nobility in what we might call their natural habitat; from household account books that have survived, which reveal everything from how much a noble house spent on spices in a year to the size of the harvest from its fields and orchards; and from archaeological excavations, which can tell us in what proximity the lord and lady of the house lived to their servants, to what people in the household used for toilet paper, to how frequently they consumed meat.

A noble household in the Middle Ages was a world unto itself. Cooks, scribes, teachers, butlers, reeves, pantlers, and other various servants worked together in a complex unit designed to attend to the needs of a noble family. This arrangement was reciprocal, in that all those who worked for the noble family were considered to be under their protection and were supplied with food and shelter—and in some cases, a salary in recompense for their labor. This relationship often extended to those peasants not directly attached to the lord's household, but who worked the fields of what was known as his manor. As we discussed in our lecture on the three orders of medieval society, in return for protection in time of siege or warfare and the right to sow and harvest their own crops, peasant farmers usually owed their lord a portion of their harvest and a certain number of days of labor per week, season, or year. Most peasants were unfree, or bound to their lord, in the institution known as serfdom. A smaller number of peasants might be free-holders, who paid a cash rent to the lord, for their lords—or in some cases, owned their land outright and practiced subsistence farming. Whether peasants were free or bound, worked the land, or practiced a trade or craft in a village or town, it is a fact of most medieval communities that they were in some way attached to—or associated with—the household of a particular lord. This way of life, as we've discussed previously, was known as manorialism.

In the modern imagination, the castle is most often associated with the idea of the noble household, but most medieval castles are far from the luxurious structures popularized in film and popular culture. Until almost the early modern period, castles were built first and foremost with defense and protection in mind. Many people are surprised to learn that many early castles were built of wood and followed the motte-and-bailey model, which we've discussed previously. According to this layout, a large, flat-topped hill surrounded by a deep ditch—the motte—would have the main structure of the nobleman's household built on top of it. Down below it, in what was usually a square enclosure, was the bailey, where most of the activity of the household—including the stabling of horses, the housing of other livestock, the quartering of servants, food storage and preparation, etc.—took place. In the 1100s and 1200s, more castles started to be built out of stone—and in some cases, the wooden motte-and-bailey structures were replaced by stone ones. Often, however, the motte—which was usually an artificial, rather than a natural, hill—couldn't maintain the weight of the stone and would start to collapse, taking part of the castle with it.

Because of this, more and more castles and other noble homes came to rely on other means of protection—deeper moats and concentric stone walls that were built so that they encircled the whole structure of the household. These walls, known as curtain walls, usually had one entrance at a fortified guardhouse, and they were often up to nine feet thick—the better to repel attacks from catapults or battering rams. Castle building in stone got a boost in the Western medieval world after the Crusades. Those who journeyed to the Holy Land saw many impressive stone keeps when they were there, and when they returned west they often brought some of these architectural ideas with them. For example, King Richard the Lionheart of England built a structure known as Chateau Gaillard—which he modeled on fortresses he'd seen while on Crusade in France at the end of the 12th century as a means of protecting and controlling certain lands that he had claimed, and which the French throne had also claimed at various times.

From its earliest days, the center of any noble household was the great hall, where many of the household staff—as well as the lord and lady—might sleep. While technically they were in the same room as the rest of the household, the lord and lady usually had a raised platform at one end of the hall separated from the rest of the chamber by a curtain or screen. As we move through the High and into the late Middle Ages, this area might become a separate room—usually placed above the great hall and occasionally able to be accessed from outside the hall by a set of stairs that were running along the outside wall. This room was usually called a solar. By the late Middle Ages, a lord and lady usually had quarters entirely separate from the main hall; they might sleep there in a curtained, four-poster bed while servants slept nearby in the same room—often on a cot by the fire. This was so that should the lord or lady need anything during the night, a servant would be there to see to their needs immediately. Privacy is a relatively modern invention and conception, as this evidence and the layout in general of great households suggests. Our modern conception of a palace with long grand hallways off of which numerous equally grand chambers may be accessed has little in common with the reality of medieval buildings. Although there was a great hall, this was simply a large chamber, and hallways or passages similar to what we see in modern architecture don't exist—one room simply opens on to another, on to another, on to another. The only real privacy might be found in a very small room that opened off the lord or lady's chamber and which was called the closet. Rather than a place for storing clothes, this room might be where the lord and lady went to read or pray—and was perhaps the one place where they might be truly alone.

Clothes themselves, on the other hand, were early on stored next to the place in the castle where one went to deal with the call of nature. In medieval castles, the toilet was often simply a chute cut through the castle wall, which emptied into the moat. A wooden toilet seat might be placed over the simple opening—and if you were in a very posh household, it might even be padded. There was no toilet paper, so soft plant leaves or even old cloths might be used. The most common name for the toilet in the medieval world was the *garderobe*, a word that comes from the French *garder*, meaning "to keep"—and the word "robe," which refers to the main article or clothing, a long tunic-like piece, that was sort of standard issue for both men and women. So literally, the word *garderobe* means "to keep clothes," and very often clothes were actually kept near the *garderobe* because it was thought that the smell in that part of the castle kept fleas away—these and other similar pests, like lice, were a bothersome fact of life in the medieval world, no matter one's social rank.

From the central structure of the noble household—the great hall—other buildings would usually radiate outward. Construction of these additional chambers might happen over a period of years or even centuries—as storage rooms, kitchens, chapels, guest chambers, servants' quarters, stables, and other buildings were added to the main structure. It is not until the early modern period that grand estate houses, built all at once according to a fully formed plan, begin to appear.

The day in the noble household began at daybreak and was typically busy and filled with tasks ranging from the most mundane to those critically important to the survival of the family and the household. In most noble households, hearing Mass was the first order of the day, after which a light meal was usually eaten. Most noble households had their own chaplain who was responsible for the spiritual well being of the castle. He might also serve as the tutor for the family's children—and in noble houses, very often both young boys and girls might receive an education.

After Mass and a light meal, the lord and lady usually went about their separate pursuits. The lord would usually meet with his stewards and other attendants to conduct business or deal with any matters arising among the peasants living on his manor. Depending on his wealth and status, the lord might have more than one manor to oversee. The lord's right-hand man was usually the head steward, a position also known as seneschal—especially in royal households. It was an important position of high honor, as the legends of King Arthur suggest. The story has it that when the young Arthur became king, he asked his foster father, Sir Ector, if he had any requests. Ector said the only thing that he wanted was for Arthur to name Ector's son and Arthur's foster brother, Sir Kay, as his seneschal. In the case of the Arthurian legend, seneschal was a largely ceremonial position, but on most manors the seneschal had a lot to do. If the lord had more than one manor, the seneschal would usually travel to oversee them a few times a year. He would also usually keep track of the lord's money, oversee his other high-ranking servants, and deal with issues surrounding the manor court—which we'll discuss in a moment.

Another servant the lord might consult with on a given day was his bailiff. Although the bailiff usually answered directly to the seneschal, the lord might also confer with him about matters such as which crops to plant and when, the hiring of servants or craftspeople to perform particular functions or make repairs to the buildings or equipment of the manor, and whether or not the peasants were obeying the laws of the manor. When it came to the law, the lord was ultimately responsible for overseeing the peace of his particular realm. A few times a year, the manor court would convene. This was an opportunity for peasants to present disputes before the lord—someone's cow kept wandering onto someone else's patch of land; someone was plowing part of a strip of land that was not legally his; and other similar concerns. Sometimes the lord made the decisions on his own, and sometimes there was a panel of villagers—an early version of a jury—who listened to the disputes and helped pass judgments and assign fines and punishments.

A third servant on which a noble lord depended quite heavily was the reeve. The reeve usually assisted the bailiff with keeping a careful tally—often on a tally stick, which he would mark with notches—of all crops, animals, and other foodstuffs produced by the manor. In a smaller household, one man might fulfill all three functions of seneschal, bailiff, and reeve; bigger estates might have multiple people working in these positions. The reeve used a tally stick, rather than a written document, to keep track of the estate—because, in most cases, the person holding the position of reeve was functionally illiterate. Tally sticks that survive are fascinating voices from the medieval world, as they can be quite complex and suggest the ingenuity and intelligence of the medieval mind; they are an excellent reminder that intelligence and education are not the same thing.

On days on which he wasn't preoccupied with the running of the estate, and depending if he had guests visiting, the lord might go out hunting—an activity that served both as entertainment and as a means of procuring meat for the table. Many noble estates were surrounded by forest—and, in most cases, the so-called animals of the hunt, which lived in the forest, were off-limits to all but the lord and his noble guests. Fines and punishments for peasants who secretly killed deer or wild boar could be quite severe, up to and including death.

The lady was responsible for much of the running of the main household itself. Very often she would have account books of her own, in which she would keep track of monies spent on foodstuffs, cloth, cookware, and similar items. When not occupied with these tasks, she would usually amuse herself with some embroidery or other refined pastime. Very often she would have as companions the noble daughters of other households who had been sent to her home for fostering—something we'll discuss in a little more detail in our lecture on childhood in the Middle Ages.

By far, the most important event of the day was dining, and there were more or less elaborate processes for the preparation and serving of food depending on whether it was a feast day or holiday, if there were guests staying in the household, and the rank of those guests. The main meal of the day—dinner—usually took place between 10 AM and noon and might involve several courses. Menus varied according to the seasons and were prepared by a team of kitchen workers. The kitchen itself was usually some distance from the main hall because of concerns about fire. We'll discuss the customs of feasting in more detail in our lecture on medieval food and drink, but for our purposes today I think it's interesting to note that dining took place in the great hall, and that usually the lord and lady would sit up on a platform at the end of the hall—facing their other guests, who would be seated below them at trestle tables, and these were flat tabletops that would be set on top of a sawhorse-like platform with benches pulled up for seats. When the meal was over, the tables could be cleared away to make space for other activities in the hall—such as dancing or a musical performance. The further you were seated away from the lord and lady, the lower down the social ladder you were. Salt was one of the most frequently used and prized spices of the medieval world, and it was usually set on the tables in limited quantities at a medieval feast. Often, only the uppermost tables would be given the honor of being provided with salt for their food—hence the phrase "below the salt," which means to be of low rank. If you were seated below the salt in a great hall, you were not on a par with those guests seated even with the salt; the highestranking guests sat at the head table with the lord and lady—and presumably plenty of salt.

The character of Geoffrey Chaucer's Franklin from his *Canterbury Tales* provides us with a glimpse of what a high-ranking member of society might consume and in what style he might consume it. The word "Franklin" in this instance refers to a wealthy landowner. Although in the earlier period noble status and a wealthy household went together, as we noted in our lecture on the three orders of medieval society, by the time Chaucer was writing there were many wealthy people who were not nobles. These were first to be found among the merchant classes—and as time went on, many of these people in turn acquired land and estates. The Franklin is one of these upwardly mobile members of the bourgeoisie, and the details Chaucer gives us about the goings on in his hall give us a glimpse of what life was like in a wealthy household. The Franklin is what we might in modern parlance refer to as a foodie. Chaucer tells us that "withoute bake mete was nevere his hous, Of fissh and flessh, and that so plenteous It snewed in his hous of mete and drynke"—or in other words: "his house was so plentifully supplied that it seemed to be snowing food and drink there." A really interesting detail is that, according to Chaucer: "His table dormant in his halle alway/Stood redy covered al the longe day." A "table dormant" is the opposite of the trestle tables to be found in most medieval households. A table dormant is one that was not ever disassembled to make room for other activities, and the fact that it stands covered with a cloth, ready for the next meal, suggests that not only the Franklin takes eating seriously, but also that he has a room especially set aside for this activity—something not at all common, even among noble households in the early and High Middle Ages.

Another very wonderful source of information comes from the medieval manuscript known as the *Luttrell Psalter*, one of the richest witnesses of daily life in the medieval period. A Psalter was a book that contained the psalms from the Bible and might often contain—as this manuscript does—other items, like a calendar of saints' days and church festivals. What sets the *Luttrell Psalter* apart from other similar works from the medieval world is its lavish decorations. It was commissioned by Sir Geoffrey Luttrell and completed some time in the second quarter of the 14th century, and it was a work that clearly took months—if not, perhaps, years—to complete. As was the case with so many so-called luxury manuscripts in the medieval world, it is more of a status symbol and a monument to the man who commissioned it than it is anything else. Among the many scenes of daily life it depicts, it devotes significant space to the activity of eating. We see kitchen stewards—almost all men—chopping and cooking vegetables, roasting different kinds of meats on a rotisserie and on skewers, carving the meat, and then serving it to the family who are seated at what is clearly depicted as a trestle table. The scene is notable for such details as the shared dishes set between guests; the presence of spoons and knives on the table, but no forks—those were not in general use yet; and the light-colored bread, the finest quality, that is visible on the table.

The *Luttrell Psalter* was never completed. We're not sure why, although some scholars speculate that either Lady Luttrell's death in 1340 or Sir Geoffrey's in 1345 may have ended work on the manuscript. It's also possible that the death of the scribe himself—as evidence suggests that a single hand was responsible for the writing throughout—may have brought the project to a conclusion. In any event, scholars of the medieval period are endlessly grateful for the incredible detail with which daily life is depicted in the margins of the *Psalter*, as it gives us vital information about everyday activities in the medieval world. Sir Geoffrey Luttrell would most likely be happy knowing that the commissioning of this manuscript achieved one of his main desires—his family name is now immortalized, at least for those who study the Middle Ages and medieval manuscripts.

Interestingly, an area that is depicted in great detail in the pages of the manuscript is agriculture—especially the mainly peasant labor of plowing, sowing, and harvesting crops. As I suggested earlier in this lecture, one of the greatest responsibilities—and potentially lucrative activities—of a nobleman was to oversee the peasants who lived on his manor and who were under his protection. Although the lord would not usually participate directly in the activity of planting and harvesting, a good lord needed to have an awareness of the varieties of labor that went into producing the food on which he and the inhabitants of his manor lived.

Lords also had the right to demand a complex range of rents from their tenants. Depending on their relationship with their lord, the serfs who were bound to the lord and his manor generally owed a certain number of days of labor per week, and per season, and per year working in the lord's fields. They also were usually required to give the lord a certain percentage of the harvest from the strips of land they held from him and which they worked to feed themselves. My students are often amused to discover that death taxes are not a modern invention. As I mentioned in an earlier lecture, when the head of a peasant family passed away, his kin were usually required to make a payment to the lord called a *heriot*, which was usually equivalent to the best beast the family possessed—usually a pig or a sheep. The logic here was that since the lord was going to be losing an able-bodied laborer with the death of his serf, the family would need to make up for the loss of the pair of hands with some sort of equivalent payment. A similar philosophy resulted in the serfs of a lord needing to ask permission if they wished to marry—particularly if they wished to marry a serf on another manor or a craftsman who plied a trade in the village, as the movement of a serf away from the manor, again meant a loss in productivity. If permission to marry was granted, the family had to pay a tax known as the *merchet*, which we've also previously discussed.

By the way, I should note here that the idea that the lord of a manor had the right to sleep with any woman of his manor on her wedding night, before her groom did—something sometimes called the *jus prima noctae* or the *droit de cuissage*, which translates to something like "the right of the first night"— this idea is just plain false. It's something that later centuries dreamed up to try and emphasize the difference of their age from the imagined barbarism of the medieval world—and something that Hollywood has latched onto as a plot device in any number of movies. But the right of the first night—along with chastity belts and various torture devices—is a fable a later age made up about an earlier one.

But in any event, being lord of a well-run and prosperous manor could be quite lucrative. At times, this led to armed conflict between nobles who wished to claim possession of a particularly productive community of peasants. These so-called private wars, between one nobleman and another, would be a problem throughout the Middle Ages, as they disrupted life on the manor. As is the case with so much in the medieval world, it was the peasants—the "everyone else" of medieval society—who were usually the most adversely affected by these events.

The entrenched hierarchical structure of medieval society and the stranglehold the lords held over their peasants changed dramatically in the middle of the 14th century, when the Black Death—to which we'll devote an entire lecture soon—wiped out at least a third to a half of the population of the medieval world. Given that peasants were 90 to 95 percent of the medieval population, this stratum of the three-estates model was obviously the hardest hit—which meant that almost overnight, lords were now desperate for enough bodies to work their farmland. In the aftermath of the plague, field after field lay fallow—with no one to work the land. Peasants discovered that they were so in demand as laborers, they could demand payment and benefits previously unavailable to them—and pretty soon they did, often leaving the manors on which they and their ancestors had lived from what must have seemed like time immemorial to head down the road and see if another lord might be willing to pay them more for their labor than their own lord.

Although there were attempts to hold on to the pre-plague social structure, the three-estates model would continue to hold force as an ideal—even after it was no longer a practical reality. Before the plague, there was a land crunch in the medieval world. Afterward, there was an abundance of land, freedom to move between classes as never before, and plenty of ingenious individuals eager to take advantage of this opportunity.

In our next lecture, we're going to return to what life was like on a medieval manor. But this time, we're going to approach it from the opposite perspective than that which we've taken today—we're going to see what life was like in the medieval village, the type of community in which the majority of the population of the medieval world resided.

Daily Life in a Medieval Village
Lecture 23

> Many villages came into being due to their proximity to the manor of a nobleman—to whom most of the villagers owed service. For most of the Middle Ages, the lives of members of the first and third orders of medieval society were thus inextricably intertwined, even as the realities of their daily existence were radically different from one another.

The majority of the population of the Middle Ages lived in rural, agrarian communities typically called villages. The medieval village was often a small cluster of dwellings surrounded by fields in which crops were planted on a rotating basis. It was usually attached to a manor and was home to agricultural laborers, brewers, millers, blacksmiths, tanners, butchers, and others who practiced a variety of occupations. Although very little textual evidence describing village life survives, archaeological excavations at villages such as Wharram Percy, along with pictorial evidence from manuscripts such as *The Luttrell Psalter*, help paint a picture of the medieval village as place brimming with life and characters.

In the High Middle Ages and beyond, most villagers fell into one of two categories—those who were free, called freeholders, and those who were not, called serfs. Slavery had disappeared by about the year 1000. Freeholders were responsible for farming their own land. Serfs might own some of their own land, hold land from their lords from which they paid the lord a percent of their harvest, and owe the lord labor on his lands. Although it might seem strange, if one were to ask a medieval villager if he would prefer to be a freeholder with a small amount of land or a serf with large quantities of land, he would likely choose the latter.

Medieval village life was full of bustle, sights, sounds, and smells. Although they did not engage in modern hygiene practices, medieval people did bathe regularly and take care of their teeth. Villagers tended to live in one of two types of houses: the cottage or the longhouse. The houses had a toft, or fenced front yard, where the household animals resided. Behind the house was the garden, or croft, similar to today's kitchen garden. Most cottages were simple

Longhouses, like this Viking farmhouse, housed both families and, in cold weather, their livestock.

one-room structures; longhouses tended to be a bit larger to accommodate a family's animals when the weather turned cold. Most cottages had a central hearth with a small hole in the thatched roof to allow smoke to escape; the fireplace was a relatively late invention. Most homes were built of wood, often using the wattle-and-daub method. The day began early in the medieval village, as people rose and went to work with the rising of the Sun. Life as a peasant meant a life of physical labor, most of it agricultural.

Most of our information about medieval village life comes from archaeological excavations at villages such as Wharram Percy and Elton.

The Luttrell Psalter, a luxury manuscript commissioned by Geoffrey Luttrell, includes numerous illustrations depicting everyday life for the common person in the medieval period. Farm implements and techniques give one an idea of the rigors of agricultural work. Other images offer an idea of daily tasks such as cooking and tending to other necessities. The psalter's illustrations also depict people pursuing various amusements during their free time.

Most of our information about medieval village life comes from archaeological excavations at villages such as Wharram Percy and Elton, which stand as two contrasting examples of how medieval villages might be structured and oriented. Wharram Percy seems to have been laid out according to a plan, with homes and farmland placed regularly and equally around the village church. Elton, in contrast, seems to have come into being somewhat haphazardly, with its multiple hubs and houses facing any which way.

By the 15th century, the medieval village was on the decline. Many people were attracted to the growing towns and cities. The devastating effects of the plague had ravaged the populations of many villages and wiped some off the map completely. The enclosure movement—whereby much land previously reserved for farming was given over to sheep grazing—hastened the decline of the medieval village. ∎

Suggested Reading

Hanawalt, *The Ties That Bound.*

Jones, *Medieval Lives.*

Questions to Consider

1. In what ways was life in a medieval village similar to modern rural life? In what ways was it significantly different?

2. How did citizens of a medieval village define and identify themselves, especially in contrast with those who lived in urban centers?

Daily Life in a Medieval Village
Lecture 23—Transcript

Welcome back. In our last lecture we discussed what life was like in a noble household in the medieval world. For a large portion of the period, a system known as manorialism was the predominant way of life. In this system, various peasant farmers and laborers lived and worked on a lord's manor, paying him cash or in-kind rents in exchange for his protection. Last time we talked about the activities of the life of a nobleman—including overseeing the peasants who were bound to him through the system known as serfdom. We discussed the type of structures the lord and his family lived in—usually castles or strongly built manor houses with defense, rather than comfort, first in mind. We also spent some time discussing what was arguably the central activity in the central place of the noble life—feasting in the great hall.

Today we're going to explore many of the same issues and preoccupations we discussed last time, but we're going to examine them from another perspective—from that of the peasants. The majority of the medieval population—over 90 percent of the inhabitants of the medieval world—lived a rural, agrarian life, the center of which was the village. Villages were usually small clusters of dwellings surrounded by strips of farmland that were planted and harvested on a rotating basis. In addition to families who made their living primarily from agriculture, the medieval village included brewers, millers, blacksmiths, tanners, butchers, bakers, and others who filled various occupations. Many villages came into being due to their proximity to the manor of a nobleman—to whom most of the villagers owed service. For most of the Middle Ages, the lives of members of the first and third orders of medieval society were thus inextricably intertwined, even as the realities of their daily existence were radically different from one another—and, in many cases, as far apart from one another as was possible in the medieval world.

In the High Middle Ages and beyond, most villagers fell into two categories—those who were free and those who were unfree or serfs. Slavery—meaning true servitude, or bondage, a system in which people were literally property—had disappeared by about the year 1000 for reasons that are not entirely clear. As I suggested in a previous lecture, much of the decline of slavery may simply have been due to economic causes. Although slaves were property and could theoretically be worked as hard as an owner wished, they still needed to be fed, clothed, and housed in decent fashion if an owner wanted them to continue to be able to labor for him. Eventually it's theorized the costs of such a system outweighed any benefits to be had—it was replaced by that element of the feudal system known as serfdom. Technically, serfs were unfree—they were bound to the lord on whose manor they lived, and they owed him certain obligations and fees in exchange for the right to hold land from him and to work it. Although most peasants in the medieval world were serfs, there were a few non-serfs—known as free-holders—who held and were responsible for farming their own land. Serfdom, however, is much more complicated than questions of being free or unfree.

Serfs might own some of their own land, but they would usually hold most of the land they worked from their lord. In medieval legal terminology, land that belonged to one individual but was given to another to be worked was described as being held in fee from the lord. As rent, peasants usually paid the lord a percent of their harvest, and additionally they would usually owe the lord a certain number of days of labor per week or season on the lord's own lands—which were known as the lord's *demesne*.

Although it might seem strange to most Americans today, if one were to ask a medieval villager if he would prefer to be a freeman with a small amount of land to work, or unfree with large quantities of land, he would almost always choose to be unfree and in control of large amounts of land. The particularly modern and American idea of being able to work one's way up from nothing really couldn't obtain in the medieval world, although there were some exceptional cases—but they prove the rule more than contradict it, really. By the end of the High Middle Ages, the medieval world was in a land crunch, and most freemen would gladly have accepted serfdom if it meant having more land to work. Increasing the amount of land that was able to be brought under the plow involved the difficult and labor-intensive task of *assarting*—or clearing woodland so that it could be farmed. This was unpleasant work and undertaken only when really necessary. But as the population of the medieval world grew, assarting became more and more necessary, and the amount of forested land was diminishing as we head into the late Middle Ages. This changed significantly after the Black Death, when the land crunch disappeared almost over night—something we'll talk about at greater length in a later lecture.

As we discussed last time, being a serf also meant that one was subject to a bewildering array of taxes that one's lord could demand. Last time we discussed the *heriot* tax—a payment of what was usually the best beast to the lord on the occasion of the death of a member of a peasant household. We also discussed *merchet*—a tax paid upon the marriage of a serf. In addition, the lord had a right to levy what's called a *tallage*, and this was a tax that he could essentially demand at almost any time, for almost any reason—such was his right as lord of the manor.

Medieval village life was full of bustle and sights, sounds—and especially, smells. Houses tended to be clustered together in a central kind of node, with fields surrounding them, in what has come to be called the open field system. Without a doubt, people were always in each other's business. In some cases, houses would be built right up against one another, and livestock and people were in close proximity. You would see, hear, and smell your neighbor, your neighbor's children, and your neighbor's animals. The sound of conversation, church bells ringing, dogs barking, children crying, roosters crowing—these were all typical elements of life in a medieval village.

I should pause here and note that while in addition to hearing your neighbor and his business, you were often smelling it, too. The idea that medieval people never bathed is a myth. Granted, they bathed far less frequently than we do in the modern world, but we know, for example, that people in the medieval world did consider baths important, because some medieval penitentials—and these were guides that told what kind of penance someone should do for committing particular sins—occasionally made forgoing a bath a punishment. In the warmer months, people would do what was simplest and go down to the river—most medieval villages were situated near one— to get clean. For soap they used lye, a combination of animal fat and ashes, which was quite effective at getting the dirt off. Bathing in winter was a more daunting prospect. Usually a barrel would be filled with heated water, and in order to avoid waste it would be used by every family member. Some villages even had bath houses, where one could pay a fee to use the facilities and get clean—although that is probably a relative term when we compare then and now. Nobles maybe bathed a little more often than peasants and similarly used a wooden barrel, which they might line with fabric, so as to avoid getting splinters. We have images from some medieval manuscripts that depict nobles seated in what looks like an early version of a hot tub while servants attend them and assist them with washing. Nobles also might have morepleasant soaps—made of olive oil and fragrant herbs, for example—that had to come from some distance away.

Medieval people—from peasants to nobles—also made an effort to practice dental hygiene. Cloths or twigs might be used to brush teeth, and we have evidence that many people used a kind of toothpaste made out of a ground-up metal known as alum, some flour, honey, and usually mint. Still, despite these efforts at cleanliness, we can be sure that the majority of the people in the medieval world, were we to encounter them today, would be an assault on our modern sense of smell.

Villagers tended to live in one of two types of houses: the cottage or the longhouse. Almost all village homes, whether cottage or longhouse, had a toft—or what we might think of as a front yard—that faced the street. This was where the household animals resided, sometimes in their pens, but there were some types of animals—especially pigs—that were generally allowed to roam freely. Although there was a risk of one's pig being stolen by an unscrupulous neighbor, the interconnectedness of village life meant that essentially everyone knew everyone else's business and property. It was actually more economical to let pigs wander freely—they could then feed themselves with refuse, or usually on the acorns to be found in the forests, which surrounded most villages, and which were difficult to make edible for human consumption. Such forage was known as *pannage*. When it was butchering time, most peasants would simply head out and look for their pig—usually individually recognizable or sometimes marked with a brand or other identifier—and they would bring it home for slaughter.

Behind the house was the garden, or croft, in which the villagers might grow vegetables or maintain what we would think of today as a kitchen garden. As we'll discuss in our lecture on food and drink, which is coming up soon, surviving recipes might suggest that medieval people ate very little in the way of vegetables and other produce—but, in fact, it signifies quite the opposite.

Recipes would, as a rule, only be written down for dishes that were not prepared regularly. Most peasants would pick some produce from their croft every day there was some available and prepare it as part of their daily meal. The fact that so many medieval recipes concern dishes that were made with meat, and the fact that this indicates a relative rarity in terms of preparation, also underscores another fact of life for the medieval peasant population: a general dearth of protein. The staple food for medieval peasants was bread—usually dark and hard, sometimes needing to be dipped in ale to soften it sufficiently for chewing—and also a dish called pottage, which consisted of a kind of milky stew with cereal grains and essentially anything else that could be put into the pot to fill one's belly. In addition to bread, pottage, and vegetables, medieval peasants subsisted on dairy products, eggs, and occasionally bacon or fish, for the most part. However, while the medieval diet might have been deficient in some respects when compared to a modern diet, in many ways it was healthier—bread tended to be more nutritious with more good fiber, and the diet was pretty low fat. All animals were essentially freerange; they were leaner than meat and poultry are today.

Like their diet, the dwellings of most medieval people were similarly simple. Most cottages were basic one-room structures. Longhouses tended to be a bit larger, mostly to provide space to accommodate the families' animals inside when the weather turned cold. The presence of the animals inside increased the warmth of a peasant's home, even if it also simultaneously increased the smell. In some cases, the animal section and people section of a peasant home were separated by a manure trench, which was intended to keep animals from wandering over to the other side—especially at night when the family had bedded down. Some cottages—like some noble great halls—had an upper loft-like room called a solar, where the husband and wife might sleep and enjoy a modicum of privacy. But still, privacy as we think of it today really did not exist in the medieval world.

Most cottages had a central hearth, with a small hole in the thatched roof to allow smoke to escape—the fireplace was a relatively late invention. Consequently, most medieval peasant households were dim and smoky, and the thatch often rotted and needed to be replaced. The thatch was also prime living space for insects, rats, and other vermin—some of which might fall out of the thatch on to the sleeping family at night, never a pleasant prospect. In almost all medieval villages, the majority of the houses were made of wood and used what's called the wattle and daub method. Branches were woven through a wooden frame—then covered over with a mixture of mud to close in the spaces. The whole thing might then be covered with lime to make the house a little more rainproof. No matter what, however, medieval peasant houses tended to be relatively insubstantial and needed to be replaced—usually actually completely rebuilt—about once a generation. Their nature was such that the medieval form of breaking and entering was exactly that—thieves could literally break open the wall of the house in order to steal from it. Floors of peasant dwellings tended to be made of earth. Both peasants and nobles would tend to use rushes, or fresh straw, as a floor covering. Once the rushes got too dirty or moldy, they could simply be swept out and replaced with fresh ones.

The day began early in the medieval village, as people rose and went to work with the rising of the sun. Similarly, the day pretty much tended to end when daylight was gone; candles and other means of artificial light were expensive. Most candles were made of tallow—animal fat—and thus gave off an unpleasant smell. Nicer-smelling beeswax candles were expensive and usually only possessed by the nobility.

As the above quick summary suggests, life as a peasant in a medieval village meant a life of physical labor—most of it involving agriculture. In addition to those working in the fields, bakers, millers, butchers, chandlers (the official name for a candle-maker), and other craftspeople rose early to begin the day. It's safe to say that sleeping in was not a common occurrence in the medieval world. Much of what we know about medieval village life comes from the *Luttrell Psalter*, a luxury manuscript commissioned by the very wealthy Geoffrey Luttrell, which we discussed a little bit last time in our lecture on life in a noble household. Although commissioned by and written for a nobleman, it also includes numerous illustrations that depict what everyday life was like for the common man in the medieval period.

Farm implements and techniques, as depicted in the *Luttrell Psalter*, give one an idea of the rigors of agricultural work. In a sequence of images, starting on folio 170 of the manuscript, we see the cycle of planting and harvesting. It begins with plowing, an arduous task that required two people and a team of oxen. Next comes sowing—and here in the manuscript, a man is depicted walking along the strip of plowed land, a basket of seeds slung over his shoulder. He's accompanied by what appears to be a specially trained dog who chases off birds who try and snatch up the seed. The next step would be harrowing, or covering, the seeds with a layer of soil. Once again, this is at least a two-person job—one man guides the horse, who pulls the harrow over the ground; while another, armed with a sling and stones, continues to try and keep the greedy birds at bay. Next, any clods of soil need to be broken up—and here we see an image of what appear to be an elderly couple with mallets breaking up each clod individually. The next image in the sequence shows a man and a woman weeding the crops, followed by what literally appears to be back-breaking work—the reaping of the crops, gathering them into sheaves, and stacking them. The people depicted in this sequence are literally bent over, bowed at the waist, seeming to stagger under the effort of finishing the harvest. Once the sheaves are gathered, they're loaded onto a wagon, and we see a group villagers—many of them behind the wagon—putting their weight into it, trying to get their precious cargo to the threshing barn. The work is not over yet, as the wheat would need to be beaten with implements known as flails, a sort of double-jointed stick—and again, this needed to happen by hand—and then the wheat would be separated from the chaff by tossing it up in the air, so that the lighter chaff would blow away and the heavier grain would fall to the ground. Grinding the grain would also have to happen before it was in any sort of condition to prepare as food, and then some of the precious harvest would need to be set aside as seed for the planting of next year's crop. I am tired just describing these images to you.

Other images offer an idea of how daily tasks—such as cooking and tending to other necessary activities—were performed. We talked last time about the depiction of the preparation, carving, and serving of various meats and vegetables. In the pages of the *Luttrell Salter* we also find lavishly detailed images of people feeding chickens—with the interesting detail that one of the hens is tethered by her leg. Other scenes show people gathering sheep into the fold and milking them, catching wild birds, tending geese, setting fish traps, and all other manner of activities that went toward making survival possible.

While the preceding description certainly makes it sound as if the world of the medieval peasant was all work and no play, the *Luttrell Psalter*'s illustrations also depict people finding time to enjoy themselves with various amusements during their free time. We see what clearly is a picture of two nobles seated in a garden, enjoying what looks exactly like a game of backgammon. Peasants are also depicted as participating in a number of games that seem to involve balls and sticks of some kind—clearly some sort of team sport, although no one is exactly sure about the rules of the games they are depicted as playing.

Life in the village followed a consistent pattern, with the seasonal and liturgical year in close step with one another. Church feast days provided an occasion for merrymaking, and it has been suggested by more than one academic that the important dates of the church calendar had less to do with historical events in the life of Jesus or particular saints than they did with the cycle of plowing and harvesting. For example, as I mentioned in the first lecture, we know that the historical Jesus was not born in winter, but the winter solstice had long been a time of celebration—the nights are getting shorter! The days are getting longer! So it made a kind of sense to literally re-christen the pagan celebration of the Saturnalia as the celebration of the birth of Christ. Similarly, it may just be a wonderful coincidence that Lent—a traditional period of fasting and restraint—occurs right at the same time that the storehouses would have been most empty. That the Easter feast and the bringing in of the spring harvest often occurred at the same time simply doubled the cause for celebration.

Other festive events included fairs or markets that—depending on the size of the village and the kind and quality of goods sold there—could attract people from neighboring communities. Some villages had a weekly market—others annual or monthly ones. These were opportunities for villagers to buy and sell excess produce or crops and/or goods like pots and pans, shoes, gloves, clothing, and other necessities and luxuries.

As most medieval peasants were illiterate and very little survives in the way of documents concerning the life of a medieval village, most of our information comes either from rare witnesses like the *Luttrell Psalter*, or from archaeological excavations at villages such as Wharram Percy and Elton—both of which were villages in the England of the Middle Ages, and which stand as two contrasting examples of how medieval villages might be structured and oriented. Wharram Percy in Yorkshire, England, seems to have been laid out according to a plan.

Although occupied by people most likely since Roman times or earlier, some time in the 10th century it seems that someone carefully planned how to organize the scattered households and hamlets into what's known as a nucleated village plan. Houses were laid out in regular fashion in relationship to the village church and to two manor houses. One of the manor houses, more or less in the middle of the village, seems to have been torn down in the mid-13th century—and a new, grander one built at the far north end of the village. At the south end, the church was located—giving a nice balance to the layout. The mill was located near the church and parsonage, and a single street ran from roughly north to south through the village—linking mill, church, peasant households, and the manor house. The village was surrounded by farmland that was similarly carefully divided into regular and equal portions.

The Village of Elton, in contrast to Wharram Percy, seems to have come into being somewhat haphazardly, rather than according to any plan. Instead of one central focus—like a village green, or church, or manor house—Elton has multiple hubs. Houses were not ordered in neat rows, but seem to have grown up rather organically—facing any which way the owner might choose. The streets running through the village were afterthoughts—paths of greatest convenience made by villagers as they traveled from one location to another eventually morphed into streets. The main thoroughfare through Elton, which ran roughly parallel to the village's river, headed northeast to the towns of Peterborough and Stamford, and south toward the village of Ouse. The far southern end of the village was known—and is still known—as overend. There was a manor house here, which provided a focus for the village. But at the junction of a side road projecting west off the main road, we have another focal point for the village—the church. Heading toward the river along this side road brings us to another focal point for the village, which was known as netherend—where another manor house, village green, and mill were to be found. Wharram Percy has been a boon to archaeologists because it had been abandoned in the medieval period and then underwent regular excavations every year for about 40 years—beginning in the 1950s. By contrast, Elton has never been abandoned, and much of what we know about it comes from looking at the living, breathing village as it continues to exist to this day.

You might ask, given the insubstantial nature of most village dwellings and other buildings: "How do we know anything about the layout of any medieval village, especially one like Wharram Percy that has been abandoned for about 500 years?" After all, we have very little substantial physical evidence from the medieval world, as wood and thatch rot and decay. Much of what we know about the layout and plan of medieval villages comes from aerial photos over village sites that were deserted in the medieval period. A plan of streets and centers of activities may not be visible on the ground—but from overhead, traces remain. While the desertion of a village may have seemed like a tragedy at the time, it has been a boon for archaeologists and historians—who have fewer layers to sift through in order to reach the medieval world.

Many villages in the Middle Ages—particularly in England—were deserted, and I'm sure you're wondering why. This happened for a couple of reasons. The plague, which we'll discuss in greater detail in a later lecture, occasionally killed off entire populations—or enough of them that those few people remaining in a village were not substantial enough in terms of population to keep it running. This is not what brought about the decline of Wharram Percy, however. By the 15th century, the medieval village was on the decline. A rise in urban life had attracted many people to the growing towns and cities in the medieval world. Add to this the rise of the enclosure movement—whereby much land previously reserved for farming was given over to sheep grazing—and the end of medieval village life was in sight. The motivation for this was simple economics—it was more profitable to take farmland and turn it over to sheep for grazing, as their wool was much prized and sought after. As the enclosure movement gained prominence, more and more people who had once lived a rural, agrarian life began to flock to the cities in search of employment and opportunity. This, apparently, is what brought Wharram Percy to the end of its medieval existence.

As the medieval village declined, medieval urban life began booming. For the first time since the end of the Roman Empire, we see a significant percentage of the medieval world living in urban centers. What life was like in a medieval city will be the subject of our next lecture.

Medieval City Life
Lecture 24

As the Roman Empire declined in the 4th and 5th centuries—so, too, did urban life. There would be no true cities in the medieval West again for at least 500 years. … As we head toward the 14th century, the medieval world is in a land crunch—there are more people and not as many places to put them, a fact that contributes markedly to a revival of urban life not seen since the days of the Roman Empire.

In the early Middle Ages, urban life virtually disappeared. In the High Middle Ages, advancements in agriculture, in conjunction with a doubling of the population between 1000 and 1300, led to reurbanization of the medieval landscape. As urban life revived, the traditional three-estates model of medieval society found itself under considerable pressure. The new merchant class became a powerful force; many of its members achieved wealth on par with or exceeding that of many nobles, leading to the first real possibility for upward social mobility. Land- and cash-poor nobles, eager for wealth, began to arrange marriages with members of the merchant class, who were themselves eager for titles and noble status. While London and Paris had somewhere between 25,000 and 50,000 citizens by the end of the High Middle Ages, the greatest concentration of urban centers was found on the Italian peninsula: Florence, Bologna, Padua, Genoa, Milan, and Venice, which all had grown wealthy through trade.

The 14th century saw a revival of urban life in Europe. In some cities, medieval buildings and streets survive to this day.

Life in a medieval town was distinctly different from life in the rural, agrarian countryside, although technically those who worked the land and those who worked in the city were members of the same estate. One of the most noticeable differences was proximity to one's neighbor: Houses leaned right up against one another, and sometimes different families shared a single household. The problem of removing waste and refuse was one of the major preoccupations of town governments. Although villages certainly had crafts- and tradesmen, cities had them in greater abundance, and practitioners often grouped together on a single street, which was then named for the occupation. Most trades- and craftspeople lived above a street-level shop. Trades such as tanning, fulling and dyeing cloth, and butchering produced strong and unpleasant smells, so these activities often took place far from the center of town.

Tradesmen were, by the late Middle Ages, strictly regulated by the charters of their guilds. Medieval guilds were like a cross between the modern labor union, trade school, and fraternity. They trained apprentices, enforced quality standards and workers' rights, and gave financial support to sick and injured members. Guilds were also social organizations, holding parties and celebrations, and many developed secret rites. In England they were well known for the annual staging of mystery plays, which depicted various episodes from the Bible.

Although guilds were one of the most powerful forces in medieval city life, they were theoretically subject to the dictates of the town government.

Although guilds were one of the most powerful forces in medieval city life, they were theoretically subject to the dictates of the town government, which was responsible for the day-to-day health and safety of the townspeople. Town government officials built and maintained defensive walls, instituted the night watch, and assigned regular days for the sale of particular good and services. In Italy, individual towns formed communes for protection and defense. Various factions sought to gain control of the towns' elected councils; in particular the *popolo grosso*—the "fat people," the wealthiest—and the *popolo minuto*—

the "little people"—engaged in never-ending power struggles in towns like Siena and Venice.

As we move from the High to the late Middle Ages, we see medieval townspeople becoming less and less like their rural counterparts. Due to the demands of business and industry, many medieval townspeople were literate and had a grasp of mathematics and economics; there was also an increasing demand for schools and educational opportunities for the children of the urban bourgeoisie. While farming peasants still thought of themselves as functioning within a feudal hierarchy, townspeople tended to think of their relationships in horizontal, rather than vertical, terms. The revivification of urban life would profoundly affect all areas of the medieval world. Religious practices, social order, the economy, warfare, and the arts would all undergo significant transformations within the bounds of the medieval city walls. ■

Suggested Reading

Frugoni, *A Day in a Medieval City*.

Gies and Gies, *Daily Life in Medieval Times*.

Questions to Consider

1. What aspects of urban living declined with the end of the Roman Empire? What social conditions needed to exist for urban centers to develop in the medieval world?

2. How did medieval town life affect the social model of the three estates? How did urbanization benefit medieval society? In what ways did it undermine certain medieval institutions?

Medieval City Life
Lecture 24—Transcript

Welcome back. In our last two lectures we discussed what daily life in the medieval world was like in a noble household and in a village—two kinds of living arrangements that usually were found paired together, as a nobleman's estate or estates often existed symbiotically with a village. In a system that came to be known as manorialism, many of those peasants who lived in a village were bound to a lord as serfs—and thus owed him labor and a portion of their crops in exchange for the lord's protection in times of warfare or famine. The other industries of the village—such as baking, clothmaking, milling, and brewing—contributed to the economic life of the manor, although the primary profession for the majority of the people living in the medieval world was agriculture. Today we're going to talk about a third kind of living situation that existed in the medieval world—the life of the city.

As the Roman Empire declined in the 4th and 5th centuries—so, too, did urban life. There would be no true cities in the medieval West again for at least 500 years. In the High Middle Ages, technological advancements—in conjunction with an explosive growth in population—led to a re-urbanization of the medieval landscape. Advances in agriculture, such as the use of the heavy plow, padded horse-collars, and the practice of shoeing horses—many of which innovations may have ultimately made their way to the West from Asia—meant that crop yields became higher and a larger population could be sustained. As you may recall from a previous lecture, it is estimated that between the year 1000 and the year 1300 the population of the medieval world practically doubled in size—from about 38 million people to about 72 million people. This increase in population is part of what spurred expansionist movements, like the Saxon *Drang nach Osten*—or "push to the east"—and the movements of peoples like the Normans, who spread throughout the medieval world and whose influence helped to make disparate groups and societies in the medieval world a little more alike. As you'll also remember from a previous lecture, as we head toward the 14th century, the medieval world is in a land crunch—there are more people and not as many places to put them, a fact that contributes markedly to a revival of urban life not seen since the days of the Roman Empire.

As urban life revived, the traditional three-estates model of medieval society—those who fought, those who prayed, and those who worked—found itself under considerable pressure. A new class, the merchant class, became a powerful force in medieval society. Many of its members achieved wealth on par with, or even exceeding that, of many nobles—a situation that led to the first real possibility for movement among the three estates. Land- and cash-poor nobles, eager for wealth, began to arrange marriages with members of the merchant class—who were themselves eager for titles and noble status. We see this kind of upward mobility demonstrated in the lives of medieval people such as Geoffrey Chaucer, whom we've discussed at great length elsewhere in this course. The son of a vintner, someone who imported and sold wine, Chaucer used his family's money to procure an education that would give him the means to make himself noticed and popular with members of the noble class—particularly John of Gaunt, son of King Edward III and the richest man in England in his day. This helped Chaucer procure government posts, which in turn led to greater wealth—and eventually, his granddaughter would marry into the nobility itself. Many merchants became so wealthy that they were able to dress themselves in fashions and fabrics once only available to the noble classes because of their expense. As we'll discuss at greater length in our lecture on medieval fashion, this led to the passage in many places of what were called sumptuary laws, which dictated things like what kinds of furs, how much gold trim, and what style of headdress could be worn by non-nobles. This concern was particularly acute in medieval cities, as opposed to in the countryside, for in the city, nobles, merchants, laborers, and beggars all might live, work, and play in the same space—while in the more rural parts of the medieval world there was a more obvious demarcation between noble and peasant spaces.

Chaucer is most associated with the city of London, which by the 13th century had an estimated population of more than 25,000 people. Other major urban centers in the medieval world also had late 13th century populations of significant size. Paris had over 50,000 residents. Ghent was running a close second to Paris with about 40,000 people, its growth fueled by the manufacture and export of woolen goods. But by far the most populous and most urbanized cities were to be found in the South, near the Mediterranean. Bologna and Palermo each had about 50,0000 inhabitants, while Genoa and Milan each had well over that number. Venice was the most populous, with around 100,000 residents. Although it might seem significant that the greatest number of urban centers were to be found in what had once been the heartland of the Roman Empire, the legacy of Rome and the memory of the empire had less to do with the revivification of urban life than did the geography of Italy, in conjunction with the presence of a group known as the Lombards.

We don't know much about the Lombards, except that they were a Germanic people who had invaded the Italian Peninsula from the North starting around the 6th century, and their name may have come from the Latin *longbardi* meaning "longbeards." They controlled the interior of the Italian Peninsula until about the late 8th century. It was no accident, then, that most of the urban centers grew up in places like Venice or along the Amalfi Coast. The sites of these cities were difficult to access by land, but easily accessed by sea, which helped keep the Lombards—no seafarers they—at bay and also, of necessity, encouraged the citizens of these cities to become excellent seafarers. As early as the 10th century, merchants and traders were doing business throughout the Mediterranean, and they were doing an especially prosperous trade in the East, in Constantinople, the capital of Byzantium, which is the former eastern half of the Roman Empire. The money to be made by trading in turn made many of these Italian cities and their inhabitants quite prosperous, which would lead eventually to the development of what historians have come to call the Italian city-states, with many, many Italian cities—like Siena and Firenze, or Florence—becoming principalities unto themselves.

Life in a medieval town was distinctly different from life in the rural, agrarian countryside—although technically, at least at first, those who worked the land and those who lived and worked in the city were considered members of the same estate. One of the most noticeable differences would be in terms of proximity to one's neighbor. The sheer number of people resulted in houses leaning right up against one another, or even many different families sharing a single household. If you were to walk through a medieval city, you would notice that in many parts of the city it would be quite dark, even if it was the middle of the day. This was because of the practice of building structures whose upper stories were each just a little bit bigger than the ones below—a means of trying to carve out extra space where there really wasn't much to be had. So you have a situation in which at the upper levels of a street, houses or buildings on opposite sides of the street might come together and actually touch one another at the top. This blocked out sunlight, obviously, as well as keeping smells and noise—neither of which were usually pleasant—contained within the street. To start with, some streets were not more than 10 feet wide, so you can only imagine how these factors all contributed to a particularly strong sensory experience.

The sheer numbers of people and the close proximity in which they lived would produce a related problem—what to do with waste and refuse—and solving this problem was one of the major preoccupations of town governments. In most cities, chamber pots would simply be emptied out of upper stories into the street. If the person doing the emptying was being considerate, he or she might shout a warning—*gardez l'eau* in French, which became "gardy loo" in England, and which meant "look out for the water." Still, if you were walking along a street in a medieval city, you would have been wise to look up frequently—in addition to looking down to avoid piles of garbage, human waste, and effectively negotiate what would become a river of mud during rainstorms, as very few streets were paved. Some cities finally passed laws requiring shopkeepers and householders to keep the area in front of their homes and shops—which were usually one and the same—clean, at least on fair or market days, at which time large numbers of people might be coming into the city from outside.

Although villages certainly had crafts and tradespeople—such as bakers and blacksmiths—cities had people practicing these trades in greater abundance. Indeed, street names in medieval cities often indicated the major trade that was practiced there. Practitioners of a single trade—such as metal workers or tailors—were often grouped together on a single street. As I just noted, in many medieval cities, houses and businesses occupied the same building. A typical layout of a home of a craftsman in a medieval city might have the first floor devoted to the business. Very often, this level would have a large shuttered window—with two shutters opening toward the street, one opening up and one down—that could be bolted on the inside. The lower shutter could be propped on supports and serve as a display area for goods and wares. Beside this, the main entrance would usually stand open during business hours, and those walking by could see the craftsman hard at work inside. Many cities had laws prohibiting craftspeople from aggressively soliciting business from passersby, and some had laws forbidding merchants and other craftspeople from approaching potential buyers who were examining a neighbor's goods. At the back of the first level of a medieval cityperson's home/business might be another workroom, a place for storage, and sleeping quarters for any apprentices to the craft.

The second floor of the building usually housed the main living space—the equivalent of the great hall in a noble household—where most of the activity of the household, especially dining, would take place. On this second level, or sometimes on the first, and occasionally in an outbuilding at a remove from the main structure, cooking would be done. The risk of fire—especially in crowded quarters full of aging structures made of wood—was always great. So many medieval townspeople took precautions when it came to using fire, although obviously this was the only means of heating a house— so fireplaces or hearths of some kind were necessary in most of the rooms. The upper floors of a craftsman's home and workplace were usually sleeping quarters for the family, and occasionally, if they were well to do, for their servants—who would usually occupy what we might think of as attic space.

Some trades, such as tanning (which is the treating of hides to turn them into wearable leather goods), fulling, and dyeing (treating cloth so that it could be made into colorful clothes), and butchering were occupations that often produced strong and unpleasant smells. For this reason, those who practiced these trades often had their workshops a great distance from the center of the town, usually near a river, which would serve as a de facto garbage dump for the large amounts of waste many of these occupations— especially butchering—could produce. If you think about it, given what went in to rivers, it made sense that most medieval people drank beverages like ale or wine that were fermented, as fermentation was a great bacteria killer. While plain water was certainly drunk by plenty of medieval people, there seems to have been attention paid to the source of that water—spring water, for example, was thought to be the most pleasant tasting.

Those who practiced certain trades were, by the late Middle Ages, strictly regulated by the charters of the guilds of that particular occupation. Medieval guilds look something like a cross between the modern labor union, a trade school, and a fraternity. Guilds set standards for training of new apprentices—

including number of years of apprenticeship, hours to be worked, and the standards that needed to be met in order to advance from apprentice to journeyman to master. They also had the power to make sure that all of the guild's members were not producing substandard goods, and they cared for their elderly or ill members when it was required. Guilds were also social organizations, holding parties and celebrations, and many developed secret initiations and other rites. In England, guilds became particularly associated with the production of what were known as mystery plays or cycle dramas. These were a series of short dramatic pieces that would be performed on the backs of wagons. The wagons would roll through the town, stopping at designated spots—the actors with the wagon would perform their particular play and then move on to the next designated stopping point. Over the course of a day, dozens of plays depicting important stories from the Bible would be performed for an eager audience. Each guild was usually responsible for a particular play each year, and the association of a certain guild with a certain dramatic piece shows that medieval people definitely had a sense of humor. For example, in the medieval English town of Chester, the waterdrawers— the guild that brought clean water into the city—performed the play of Noah and his wife. The bakers staged the Last Supper. The Crucifixion? That was staged by the ironmongers—who, among other things, made nails.

Although guilds were one of the most powerful forces in medieval city life, they were theoretically subject to the dictates of the town government, which was responsible for the day-to-day health and safety of the townspeople. Town government officials dealt with the building of defensive walls, the institution of a night watch, and assigning regular days for the sale of particular goods and services. As we've already discussed, sanitation was a particular concern, and medieval towns came up with interesting ways to deal with this situation. One striking example comes from Siena, which made the position of sanitation official attractive in that this person had the right to collect excise taxes from the homes and businesses on the piazza del campo, the central square, and the streets adjacent to it. In fact, this position was so attractive that several people bid for the right to hold it for a year. In addition to the taxes, this sanitation official was permitted to collect. The public record for October of 1296 in Siena further asserts that in exchange for cleaning refuse and garbage off the streets, the holder of this office had the right to be a town crier—meaning that he could do some advertising with his voice, such as announcing livestock for sale, objects that had been lost, and alerting citizens to holidays and to the creation of certain emergency governing bodies.

This profession of crier was strictly regulated in order to prevent anyone and everyone from announcing anything and everything. This particular citizen who had managed to become the Sienese sanitation official, although granted the privilege of crying, was at the bottom of the hierarchy of criers— he was one of the *gridatori*. At the top were the *banditori*, the official heralds of the commune who announced the decisions of the town council plus judicial sentences and other such important matters. Below them were the town messengers, who carried letters on official town business between city members and occasionally would carry letters between various private individuals. Although the holder of the sanitation office was most likely a gridatori, on the lowest rung of the criers, the benefits from this position must have been significant if people were willing to pay money for the privilege of holding it.

One interesting note about the sanitation officer in Siena: He was also given the right to keep a sow and four piglets in the piazza, where they could feed on the grain that had been spilled there—a common occurrence in any place where buying and selling of food took place. In fact, pigs were some of the most frequently used sanitation workers throughout the medieval world, as they would often eat that which most humans considered garbage and had thrown out into the street. In our last lecture, we talked about the tradition in a medieval village of letting pigs roam loose in the streets and in the nearby forests, where the forage they consumed was referred to as *pannage*. In cities throughout the medieval world, pigs performed a similar function—they kept the streets relatively clean, and in return they ate and fattened themselves up for free. It wasn't a perfect solution to a noisome problem, but it helped some.

As many of the examples I've given you in this lecture suggest, the growing power of urban centers in the High to late Middle Ages is particularly visible in Italy. In fact, between the year 1000 and the year 1450, the Italian region was the most economically and culturally advanced in the medieval world. That wealth was based primarily on trade—merchants traveling to the East brought back silks, spices, and other desirable commodities. Certain Italian cities and towns became known for the manufacture and export of particular goods. Florence became renowned for the quality of its finished cloth—Milan for armor and armaments. Several towns, including Siena, were known as centers of banking. Another source of income for medieval towns came with the advent of the Crusades.

As I've mentioned before, travel to the Holy Land was a lot quicker by sea than it was overland—and Italy, with its location and its reputation for seafaring, was the logical jumping-off point for a travel to the land of Outremer. Italian shipping outfits made a significant income from ferrying Crusaders to the Holy Land as well as pilgrims who wished to travel there for non-military reasons. All of this Italian wealth necessarily attracted attention. For several centuries there was a struggle between the papacy and the Holy Roman Empire—which at this time was essentially the German Empire—to try and control the region of Italy. The Italian city-states, however, were for most of the medieval period fiercely independent, proud, and patriotic—a combination of traits that ultimately foiled most attempts of the papacy and the Holy Roman Empire to gain control over them.

One thing that marks Italian urban life in particular was the rise of the communal movement, where individual towns formed what are called communes for protection and defense from other urban communities, as well as from the agents of the pope and the Holy Roman Emperor. The communal movement had its origins in the 12th century and was essentially an association that all the businessmen in the town swore to participate in. Communes came into existence outside of Italy as well, but they had their fullest expression on the Italian Peninsula. In medieval cities, most members of the commune were middle-class, but some nobles who conducted business in the cities joined as well. Communes tended to protect the economic interests of business people against both secular and religious leaders—a fact that many factions of the church found somewhat threatening, and something that was regarded by many as threatening the entire social order, as prior to the 12th century, most cities were governed by a local lord or a bishop. With the communal movement, the voice of the people—the third estate of the three-estates model—was more prominent in the running of the city's affairs. The communes were overseen by town councils, to which people were elected to serve—but essentially, every adult male was expected to participate in the governing of the city.

The town councils were one of the major powers in medieval cities, and different members of the citizenry were always trying to control them. At the top of the social ladder in medieval cities in Italy were the wealthy merchants and bankers who were known as the *popolo grosso* or "fat people." Those citizens who labored at trades or crafts were known as the *popolo minuto* or "little people." These two factions, both before the advent of the communal movement and after it, were constantly at odds with one another.

As we move from the High to the late Middle Ages, we see medieval townspeople becoming less and less like their rural peasant counterparts. Due to the demands of business and industry, many medieval townspeople were literate and had a grasp of mathematics and economics. There was also an increasing demand for schools and educational opportunities for the children of the urban bourgeoisie. It became the norm, rather than the exception, for the children of merchants to attend school and become educated. City life also became an area where upward mobility was possible, even for those born into serfdom. Legally speaking, a serf from a manor was considered free and no longer bound to his lord if he ran away and managed to survive in the city for a year and a day without his lord fetching him back and without starving to death. Plenty of serfs left their manors and sought employment in the city, where they usually filled the least desirable jobs—assisting tanners, fullers, and butchers with their more unpleasant tasks, for example.

For those who left the manor, city life would have been a radically different way of life in many respects. While peasants farming the manor of the lord in the countryside still thought of themselves as functioning within that hierarchical relationship matrix we often refer to as feudalism, merchants and craftspeople in the towns tended to think of their relationships with others in horizontal, rather than vertical, terms. A good example of this is William Caxton, a late medieval Englishman who established the first printing press in England, and about whom we've already talked a little, and about whom we'll talk more. Caxton was a commoner from the countryside in Kent, some way from London, but in his business he interacted with people from all strata of society: from royals, to educated merchants, to the lower classes that would have supplied him with the basic necessities for his trade—like paper, and ink, and parchment. Significantly, although the printing press was revolutionizing the late medieval world in that it was making books affordable at the same time that more and more people were becoming literate and able to purchase such items, Caxton did not put all his eggs in one basket. A true entrepreneur, the first of his kind in England, he also continued to be active in the luxury book trade, procuring manuscripts—laboriously hand-copied and also gloriously decorated—for noble clients who considered these to be the best and only kind of books worth having. Relatively soon after its creation, the occupation of printer would become one of the most important jobs plied in a medieval city—as government edicts, statutes, and proclamations, not to mention documents pertaining to law and business, could be more efficiently and economically produced by the print shop than by the scribe copying by hand.

The revivification of urban life would profoundly affect all areas of the medieval world—religious practices, social order, the economy, warfare, and the arts would all undergo significant transformations within the bounds of the medieval city walls. From the cities, new ideas and ways of doing things would spread into the countryside, until by the end of the Middle Ages, the three-estates model and its attendant philosophies would be, for all practical purposes, just that—philosophies or ways of thinking that bore little resemblance to what we might call real life.

So in our last three lectures, we've examined three different types of medieval living situations: that which we'd find at the top of the social ladder—in a noble household; at the bottom—in the peasant's village dwelling; and finally, today we've explored the medieval city, whose inhabitants might come from all social strata and encompass almost every occupation. We've talked about what kind of houses medieval people lived in, the kind of work they did, and in our next lecture we're going to explore one of the most fascinating and important concerns and activities of people of the Middle Ages—eating and drinking. Although it has been a widely held belief that medieval cuisine was tasteless, bland, or just plain not good, research and re-creation of medieval cooking techniques and recipes has revealed the food of the medieval world could be abundant in its variety, ingenious in its preparation, and delicious.

Food and Drink
Lecture 25

Imagine, if you will, a world without chocolate … a world without coffee. But that was the medieval world. It was also a world without tomatoes, or corn, or even potatoes. There is no sugar in the medieval world until quite late in the period. It is, in so many ways, a world whose tastes and smells are vastly different from our own.

Although the medieval world lacked many foods that most of us consider fundamental to our culinary and dining experiences, people in the Middle Ages were not condemned to bland, bad tasting, or spoiled food. Medieval cuisine could be both delicious and innovative. Any study of medieval food and drink will be skewed by the surviving evidence. Recipes preserved in household books or otherwise written down were not typical, everyday fare but rather special-occasion dishes, more complicated than the food eaten regularly. The recipes preserved tend to be heavily weighted toward meat, poultry, and fish, with little mention of vegetables, so for a time it was believed that medieval people ate very little in that way; in fact, the opposite is true. Vegetables were so much a part of the daily diet that there was little or no need to preserve instructions for their preparation.

By far the most important foodstuff in the medieval world was bread. Medieval bread was most likely denser and browner than most bread consumed today, and extra ingredients were occasionally added to give it more heft. Although bread was eaten daily and with almost every meal, very few people baked their own; they would take grain to the local miller to be ground, prepare the raw dough, and then bring that to the baker's for baking. Large slabs of bread, called trenchers, were also used as dishes. Once a meal was over, the diner could consume the plate, which had sopped up many sauces and flavors.

Perhaps the most notable difference between medieval and modern cuisine is the use of spices. As the account books of great medieval households show, spices and sweeteners were greatly prized, and careful track was kept of how much was used and when. As today, salt and pepper were the most commonly used spices. Salt was especially valued because it could be used to preserve meat. Spices favored by medieval cooks that remain relatively little used in modern Western cuisine include mace, galingale, cardamom, spikenard, and saffron. Honey was the primary sweetener. Sugar was a late arrival, meaning that for most of the Middle Ages, tooth decay was relatively rare.

Honey was the primary sweetener. Sugar was a late arrival, meaning that for most of the Middle Ages, tooth decay was relatively rare.

A medieval feast was a special occasion, primarily for the nobility, with certain conventions of hospitality and good manners. Everyone brought his or her own knife—forks were not yet in common use—and tablecloths doubled as napkins; at major feasts, the cloths would be changed between courses. Several medieval authors, including Chaucer, describe proper behavior at a feast. While the nobility enjoyed a diet heavy in protein, peasants tended to eat a diet heavy in vegetables. As long as planting and harvesting were not disrupted by drought, warfare, uncooperative weather, and so on, medieval people enjoyed a diet that was in some respects healthier than ours.

When it came to beverages, the safest choice in the medieval world was something alcoholic. Water was in many instances unsafe to drink, given that rivers were the garbage dumps of the day. Well water was a bit safer, but due to poor understanding of hygiene and sanitation, this water could also be contaminated, especially by human and animal waste. Brewing ale became a necessary and lucrative activity, especially for women. The drink of choice among the upper classes was wine, although until the 18th century, all wine was drunk young. Mead, made of fermented honey, was most commonly drunk in Scandinavian societies. ■

Suggested Reading

Hieatt and Butler, *Pleyn Delit*.

Scully, *The Art of Cookery in the Middle Ages*.

1. What kinds of misconceptions do modern people tend to hold concerning medieval cuisine? What are the sources of these misapprehensions?

2. How did medieval tastes differ markedly from modern ones? How important were food and dining in medieval culture compared to modern culture?

Food and Drink
Lecture 25—Transcript

Welcome back. In our last three lectures, we explored medieval life in a noble household, a village, and a city. Each of the lifestyles of the inhabitants of these various spaces had its own unique characteristics and issues, but one thing common to all classes was a need for—and a delight in—preparing food. In today's lecture, we're going to explore the gustatory habits of medieval people, and we'll discover that the inhabitants of the medieval world could be skilled chefs and discriminating consumers—although their tastes might be a bit different from ours.

Imagine, if you will, a world without chocolate. For many of us, this is a distressing idea. Even worse for many of us would be to try and imagine a world without coffee. But that was the medieval world. It was also a world without tomatoes, or corn, or even potatoes. There is no sugar in the medieval world until quite late in the period. It is, in so many ways, a world whose tastes and smells are vastly different from our own. At the same time, there is no truth to the longstanding idea that medieval food was, as a rule, foul-tasting swill—nor is it true that medieval meats were often heavily spiced in order to cover up any odor of rot. People then and people today are largely the same, and medieval people would have become ill from eating rotten food—spiced or not—just as any person living in the 21st century would. But it is true that spices were particularly prized and sought after, and it is true also that medieval European taste buds seem to have preferred tastes quite different from those of people living in the Western world today. Still, as anyone who has ever attended an authentic medieval feast can attest, there is much in the way of good—and even delicious—medieval cuisine, and medieval cooks were some of the most skillful, resourceful, and inventive artisans of their time.

The first thing we have to remember is how little medieval people had in the way of what we might call modern conveniences. There are no refrigerators, no stoves with burners that could be turned up and down, and certainly no microwave ovens. Most cooking was done over an open flame, sometimes in an enormous fireplace, and the risk of fire was always significant. In great households, the kitchen was usually in a separate building, perhaps connected to the main house by a covered walkway. Given these constraints, one might be forgiven for wondering if medieval people only rarely had a good, hot meal. Yet, documentary and archaeological evidence testify both to the cleverness and talent of medieval cooks, particularly in terms of preparing dishes both tasty to eat and beautiful to behold—as we will see in a moment.

Any study of medieval habits of eating is necessarily skewed or biased by the kind of evidence we have at our disposal. First of all, from the earlier period we have very little concrete evidence except for that which comes from a relatively new field of investigation—archaeological excrement studies. This kind of investigation can give us some idea of the diet of medieval people—based on evidence such as fruit pips or seeds, etc.—but by no means is the picture complete.

We also have very little in the way of recipes that were written down—the earliest manuscripts that we might refer to as cookbooks come from near the end of the 13th century, and there aren't many of these. Even the evidence within these manuscripts must be viewed cautiously, as it in no way can be said to represent the cooking habits of all or even most of medieval society. As you'll recall from an earlier lecture, the process of producing even a single manuscript page was incredibly labor-intensive and time-consuming, so any manuscript pages that were devoted to something as quotidian as cooking would almost certainly be the property of wealthy noble households—and even then, the recipes included almost certainly did not represent everyday eating habits. As anyone who has spent any amount of time cooking knows, foods that one makes frequently don't require instruction—you know the recipe and cooking procedures by heart. But dishes that are not made often—that are expensive, or elaborate, or reserved only for feast days—these are the recipes that would be written down in medieval cookbooks, as it is only when dealing with something unfamiliar or novel that a medieval cook would need to consult an authority. This would explain why the documentary evidence for medieval cooking seems to emphasize meat dishes, with almost no recipes for fruit or vegetable dishes. Many people once thought that this meant that medieval people ate very little in the way of fruits or vegetables. On the contrary—the lack of mention of these foods in medieval recipe collections indicates exactly the opposite. Most households in Western Europe in the Middle Ages—even that of the poorest peasant—would have a vegetable garden in close proximity to wherever the cooking was done. Fruit trees and berry-producing plants and shrubs might also be in abundance. With no refrigeration and no modern canning or preserving techniques, medieval people ate seasonally, and most likely prepared fruit and vegetable dishes every day that such foods were in season. In order to procure these items, all they had to do in most instances was walk outside. Thus, there'd be no reason to write down, for example, how one might cook and season carrots, or make vegetable soup, because it was something that was done on such a regular basis.

The same is true of that most fundamental of foods in the medieval diet: bread. This food staple is called the staff of life for good reason—it might be eaten with every meal, and occasionally, it was the meal. Medieval bread, however, was very different from what we might think of when we think of a loaf of bread today. For one thing, it was probably significantly denser and chewier than the bread you find at the grocery store, because although medieval bakers did have rising agents that they added to the dough, they aren't the same as the dry yeasts used in most bread nowadays. The grain would have been coarser—and often, especially in times of extreme hunger or famine, items like beans, or nuts, and even tree bark would be added to the dough mixture in order to give the bread more heft. Evidence of the status and power of bakers guilds from the late medieval period demonstrates that most people did not bake their own bread, but either purchased it from a baker, or paid a fee to bake one's own bread in a communal oven. The use of communal ovens was a practical matter, when one considers the space an oven would take up and how much fuel one needs to heat an oven to the right temperature for baking bread. It was far more economical for one person or group of people to maintain the oven and charge people for using it. Before one could bring one's dough to the oven for baking, however, one had to have one's grain ground into flour. This involved a visit to the miller, who—like the baker—maintained the equipment necessary for this first step in bread baking and charged a fee for its use—the infamous soke, which we've already discussed on a few occasions.

There were different types of bread. White bread was considered by many the best bread because it was usually made of finer flour, which took much longer to produce since the grains needed to be sifted through an item called a bolting cloth—and usually more than once in order to get rid of the bran and germ of the bread and leave behind only the finest white grains. Because it was more labor-intensive, white bread certainly cost more and was most often seen on the tables of nobles or very rich merchants. At a feast there would be a few communal loaves at the table, and the highest-ranking person at the table or guest of honor would get first crack at the loaf, usually taking the best portion for himself—from whence most likely comes the association of the phrase "upper crust" with those in the upper echelons of society.

Bread had multiple uses beyond the nutrition it provided. Often at a feast, instead of a plate one might be given a slab of so-called trencher bread. This bread would be of lower quality than that meant primarily for consumption—and most likely somewhat stale and crusty. Because diners ate from communal bowls at a feast, the trencher was a place where one could place whatever item of food one had taken from one of these communal dishes. The bread acted as a natural absorber or container for the sauces—many of them quite strong—that accompanied some of the more flavorful dishes at a feast. At the end of the feast one had the option of eating the nowsoft trencher, or else throwing it to one of the many dogs sure to be roaming the feasting hall.

So what else did medieval people eat at these feasts? Some type of meat was usually served, but as a general rule very few people, except the exceedingly wealthy, ate meat on a regular basis. Protein was more frequently consumed in the form of beans, milk products—like cheeses, and poultry. Even at the wealthiest table in the land, however, the meat would in most cases taste somewhat different than what people today are accustomed to. We have to remember that all livestock in the Middle Ages are pretty much freerange—even though they might actually sleep inside a farmer's cottage at night for protection against either thieves, or the cold, or both. Most livestock raised to provide food in the medieval world, scholars estimate that the ratio of fat to muscle was about 1 to 3. Tastes in the Western world today seem to prefer the inverse, or a ratio of fat to muscle that is 3 to 1. So, as a rule, medieval meat was leaner than modern meat.

However, as important as meat dishes were at most medieval feasts, medieval dining moved in step with both the change of seasons and the church calendar—which forbade meat on many specific occasions. Because of this, there was quite an industry involved in providing fish for the tables of medieval people—and as a rule, people in the Middle Ages seem to have had different tastes when it came to fish. Eels, for example, appear frequently in those cookbooks that survive. King Henry I of England is almost always described as having died after consuming "a surfeit of lampreys," a kind of eel to which he seemed particularly partial. Many great houses kept fishponds stocked so that they would have an ample supply of fish on those religious days when eating flesh was forbidden. One of the clauses of the Magna Carta actually deals specifically with the number of fish weirs, or fish traps, set in the River Thames. There was very little regulation, and many boats found themselves entangled or otherwise damaged by coming into contact with these traps, and the peers of the realm felt that the implementation of some sort of rules was in order.

Preparation of flesh, fowl, and fish often involved combinations of ingredients and flavors we'd be unlikely to run across today—although most scholars would agree that salt and pepper were the most common spices. Indeed, household account books from the later medieval period keep careful record of quantities and amounts paid for these spices. Salt was considered so valuable that in the late antique world people were sometimes paid with it—the word "salt" and our modern word "salary" have the same root because of this. Salt was also prized because salting meat was one of the main ways of preserving it for consumption at a later date. Ginger, cloves, nutmeg, cinnamon, and cumin make frequent appearances in recipe books. Other spices with which modern cooks may not be overly familiar—but that medieval cooks seemed to have used with some regularity—include mace, galingale, cardamom, spikenard, and what is arguably the mother of all spices—saffron.

Saffron was by far the most useful ingredient at a medieval chef's disposal when he wanted to make an impression. It has a unique flavor and, more importantly, the ability to change the color of a dish—and it is still to this day, in terms of price per pound, the most expensive item in any grocery store. Many of these spices traveled long distances—often all the way from the Middle East or beyond—and thus they were quite expensive and didn't come into extensive general use until late in the period, as far as we can surmise. One item that was introduced to the medieval world quite late was sugar. For most of the Middle Ages, honey performed the task of sweetening dishes, which meant that medieval taste buds were not accustomed to the kind of sugary sweetness we associate with most desserts now, and it also means that medieval people were less prone to tooth decay.

When preparing a dish for a feast, cooks were expected to provide some sort of marvel or edible delight with which to amuse and entertain the guests. Very often these displays of talent would take the form of some fantastic feat of presentation. We hear of chefs cooking peacocks or swans and then re-dressing the cooked fowl in their original feathers for presentation to the table. The children's nursery rhyme about 4 and 20 blackbirds baked in a pie would seem to have some truth to it, as there are accounts of live birds—usually doves—being brought to the table inside a pie crust and then flying out when the host was asked to cut into the pie.

There were no forks as we know them in the medieval period. When invited to a feast, everyone was expected to bring his or her own knife, which could be used for spearing food from a serving platter and bringing it to one's own trencher, as well as bringing the food to one's mouth. Two people sitting side-by-side at a feast might share a single cup for drinking, but it was considered bad manners to drink from the cup if one had a lot of grease on one's upper lip, or to back wash in the cup—that was considered especially bad. Before the feast, there was often an elaborate hand-washing ritual—a pair of servants might move around the table with an ewer of water, a bowl, and towel, and each guest was expected to wash his or her hands before the feast began. Although medieval people did not really grasp the concept of germs, it was still considered bad manners to reach into a communal dish with unclean hands. Several important literary works from the Middle Ages describe proper manners at a feast. Geoffrey Chaucer's Prioress in the *Canterbury Tales*, for example, is described as being a very tidy eater in a passage that seems to have been heavily influenced by the French poem *The Romance of the Rose*, written in the 13th century. This poem includes a lengthy section on proper behavior at the table. Other texts instruct diners not to dip food directly into the salt cellar, but rather to bring salt to one's own trencher. Neither should one talk with one's mouth full, get drunk, or fall asleep during the feast—as this was considered bad manners. As we've already discussed, another of Chaucer's characters, the Franklin, takes great delight in dining—so much so that Chaucer tells us it "snewed mete and drinke in his hous" (it "snowed meat and drink in his house") .

The Franklin is also described as having a "table dormant"—a table that was always set and ready for eating, something unusual in an age when most people ate at trestle tables that could be easily disassembled. This would certainly be the case in the homes of peasants, which were often only one room. Space was at a premium, so it was often necessary to be able to move a dining surface out of the way, if one had one at all. Peasant cooking was a great deal simpler than the food seen at the great feasts in a noble household, and was often of the one-pot variety. One of the diet staples for this group of people was something called pottage, which we've already discussed, and which calls to mind some sad, watery, grey version of porridge or gruel, but which could actually be quite tasty and even creamy. Into this went vegetables, a bit of meat if it could be had, and then some sort of grains—or, on occasion, stale bread, which when softened, cooked, and plumped up, served to make this dish quite rich and creamy.

On the whole, medieval people ate a fairly healthy diet when times were good. Even peasants would have access to all kinds of healthy food simply by walking out the door and into their garden. But those good times were precarious, and the threat of starvation was always very present and very real—all the more reason, perhaps, for them to celebrate with a big feast when there was plenty of food to be had. Speaking of celebrating—we should talk a little bit about what medieval people drank. Water, as a rule, was not the safest thing to put in your body unless it had been boiled, fermented, or obtained from some known pure source—like a spring. Rivers were the medieval garbage dump. As we've already discussed, it was in rivers that all kinds of trades, and craftspeople, and farmers disposed of waste. Butchers, tanners, and others used the river as a means of disposing of refuse. Many medieval castles positioned their latrines, the *garderobes*, so that they were directly over the river. So you can imagine that if you were downriver from any of this, the river would not be the place from which you'd want to get your water. In fact, some medieval recipes specifically occasionally call for spring water, as it was understood to be the best and the purest. Communal wells in villages were better sources of water, but poor understanding of hygiene and sanitation meant that often the medieval version of the outhouse might be positioned close enough to a well to contaminate the water. The safest thing to drink in the medieval world was ale, mead, or wine. In fact, just as the baker might do a steady business supplying bread or allowing people to use his communal oven, many medieval women found brewing to be a lucrative venture—producing ale, often out of their own homes, and selling it to the public.

Students always ask me how it would be possible for someone to consume ale constantly and not become dehydrated, and the answer is that most potent potables in the medieval period had a significantly lower alcohol content than their modern counterparts. It was enough to kill all kinds of bacteria, even if people living in the Middle Ages didn't quite understand the mechanism behind this—but it was not enough, usually, to severely dehydrate someone. People did drink non-alcoholic beverages—water, especially if one could get it from a pure source, and milk. Fruits such as apples and strawberries also provided hydration, as did some vegetables.

Wine was considered the most desirable and upper-class of medieval alcoholic beverages, but until the 18th century there was no wine bottling and storage as we know it today. The use of corks to keep wine fresh wasn't common practice until the 18th century, so all wine was drunk when young and usually kept in a large vat known as a butt. The wooden butts often helped impart a particular flavor to the wine that sat in it—something that medieval people recognized, often choosing butts made of particular woods for the storage of particular wines. Even today, many people feel that the proper beverage to accompany particular cuisines, such as Greek, is a kind of wine known as retsina, a name that recalls wine that absorbed the flavor of the pine resin from the butt in which it was kept.

In great households, there would be a separate storage room known as the buttery, where these vats were kept. Although many people might logically assume that a buttery is where one would keep butter—that is not the case. This is also the origin of the word "butler." In more recent times, the title of butler has been used for a male household servant—often the head servant in a household. Originally, the butler was the serving man responsible for looking after the butts of wine. A butt of wine is one of the most famous elements of Shakespeare's play *Richard III*, as the character of the duke of Clarence is executed by being drowned in a butt of Malmsey wine.

Then, as now, different regions were known for producing different types and flavors of wine. The region around what is Germany today was particularly known for its white wines, while red wines from the South were held in high esteem. Wine was perhaps the most popular and common table beverage of the whole medieval period, and one thing working in its favor is that grape vines would grow in soil that was usually useless for growing other crops. When the climate was right, it was fairly simple to cultivate and tend to these crops. Even after wine had turned and was no longer considered fit for straight consumption at the table, it could be used in cooking to impart strong flavors—much as one uses vinegar today.

The third alcoholic beverage after wine and ale that was commonly consumed in the Middle Ages was mead. As, for most of the period, honey was the primary sweetener used in food preparation—sugar being unknown to many or too expensive due to its exotic provenance—bee-keeping and honey production were two important occupations. After it had fermented, honey produced the alcoholic beverage known as mead. Mead is most frequently found in northern European and Scandinavian communities—places where grape vines would not easily grow. As we discussed in an earlier lecture, the center of almost any Germanic community, particularly in the early medieval period, was the mead hall. Here, the drinking of mead was often ceremonial with the drinking horn—in many cases, this was made from the horns of a huge, now-extinct kind of cattle called an aurochs. This horn would be passed ceremoniously around the hall by the queen or highest-ranking noblewoman of the community. Such a moment happens in the Old English poem *Beowulf*, when Queen Wealtheow, wife of Hrothgar, King of the Danes, brings the drinking horn to the hero Beowulf as a symbol of welcome and of thanks for his assistance in fighting the monster Grendel.

So, as I hope this brief overview has suggested, medieval food was far from bland or uninspiring. In many respects, when food was plentiful and crops were not poor due to bad weather or insect infestation, medieval people ate a healthier diet than many of us in the West today. Most of the population ate a diet heavy with fruits and vegetables—with beans, poultry, fish, and dairy products providing necessary protein. Nobles enjoyed an even more varied diet, with a variety of meats—most of which were considerably leaner than those raised commercially today—complementing the typical vegetables, fruits, and dairy products. Bread, the number one most important food in the medieval world, was also healthier in that it had a much-higher fiber content. In fact, some scholars have gone so far as to suggest that medieval people were getting altogether too much fiber in their diets—whereas in the modern period many people have the opposite problem. Medieval people ate seasonally, and their schedule of food consumption followed a fairly regular calendar—dictated both by nature and its seasons, as well as the church and its particular feast and fast days.

Although food preparation equipment was rudimentary by today's standards, medieval cooks displayed an inventiveness and skill that would be the envy of many famous chefs today. The preparation and consumption of food was a huge component of daily life in the medieval world. Peasant families worked together to plant and harvest. Those who helped transform crops from the ground into food on the table—such as millers and bakers—held an important place in medieval society—even if they might often be viewed as taking unfair advantage of that position. A medieval feast was an opportunity for demonstrations of hospitality, friendship, and generosity to the poor— who might wait outside the feasting hall to be given whatever leftovers there were as the event came to a close.

A medieval feast was not just a time for eating—it was a time for socializing and entertaining as well. In our next lecture, we will discuss some of the ways that medieval people amused themselves—both in large groups, as at a feast; and in smaller gatherings, where people might occupy themselves with playing board games and the like. Next time, we will also hear a little bit more of what we might call the soundtrack of the medieval world, as we explore the kinds of musical instruments typical of Europe in the Middle Ages—and the songs and dances popular throughout the period.

Music and Entertainment
Lecture 26

While the medieval world and its people seem in many ways very different and far removed from the modern world and our own experiences, in most respects they were very similar to us—particularly with respect to their desire and enthusiasm for musical entertainment and diversions of other types.

Medieval people engaged in a variety of activities to fill their leisure time. Music was a popular diversion, although the instruments used—such as the shawm, lute, psaltery, gemshorn, and rebec—produced sounds and melodies that might sound unusual to the modern ear. Very little popular music has survived from the Middle Ages, but manuscript drawings, archaeological finds, and literary references tell us they enjoyed musical entertainment ranging from large formal groups of musicians to itinerant minstrels. We have clear evidence of the importance of music in medieval church services, where it was a major component of the Mass.

The account books of many great households show significant sums paid for musical entertainment at feasts. In parts of Europe, most notably Occitania (part of France) and later England, the traveling minstrel, or troubadour, was able to make a living moving from great household to great household, providing entertainment for its occupants. Medieval musical instruments, while similar in many respects to modern instruments, produced musical sounds that may sound strangely foreign to our modern ears. Standard instruments included the lute, vielle, recorder, rebec, shawm, drum, and crumhorn. Because musical notation that includes rhythm is a relatively late development, often we simply have to guess when reconstructing medieval songs and dances.

In addition to music, medieval people had a variety of gaming activities to occupy their leisure time. Perhaps the oldest and simplest game of luck was dice. Records show people brought to court over dice-gambling debts, and archeologists have found evidence of cheating—namely, weighted dice. Board games such as nine man's morris, fox and geese, and the seemingly unpronounceable Welsh game gwyddbwyll, many of which seem to be some variation on checkers or backgammon, were popular throughout the medieval world. By far, however, the most popular board game of the medieval world was chess, which originated in the Arab world. William Caxton, the first printer in England, printed *The Game and Playe of Chesse* in the late 15th century.

Although we often do not think of true theater performances as coming into existence until the 16th century with the construction of purpose-built theaters like the Globe, drama and theater were common pastimes in the medieval world. Medieval drama had its origins in liturgical drama, plays that occurred in church, usually on important feast days, and involved acting out biblical scenes for

The most popular board game of the medieval world was chess, which originated in the Arab world.

a congregation that could not understand the Latin of the standard Bible. This evolved, particularly in England, into the Corpus Christi dramatic performances, wherein the entire story of the Bible would be performed over the course of one day. A third kind of dramatic performance—one for which we have the least surviving evidence—would be given by a troupe of traveling players whose repertoire would include religious material and nonreligious, popular stories. Such traveling players could only move about the country if they were officially members of a lord's household and bore his badge to prove it. The lord, in return for his sanction of their itinerant life, expected his players to return to his estate at Christmas and other holidays to entertain guests and family. With the creation of permanent structures for dramatic performance in the 16th century, drama flourished in a way that it could not have in the medieval world. ■

Suggested Reading

Gies and Gies, *Daily Life in Medieval Times*.

Jones, *Medieval Lives*.

1. What does the evidence about recreation and leisure in the medieval world suggest about the nature of the societies of the Middle Ages? What surprises you about these activities and pastimes?

2. Do you see any continuities between medieval musical tastes and modern ones? What might account for these differences and similarities?

Music and Entertainment
Lecture 26—Transcript

Welcome back. In our last lecture, we discussed medieval food and drink and dispelled the long-held belief that medieval food was neither tasty nor nutritious. Although medieval tastes were certainly a bit different from modern ones, re-creation of medieval recipes demonstrates that medieval cooks could be as inventive and skilled as any celebrity chef cooking today. In many respects, the majority of the medieval population ate a healthier diet than that which most people in the modern world eat. Their diet was necessarily largely vegetarian, with the exception of the members of the noble classes—and when they did eat meat it tended to be much leaner than modern cuts.

Getting enough to eat, however, was a major preoccupation for most inhabitants of the medieval world, and thus it is no surprise that eating was a particularly important part of the day, and that feasts would be an occasion of great revelry and celebration. Although the food was the main attraction at a medieval feast, entertainers—particularly of the musical variety—also amused the guests as they dined. While the medieval world and its people seem in many ways very different and far removed from the modern world and our own experiences, in most respects they were very similar to us—particularly with respect to their desire and enthusiasm for musical entertainment and diversions of other types.

Although very little has survived in the way of popular music—manuscript drawings, archaeological finds, and literary references tell us that people living in the medieval world enjoyed musical entertainment that ranged from large formal groups of musicians playing for feasts, to itinerant minstrels who made their living traveling from town to town. One area in which we do see clear evidence of the importance of music is in medieval church services, where religious music was a major component of the Mass. As I indicated in the introduction to this lecture, music was also believed to be an important component of a large feast, and the account books of many great households show significant sums paid for musical entertainment at these events. In certain parts of Europe—most notably that part of southern France that was known as Occitania, and later, in England—the traveling minstrel or troubadour was able to make a living moving from great household to great household and providing entertainment for its occupants.

There were all types of minstrels—from those who were attached to great houses and performed in verse, noble and exciting stories of martial prowess, and those who made their living by singing bawdy songs, doing acrobatics, and farting. At the more refined end of the spectrum, these songs performed and the stories told were sometimes known as *chansons de gestes*—or literally, "songs of deeds"—and they tended to focus on heroic and honorable feats of knightly valor. At the lower end of the spectrum, some minstrels told risqué stories that involved lots of sex and farting. But it would be a mistake to think that upper-class people only liked upper-class entertainment and vice versa. Peasants enjoyed hearing about knights, and ladies, and kings—and some kings and other nobles seemed to have enjoyed what we might consider bawdy or vulgar humor. For example, one of King Henry II's favorite minstrels was granted 30 acres of land for his ability to perform what the records refer to as "a leap, a whistle, and a fart." This land was granted to the minstrel Roland le Pettour and his descendents as long as Roland—and later, his heirs—showed up at court on Christmas Day to perform his extraordinary talent.

Music was popular among all classes in the medieval world. Medieval musical instruments, while similar in many respects to modern instruments, produced sounds that may seem strangely foreign to our modern ears. Standard instruments found in any medieval group playing popular music might include the lute—which was a four- or five-string instrument that looks a little like an acoustic guitar, and which was an import from the Arab world. Another instrument was known as the vielle, and it was somewhat like a violin or a viola. Also popular was the recorder, a woodwind instrument that looks pretty much like the modern instrument of the same name. It usually had seven holes down its front and a thumb-hole at the back—fingering the holes singly or in various combinations produced different notes. Drums of all types provided rhythm then as now.

Some less familiar instruments are the rebec, the shawm, and the crumhorn. The rebec, like the lute, comes originally from the Arab world and is a version of an instrument known as a rebab. The medieval rebec was a three-stringed instrument that looked a little like a violin and was played with a bow. The shawm was a woodwind, like the recorder—and it, too, came from the Arab world. Although the shawm is considered the ancestor of the modern oboe, in its medieval form it had a more piercing sound than the modern oboe. The shawm was a single-reed instrument—and as such, was quite loud. Generally, it was reserved for outdoor performances. Indoors the part played by the shawm might be taken over by the crumhorn, a curved woodwind with a double reed. The crumhorn is distinctive in the buzzing noise it makes—a little bit like a kazoo.

Other popular medieval instruments include the hurdy-gurdy, which was a stringed instrument that was played by turning a wheel, so that the hand-bowing motion typically used with a stringed instrument is replaced by a movement that is mechanical—generated by the rotating action. Also always popular with medieval musicians and listeners was the bagpipe, which is much the same now as it was then—and the organetto, which looked a little like a miniature pipe organ. Air was generated by pushing on a bellows, and this was translated into sound by the pushing of a button associated with a particular pipe. Of course, at its most basic, a pipe and a drum—sometimes called a tabor—could provide both rhythm and melody.

Because musical notation that includes rhythm is a relatively late development, often we simply have to guess when reconstructing medieval songs and dances. Here are a few clips of modern recreations of medieval songs, just so you can get a feel for what some of the more popular music may have sounded like. In this first selection, you'll notice the dominance of the sound of piping and drums. [Music.]

In this second selection, you'll hear some more piping, but there is more emphasis on stringed instruments like the lute, viol, or rebec. [Music.] In this next clip, you can hear some of the deeper sounding woodwinds, like the crumhorn. [Music.]

In this final clip, you can hear some instruments that were the ancestors of the modern piano—meaning they were stringed and music was generated not by strumming, plucking, or bowing across the strings, but by striking them. Medieval instruments in this group include the harpsichord and the dulcimer. [Music.]

In addition to music, medieval people had a variety of gaming activities to occupy their leisure time. Perhaps the oldest and simplest game of luck was dice. Dice were relatively easy to fashion—out of wood, or animal bone maybe—and they were easily transportable. You could have a dice game practically anywhere, although evidence suggests that taverns and pubs were particular places where people might play at dicing. It also produced what might be some of the earliest recorded instances of gambling addiction. Court records show individuals brought before the court for failing to pay what they owed after a round of gambling with dice, and many of the same individuals show up in the records repeatedly. Archaeology shows that cheating at games of chance was occurring even before the Middle Ages, as several pairs of weighted dice have been discovered on archaeological digs. In fact, excavations in the ancient Roman city of Pompeii—destroyed when Mount Vesuvius erupted in A.D. 79—have turned up weighted dice, which would tend to land on certain numbers whenever thrown, thus allowing the thrower—as long as he was in the know—to cheat.

Board games—such as Nine Man's Morris, or Fox and Geese, and the seemingly unpronounceable Welsh game spelled g-w-y-b-y-d-dy- l-l and pronounced something like "gooy-boythill," many of which seem to be some variation on checkers or backgammon—were popular throughout the medieval world. We have found Nine Man's Morris boards scratched into rocks, on the backs of boards of other games—and perhaps most amusingly, carved into church pews. The layout of a Nine Man's Morris board was relatively simple—three concentric squares, with four lines linking the squares, and dots at the corners. Each player has nine men and may place them on any open dot on the board. The object of the game is to collect all of your opponent's men, which you accomplish by forming mills—which are three of one player's markers all in a row. For every mill formed, the opposing player loses a piece, and it cannot be returned to the board. There were several more or less complicated variations on this game, including Three Man's Morris up to Twelve Man's Morris.

By far, however, the most popular board game of the medieval world was chess. As far as we can tell, chess seems to have originated in India, with versions of it being played as early as the 6th century. From there it moved into the Arab world, and this seems to be the main avenue by which it made its way to the medieval European world—as did so many other developments in math, science, and medicine, as we will see in later lectures. In the 10th century, chess was introduced to the Iberian Peninsula in what is modern-day Spain, and from there it seems to have spread to the rest of Europe. Although many of us today might think of chess as a slow-moving game, in its original medieval form it moved even more slowly. Originally, the piece that we call the queen today was called a minister, or some equivalent term, and this piece had very limited movement—usually one square in any direction. In the 15th century, however, the queen was given the powers of movement she enjoys today—an innovation that considerably livened up chess play. Chess shortly after this development was often called queen's chess in order to distinguish it from the earlier form of chess.

A mark of the importance of chess in the medieval world is that William Caxton, the first printer in England, chose to print a book entitled *The Game and Playe of Chesse* in the late 15th century. We've talked a little bit about Caxton prior to this. He is one of my particular interests, in that he represents what seems to be a truly medieval personality—if we can say that such a thing really exists. A deeply religious man, he was in many ways very conservative—and in many others, he was a remarkable entrepreneur and innovator. He left his home in the country—in the section of Kent, England, known as the Weald—and he traveled to the Continent, where he learned about this new-fangled invention called the printing press. After returning to England, he set up his business in Westminster, printing a variety of books in English—many of which he himself had translated out of their original languages.

But he began his printing enterprise before returning to England, actually. While still on the Continent, where he had learned this new trade—probably in the Belgian town of Bruges—the first book printed in English came off Caxton's press. This was an English version of the story of Troy and the legendary hero Aeneas. About 1474 or 75, Caxton completed his translation of a book very popular on the Continent, but virtually unknown in England at the time, and he set about printing it. That book was *The Game of Chess* and was written by one Jacob de Cessolis as an allegory, using the game of chess to illustrate important life lessons.

The basic premise of the book is that an evil king is brought under control by one of his advisors who teaches him how to play chess. The advisor then proceeds to explain all the figures on the chessboard, carefully detailing social position and responsibilities of each and how they are to interact with each other. The idea is that the evil king learns how to be a better ruler and a better man through the study of chess—and by extension, other readers of the book may also learn important life lessons. Caxton dedicated the first edition—which he entitled *The Game and Playe of Chesse*—to George, duke of Clarence, although he is careful to state that he does not believe that the duke is in need of correction, like the evil king depicted in his book. In the second edition, Caxton removes this dedication—replacing it with a statement that he makes over and over in the prefaces and epilogues to his books. He references Saint Paul who says that everything that is written can be used to educate—or as Caxton repeatedly says: "All is wryten for our doctrine," and so he hopes that people will learn something from reading this book. That Caxton went to the time and effort to translate, set in print, and publish more than one edition of this work so early in his career underscores how popular and widespread chess had become, and how many people were easily able to understand it being used in allegorical form to teach larger life lessons.

Medieval theater also usually sought to entertain as well as instruct. Although we often do not think of true theater performances as coming into existence until the 16th century—when structures such as the Theater and the Globe, whose sole purpose was to provide a venue for dramatic performance—this is the time these structures were built—drama and theater were common pastimes in the medieval world.

Medieval drama has its origins in liturgical drama. These performances usually occurred in church, and usually on important feast days. They were generally an acting out of an important biblical scene, allowing those in the congregation who didn't understand Latin—and this would be the majority—to understand the subject of that day's sermon or Mass celebration. Interestingly, it seems that sermons were sometimes delivered in Latin—sometimes in the vernacular or common language. The thinking on the part of scholars is that usually sermons in Latin were directed toward clergy, while those in the vernacular were directed toward the lay people of the parish. It's hard to determine this split exactly, however, as many sermons that were given in the vernacular might actually be written down in Latin—they could thus be circulated among and given by different clergy who spoke a variety of different native languages. In a situation like this, essentially the Latin would be translated "on the spot" during the giving of the sermon by the priest who was celebrating the Mass.

These liturgical performances evolved into what have come to be called, particularly in England, the Corpus Christi dramatic performances, or medieval cycle drama, which we discussed a bit when we covered the topic of guilds in our lecture on life in a medieval town. In medieval cycle drama, over the course of a single day—usually but not always on the occasion of the Feast of Corpus Christi—the entire story of the Bible—more or less—would be told in a series of dramatic performances. For these performances, as you'll recall, a series of carts would be made into moving stages, and they would travel through the town—stopping at set locations to perform their particular play. Each play might be performed, say, 6 to 10 times in the course of the day. The carts rolled through the town in order, starting with dramatic representations of the Creation—or in the case of the town of Chester, the fall of Lucifer, and usually concluding with a dramatic performance of the Last Judgment. As I said previously when discussing mystery plays, various town guilds were each responsible for staging a particular play, and sometimes the associations were both deliberate and humorous—the bakers for the Last Supper, the water-drawers for Noah's flood, the ironmongers for the Crucifixion.

After liturgical drama and cycle drama there is a third kind of dramatic performance—one for which we have the least surviving evidence. This would be the type of performance given by a troupe of traveling players, whose repertoire would include religious material, but non-religious, popular stories as well. Such traveling players could only legally move about the countryside if they were officially members of a lord's household and bore his badge to prove it.

The lord, in return for this sanction of their itinerant life, would expect his players to return to his estate at Christmas and other holidays to entertain guests and family. Both the mystery plays and the popular dramatic pieces performed by itinerant traveling players would be considerably different in comparison to expectations surrounding modern drama. For the most part, when one attends a play or other type of performance in the 21st century, there is the infamous fourth wall that separates the audience from the performers. Those dramatic offerings that break the wall and address the audience directly are often considered edgy or avant-garde. In the medieval world, the situation would have been the inverse—although in cycle drama the players did have set lines, there would be much more direct address to the audience than is typical of modern drama, and much of the action would have taken place right in the mix with the crowd gathered to watch.

In order to suggest different locales with just a wagon, very often the bed of the wagon would be the main location in a dramatic performance, but the area on the ground in front of the wagon was almost always used at some point in the performance. For example, in the Chester cycle, the Three Wise Men seem to have made their way on stage not from behind a curtain on the wagon, but by walking right up through the crowd gathered to watch the performance. A traveling troupe of players would most likely engage directly even more with a gathered audience. Whether or not they ate or had a place to sleep might depend on how they interacted with a particular crowd, or maybe even a particular individual in the crowd, so traveling players needed to be particularly quick-witted and able to shift the style of their performance to something different if the particular scene they were presenting wasn't going over well. Most traveling players were paid by passing the cap after a performance—so they needed to be good. Essentially, they had to be masters of both memorized set pieces and improvisation, with a little bit of stand-up comedian thrown in.

Although drama served to both entertain and educate in the medieval world, it is not until the creation of permanent structures designated for dramatic performance in the 16th century that drama—such as that written and performed by Shakespeare—would truly begin to flourish. Still, drama—along with games and music—was an important part of the medieval world. Although we tend not to think of people in the Middle Ages as having much time to devote to leisure activities, the scant records that survive indicate that they needed relaxation and diversion just as much as modern people do. Further evidence of the fact that medieval people certainly concerned themselves with much beyond the bare necessities of survival becomes clear when we turn our attention to medieval fashion.

Although it is true that most clothing in the Middle Ages was practical and utilitarian in nature, there were fashions and fads then just as there are now, and any number of stylistic variations in garments that clearly existed only for show—many of which seem, like some things in modern fashion today, to be quite silly and impractical. So, in our next lecture, we're going to turn our attention to what medieval people wore—and how, and why, and when they wore it.

Dress and Fashion
Lecture 27

> Margery Kempe ... relates how she was a slave to fashion before she began having her spiritual encounters with Jesus Christ. ... She describes her earlier desire to be fashionable as evidence of the sinful nature she once possessed. ... Clothing could be used to announce to the world something about Margery's spiritual state—her outer covering said something about her inner soul.

Although very little clothing has survived from the medieval period, pictures in medieval manuscripts and entries in household account books give us some idea of what medieval clothing was like. Imagine a world without zippers, in which a lady might sew the sleeves of her gown on every day and unstitch them at night, and in which one's head was almost never without some sort of covering. Although basic articles of clothing were similar in style for most classes, the quality, color, and ornamentation of dress often served as indicators of social status. Sumptuary laws restricting the amount and kind of fur trimmings or the color of clothing indicate a concern that wealthy, nonnoble merchants might be mistaken for nobility. While function was their primary concern, people in the Middle Ages were also quite fashion conscious.

Although there was striking uniformity of fashion throughout the Middle Ages, there were also some remarkable and original variations as the period progressed, especially among members of the noble classes and those who aspired to move up in society—usually the merchants. The basic article of clothing for both men and women, peasant and noble, was the tunic with sleeves. It was usually ankle length for women and knee length for men. Under the tunic, which was usually wool, might be a linen cotte, or kirtle, and over those, a surcoat might be worn. The other universal element was some sort of head covering, ranging from a simple cap to an elaborate women's headdress using wire or other supports to maintain its shape.

By the end of the medieval period, the wardrobes of men and women had become a little more developed and elaborate. As undergarments, a man wore a shirt, or chemise, and hose, or chausses, which were somewhere between trousers and tights. Over his shirt he wore a doublet, and over this a sort of gown, or robe. In cold weather, he might add a cloak or cape. By the end of the Middle Ages, a woman also wore hose, and as an undergarment a smock, or chemise. Over this she might wear a kirtle, and on top of this a gown or robe. In cold weather, she would add another layer, such as a mantle, or manteau.

The greatest differences in medieval fashion are not seen across time but rather across class. Without a doubt, peasant clothing was the simplest and most practical, as its wearers were usually engaged in manual labor. Manuscript illuminations depicting peasants laboring in the fields often show them barefoot, with the long ends of their robes tucked up around their waists for ease of movement. Shoes were often made of leather that provided little protection against the elements, particularly muddy streets, so peasant and noble alike might strap wooden platform clogs on over their shoes to avoid the mud and the damp.

We tend to see the greatest fashion variety among the noble classes, including fashion for the sake of fashion—that is, impractical clothing that announces its wearer's wealth. Many women's fashions included dresses with sleeves that would need to sewn onto the gown each morning—a task requiring the help of a maidservant. Women of the upper classes also wore elaborate headdresses, many of them constructed out of wire and several pounds of cloth, making them look like ships under full sail. By far the greatest indicator of nobility was the use of jewels and fur as clothing adornments. As the merchant class grew in wealth and power in the High and late Middle Ages, many of its members sought to imitate the style and dress of the noble classes. This situation led to the passage of sumptuary laws, which restricted certain types of clothing and accessories to members of certain classes. ∎

Suggested Reading

Gies and Gies, *Daily Life in Medieval Times*.

Piponnier and Mane, *Dress in the Middle Ages*.

Questions to Consider

1. What role did medieval fashion play in relationship to social status? How did functionality intersect with aesthetics?

2. What impact did contact with foreign cultures have on medieval fashion sense? How and why might fashions vary from place to place and time to time?

Dress and Fashion
Lecture 27—Transcript

Welcome back. In our last lecture, we discussed some of the leisure activities enjoyed by people living in the medieval world. We explored some of the board games they enjoyed—such as chess, backgammon, and Nine Man's Morris—the music they listened to, and the dramatic productions they watched for entertainment. Today we're going to turn to a topic that might similarly be categorized as something that occupied the free time of medieval people—and this is fashion. While it is certainly the case that people living in the Middle Ages tended to dress with practicality first in mind, there were plenty of clothing trends and fads in the Middle Ages that had absolutely nothing to do with function and everything to do with flair.

For example, Chaucer's Wife of Bath, whom we've already discussed in a few lectures, has special mention made of her head covering. Chaucer's narrator tells us that "Hir coverchiefs ful fyne weren of ground/I dorste swere they weyeden ten pound/that on a Sonday weren upon hir heed" or in other words: "On Sundays, the Wife wears an elaborate head covering of fine-quality cloth that must have weighed at least ten pounds." Margery Kempe, the late medieval Englishwoman we discussed in a few of our previous lectures, relates how she was a slave to fashion before she began having her spiritual encounters with Jesus Christ. According to Kempe, she used to wear her skirts in the latest slashed style. What this means is that she might have an underskirt that was a bright or striking color; the top skirt she wore would have strategically placed slashes in it that would allow the bright underskirt to show through.

She also, she tells her readers, wore fancy headdresses with tippets on them—essentially decorative flourishes—and she describes her earlier desire to be fashionable as evidence of the sinful nature she once possessed. It is perhaps not surprising, then, that when she dedicates her life to Christ, she dresses all in white, a color generally reserved for virgins—which given her 14 children, Margery certainly was not. What's significant here is the way in which clothing could be used to announce to the world something about Margery's spiritual state—her outer covering said something about her inner soul. As the example of Margery Kempe suggests, clothing in the Middle

Ages served functions far beyond simply covering bodies and keeping them warm.

For all this, however, compared to today's fast-paced world of fashion, the costumes and dress of the Middle Ages might seem a little boring and static. Relatively speaking, little changed in terms of clothing styles in the medieval world as compared to the great variety of fabrics, styles, and colors that are such an intrinsic part of modern dress. Still, although there exists a strikingly uniform fashion style throughout the Middle Ages, there were some remarkable and original variations as the period progressed—especially among members of the noble classes, and those who aspired to move up in society, usually the merchants. Today we're going to begin our discussion with the basics of medieval dress, and then we're going to explore some of the more outlandish styles and fashions that tend to leave quite a memorable impression when they're described or depicted in the art and literature of the period.

The basic article of clothing for both men and women—peasant and noble—for most of the Middle Ages was the tunic with sleeves. The tunic was usually worn at the ankle for women, and close to the knee for men, and it was usually made out of wool—the most commonly used fabric in the medieval world. Under the tunic might be a linen *cotte*, or "kirtle." As a general rule, wool was used for outer garments, and linen—made from the woven fibers of the flax plant—was used for undergarments, as it was less scratchy against the skin than wool was. Interestingly, it seems that having new undergarments was not necessarily considered a good or desirable thing, which makes a kind of sense if you think about it. Just as items like flannel sheets get softer over time and with each use and washing—so, too, did linen undergarments become gentler to the skin over time. But underwear in the way that we think of it today did not really exist in the medieval period.

Depending on the weather and time of year, over this whole outfit something called a surcoat might be worn. This was similar in its basic shape and style to the tunic, but the surcoat tended to be sleeveless, so that the sleeves of the tunic showed through. If it was really cold—and you were noble or wealthy enough—a heavy outer garment known as a mantle and sometimes made from, or trimmed with, fur might be worn.

The other universal element of clothing for people in the medieval world was some sort of head covering. This might range from a simple cap to an elaborate woman's headdress that made use of wire or other supports to maintain its shape. The wearing of something on one's head was practical in that it kept one's hair out of one's eyes and face, and it provided warmth—as humans tend to lose as much as 30 percent of their body heat from their heads. It also meant that most medieval people did not have to worry about that modern issue of concern—the bad hair day. Most peasant men—and some women—for much of the period wore a head covering known as a capuchon, which was more like a hood than a hat or cap, and which covered essentially all of the person's head—with the portion around the neck serving a function similar to a scarf. In the earlier part of the period, most women wore head coverings known as wimples that concealed the head and neck, leaving the face bare—these pieces of clothing are very similar to the kinds of headdress many people envision when they think of the wardrobe of a Catholic nun today.

After the 13th century, as we move into the late medieval period, women's headdresses became more and more elaborate, as the description of the Wife of Bath's headgear, which we mentioned at the beginning of this lecture, would seem to suggest. In some cases, wire supports were used to hold up what became larger and more elaborate confections of cloth. One style of draped headgear was often referred to as the butterfly veil, as wires worn on the head made the cloth take the form of what looked like butterfly wings. Perhaps the most dramatic and memorable head covering from the medieval world was something called a hennin, which was a tall, cone-shaped hat that occasionally had some gauzy fabric attached to it.

By the end of the medieval period, the wardrobe of medieval men and women had become a little more developed and elaborate. As undergarments, men wore a shirt, or chemise, and hose (which were also called chausses), and these hose were somewhat between trousers and tights to our modern way of thinking. Over his shirt, the medieval man would usually wear a piece of clothing called a doublet, and over this a sort of gown or robe. In cold weather, he might add a cloak or cape. Over time, the doublets got shorter and the hose longer; the form-fitting nature of this kind of outfit was considered somewhat scandalous by many—especially those who were members of the clergy—and we find many religious leaders castigating those who wore such clothing. Indeed, the court of William II of England—who was also sometimes called William Rufus because he had red hair, and *rufus* is a Latin word meaning "red"—his court regularly was regarded as a den of sin, lustfulness, and iniquity. Scholars and critics, such as the 11th-century cleric Peter Damian, critiqued the practices of William II's court—calling particular attention to the scandalous dress many members of the court were reported as wearing.

By the end of the Middle Ages, a woman also wore hose—as the example of the Wife of Bath again confirms. Chaucer tells us that "Hir hosen weren of fyn scarlet reed/Ful streite yteyd, and shoes ful moyste and newe," or in other words, that "She is wearing bright red hose that are tied up tight." We have to remember that the Middle Ages is an age before elastic waistbands, so both men and women who wore hose would usually keep them up by tying them around their waists. Although Chaucer does not describe this next part of female dress, the Wife most likely had on some sort of undergarment, which would be called a smock or chemise. Over this she might wear a kirtle, and then on top of this a gown or robe. In cold weather she, too, like a medieval man would add another layer—such as a mantle, or *manteau*. Both men and women usually wore a belt of some kind, from which might be hung keys or pouches for holding money—or perhaps tools important to one's occupation.

The greatest difference and distinction in medieval fashion is not necessarily to be found when comparing time periods within the Middle Ages, but rather by comparing the fashions of the various classes at any one time. Without a doubt, peasant clothing was the simplest and most practical, as its wearers were usually engaged in manual labor. Manuscript illuminations depicting peasants laboring in the fields often show them barefoot, with the long ends of their robes tucked up and tied around their waists for ease of movement. When not working in the fields, peasants—and nobles alike—might wear shoes. As is the case today, some shoes could be quite practical, and some could be ridiculously unpractical. The majority of medieval people wore simple shoes made of leather that fitted closely to the foot, somewhat resembling slippers. Those people who rode horses regularly sometimes wore boots known as buskins—which were about thigh-high, and which fastened to one's outer garments by means of buckles or similar types of closures. Whether slipper-shoes or boots, footwear was most often made of leather that provided little protection against the elements, particularly muddy streets. In order to protect their feet and their shoes, medieval people might strap wooden platforms—known as pattens—on over their shoes to avoid the mud and the damp. The pattens were kind of like a small wooden platform that fastened over regular shoes, elevating people a bit so that they could navigate muddy thoroughfares more easily.

Although almost everyone wore leather shoes, the quality of the leather tended to vary by social class. Particularly supple leather—known as Cordovan because of its association with Cordoba, Spain—was prized as especially comfortable footwear. You could be sure that most nobles would not wear their Cordovan shoes outside in inclement weather, even with pattens on. Even more limiting in terms of moving about the medieval world were extremely long, pointed-toe shoes known as *poulaines* or *crakows*, which were just briefly in fashion as men's footwear in the 15th century. I say briefly because it was not too long before even those nobles who liked the message sent by shoes that were ridiculously impractical realized that they were going to look like idiots if they kept tripping over their own feet, or had to walk sideways in order to mount a staircase.

It is among the noble classes that we tend to see the greatest variety, and fashion for the sake of fashion—i.e., clothing that is impractical and thus announces that the wearer is wealthy. One of the places where this distinction often was emphatically made was in the area of sleeves. A safe rule of thumb: the bigger the sleeves, the wealthier the person who wore them. Some manuscript images depict medieval people clothed in outfits that have enormous sleeves. In more than a few cases, we have images that show servants holding back the sleeves in order to allow the wearer of the garment to wash his or her hands. Reaching across the table for the salt meant that nobles who wore such garments would usually need to use one hand to hold back the sleeve of the arm that was reaching for the salt cellar or a particular morsel of food in order to keep from dragging one's clothing through one's dinner. A particular garment known as the houppelande and which was in fashion only relatively briefly—from about the middle of the 14th to the middle of the 15th century—had as its defining characteristic enormous sleeves and was worn by both men and women. With a closure in the front, on women it was always worn down to the ankle, while some men wore houppelandes that were half-length.

If excessively large sleeves could signal wealth and status, so could their opposite. For example, some women's fashions included dresses with tightly fitting sleeves that would need to be sewn on to the gown each morning—a task requiring the help of a maidservant. In other instances, the sleeves might have lacings that, when done up, kept them close to the arm—and thus, out of the way. Again, lacings on the sleeves, while theoretically manageable by a single individual, could most easily be done up if one had maidservants to assist one. The idea of certain styles of close-fitting sleeves as a marker of nobility or wealth gets support from Sir Thomas Malory's *Morte d'Arthur*—the 15th-century retelling of the legend of King Arthur—which we've already discussed at some length. In one scene in the text, a tournament is held, and several noble and beautiful ladies turn out to watch. Among them is a young woman who is identified only as the Maiden with the Small Sleeves. Her title suggests both that tightly fitted sleeves were rare and that they could be markers of wealth and class.

Even more than peasant women, women of the upper classes wore elaborate headdresses, many of them constructed out of frameworks of wood or wire and several pounds of cloth—making them look like ships under full sail. By far the greatest indicator of nobility was the use of jewels and fur as clothing adornments. As we saw in our lecture on heraldry, or the science of coats of arms, furs were particularly associated with the nobility in that they could be represented as one of the layers on a coat of arms. One of the furs most commonly used was ermine, which comes from the winter coat of an animal known as the stoat while it is still an adolescent. Ermine is a white fur with distinct black markings. Miniver, an all white fur, comes from the same animal but at a different time in its lifecycle. Vair was the fur of the European squirrel and was distinguished by a shield-shaped white belly that was encircled by gray. In addition to these three furs that were represented in heraldic devices, others—such as marten, which was a dark fur that came from a type of weasel—also became highly prized.

While nobles also wore garments made of wool and linen for the most part, in addition to the luxury of furs there were a variety of silks that, for most of the medieval period, were only affordable to the upper classes. There were no silkworms in Europe at this time, so any silk fabrics had to come from long distances. Usually they were purchased by Italian merchants who did business in the cosmopolitan city of Constantinople—which, as we've previously discussed, was at a trading crossroads in terms of both maritime and overland trade. Here the most exotic goods from all over the known world could be bought and sold. As I said, it was mostly Italian merchants who originally brought silks back to the European West. The journey they had traveled necessarily made them expensive—and thus, they became markers of noble and wealthy status. After a time, silk began to be produced in Italy and in Spain. Cotton, originally introduced into Muslim Spain, Al-Andalus, by the Arab populations there who had imported it from India, eventually it was manufactured in France, Italy, and the Netherlands.

As the merchant class grew in wealth and power in the High and late Middle Ages, many of its members sought to imitate the style and dress of the noble classes. The fact that the Wife of Bath is described as wearing a headdress, weighing more than 10 pounds, points once again to the ways in which members of the merchant class were trying to imitate the clothing and behaviors of members of the nobility. This situation led to the passage of laws known as sumptuary laws, which restricted certain types of clothing and accessories to members of certain classes.

Originally, sumptuary laws were most likely intended to identify people on the fringes of mainstream medieval society—Jews, Muslims, lepers. Efforts were made to make lepers wear distinctive clothing—usually long, fastened capes. But more effective as a means of distinction was the law that lepers, as they moved from place to place in their communities or throughout the medieval world, needed to constantly be shaking a rattle or working a wooden clapper of some kind, so that the noise would alert people at some distance of the menace that was coming their way. The Fourth Lateran Council of 1215, which we've already talked about at length in an earlier lecture, also ruled that Muslims and Jews had to wear some kind of distinctive marking on their clothes so that they could be easily distinguished from the rest of the population. The reasoning behind this, as stated in the specific Lateran canon in which this edict was issued, was that it had become difficult to tell the difference between Christians, Muslims, and Jews, and there was concern that there might be "accidental" intermarriage between the groups— something that was thought to be quite perilous for the immortal soul of any Christian who engaged in such a union.

Sumptuary laws that were more concerned with divisions between classes than between the sick and the healthy, or between members of particular religious faiths, really came into being in the late Middle Ages when, as I've suggested already, the noble classes were really starting to feel the bourgeoisie breathing down their necks. For example, in 1336, King Edward III of England issued a decree that stated that any one below the rank of gentleman or knight—and these are the lowest rungs on the ladder of nobility—caught wearing footwear that had spikes or points more than two inches long had to pay a fine of 40 pence. In 1337, another law was passed—restricting the wearing of certain kinds and amounts of fur to certain social groups. Edward III wasn't done, however, and in 1363 even more comprehensive sumptuary laws were passed. Among their various provisions, these laws restricted the wearing of the most luxurious of fabrics and colors—namely gold and purple silk—to members of the royal family. These laws similarly restricted the wearing of certain kinds of fur to specific ranks within the nobility— for example, the wife or daughter of a knight was expressly forbidden to wear sable. The wearing of fur of any kind was denied to the members of a knight's family unless that knight's income exceeded 200 marks a year. The wives and daughters of craftsmen were not allowed to wear veils of silk, and those women in the families of men who fell into the general category of laborers were forbidden from wearing girdles that were decorated with gold or silver.

A quick word about girdles—in the Middle Ages, the term "girdle" does not refer to what most modern people think of as what we might call a foundation garment. A girdle was more like a decorative sash worn around the waist. Perhaps the most famous piece of clothing from the Middle Ages is the green girdle that King Arthur's nephew, Sir Gawain, accepts as a gift from a sly noblewoman in the literary masterpiece known as *Sir Gawain and the Green Knight*. The fact that Gawain and the other Knights of the Round Table adopt this piece of clothing as part of their distinctive noble uniform at the end of the tale emphasizes that this is not a girdle in the way we might conceive of it today.

It wasn't just laborers and craftsmen whose dress was regulated. Even servants—whom we might not think would have the money to buy clothes that suggested a higher rank than they possessed—had restrictions placed on them. For example, women of the servant class were not allowed to wear veils that had a value of more than 12 pence. In many places, prostitutes were also required to wear special clothing—often a style of headdress or cloak that would identify the occupation that they plied.

Approximately 100 years or so after Edward III first issued restrictions on dress in England, Duke Amadeus VIII of Savoy, which is in modern-day France, issued the so-called *Statutes of Savoy* that attempted to regulate fashion and styles of dress. In addition to being duke of Savoy, Amadeus VIII also has the distinction of being the last antipope elected, in sort of a hangover from the papal schism—which we discussed in an earlier lecture. Amadeus VIII assumed the papacy as Pope Felix V in 1439, but relinquished his position and acknowledged the pope in Rome at this time, Nicholas V, as the true pope—for which gracious act he was not excommunicated, but was instead allowed to become a cardinal.

In any event, before his foray into religion, Duke Amadeus issued the most comprehensive set of sumptuary laws the medieval world had ever seen. Duke Amadeus moved far beyond the basic division of medieval society into three groups—the nobles, the clergy, and "the everyone else." Depending on how you count, Duke Amadeus has divided his society into almost 40 distinct tiers. Among the myriad rules and regulations the duke laid out was the injunction forbidding members of the peasant class to wear articles of clothing that were made of two different fabrics. In the *Statutes of Savoy*, the quality, color, cut, and cost of the clothing worn by members of various social ranks was strictly regulated. Everyone from dukes to knights to gentlemen to lawyers to artisans, craftspeople, and agricultural workers were told exactly what they could and could not wear. Everything from style of headdress to quality of footwear was dictated.

The *Statutes of Savoy* are in some way a last gasp uttered by the three-estates model, and in its strictures we can see an attempt to hang on to class divisions in a society that had by and large already given up such distinctions as impractical and unworkable. Although sumptuary laws would continue to be issued by rulers of various nations well into the early modern period, the fact that there was a perceived need to issue them at all during the Middle Ages points to the beginnings of the transformation of the medieval world into something new.

So as we can see, medieval people were no less susceptible to trends and fads that seemed to border on the ridiculous than modern people are. We can see also how clothes then and clothes today could function as a sort of status symbol—so much so that those at the top of the social order wanted to prevent people lower down in the hierarchy from appearing to be higher-ranking individuals than they actually were.

As the last two lectures have demonstrated, medieval people engaged in all sorts of leisure activities, pursuits, and interests that went beyond the mere effort to survive. Although it is certainly true that in most respects life in the medieval world was more difficult than it is in the modern one, that doesn't mean that people in the Middle Ages were all a grim, humorless lot—focused only on the basic necessities of life, as has so often been the popular misconception. Medieval people liked games, and play, and showing off their wealth and status just as much as people today do.

But in our next lecture, we're going to turn away from what we might think of as the extras of life in the Middle Ages and focus on a more serious topic: medicine. Some well-known medical treatments in the medieval period have long had a reputation as often causing more harm than good—the practice of bloodletting, for example. But modern science has proven that some treatments and cures from the Middle Ages are, in fact, efficacious. Evidence suggests that healers and physicians in the medieval period were, in many cases, quite knowledgeable when it came to treating certain conditions and diseases. In our next lecture, we will explore medieval medical theory, the development of a curriculum at the first medical schools in the medieval world, and the specific practices that a patient in the Middle Ages might experience as part of a treatment or cure.

Medieval Medicine
Lecture 28

Most of the medical advances made in the European West during the Middle Ages came from the discovery or translation of Greek or Arabic medical texts. ... As the 16th century, the three great authorities of medieval medicine are represented as two Greeks—Hippocrates and Galen—and a practitioner from the Muslim world—a man called Ibn Sina, or Avicenna.

To the modern individual, medieval medicine might seem an odd mix of superstition, folk remedies, astrology, and religious beliefs. Much medical practice in the Middle Ages was based on the theory of the four humors of the body. These humors—blood, yellow bile, black bile, and phlegm—were thought to be produced by various organs, and the theory was that they needed to be in balance to ensure good health. Although many medieval folk remedies—such as the use of leeches—have been proven by modern medicine to have some beneficial effects, other medieval practices—such as bloodletting—were likely to do more harm than good.

The medieval West lagged behind Byzantium and the Muslim world when it came to the practice of medicine, and many of the advances in the medieval world came in the 11th century with the foundation of educational institutions devoted to the study of medicine, particularly in Italy, as well as the translation Greek and Arabic medical texts, such as that by the Islamic scholar Avicenna, into Latin or Western medieval vernacular languages.

The three most important experts on medicine in the Middle Ages were Avicenna and the ancient Greek scholars Hippocrates and Galen. At its core, the practice of medicine in the medieval world was Galenic—that is, based on the theories of Galen. At the center of Galenic theory was the idea of balancing the four humors—blood, phlegm, black bile, and yellow bile. The body also needed to be in balance in terms of heat, cold, moisture, and dryness. Galenic theory held that there were two critical elements in diagnosing an illness: the examination of urine and the checking of the pulse.

In the early Middle Ages, there was very little in the way of formal medical training in Western Europe; most medical knowledge was passed down orally. We start to see a shift in medical training and education in the 10th century. An interest in studying the theory and practice of medicine in a structured setting sprang up in the Mediterranean basin, particularly in the Italian towns of Salerno and Bologna. It is not surprising that this occurred first in the Italian city-states, as many of these had longstanding trading relationships with the Byzantine and Muslim worlds and were thus exposed to their medical texts and practices. Through Italian medical institutions, the medieval world first became aware of the theories of the brilliant Islamic scholar Avicenna, who based his theories on Galenic medicine and produced a compendium of all medical and pharmacological information available at that time.

From Salerno came the most important group of medical texts, known as the *Articella*, which would serve as the core of any medieval medical education from the 12th to the 16th centuries.

In the early part of the High Middle Ages, a Salernitan medical education—focused on practical matters of diagnosis and healing—was the best available. From Salerno came the most important group of medical texts, known as the *Articella*, which would serve as the core of any medieval medical education from the 12th to the 16th centuries. Salerno was unusual in its liberality; both men and women were allowed to study there, as were various non-Christians, including Jews and Muslims. Nowhere else were such freedoms allowed to minority groups. After the 12th century, the curriculum at Salerno became increasingly focused on theorizing medicine and the natural world, so that those who studied there not only referred to themselves as *medici*, or healers, but also as *physici*, or scholars.

Although medieval Western medicine generally lagged behind Byzantine and Muslim medicine, there was one area where physicians in the medieval European world made significant contributions and advances: surgery. Muslim texts had long shied away from the practical study of surgical procedures. Thus, when the schools at Salerno and Bologna began to include dissection and surgical procedures in their curriculum, Western medicine made some important advances. Prior to the 13th century, a community's barber was frequently also its surgeon, simply because he had the requisite tools on hand. By the 13th century, however, surgery had become a legitimate field of medical study.

In the late Middle Ages, medical training became more formalized and structured. The real explosion of medical advancements, however, came in the 16th century, during the early modern period. Many of these later advances were due to the discovery of hitherto unknown medical texts and the ability to quickly make such information available via the printing press. The innovation and advances in medicine in the early modern period were largely dependent on two medieval inventions: the university system, which formalized the study of medicine, and the printing press, which first came into use in the medieval world in the early 15th century. ∎

Suggested Reading

Glick, Livesey, and Wallis, *Medieval Science, Technology, and Medicine*.

Grant, *The Foundations of Modern Science in the Middle Ages*.

Questions to Consider

1. How did the theory and practice of medieval medicine demonstrate continuity with the world of classical antiquity? How did it differ from classical ideas about science and healing?

2. Why was medieval Italy so forward thinking in terms of those it admitted—women, Jews, and so forth—to the study and practice of medicine in its university system?

Medieval Medicine
Lecture 28—Transcript

Welcome back. In our last lecture, we discussed conventions of medieval fashion—from the basic necessities in terms of clothing to the many impractical trends and fads that were popular at various times. Today, we're going to move from the frivolous to the deadly serious and talk about matters of life and death—specifically, the ways in which medical practices in the Middle Ages worked to cure the sick, ease the suffering of those in pain, and help preserve the health of everyone else.

To the modern individual, the phrase "medieval medicine," might seem to be a contradiction in terms, as much medical practice in the medieval world relied at least in part—or sometimes quite heavily—on superstition, astrology, and prayers to individual saints for intercession and healing. Some widespread practices—such as bloodletting—certainly often did more harm than good. Others, however, such as the application of leeches on affected body parts, have been proven by modern science to be efficacious in treating certain conditions. Certainly many folk remedies produced positive results, and knowledge of these remedies was surely passed down—usually orally—from generation to generation.

But it cannot be denied that in the Middle Ages, Europe lagged far behind the Byzantine and Muslim worlds when it came to medical theory, training, and practice. In part, this is because the Middle East and the former eastern half of the Roman Empire had greater access to—and a continuous relationship with—medical texts from ancient Greece, the source and origin of medical study in the medieval world. Indeed, most of the medical advances made in the European West during the Middle Ages came from the discovery or translation of Greek or Arabic medical texts—rather than what we might call any innovation of Western medical practitioners.

It is significant that as late as the 16th century, the three great authorities of medieval medicine are represented as two Greeks—Hippocrates and Galen—and a practitioner from the Muslim world—a man called Ibn Sina, or Avicenna. This influence has been profound, as medical professionals to this day take what is called the Hippocratic Oath, named after Hippocrates—a

Greek physician who lived sometime around the 5ᵗʰ and 4ᵗʰ centuries B.C. Hippocrates has been credited with instituting a form of medical practice that was relatively free from superstition, and which focused on things such as diet and environment in treating patients. As famous as Hippocrates was as a medical practitioner, we have no texts that seem to have been written by him—although there are later texts that claim to include much of his philosophy and theory concerning medicine.

While Hippocrates loomed large in the minds of those who practiced medicine in the medieval world, this ancient Greek physician was made accessible to the medieval European West through the work of Galen—another Greek physician who lived in the 2ⁿᵈ century A.D. Galen was a prolific writer, and using Hippocratic theory as a foundation, Galen produced an immense body of medical literature covering everything from anatomy to pharmacology to physiology to medical ethics. It would not be an exaggeration to say that at its root, all medical theory and practice in the medieval world was Galenic in nature. Thus, we need to take a moment to explore exactly what this medical theory consisted of.

At the center of Galenic theory is the idea of the four humors. Galen and those who followed him held that the body would be healthy as long as it maintained a balance between heat, cold, dryness, and moisture. Diet was important here, as it was believed that all foods were made up of at least one of the four elements of fire, air, earth, and water—and after they were consumed, they were transformed into one of the four humors: blood, phlegm, black bile, and yellow bile. Medieval diagnosis might take into consideration the complexion of the patient, meaning an attempt to determine how his or her humors were balanced. Thus, someone with an excess of blood might be described as sanguine, and bloodletting would be prescribed in order to try and bring the humors back into balance. Care had to be taken as to where the bloodletting incision should be made, and many medical texts offer complex diagrams as to where an incision for bloodletting should be made—dependent upon the particulars of the patient's illness. Most of the bloodletting was very often harmless—especially if applied to healthy bodies. But in many cases, it almost certainly did more harm than good.

A person who had an excess of yellow bile, which was believed to be produced by the liver and held in the gall bladder, might be referred to as choleric—as having an excess of choler, which is another term for yellow bile. Black bile was also believed to be produced by the liver, but it was held in the spleen, according to medieval medical theory. A person with an excess of black bile was believed to tend toward melancholy behavior and feelings. "Phlegm" seems to be a catchall term for any whitish or colorless bodily secretion, with the exception of breast milk and semen—both of which were believed to be blood transformed. Bloodletting was one way to try and regulate the humors, but there were others. Many medical texts—including one of the most famous, that known as the *Secretum Secretorum*—are full of recipes for laxatives and emetives, suggesting again the interest in purging the body of excess humors.

If Galenic medical theory was founded on the idea of the four humors, then Galenic diagnosis and practice had as its most important elements two things—the checking of the pulse, and the examination of urine. For medieval medical practitioners by far the most important tool was the urine glass, the most ubiquitous symbol of the medieval doctor. In the version of Chaucer's *Canterbury Tales* found in that most beautiful manuscript known as the *Ellesmere Chaucer*, the pilgrim character of the physician is depicted as riding off to Canterbury with his urine glass plainly visible. Some medieval medical texts suggest that there were 20 different gradations of urine color, and they offered an explanation as to what kinds of afflictions might cause certain changes in color—and what treatment might then be called for.

One common treatment, especially in the earlier medieval period, was something known as cautery. To think of it in modern terms, cautery is essentially a combination of acupressure and hot stone massage—very hot stone massage that occasionally might leave a burn mark on the patient's skin. A hot iron would be placed on a particular part of the body in an attempt to regulate the humors by focusing on that specific body part. Many medical texts—several from the 9th century—offer detailed anatomical drawings depicting the appropriate points at which a hot iron should be applied to the body for a variety of ailments. Another medieval medical practice thought to operate along the same lines—and which has come back into vogue in modern times—is the practice of cupping, where a small heated cup is placed on a location on the body. A vacuum is created, and this supposedly draws excess humors to the surface and away from the internal organs they might be affecting negatively.

In the early Middle Ages in Western Europe there was very little in the way of formal medical training. Cures, treatments, and recipes for medicinal compounds were usually handed down by word of mouth, and those who treated the sick or the injured were referred to as healers—or sometimes the term "leech" was used, as the leech was one of the most important treatments the medieval healer had at his or her command. This word was sometimes used to indicate the person who employed the humble leech—and I should add here that in this case, at least, medieval people knew what they were about, as modern science and medicine continue to use leeches to this day in certain situations. While little of this early medical knowledge was written down, we do have a fascinating medical text from 9th-century England that provides a tantalizing window onto early medieval practices. This manuscript, which has come to be called *Bald's Leechbook*, is divided into two sections. The first deals with external maladies—broken bones and the like—while the second deals with internal medical issues. The text seems to include both some medical knowledge handed down from antiquity, as well as what we would call folk remedies. *Bald's* text also contains the earliest known reference to plastic surgery in the medieval world in a section that discusses treatment for a harelip.

In the 10th century, as we head into the High Middle Ages, we start to see a shift in the medieval world in terms of attitudes toward studying medicine. An interest in the theory and practice of medicine, as well as the training of physicians and healers, sprang up in the Mediterranean basin—most notably in Italy in Salerno and Bologna, where the greatest institutions of medical learning the medieval Western world had ever known came into being. It is not terribly surprising that this should happen in Italy. The various Italian city-states had always been active in trading, and there was a serious amount of cultural exchange between this part of Europe, the former eastern half of the Roman Empire, and the Muslim world. Most significantly, Arabic medical texts found their way to Italy.

Perhaps the most important of these was written by a man I've already mentioned: Abu Ali al-Husayan ibn Abd Allah ibn Sina—known to the West as Avicenna. Considered by many the most important figure in the fields of philosophy, science, and medicine in the Muslim world, he was a 10th-century Persian who, by all accounts, was a genius—memorizing the Koran by age 10 and curing the ruler Nuh ibn Mansur of an illness while he was still a teenager.

Over the course of his career, Avicenna wrote over 400 works; around half of them still survive today. He draws heavily on Galen, but goes far beyond Galen's theory of the humors to produce a compendium of virtually all medical and pharmacological information available at that time. When his work was translated out of Arabic in the 12th century, it only helped increase the prestige and excellence of the medical curriculum at universities in Salerno, Bologna, and Montpellier.

It is at Salerno that the story of medieval medicine in the West really begins. Salerno to this day is referred to as the *Civitas Hippocratica* ("the Hippocratic state") indicating its pride in a long tradition of the instruction and practice of medicine. Although as the Middle Ages moved toward their close, Salerno would become somewhat overshadowed by the medical schools of Bologna, Montpellier, and Paris—starting in the 10th century, it became the most important medical center in all of the medieval world. In the early Middle Ages, what you have is medical practitioners and students wishing to learn this art, and it was often considered an art, rather than a science. These people came together rather informally to share knowledge and to be instructed. This, incidentally—as we've already mentioned—is how all medieval universities effectively got their start. A group of scholars, generally known as masters, tended to gather in one place: Paris, or Oxford—or in this case, Salerno. These established scholars might debate with one another and share information, and this in turn attracted students who wished to learn from these masters. Eventually, this situation became regularized and ritualized, and out of it evolved the university as we know it today.

In terms of medical knowledge, we call the period prior to the 12th century early Salerno, and this period is notable for its emphasis on practical function and healing. The 12th century marks the start of the period known as High Salerno, and it is in this period that most of the very important medical texts that would come to be the foundation of medieval medical instruction would come to be compiled. The most important of these texts, the core of a medieval medical education, were referred to as the *Articella*. The name *Articella*—meaning "Little Art"—was given to a group of Greek and Arabic texts that were the foundation of all medical learning from the 12th to the 16th centuries. The *Articella* contained works by famous medical authorities such as Johannitius, Hippocrates, and Galen, among others. Later, commentaries on these texts by some of the greatest medical masters—such as Bartholomaeus of Salerno in the 12th century—also become an important part of the *Articella*, as did the newly translated works of Avicenna, and the commentaries on Avicenna and Galen by another prominent Arabic scholar, Ibn Rushd—known as Averroes, who was born in Cordova in what is today Spain in the 12th century. Remember that Spain was Muslim for much of the medieval period, and thus served as an important contact point for books and knowledge coming from the Islamic world into Europe.

For a time, Salerno was the most famous and prestigious medical institute in the medieval world, drawing would-be students from all over Europe. There is a story told by Orderic Vitalis, a Norman historian of the 12th century. He relates how a monk went to Salerno thinking himself a highly educated man, wishing to increase his already ample store of knowledge and learning. When he arrived, however, he found that he knew less about medical matters than a woman who was also studying at Salerno, and he was ashamed to find that he could be bested in a matter of intellect and education by any number of women who were pursuing studies at Salerno. The interesting thing about this story is that it demonstrates that women were able to attend classes and were granted medical degrees from the university. People of different faiths—including Jews and Muslims—also studied here, although they were not allowed to hold positions as masters of the university.

It is out of Salerno in the 12th century that three remarkable texts dealing with women's medical issues come. What's more, they are believed—very firmly in the case of at least one of them—to have been authored by a woman named either Trota or Trotula. These three texts are now usually grouped together under the name *Trotula*. Based on older texts, many of which were written in Arabic, the *Trotula* includes many short selections on medical issues particularly affecting women. What's really remarkable about the *Trotula*, however, is the wealth of practical medical experience it demonstrates, as well as the fact that it includes some of the most detailed anatomical drawings of women that had existed up to that point in the medieval medical tradition. Although it has often been the stereotype that women's medical issues were attended to by women—usually midwives—and that women medical practitioners did not treat men, evidence from the period suggests this is not the case. Yes, midwives—those who attended a birth—were almost always women, but as we move into the later Middle Ages we see an explosion of texts on gynecology authored by men—focusing on everything from the difficulties of staying chaste to how best to expel a dead fetus and other similar issues for which practical information was a must. Women were much more than just midwives, despite the common perception to the contrary. They were very often healers in their own rights and also served the medical profession as apothecaries—and sometimes even surgeons.

After the 12th century, Salernitan doctors became more and more interested in medical theory, as distinct from medical practice, indicating an increasing desire to understand the reason behind many medical symptoms—the idea being that this understanding would help, ultimately, in the treating of various ailments. Scholars at Salerno in the later Middle Ages began to refer to themselves not just as *medici*, as "healers," but as *medici et phisici*— "healers and scholars of the natural world"—and it is from that word *phisici* that we get our modern word "physician." Although the medical curriculum at Salerno and the other great universities of the medieval world was based heavily on the knowledge contained in texts from Classical and from the Muslim world, there was one area in which medieval European physicians and scholars were able to make some breakthroughs—and this, notably, was in the areas of dissection and surgery. Muslim texts had shied away from using dissection, basing discussions of anatomy, etc., on earlier Classical works, or on evidence from the animal world—so when dissection and its attendant field of study, autopsy, became part of the curriculum at Salerno and Bologna, some important advances were made.

Prior to this, surgeons were viewed less as healers or philosophers of medicine and viewed more as one might view a craftsman—such as a blacksmith. Very often, the local surgeon was also the local barber, due to the simple fact that he would have the right tools for bloodletting and amputation. But as we move through the 13th century, surgery comes to be thought of as a legitimate medical field—and one that should be practiced by trained surgeons, rather than the local barber.

The skills necessary for surgery were learned in part through the study of dissection. Dissection of animals was the most common form practiced—then students moved on to cadavers, usually of criminals. The dissection of human bodies starts to occur with some regularity in the medieval world at the end of the 13th century and is a hugely important occurrence, as dissection had not been regularly practiced since the Hellenistic period. This probably happened in part because of the widespread proliferation of Galenic texts—many of which made reference to dissection as the means by which the information conveyed had been studied and tested. In 1297, Pope Boniface issued a decree called *Detestande feritatis*, which forbade dismembering and boiling down a corpse in order to make for easy transport. Although he did not explicitly mention dissection for medical purposes, the effect of his decree could be felt among the medical community. There's nothing necessarily inherently un- Christian about dissection. Indeed, the evisceration and embalming of bodies of important figures like kings, bishops, etc., was quite common—especially if they were going to lie in state after their deaths. But it was not really until the late 14th and 15th centuries that the practice of dissection spread out from the Mediterranean basin. In order to get cadavers, one usually had to rely on hanged criminals, and the dissections themselves were only able to be performed in a limited time period. For example, in Padua no dissections were allowed after February, as there was no means to preserve a corpse once the weather turned warm.

For all the emphasis on logic and rationality that we find at medieval medical institutions, we must remember that much of medieval medicine might strike us as irrational and superstitious—especially when we look at the practical, rather than theoretical, application of medical principles. When a physician prescribed a medication was often as important as what he prescribed, as the alignment of the planets and stars was considered to play a role in how effective a particular treatment might be. Never underestimate the significance of magic in medieval medicine. Many recipes for medicines also included charms that should be said or other incantations that were to help with the process of aiding the ailing patient. Very often, there was a tendency to see some afflictions or ailments as being a mark of God's anger. Frequently, medical treatment would call for the practical application of a medicine or treatment, while also demanding a prayer be made to a particular saint. For example, the patron saint for sufferers of hemorrhoids was Saint Fiacre, a 7[th]century Irishman. People suffering from headaches had a few saints to pray to, including Saint Ubald and Saint Teresa of Avila. A medieval doctor might also prescribe a visit to a saint's shrine (as we discussed in our lecture on pilgrimage) for healing.

Although university learning became important, medical knowledge and skills might be acquired in a variety of ways, including apprenticeship (either formal or informal), personal experience, and general knowledge of folklore—the kind of superstitious beliefs that held that burying a potato at the full moon will help one get rid of warts. With recent documentation of how the placebo effect works, who's to say that in some instances these cures didn't function? For some levels of training, Latin literacy was a necessity; for others, vernacular literacy would suffice; and for many, certainly, no literacy at all would be necessary—pure and simple observation, experience, and memorization were all that were really required to make a good healer.

As we move toward the end of the Middle Ages, medical training becomes more formalized and institutionalized, although there were some variations from university to university. In Montpellier in the 13th century, a bachelor of medicine degree could be attained after three and a half years of study plus six months of practical experience treating patients. In the 14th century, a papal bull decreed that the course of study should be six years, with an eight-month practicum. In Bologna, medical students in the 15th century needed to spend three years each on the study of philosophy and astronomy/astrology—they're essentially the same thing in the medieval world—and then four years on the theoretical study of medicine plus another four of practical experience.

There may be a little confusion in terminology here. "Master" officially meant a university graduate or instructor scholar in any subject, but could also be a term of respect. "Doctor" could be used to describe any university graduate, not just in medicine. This terminology remains today. For example, my highest degree is the Ph.D., which stands for the Latin form of the words "Doctor of Philosophy," but my degree is actually in medieval studies—so I am technically a Doctor of Medieval Studies. A law degree, often referred to as a J.D., simply means "Doctor of Jurisprudence," or someone who has mastered the study of law. The term used to denote someone who practiced healing varied from place to place. In its Latin form, *medicus* was used. *Physicus* signaled someone who had medical education but was more inclined toward the study of natural philosophy. Although members of the clergy quite often practiced healing and surgery—after all, monasteries were some of the most important repositories of medical knowledge—after the 13th century, the range of their abilities became somewhat limited, especially after the decree of the Fourth Lateran Council in 1215 that forbade clergy to practice surgery or cautery, although a few practitioners did get papal dispensations.

In the 16th century, in what many scholars refer to as the early modern period, those who were interested in medicine wanted to get back to the original Greeks and not rely on translations into Latin or out of Arabic. The 16th century also saw a remarkable series of medical advances—especially in surgery, which ironically came from the enlarged scale of warfare in the period. Military conflicts involved greater numbers of warriors who might be injured in novel ways. Battlefield training provided a wealth of knowledge and practical experience for medical professionals—especially surgeons.

Some scholars have seen medical advances that occurred in 16th century Europe as signaling a break with the past—as emphasizing the superiority of the early modern period over the medieval. It is true that there was explosive growth, especially in the areas of anatomical, botanical, and medicinal research—in part due to the discovery of Greek texts unknown to the medieval world, which contained important information. With the widespread use of the printing press and paper, medical information and discoveries could be disseminated quickly and to a great many people. But while some have seen a break, advances in early modern medicine are part of a transformation that owes much to the development of the university system in the medieval world, a process that was beginning as early as the 12th century.

Although many medieval medical treatments arguably did more harm than good, some have been proven by modern medicine to be at least somewhat efficacious in treating certain diseases and afflictions. There was one major medical disaster that swept through the medieval world, however, against which nothing seemed to have any preventive or curative effect. This was the outbreak of plague in the 14th century that later generations would refer to as the Black Death. Perhaps no single event would have a greater impact on the entire social fabric of the medieval world, and it is to this subject that we turn in our next lecture.

The Black Death and its Effects
Lecture 29

"Because of the growing strength of this disease it has come to pass that, for fear of infection, no doctor will visit the sick … nor will the father visit the son, the mother the daughter, the brother the brother, the son the father, the friend the friend, the acquaintance the acquaintance, nor anyone a blood relation—unless, that is, they wished to die suddenly along with them, or follow them at once."

—Louis Helygen, a medieval witness to the Black Death

As the medieval world headed into the 14th century, a land crunch began due to unprecedented population growth. This land crunch, combined with the climactic changes called the Little Ice Age, contributed to a famine in 1315 that killed up to 10 percent of the population in certain areas. Those who survived were usually in less than robust health. Some scholars feel that overcrowding, especially in cities, in combination with food shortages and the resulting general ill health, gave the plague that swept through the medieval world in the 14th century a particularly profound impact. This event was never actually called the Black Death during the medieval period. Those who lived through it tended to refer to it as blue sickness (because of the bluish-colored bruises some victims developed) or the great mortality.

Although there is some disagreement, most scholars think the cause of the Black Death was an outbreak of bubonic plague. Caused by the *Yersinia pestis* bacterium, which is generally carried by fleas on rats, bubonic plague traveled to the medieval world from Asia along trade routes. Ecological changes in Asia during the 14th century drove rodents out of their natural habitats and into closer proximity with humans, so plague could cross over into the human population. Plague was active in central Asia in the 1330s, and one of its worst aspects was that people knew it was coming; although they didn't understand the method of transmission, sources indicate that people west of an outbreak recognized it was heading their way.

There were three types of plague: bubonic, septicemic, and pneumonic. The bubonic type was named for the large swelled lumps, or buboes, that appeared on the sick around the lymph nodes in the groin or armpit area. This form was usually transmitted by the bite of an infected flea. Septicemic plague attacked the blood and had as its only benefit that death came more swiftly than for victims of the bubonic type, who lived for days in agony before vomiting blood and dying. A third type, pneumonic, was perhaps the most deadly in that it could be spread through the air. Death was even swifter than with septicemic plague—often in just a few hours. A cure for the plague was not discovered until the 19th century, but that didn't stop people living in the medieval world from trying to find treatments and preventive measures.

The lancing of buboes was considered the only real intervention available once bubonic plague had manifested. Many people carried flowers or otherwise pleasant-smelling items near their noses in the belief that the pleasant smell would counter the presence of plague.

Many religious and lay people alike regarded the plague as divine retribution for humanity's sins.

Contemporary accounts paint a grim picture of understanding and reaction to the plague. Fear and panic led some to blame communities on the fringes of mainstream medieval society—Jews, lepers, and the like—for causing the plague. Some scientists blamed a particular alignment of planets for corrupting the air. Many religious and lay people alike regarded the plague as divine retribution for humanity's sins. This gave rise to the flagellant movement, in which groups of people would walk from town to town, whipping themselves, to try and atone for their sins by punishing their flesh.

From a cultural standpoint, the Black Death had a profound effect on art, the practice of memorialization, and social and economic matters. An artistic theme known as the *danse macabre* began to show up in churches, cloisters, and other sites. A cult of the dead that emphasized the memory of the departed had been in existence well before the 14th century, but it achieved new popularity. Social and economic changes that had already begun were hastened along, especially given that plague outbreaks recurred every generation or so well into the 16th century and beyond. ∎

Suggested Reading

Herlihy, *The Black Death and the Transformation of the West*.

Horrox, *The Black Death*.

Questions to Consider

1. How might European society have developed differently if the Black Death had never occurred?

2. What do the multiplicity of reactions to the plague tell us about the complexity of medieval society and the mindset of people living in the medieval world?

The Black Death and its Effects
Lecture 29—Transcript

Welcome back. In our last lecture, we discussed how medicine was understood and practiced in the medieval world. Based primarily on the medical theory of the four humors as laid forth by the Classical scholar of medicine known as Galen, medieval medicine involved techniques and approaches that might seem somewhat barbarous to us today—such as the use of leeches, or cautery—which was the application of heated pokers to various parts of the body. But modern science has proved the efficaciousness of many medieval techniques of healing. At the same time that medieval doctors and healers were able to cope with and treat a variety of diseases and afflictions successfully, there were some medical issues that proved beyond the capabilities of any practitioner of medicine in the Middle Ages.

Perhaps the most notable and devastating of the many diseases that ravaged the medieval world was the plague, or Black Death. When it swept through the West in the 14th century, the plague left a path of destruction and death in its wake. There was seemingly no way to avoid it, and it did not discriminate: old, young, rich, powerful, weak, pious and not—it took them all. Today we're going to examine the Black Death and its far-reaching impact on the medieval world. It is safe to say that once the plague had ravaged its way through Western Europe, nothing in the medieval world would ever be the same again.

But before we get to talking about the plague itself, we need to back up a bit and examine what living conditions were like in the halfcentury or so before the plague made its appearance in the West, as living conditions in the medieval world arguably contributed somewhat to the plague's devastating impact. As the medieval world headed into the 14th century, there was the beginning of a land crunch due to unprecedented population growth. As we've discussed in a previous lecture, the population of the medieval world almost doubled between the year 1000 and the year 1300. With so many more people, land was soon in short supply. This land crunch contributed in part to a famine in 1315 that killed up to 10 percent of the population in certain areas. Those who survived were, not surprisingly, usually in less than robust health. The famine was caused in part by the start of a period known as the Little Ice Age.

This began in the 12th century and lasted through the 14th, with repercussions felt well into the 16th century. Just as the warm period, or Little Optimum, had contributed to the population increase starting around the year 1000, the Little Ice Age would have the opposite effect. Although the change in overall mean temperature was slight—no more than a few degrees—the impact from this slight change was hugely significant. It resulted in more rain, shorter growing seasons, and unexpected frosts in late spring and early fall—all of which negatively affected food production. Some scholars feel that overcrowding—especially in cities—in combination with food shortages and the resulting general ill health caused the plague that swept through the medieval world in the 14th century to have a particularly profound impact.

I should pause here and note that although most modern scholars refer to this event as the Black Death, it was never actually called this during the medieval period. Those who lived through it tended to refer to it as blue sickness, or the great mortality, or the great pestilence. The description "blue sickness" may refer to the bluishcolored bruise-like marks that many victims were said to have developed on various parts of their bodies, although no one is entirely sure about this. Because "Black Death" is the phrase commonly used to describe this devastating event, I will continue to use this term today—even though it is somewhat anachronistic to do so.

Although there is some disagreement, most scholars agree that the cause of the Black Death was plague, most commonly known as bubonic plague. Infection was most likely caused by a bacterium known as the *Yersinia pestis* bacterium, which is generally carried by fleas on rats. In the 14th century, the time of the most serious outbreak, it appears that the plague traveled to the medieval world from Asia along trade routes. Plague has long existed and continues to exist in the modern world, especially among rodent populations. What was unusual in the 14th century is that this disease moved into the human population and that it did so, so virulently and devastatingly. Today there might be an occasional case of plague in humans—no more than a few every few years, at most—and modern medicine can usually treat the disease if it is diagnosed in time. Still, transmission to humans is very rare and seemingly difficult—a fact that has led some scholars to surmise that the plague of the medieval world is different from the plague that exists today—that perhaps the bacteria mutated over time into a form less harmful to humans. A few scholars believe that a different disease entirely was to blame for the death and destruction that so altered medieval society.

Most scholars, however, tend to believe that the culprit behind the Black Death was plague. They theorize that there was a sort of perfect storm of events that allowed plague to jump from the animal to human population so easily—and to infect that population so rapidly. Ecological changes in Asia during the 14th century drove rodents out of their natural habitats and into closer proximity with humans. The fleas that carried the plague bacterium then most likely moved to humans or animals that lived in close contact with humans once their primary hosts—rats—had succumbed to the disease. Plague was active in central Asia in the 1330s, and one of the worst aspects of it was that people knew it was coming their direction.

Although they didn't fully understand the method of transmission, sources indicate that people west of an outbreak recognized it was heading their way. Letters from people in infected regions warned others to the west and north of the dangers of plague. For example, a musician named Louis Heyligen who was a member of the household of Cardinal Giovanni Colonna in the French city of Avignon, wrote a letter to friends in the Belgian town of Bruges telling them of the plague a year before it actually appeared in that town. Some travelers—usually religious pilgrims—came home with horror stories of disease and death. As a result, many towns—especially in England, where the plague didn't appear in full force until 1348—took measures to try and prevent the plague from gaining a foothold in their communities. These efforts took the form of prayer, lifestyle changes—such as altering eating and drinking habits—and the performance of penance, to name just a few.

Often, however, any measures taken were fruitless, as medieval people didn't fully understand how diseases were transmitted, and often they attributed supernatural causes—the alignment of the planets, or earthquakes—to the outbreak of plague. Still, medieval people did have a sense that the plague must have been transmitted by some means, and they knew that it was coming from the East. Another account from the city of Avignon relates how people living there refused to purchase or eat any spices that had recently come from the East along trade routes out of fear that the infection might somehow be spread that way—a not unreasonable assumption.

There were three types of plague: bubonic, septicemic, and pneumonic. The bubonic type was named for the large swollen lumps, or buboes, that would appear on an infected person around the lymph nodes in the groin or armpit area, and this seemed to be the most common form of the plague in the 14th century. Bubonic plague was usually transmitted by the bite of an infected flea. Contemporary accounts suggest that sometimes the buboes would burst, and sometimes they were lanced by medical practitioners who believed that the bubo was evidence that the body was trying to expel the disease—and so they thought to help that process along. The smell and discharge from these ruptured buboes was reportedly quite vile and noxious. The only benefit to contracting this form of plague, if we can imagine such a thing, was that this was seemingly the only form of plague from which it was possible to recover. We have significant evidence to suggest that some people did, in fact, recover after having contracted this form of the disease.

Septicemic plague attacked the blood, and had as its only benefit that death came more swiftly than it did for victims of the bubonic type—many of whom lived for days in agony before vomiting blood and dying. This form also seems most likely to have been contracted through the bite of an infected flea.

A third type, pneumonic, was perhaps the most deadly in that it could be spread through the air, and it could be spread from person to person. An infected person could cough up droplets of the bacterium and pass it on to someone else; a flea bite was not necessary to transmit the disease. Death was even swifter than with septicemic plague—often in just a few hours. Numerous medieval accounts tell of people who seemed hale and healthy in the morning, but who had dropped dead by the afternoon. An oft repeated set piece in plague narratives tells of a man who went to his confessor to be absolved of his sins, or someone who paid a visit to a lawyer to try and set his affairs in order, or someone who wished to spend what modern people might call quality time with family in the face of the threat of this disease. The end of all these stories is usually the same—the main player in the story dies, and he takes along with him his priest, or his lawyer, or his entire family. Although for a time, some scholars thought it was an exaggeration, it now seems likely that entire households might die in the space of a few weeks, or days—or even hours. Other similarly frightening stories also seem to have had some truth to them. Some accounts relate how there were so many deaths and so many funerals—there were not enough priests to perform burial services. Church graveyards were overwhelmed, leading to the creation of mass graves. Long trenches would be dug, bodies laid along the bottom, and a thin layer of soil made to cover them—another layer of bodies would be placed on top of this, and so on, until the pit was full. The resulting stench coming from these mass graves was reportedly so overwhelming that many people avoided walking past graveyards if at all possible.

Other even more heart-wrenching stories tell of family members abandoning one another once one of them showed signs of infection—as Louis Helygen noted in his letter detailing the plague in Avignon:

> Because of the growing strength of this disease it has come to pass that, for fear of infection, no doctor will visit the sick … nor will the father visit the son, the mother the daughter, the brother the brother, the son the father, the friend the friend, the acquaintance the acquaintance, nor anyone a blood relation—unless, that is, they wished to die suddenly along with them, or follow them at once.

Plague was also the main element in what may be one of the earliest examples of germ warfare. As we've discussed in several previous lectures, the Italian city-states had one of the strongest and most wide-ranging maritime mercantile presences in the medieval world. Thus, some of the first people from the Western medieval world to encounter the plague were Italian merchants who were doing business in the Byzantine city of Tana in 1343. In the face of an invasion by a group of people known as Tartars, the merchants fled to the walled city of Jaffa, where they holed up to wait out the siege. For a time, it looked as if luck was on their side—plague swept through the Tartar forces, killing huge numbers of them, while the merchants in the city seemed to have avoided this greatest threat. But then, before they gave up the siege, the Tartars lobbed one last series of missiles over the walls of the city—they loaded up their catapults with the dead bodies of plague victims and launched them into the city. In an account of the plague written by an Italian lawyer named Gabriele de Mussis, the author relates what happened:

> What seemed like mountains of dead were thrown into the city ... and soon the rotting corpses tainted the air and poisoned the water supply, and the stench was so overwhelming that hardly one in several thousand was in a position to flee the remains of the Tartar army. Moreover, one infected man could carry the poison to others, and infect people and places with the disease by look alone. No one knew, or could discover, a means of defence.

Again, it seems that neither the attacking army nor the writer who described their actions fully understood how the disease might be transmitted by corpses. The original intent of the Tartars seems to have been to overwhelm their enemy with the stench of dead bodies, and not to infect them with plague. De Mussis's statement that one could contract the disease simply by looking at the bodies underscores the hysteria surrounding the movement of the plague through the medieval world. Indeed, it was the inability to fully understand how the plague was transmitted that contributed to the horror it possessed in the minds of the inhabitants of the medieval world.

A cure for the plague was not found until the 19th century, but that didn't stop people in the medieval world from trying to find treatments and preventive measures. As I noted earlier, records indicate that with bubonic plague, the lancing of buboes was considered the only real intervention available once plague had manifested itself. In many instances, once a person showed signs of developing plague they were, on many occasions, abandoned. Attention thus turned to ideas about how to prevent infection, but here as well the incompleteness of medieval medical theory led people to take what we would probably think of as some odd measures by modern standards. For example, belief that the plague was the result of a miasma that spread through the air led many people to carry flowers or otherwise pleasant-smelling items near their noses in the belief that the pleasant odor would counter the presence of plague.

There were some doctors who treated the plague—some who labored to bring comfort to those who were suffering from this disease, demonstrating that medieval people were as capable of compassion and a commitment to a perceived sacred duty as modern people. Indeed, given the lack of efficacious remedies and the virulence of the disease, those physicians who were willing to enter the sick room of plague victims were brave indeed, and many were held in high esteem. When they did treat those patients, they were also rather scary looking. Some illustrations and woodcuts from the period depict plague doctors wearing a special headpiece—what was essentially a mask with what looked like a long bird's beak attached at the nose. Inside this beak would be placed flowers, or herbs, or some other item with a sweet smell—as it was thought that this could help prevent transmission. The masks of plague doctors probably did provide some measure of protection, but only because they offered some level of physical barrier between healer and patient—much like surgical masks do today.

In the face of such a terrifying and seemingly unstoppable enemy, contemporary accounts not surprisingly paint a grim picture of understanding and reaction to the plague. Fear and panic led some to blame communities on the fringes of mainstream medieval society—Jews, lepers, and the like—for somehow causing the plague. Numerous accounts tell of accusations leveled against Jewish communities—accusing them of deliberately poisoning wells, or practicing some kind of witchcraft that brought the plague down on the medieval world. In horrific episodes that recall the atrocities of the First Crusade, entire Jewish communities were slaughtered by Christians who thought they were responsible for the Great Mortality. Some Jews were made to "confess" under torture to conspiring to spread the plague—evidence that the more zealous and hysterical inhabitants of the medieval world seized upon to justify the wholesale slaughter of entire Jewish communities. So great was the prejudice against Jewish communities that in 1348 Pope Clement had to issue an injunction forbidding the killing of Jews in an attempt to calm the widespread hysteria. In early 1349, the government leaders of the German town of Cologne took the unusual step of publicly announcing their collective belief that the Jews living in their community were innocent of any crimes in an attempt to protect them. It was all for naught—later that year, the entire Jewish population of Cologne was burned. Similar atrocities occurred almost every place in the medieval world where there was a significant Jewish population.

There were other explanations for the cause of the plague. Some people blamed a particular alignment of planets, or similar phenomenon, for corrupting the air. But most people, religious and lay alike, regarded the plague as divine retribution for humanity's sins. Some religious leaders singled out particular behaviors. Everything from the staging of elaborate tournaments, to scandalous new fashions, to lack of parental discipline was at one point or another identified by clerics as having angered God—who had brought down plague upon the world to punish humanity for this behavior. This theory sometimes proved untenable, as plague certainly did not attack only sinners. Many of its victims, especially in the outbreaks that occurred after the initial one of the mid-14th century, were children—arguably the most innocent members of society. Most of those who blamed the plague on the sinfulness of mankind tried to avoid citing specific behaviors—and instead suggested that it was a general moral decline that had brought on God's wrath, and the seemingly indiscriminate selection of victims was in its own way a kind of punishment. The idea here was that the death of good and innocent people would be much more of a catalyst for society as a whole to shape up than if the plague only affected those who were truly sinful. The medieval world needed to wake up and address a crisis of sin, and this was going to happen more quickly if everyone had the potential to become subject to the disease God had visited upon the world.

Beliefs such as this gave rise to several widespread penitential activities and movements. For example, there was a significant increase in the number of people going on pilgrimage, and there was an increase also in the size of the offerings they tended to make at religious sites and shrines. The pope recognized both the increase in religious pilgrims and the terror from which their travels sprang. In response to those trends, he declared the year 1350 to be a jubilee year—in which any pilgrim making the journey to Rome would receive what is known as a plenary indulgence. Religious indulgences were an often controversial issue in the medieval world, as what being granted an indulgence meant was that the penitent was absolved from having to perform penance for certain sins committed.

A plenary indulgence meant that the penitent, in the eyes of the church, was considered to have completed the required penance for all sins that may have been committed in the penitent's lifetime. As you might imagine, this was quite the motivation for those concerned about the state of their immortal souls, and it also served to provide a measure of comfort during the terrifying days of the plague. Thus, in 1350, a person who made a pilgrimage to Rome might still live in fear of the plague, but they could rest easy in the knowledge that if the plague did claim them they would not be going to hell.

On the fringes were more extreme and bizarre movements that sought to find a way to appease God's wrath. One of these was the flagellant movement, in which groups of people would walk from town to town, whipping themselves, to try and atone for their sins by punishing their flesh. This very public spectacle intended to recall Christ's crucifixion. At the other extreme, some people engaged in bouts of drunkenness and debauchery, feeling as if the end of the world had come. Indeed, one chronicler who recorded the horrors of the Black Death seemed so certain that this was the end of days, he noted that he had left a few blank pages in his text for someone else to add to, should there happen to be "anyone left alive." From a cultural standpoint, the Black Death had a profound effect on art, the practice of memorialization, and social and economic matters. An artistic theme known as the *danse macabre*—or "dance of death"—began to show up with some regularity in churches, cloisters, and other sites. Most of the surviving examples are from about a century after the first outbreak of plague, and they suggest that the inhabitants of the medieval world—after enduring wave after wave of plague every generation or so—were coming to terms with the seeming arbitrary quality of the plague by creating artistic representations of death. In many of these frescoes, book illuminations, and the like, death is represented as a skeleton who is taking by the hands other skeletal figures and leading them in a dance. The figures that death leads away are often dressed in apparel that suggests all stations and strata of medieval life—from kings to popes to plowmen, from old people to young children—death claims them all. A cult of the dead that emphasized the memory of those who had departed had been in existence well before the 14th century, but it achieved new popularity and participants with the advent of the Black Death.

Social and economic changes that were already starting to occur were hastened along by the effects of the plague—especially given that outbreaks would recur every generation or so well into the 16th century and beyond. Demographically speaking, the plague was a disaster for the medieval world. After a long period of growth, the population dropped dramatically. Significant recovery in terms of demographic numbers would not really happen until well into the early modern period. One reason for this was that, in addition to killing off members of society of reproductive age, the plague also attacked a section of the population of the medieval world that was already prone to high mortality rates: children. The ravages of the plague meant that even fewer children than before were growing up and themselves reproducing. On the other hand, for those who did survive the plague, life was much better in many respects than it had been before. Suddenly, there was land aplenty—while in the early 14th century, the medieval world had been in a land crunch.

The horrors of the plague were quite real and quite potent, and knowledge of this devastating event added fuel to scholarly thinking about what life for medieval people was like—and what their attitudes toward life, death, and their own mortality must have been. As I noted in the first lecture of this course, my students are often surprised when I provide them with examples of jokes or humorous tales from the period. Their thinking tends to be that because life in the medieval world was seemingly constantly under threat from disease, famine, war, and other ills, medieval people were a grim lot—going about the business of daily survival with their heads down and not doing a whole lot in the way of merrymaking or laughing. But as the jokes I provide my students suggest this was not the everyday reality for medieval people.

A similar theory long held sway when it came to the idea of children or childhood in the Middle Ages. Even before the plague, childhood mortality rates were astronomical by modern standards. How could it be, modern scholars wondered, that people could possibly form affectionate attachments to children when they knew full well that most of them would not make it past age five? The event that today we call the Black Death seemingly only added support to the thinking that medieval people did not really love their children, nor did they have any concept of childhood like we do today. But just as the examples of the jokes that I gave in the first lecture suggest that, in fact, medieval people did do a fair amount of laughing and were no more unhappy than modern people—so, too, is there a plethora of evidence that inhabitants of the medieval world understood childhood as a specific stage of development, and that they loved their children deeply and mourned their loss or absence. It is to the related issues of children and childhood that we will turn in our next lecture.

Childhood in the Middle Ages
Lecture 30

Lady Thomasine Tendryng, who died in 1485, was commemorated with a funeral brass that not only depicted her, but her seven children. Five of the children are dressed in shrouds, while two are represented as wearing clothing—suggesting that only two out of her seven children made it past infancy.

Until relatively recently, many people believed the concept of childhood was a thoroughly modern one and that medieval people had no such concept, nor were they emotionally attached to their children in the way that most modern people are. One of the most oft-cited pieces of evidence for this belief was the high infant mortality rate in the Middle Ages—estimated at about 30 percent. Only half of all children lived to age five, and it would not be uncommon for a medieval woman to give birth to 10 children but only see 1 or 2 survive into adulthood. Also contributing to the idea that medieval people did not feel great love for their children came from the practices of fostering and apprenticing children when they were still quite young.

Recent studies suggest that medieval people loved their children and genuinely missed and grieved for them when separated, whether due to fosterage, apprenticeship, or early death. Numerous written documents, letters, chronicles, and funerary monuments attest to their attachment and the loss they felt when their children died young. Fostering had its roots in the politically savvy idea of maintaining good relations among powerful families; often two families sent their offspring to be raised in each other's households, an exchange that ensured frequent visits between the members of each household. Among the lower classes, apprenticing a child at a young age was quite often an act of love: Apprenticeship usually guaranteed the child a bed, food, and a means of making a living that might otherwise be beyond his or her reach.

That medieval people had a clear concept of childhood is demonstrated by the popular and widespread belief, developed from the classical world, that the life of a person was divided into several distinct stages. From birth to age seven was the *infantia*, or infancy. From 7 to 14 or so was considered childhood, or *pueritia*. At about 14, a child was thought to enter adolescence (*adolescentia*). For some medieval writers, this stage ended some time in one's 20s. Depending on the thinker or writer, there were three or four more stages of adulthood, a model in which people often passed through old age and into a second childhood, ending up, essentially, right back where they had begun.

Although little survives in the way of artifacts that attest to a clear concept of childhood, the evidence we do have clearly points to an idea that is not so different from our own. Medieval children were fed a special diet, wore specially made clothes, and often slept in specially constructed cradles or children's beds. Toys similar to those children still play with today—such as dolls and spinning tops—have been discovered in archaeological excavations. Some literary texts record games and songs that were favorites of medieval children.

Although little survives in the way of artifacts that attest to a clear concept of childhood, the evidence we do have clearly points to an idea that is not so different from our own.

For all its similarities with childhood in the modern period, however, childhood in the Middle Ages was also different in various important ways. Attending school—a requirement for all children in the United States today—was an option for only a small portion of the population. Medieval children tended to begin working much younger than modern children. Perhaps the biggest difference between then and now is the age at which children were considered eligible for marriage. While the average age of marriages in the peasant and merchant classes tended to hover around 18, the formal age of consent was usually 12 for girls and 14 for boys. Some noble marriages—particularly royal ones—might occur when the boy and girl were as young as eight, although they would not be consummated until later. In practice, it was not uncommon for medieval children to become parents before they had left adolescence; thus some medieval youths were understood as existing in a sort of hybrid childhood-adulthood, a situation much less common today than it was then. ■

Suggested Reading

Orme, *Medieval Children*.

Shahar, *Childhood in the Middle Ages*.

Questions to Consider

1. In what ways do medieval concepts of childhood and adolescence differ significantly from modern ones? In what ways are they similar?

2. How did high infant mortality rates shape medieval thinking about the family unit?

Childhood in the Middle Ages
Lecture 30—Transcript

Welcome back. In our last lecture, we discussed the decimation of the population of the medieval world by the bubonic plague in the mid-14th century. Termed the "Black Death" by later scholars, the plague was carried into the medieval West by fleas that hitched a ride on rats and other animals along trade routes from the East. Once the fleas' host died, they moved onto humans, who usually would acquire the plague from a fleabite. Plague usually manifested itself in the form of swollen lymph nodes—called buboes—in the armpit and groin area. Very few people who contracted the plague survived, although a few did recover. Some historians estimate that as much as half of the medieval population was killed by the plague. Obviously, this event had a far-reaching impact, and it helped to dramatically reshape the society of the medieval world. For the majority of those who survived the plague, things were much better than they had been—there was suddenly an abundance of land and a plethora of landowners desperate for laborers to work it. But for those who lived through it, it was also a grim reminder of the fragility of life in the Middle Ages—something they had already been acutely aware of given the high mortality rates for the population of the medieval world, especially when it came to children.

When one looks at demographic data from the Middle Ages, it used to be the case that a simple calculation of life spans produced the answer that the average medieval person lived to be about 35. This number is misleading— we should not for a moment believe that otherwise healthy people were suddenly dropping dead once they hit the back side of their 30s. The data is skewed by the high infant mortality of the period. For those who made it past the first year—and especially those who made it past age five—an average life expectancy would be somewhere in the 50 to 60 year age range, with plenty of people living into their 80s, especially among the noble classes, who had access to better nutrition and a less difficult lifestyle than peasants.

In part because of what seemed to be the relatively short duration of a medieval life, until recently many people believed that the concept of childhood was a thoroughly modern one, and that medieval people had neither a similar concept, nor had they been emotionally attached to their children in the way that most modern people are. The idea was that in a world where life span was shorter and dangers such as plague, and famine, and war seemed always to be lurking, there was no time for the fun and innocence of childhood—nor was it possible or prudent to get too attached to one's children. One of the major proponents of this theory was the French historian Philippe Ariès, who in 1960 wrote the book *L'Enfant et la Vie Familiale sous l'Ancien Régime*—translated into English as *Centuries of Childhood*.

In this book he argued that before the 17th century, all children were essentially treated as smaller adults, and that there was no concept of childhood or childishness. If we look at the data, one can understand why Ariès and other historians might have believed this to be the case. Scholars estimate that for every 1,000 births in pre-industrial Europe, as many as 300 children did not survive past the first year.

Additionally, in the same period, only half of all children born survived until age five—and in most cases, it was probably less. It would not be at all uncommon for a medieval woman to give birth to 10 children, but only see one or two survive into adulthood. If you think for a moment what it would be like to have several of your children die in infancy, it would seem logical to believe that the psychological trauma of such loss meant that in order to survive it and to continue reproducing, medieval people couldn't love their children in the way that most modern 21st-century people do—the emotional toll would seem to be unbearable. To detach from one's offspring might seem a logical defense mechanism.

Another piece of evidence contributing to the idea that medieval people did not feel great love and affection for their children comes from the practices of fostering children in other households and apprenticing children to learn a trade when they were still quite young. Fostering was a practice found almost exclusively among noble families, and in this practice very young children would be sent to live in the household of another noble. Quite often, noble households might actually exchange children, with the idea being that this would help to cement bonds between the families, as they were each caring for the other's offspring. For those who lived below the noble classes, surviving records indicate that children as young as eight or nine might be sent to live in the household of a craftsman in order to learn a trade. To most modern people, fostering children out or apprenticing them to learn a trade before they had even reached their 10th birthday might at first glance seem to be cruel and unfeeling—like something out of one of Charles Dickens's books.

However, recent studies have suggested that although their attachments to their children might be different in certain respects, medieval people loved their children and genuinely missed and grieved for them if they were separated from them—whether due to fosterage, apprenticeship, or early death. Numerous pieces of evidence in the form of written documents, letters, chronicles, and funerary monuments attest to the attachment medieval people felt for their children and the loss they experienced when those children died young. For example, Lady Thomasine Tendryng, who died in 1485, was commemorated with a funeral brass that not only depicted her, but her seven children. Five of the children are dressed in shrouds, while two are represented as wearing clothing—suggesting that only two out of her seven children made it past infancy. The 13th-century chronicler Matthew Paris describes the reaction of Eleanor of Provence, wife of King Henry III of England, when their three-yearold daughter Katherine died. Although Katherine had had some sort of disability which had meant that she was unable to speak, she was obviously greatly loved by her parents. Matthew Paris tells us that after her death Queen Eleanor was absolutely inconsolable and could not be helped by either human or medical intervention.

One of the most enigmatic and carefully wrought English poems of the 14th century—known as *Pearl* and written by the same anonymous poet who composed the Arthurian classic *Sir Gawain and the Green Knight*—focuses on a speaker who is grieving the death of his young daughter. Overwhelmed by emotion, the narrator lies down upon his daughter's grave and falls asleep, whereupon he has a dream in which he sees his daughter—a child when she died, but now a grown woman in heaven. The child is usually called the pearl maiden by literary scholars—as the dreamer refers to her repeatedly as his "pearl of great price"—and she tells her father to be comforted, as she is in heaven with Jesus. Their conversation takes place across a river, which symbolizes the separation between the dreamer in his earthly realm and the Pearl maiden in her heavenly one. The maiden and her father have a long talk across that river, and in the course of their discussion she answers many of his questions, assures him of her salvation, and cautions him that he may not cross the water. But so great is the dreamer's grief that he desperately plunges into the water. Immediately upon entering the river he awakens from his dream, still mourning the loss of his child. It is clear in the poem that the Pearl maiden has attained that which any medieval Christian would want for his or her child—she is saved; she is in heaven—yet even this knowledge is not enough to assuage the dreamer's grief. He misses her so much that he disobeys the command to stay on his side of the river. When he wakes, rather than being comforted by what he has seen, if anything his longing for his dead child is even greater than it was previously.

Evidence like written documents, or funeral monuments, or even literary texts obviously tends to coalesce around the noble classes, as they were the members of society most likely to be able to afford such remembrances, and/or they were educated and able to read or write about such events. But there is evidence from the peasant classes as well, although it is more difficult to come by and interpret. Historian Barbara Hanawalt, for example, has analyzed coroners' documents for several medieval villages in her book entitled *The Ties That Bound: Peasant Families in Medieval England*. Based on the evidence, she concludes that we can see a demonstration of familial affection—particularly in terms of the relationships between parents and children—if we pay attention to cases of accidental death. She notes that when children have met with some sort of accidental death—very frequently this is some kind of drowning—the preponderance of first finders, or presumably those out looking for the missing child, are the parents—usually the mother—and she suggests that this underscores the fact that peasant women had a nurturing role.

Other pieces of evidence suggesting concern and affection for children can be found in records of churches, which record gifts that were made to the particular religious house with the stipulation that it go toward paying for masses to be said for the dead child's soul. As we discussed in an earlier lecture, in medieval religious thinking most souls had to spend some time in purgatory—where they were punished for, and cleansed of, their sins before they got to go on to heaven. It was thought that prayer performed by those still living on earth could lessen that time, and the more people praying and the more frequent the prayers, the better. Thus, a donation to a religious house meant that monks and priests would dedicate specific masses to be said for the soul of a particular individual—and very frequently, we see children being named as the beneficiaries of these masses. The lingering grief that parents who buried their children might have felt is suggested by the example of Eleanor of Castile—who sometime around 1266, gave birth to a daughter who died shortly after she entered the world. Some 20 years later, records show that Eleanor gave a donation of cloth of gold to a house of Dominican Friars in Bordeaux on the understanding that they would say prayers for her every year on the anniversary of her death.

Obviously, her love for her child was profound and long lasting. So death, obviously, is one event around which we can see evidence of affection for children. Another area in which we see affection for children—and an understanding and recognition of them as children—is in the practice of fostering. As I suggested earlier, occurring as it did in the upper echelons of society, fostering had its roots in the politically savvy idea of maintaining good relations among powerful families. Often two families would send their offspring to be raised in the household of one another, an exchange that ensured frequent visits between the members of each household. Although the parents in many instances seemed to miss their absent children, the idea seems to have been that it was a worthwhile sacrifice—as the training and connections such a child would receive would prepare him or her better for adult life.

Similarly, among the lower classes, apprenticing a child at a young age was quite often clearly an act of love, in that apprenticeship usually guaranteed the child a bed, food, and a means of making a living that might otherwise be beyond his or her reach. The child who was apprenticed to a crafts or tradesperson—like a butcher, woodworker, or blacksmith—would join the household of the socalled master of the craft, eating and sleeping with the master's family—and sometimes other apprentices. Although 12 seems to be the typical average age for apprenticeship, some medieval children were apprenticed considerably younger. Usually after about seven years of apprenticeship, the child—now an adolescent—would earn the title of journeyman. The title comes from the fact that the apprentice was now supposedly free to visit other masters to perfect his learning of the trade. Once he was ready, the journeyman would often present his best piece of work to the local guild in his craft. As we've already discussed, medieval guilds were organizations that were sort of a combination of fraternity, labor union, political action group, and social club. The leaders of the guild set standards for their particular trade or craft, and one could only practice that trade if the guild deemed one acceptable. If the journeyman's presentation to the guild was accepted, he was then granted the title of master, allowed to open his own workshop and to hire his own apprentices—and thus, the cycle would begin again.

That medieval people had a clear concept of childhood is demonstrated at least in part by the popular and widespread belief—developed from the Classical world—that the life of a person was divided into several distinct stages. From birth to age 7 was usually described as the period of *infantia*, or the infancy of a child. From 7 to 14 or so was considered the time of childhood, or *pueritia*. Around 14, the medieval person was thought to enter adolescence (*adolescentia*)—for some medieval writers, this stage ended sometime in one's 20s. Depending on the thinker or writer, there were then three or four more ages of adulthood, a model in which man often passed through old age and into a second childhood—ending up, essentially, right back where he had begun: wearing diapers, usually called clouts in the medieval world, and needing to be fed a special diet—usually a gruel like mixture often called pap, which might contain milk, grains, and other foods that had been mashed or even chewed to a watery consistency by the caregiver.

Clearly then, medieval people did not simply think of children as immature or tiny adults. Although little has survived in the way of artifacts, what evidence we do have clearly points to an idea of childhood that is not so much different from our own. In addition to the special diet that medieval children were fed, they wore specially made clothes and often slept in specially constructed cradles or children's beds. Cradles that survive from the period often have ingenious footpedals or rockers that would allow the mother to rock the cradle with her foot while she was engaged in the other activity of running the household. Sometimes a special seat, known as a cricket, was set beside the cradle for the mother to sit on while she rocked it. Other pieces of furniture seem to have had a function similar to that of walkers for toddlers today, in that they allowed children to practice pulling themselves into a standing position and taking a few steps.

Toys similar to those children still play with today—such as dolls and spinning tops—have been discovered in archaeological excavations. That classic, the hobbyhorse, is attested in numerous noble households, with evidence that sometimes the horse's head was elaborately painted and decorated so that it would look more lifelike. Ball games were also popular, including those that involved kicking or hitting a ball with some sort of stick or paddle. The balls themselves were often made out of pigs' bladders that might be filled with peas—or leather stuffed with straw, or horsehair, or wool and sewn closed into the shape of a ball. In wintertime, when the rivers froze, children might go ice skating on skates made of animal bone.

Some literary texts record games and songs that were favorites of medieval children, and very often they served an educational as well as entertainment function. For example, the call-and-response game that goes: "How many miles to Beverlyham? Eight, eight, and other eight. May I come there by daylight? Yes, if your horse be good and light" teaches math—3 x 8 is 24— and it teaches also some practical matters: It's possible to ride 24 miles on a good horse and reach your destination while it's still light out. Other rhymes and songs that seem innocent—like "Ring around a Rosy" still chanted by children today—actually have their roots in the horrors of the Black Death. In its references to flowers, the chant refers to the prevalent idea that the plague could be avoided by keeping pleasant scents near one's nose—hence the beaked, bird-like mask of plague doctors. The beak would be filled with something pleasant-smelling in an attempt to prevent transmission of the disease. The final phrase of the "Ring around a Rosy" rhyme—"Ashes, ashes; We all fall down!"—refers to the idea of "ashes to ashes, and dust to dust." As we saw in our last lecture, if the plague did anything, it reminded people of the mortality of all human beings.

For all its similarities with childhood in the modern period, however, childhood in the Middle Ages was also significantly different in various important ways. Attending school—a requirement for all children in the U.S. today—was an option for only a small portion of the population. Boys from the wealthier classes make up the greatest bulk of those who received an education. Noble boys would tend to be educated at home with a private tutor. Boys from the wealthier families of merchants and sometimes particularly well-off peasants would pay a fee to attend a church or cathedral school, where a priest or monk would be in charge of their education. As we enter the High Middle Ages, we find more and more schools being offered in towns, with educated individuals hanging signs to advertise outside their homes, and this would be where most classes took place. Children were usually taught the basics of how to read and write, some basic arithmetic, and enough Latin to understand their prayers. While abuse of children was generally abhorred, the occasional striking of a child with a switch, or even a beating, was considered par for the course when masters were trying to get children to learn their lessons—something that strikes us as quite different from the thinking about the practice of education today.

Although most families had to pay a fee, there is evidence that even in the Middle Ages there were what we might call scholarship students—poor children who were taught out of an impulse of charity. For most boys, schooling ended around 12 or 14—just about the time they were really learning a craft or trade—but around the 12th century, we have the rise of the university system, which we've discussed a little bit in some of our previous lectures. Various monastic orders—like the Dominicans—played an important part in the development of the first universities. Originally focused around the households of certain renowned masters or philosophers, universities came into being when educated boys—and they were all boys—came to the household of a master wishing to learn more—particularly in subjects like philosophy or religion. As such, universities were not so much physical places as they were clusters of people. As we discussed, again, in some earlier lectures, university curricula, fees, and class schedules came into being because students, hungry for knowledge, wanted more from their masters. They felt they weren't getting as much education as they wanted.

Girls tended to be educated at home. Often the main focus of their studies was the running of a household, with little emphasis placed on literacy or mathematics—although those girls who entered a convent might be taught to read and write and employed in the convent's scriptorium, copying manuscripts, or else they might be put to the task of keeping track of the accounts of the nunnery—a necessary and time-consuming administrative task. By the later Middle Ages, we find more and more noble girls not destined for life in the convent knowing how to read and write, and some daughters of wealthier merchant families also learned these skills.

So, although we can see that many aspects of what we think of as a typical childhood experience can be found in the medieval world, it is also true that medieval children tended to begin working much younger than modern children. Among peasant families—the largest proportion of the population, as we've discussed several times already—children often began working alongside their parents in the fields at a very young age. In that system, known as manorialism, the families of serfs who were bound to a particular lord were required not only to tender him a portion of the harvest from the lands they held from him, but also to work a certain number of days on the lord's own lands. Here, having many children was a real boon, as some family members could be sent to work the lord's land while others worked the family's own plot. In families with one or no children, certain times of the year—like harvest—could be a real cause for concern—as once you were done harvesting the lord's crops, there might not be enough daylight left or enough working days in the week for you to harvest your own. A big family meant more mouths to feed, but it also meant obligations to the lord would be easier to keep. At harvest time, everyone helped out, and school was not held so that children could assist with age-appropriate tasks—like scaring off birds who would eat the grain, or stacking sheaves of wheat, or gleaning the grains that had been left behind after the initial harvest.

This is what was happening in the countryside, in the villages. In the towns, children who had been apprenticed often took on many of the responsibilities of running a business or practicing a craft while they were still teenagers. Even if still technically journeymen or even apprentices, they might be performing the same work the master of the household did while they were still quite young.

Perhaps the biggest difference between then and now—and the factor that seems to set a limit on a range of childhood—is the age at which children were considered eligible for marriage. While the average age of marriages in the peasant and merchant classes tended to hover around 18, the formal age of consent was usually 12 for girls and 14 for boys. Some noble marriages—

particularly those arranged between royal families—might occur when the boy and girl were as young as eight years old, although these marriages would not be consummated for some years. In some cases, the young bride might go to live in her husband's household, where they would essentially spend the next few years growing up together as playmates before the union was formalized. In some cases, we have evidence that a marriage ceremony was performed as soon as the children were of legal age—12 and 14—but that consummation didn't happen until much later—something that is not surprising when we consider that according to our best medical evidence, children did not reach puberty on average until somewhere between 14 and 18 years old for most of the medieval period. In practice, what this meant was that it was not uncommon for medieval children to become parents before they had left adolescence—resulting in a situation in which medieval youths were understood as existing in a sort of hybrid childhoodadulthood, a situation much less common today than it was then.

So, as we can see from what the evidence suggests, it is not true that there was no concept of childhood in the medieval world, and it is equally not the case that medieval people didn't care deeply for their children and grieve for them when they died. On the other hand, given the realities of the medieval world, childhood wasn't imagined in quite the same way that it is in the modern world, and relationships between parents and children must have been emotionally a bit different in most instances in order for parents to survive the psychological trauma of such high infant mortality rates.

This sort of same-yet-different perspective similarly holds true for the topic of our next lecture on love and marriage in the medieval world. Although it is the case that many marriages were arranged—and technically, most medieval women were legally subordinate to their husbands and fathers—we find plenty of instances of real warmth and affection between spouses, and examples of marriages where the husband and wife appear to have treated one another as equals. We'll explore medieval ideals of love, family, and wedded life next time.

Marriage and the Family
Lecture 31

> In many respects, marriage was one of the fundamental cornerstones of medieval society, so it would make sense that those who held religious office thought it reasonable—and indeed, ideal—if marriage and its attendant issues were to come under ecclesiastical jurisdiction. Indeed, for many in the medieval world, marriage was regarded as first and foremost a method of avoiding damnation.

Although today many view the institution of marriage as enmeshed in religious practices, for most of the Middle Ages marriage was a secular institution. Couples were often married at the church door simply because it was the most visible, open space in their village. Only occasionally would any aspect of the ceremony take place inside a church; the presence of a priest—or any other witnesses—was not considered necessary until fairly late in the period, around the 12th century.

Although romantic love could be a part of a medieval marriage, this was the exception rather than the rule, and it varied depending on the social status of the parties involved. Theoretically, a marriage was not considered valid in the eyes of the church unless both parties consented, a policy that seems designed to ensure that both bride and groom felt some sort of romantic affection for the other. In reality, most marriages, especially in the upper strata of society, were more like business arrangements, designed to combine, consolidate, and maintain wealth, lands, titles, and political status for the families involved.

Medieval marriage practices varied widely depending on the time, the place, and the social status of the parties involved. In western and northern Europe, the bride and groom were usually close to one another in age, especially among peasants. Peasants attached to a manor needed their lord's permission to marry and paid a merchet, or marriage tax. In the south and Mediterranean areas, much older men tended to marry considerably younger women. Legally, by the High Middle Ages, age of consent was established as 12 for girls and 14 for boys, although the actual betrothals might happen much earlier.

Family could be a complicated institution, no matter the social status of the parties involved, and there were many laws to protect the property of the wife and offspring of the marriage. Because of the high mortality rates, remarriage and blended families were more the norm than the exception. Divorce, while rare, could and did occur, especially in instances of abuse or nonconsummation, something that was tricky to establish in court; in at least one instance, several "honest women of the parish" attempted to arouse a man with no success. When they reported their results to the court, the marriage was annulled.

Many customs and practices surrounding betrothal and marriage would seem unusual to us today. The decision to wed could involve a series of businesslike negotiations about issues like dowry; morgengabe, or "morning gift"; provisions for heirs; and so forth. More than one marriage contract fell apart because of arguments over wealth and property. Although most of the medieval population seemed to marry and separate at will, the church issued strict guidelines for behavior within the marriage, including days on which sexual intercourse was forbidden—usually because a particular day was considered holy. Love, especially in the upper strata of society, was expected to be found outside marriage. There were notable exceptions, such as King Richard II of England and his first wife Anne of Bohemia; at her death, Richard was "wild with grief," ordering the destruction of the royal residence where she died.

The political and economic reasons behind most noble marriages spurred a literary movement known as courtly love, popularized in the 12th century at the courts of Eleanor of Aquitaine and her daughter, Marie de Champagne. It most likely had its source in poetry of the Arab world. Writers such as Chrétien de Troyes and the anonymous King Arthur poets emphasized idealized adoration that never crossed the line into consummation; pledging devotion to a lady thus became a means of currying favor with her lord, as the love was understood to be innocent and pure.

Although the married couple was arguably one of the foundational elements of medieval society, a strain of antimatrimonial, misogynistic writings grew in popularity from the High to the late Middle Ages. Emphasizing the danger of lust, such writings characterized marriage as a stop-gap measure for slaking lust and preventing many people from going to hell. Central to this debate was the 13th-century French text *Le roman de la rose*; it would spark a series of written arguments for and against women, marriage, and family that came to be known as the *querelle de la rose*. In response to this movement, many elected to engage in chaste marriages, in which they married but pledged before a priest to abstain from sexual intercourse. In some instances, the husband and wife might enter monastic orders. ■

Suggested Reading

Brundage, *Law, Sex, and Christian Society in Medieval Europe*.

Wemple, *Women in Frankish Society*.

Questions to Consider

1. In what ways were medieval families different from or similar to modern families? What social, religious, and cultural factors affecting the makeup of the medieval family perhaps no longer exist today?

2. What effect might the representation of romantic love in medieval literature have had on real-life relationships?

Marriage and the Family
Lecture 31—Transcript

Welcome back. In our last lecture, we discussed what childhood was like in the medieval world. We debunked the myth that medieval people neither had a real conception of childhood, nor that they did not care deeply for their children and missed them when they were elsewhere—and mourned them when they died. At the same time, we discussed the fact that although there was certainly real affection between children and parents, the relationship necessarily had to be at least a little bit different emotionally than it is in the modern world. Infant and childhood mortality rates were so high that almost without exception, every family would suffer the loss of a child, or two, or more. In order to survive such psychological trauma, medieval people most likely could not form the same types of attachments that modern parents have with their children—although some of the examples of grieving parents we examined last time would certainly seem to indicate that some cared just as intensely for their children as any parent in the 21st century. In many respects, childhood and family relations in the medieval world were more alike to modern thinking about these matters than they were different—although they did differ in significant ways.

Today, we are going to take a similar approach to the interconnected issues of love, marriage, and the family in the medieval world—exploring the ways that medieval thinking about such matters was similar to modern thinking, and also examining instances of dramatic difference between the medieval and the modern.

Today, we tend to think of love and marriage as going naturally together—and, indeed, it is the common perception that the one does not usually occur without the other. Although romantic love could be a part of a medieval marriage, this tended to be the exception rather than the rule. In many cases, it seems that the degree of affection between the parties involved depended heavily on their social status. Although it is generalizing a bit to say so, essentially the further down the social ladder one moved, the more likely one was to be able—or want—to marry for love.

Theoretically, a marriage was not considered valid in the eyes of the church unless both parties consented—a fact that would seem designed to ensure that both bride and groom felt some sort of romantic affection for the other. The other side of the coin is that in order for a marriage to be valid all that needed to happen was that the two parties involved pledged to take one another as husband and wife. No priest or witnesses were required for a marriage to be valid—although as many court cases indicate, it was certainly helpful if there were a number of witnesses present when the words were said who could attest to the legality of the union. What specifically those words needed to be was also occasionally up for debate, but something as simple as "I, Joan, agree to take you, John, as my husband" usually sufficed.

In reality, most marriages, especially in the upper strata of society, were more like business arrangements—designed to combine, consolidate, and maintain wealth, lands, titles, and political status for the families involved. Especially when it came to royalty, the parties to be married might be pledged to one another at a very young age and have no real say in the matter. At the same time, however, even at the lower levels of the social order, economics and the benefits to be gained by either party were part of the discussion of contracting a marriage. Although it is a commonplace in fiction and film to portray poor, sympathetic, young people of the past being forced to marry against their wills, we have to realize that these young people were themselves products of the medieval world—and most likely, they would expect their marriage to be arranged by their parents, or to be contracted with practical and economic matters first and foremost. While they might have hoped to develop affection and love for their spouses, the idea of the institution of marriage was not surrounded by the lavender haze that movies, and romance novels, and greeting card companies give it today.

As we discussed briefly in our lecture on religious institutions in the High and late Middle Ages, for much of the medieval period, marriage was a purely secular institution—and weddings occurred outside the church. In the 13th century, the canons of the Fourth Lateran Council in 1215 made marriage one of the sacraments of the church—and thus, more fully under the jurisdiction of religious officials. In many respects, marriage was one of the fundamental cornerstones of medieval society, so it would make sense that those who held religious office thought it reasonable—and indeed, ideal—if marriage and its attendant issues were to come under ecclesiastical jurisdiction. Indeed, for many in the medieval world, marriage was regarded as first and foremost a method of avoiding damnation. It provided an outlet for sexual desire, provided that intercourse was engaged in with the intent to produce children. There were a host of other religious proscriptions concerning when sex was and was not permissible, but generally speaking, sex within marriage was not going to get you sent to hell or purgatory—while sex outside marriage was guaranteed to do so, in the eyes of the church.

Medieval marriage practices varied widely, depending upon time, and place, and the social status of the parties involved. In the West and North of Europe, a marriage pattern in which bride and groom were close to one another in age prevailed. This was especially true among peasant populations, where love could be the primary reason for marriage. With this pattern, we also see many young people, especially in cities and towns, marrying for the first time surprisingly late—in their early 20s usually. This would often be because those young people who lived and worked in cities like London and Paris were, in some cases, immigrants from the countryside who were in the city to learn a trade, and they needed to put in a significant amount of time in order to accrue sufficient money and status—this usually meant completing an apprenticeship—before they could marry and begin to set up their own household.

For peasants living a primarily rural, agricultural life, the issues were a little different. In the countryside, people might be married a bit younger—say, around 18. So a marriage of partners of near equal age was the norm in the North and West, but in the South—particularly in Italy—we find a different marriage pattern in which much older men—in their 30s and beyond—married much younger women—often wedding girls who were barely into their teens. This created a problem, in that you had lots and lots of young men in their 20s who wanted wives but were unable to get them—as the older, more established males of the community were claiming all the women of marriageable age. Eventually, this marriage pattern would collapse, as it led to a host of other social problems. Legally, by the High Middle Ages, laws concerning the age of consent established the age of 12 for girls and 14 for boys as the earliest at which a marriage could occur, although betrothals might happen when the parties involved were much younger—as I discussed in our last lecture on childhood.

The marriage ceremony itself was more a process than a single event and might involve all or just a few of the following steps. First, the parties needed to consent to the match. If they did, and they said the appropriate words to one another, even if no one else witnessed it, they were legally married. We see evidence of this in an episode from the life of a 15th-century English family, the Pastons, who were part of the upwardly mobile commons, who—through a combination of education and hard work—were advancing up the social ladder. One means to do this was to marry into a higher-ranking family, and the Pastons had high hopes for one daughter, Margery. Margery, it turns out, had other ideas. She exchanged marriage vows in secret with one Richard Calle, who was the family's bailiff—a competent and responsible man, but perhaps not the match they had hoped for their daughter. The Pastons tried everything to undo this marriage, and they even called in the bishop of Norwich in the hope that he would declare the marriage illegal—and thus, null and void. After interviewing the parties involved, however, the bishop said that based on their testimony, the union was, in fact, legal, and there were no impediments to it—and thus, it would have to be upheld.

Supposedly, the Pastons never spoke to Margery again—although oddly, Richard Calle was kept on as a member of the household. So the first and most crucial part of the marriage contract was the consent between the parties. After this first step, the couple might repeat their vows in front of witnesses—friends, family, and the like—and after this, the contract between the parties would be made public knowledge. In a number of court cases from late medieval London, for example, we come across individuals who, for whatever reason, seem to have changed their minds after contracting a marriage. One of the key pieces of evidence in such a case would be testimony given by neighbors as to whether the marriage had become a matter of "public voice and fame"—meaning, did the couple go around telling people that they had contracted a marriage. Such statements were considered important evidence about intent and consent of the parties involved.

The next step in this process would often be the announcing of the banns of marriage. This would take place in the church of the parties involved. The goal behind the announcement was to alert people to the marriage contracted between these two individuals, so that if anyone knew of an impediment to the union—the couple were too closely related, or one of the parties had already contracted a marriage with someone else, for example—that impediment could be made known. Today in churches that still engage in the practice of announcing banns, this occurs before the marriage ceremony—not after, as could be the case in the medieval period.

If no one came forward to state a reason why the marriage could not happen, then usually there was some sort of religious blessing or ceremony. Most often, this took place at the church door, as we've discussed in a previous lecture—although the couple might then after the blessing go inside the church to hear a nuptial Mass. Real church weddings, in the way we think of them today, were reserved for royals and the very highest members of the nobility.

Somewhere along the line, the marriage would be consummated. This might happen right after the two parties consented to the marriage contract (and in plenty of cases, it happened before), or it might be delayed until after the church blessing of the union. Not every marriage followed this pattern, obviously, and many neglected to observe certain of these steps in the process. But what we can see from the numerous steps here is that a medieval wedding was more of a process than it was a singular event.

It was expected that after the marriage, there would be children, and the couple would become a family. The family can be a complicated institution, no matter the social status of the parties involved. Although theoretically a woman was usually considered legally subject to her father and then her husband, there were many laws in place to protect the property of the wife, and mother, and of the offspring of the marriage. This was in part because of the high mortality rates in the medieval period. Remarriage and blended families were more the norm than the exception. Chaucer's Wife of Bath, you'll remember, had been married five times and widowed four. Divorce, while rare, could and did occur—especially in instances of spousal abuse or inability to consummate the union—but it was not at all like modern divorce. There were two types of divorce. The first—which was a divorce *a mensa et thoro*, which literally means a divorce "from the table and the bed"—was equivalent to a separation in modern terms. The couple no longer needed to live together, but they also could not get remarried to other people. The second kind of divorce was called in legal terms a divorce *a vinculo*, which means "from the vow or the bond"—and this was essentially an annulment.

The most common reason for an annulment would be the discovery that the couple were too closely related—they were too close in what are called degrees of consanguinity or affinity. Usually those who were second or third cousins were considered too closely related, but in the medieval period, relations by marriage—or even by godparentage—could make a marriage illegal. For example, if we have two sisters, Ann and Joan, and Ann marries a man named Peter, Joan cannot marry Peter's brother because they are now considered related by blood. Likewise, let's say a man named Michael is godparent to a boy named Christopher. When Christopher grows up, he cannot marry Michael's daughter—even though they are not blood relations. The fact that Michael is godfather to Christopher makes them blood relations in the eyes of the church. Very often, closeness in degrees of consanguinity or affinity was the excuse used by nobles to get out of marriages that were no longer advantageous or desired. Given the intermarriage among the upper classes, if one looked hard enough one could usually find a relationship that could annul the marriage if that's what one chose. Conversely, such close relationships were usually conveniently ignored if the parties and their families really wanted a particular union to take place. Terminating a marriage because of an inability to consummate the union was rare, but it did occur. In such cases, when one of the parties petitioned to end the marriage because it had not been consummated, doctors were sometimes called in to examine the woman and see if she was still a virgin. If a woman was bringing the case, claiming her husband was impotent, the situation was a bit trickier. In at least one case, the man who was charged with impotence was put into a room with several "good, honest women of the parish" who attempted to arouse him. When they failed, the court returned a judgment annulling the marriage.

There were many customs and practices surrounding betrothal and marriage in the medieval world that would seem unusual to us today. The decision to wed could involve a series of businesslike negotiations concerning such issues as the bride's dowry; the *morgengabe*, or "morning gift" that would be given to her after consummation of the union; provisions for heirs; and other issues. All of these matters could be subject to lengthy negotiations. The matter of dowry—of what property and wealth the bride would bring to the union—could be the subject of lengthy and intense discussion. On more than one occasion, the inability of the bride's family to provide a proper dowry scuttled a marriage contract that was in the works. On the other hand, there are a few examples of marriage—particularly among the nobility—when the bride's dowry is unusually small, suggesting both that her family was unable to provide a substantial dowry, and that the groom was willing to marry her regardless—perhaps a sign of marriage for love. The morgengabe was the bride's separate property once the marriage was consummated. You might remember the Thuringian princess, Radegund, from our earlier lectures on the Merovingians and Carolingians. When she married the generally reviled Clothar—against her will, as she was claimed by him as a war prize when she was just six years old—he gave her a villa in the town of Saix as her morgengabe. When she wanted out of the marriage and to become a nun, she fled to her villa as a refuge. As big of a jerk as Clothar was, the law of the morgengabe was one that even he didn't try too hard to defy.

Although it may occasionally be found within a marriage, love—especially in the upper strata of society—was something that was usually expected to be found outside of wedlock. However, there are some notable exceptions, such as King Richard II of England and his first wife, Anne of Bohemia. At her death, Richard appears to have been "wild with grief," ordering the destruction of the royal residence, Sheen, where she had died.

The political and economic reasons behind most noble marriages gave rise to a literary movement known as courtly love—popularized in the 12th century at the court of Eleanor of Aquitaine and her daughter, Marie de Champagne. Like so many other things that enriched the life of the medieval world, this ideal—in which a woman was adored by a man who placed her on an unreachable pedestal—seems to have originated in the Arab world and worked its way west with the influence of the Crusades.

Writers such as Chrétien de Troyes and the anonymous poets behind the 13th- and 14th-century stories of King Arthur emphasized courtly love as a practice in idealized adoration that was never supposed to cross the line into consummation. Pledging devotion to a lady thus became a means of currying favor with her lord, as the love was understood to be innocent and pure. So, for example, a man who wished to gain favor with a powerful lord might do so by pledging his devotion and service to the lord's wife—composing poetry that praised her various qualities and accomplishing great feats of valor in her name. By praising the lady, he was indirectly praising the lord who had been wise enough to marry such a woman—and thus, he hoped to gain some favor for himself. The story of Lancelot and Guinevere was in part so popular in the medieval period because this was a story of a relationship that had started in typical courtly fashion as chaste and devoted, but which had crossed the line. It was a fantasy for thousands of people who were unable to find love within the bonds of their marriage or consummate it without.

Although the married couple was arguably one of the foundational elements of medieval society, a strain of anti-matrimonial, misogynistic writings grew in popularity from the High to the late Middle Ages. Emphasizing the danger of lust, such writings characterized marriage as merely a stopgap measure for slaking lust and preventing many people from going to hell. For example, the 13th-century Middle English text known as *Hali Meidhead*, written for those religious women known as anchoresses, emphasizes that the ideal state of being is virginity; after that, widowhood is the next desirable state. The married state is at the bottom of this list and is characterized as a last resort for those who simply cannot control their sexual urges.

Central in this debate was the 13th-century French text known as the *Roman de la rose*, or *The Romance of the Rose*. Composed primarily by one Jean de Meun, this text was, at its end, an extended sexual allegory that mocked the traditions of courtly love and characterized women as wanton seductresses. It would spark a series of written arguments for and against women, marriage, and family that came to be known as the *querelle de la rose*, or the "quarrel of the rose." One of the participants in this quarrel was the 14th-century French writer Christine de Pisan. Born in Italy, she moved to France at a young age when her father was appointed to the court of King Charles V of France. There, she was educated and at 15 married the courtier Etienne de Castel, with whom she had three children. When she found herself unexpectedly widowed at the age of 24 with children, her mother, and other relatives to support, and with her husband's estate tied up in legal wrangling, Christine turned to writing to support herself. She started with poems and ballads, but was soon making a living writing less typically feminine texts—including tracts on warfare and military strategy. She became involved in the *querelle de la rose* as a vociferous advocate for women—although she was not, as many modern scholars tend to think, some kind of proto-feminist. Although Christine de Pisan was an independent woman who made her own living and way in the world once her husband was gone, she did not think this was an ideal situation. In her thinking, the ideal situation was that women should be supported by their husbands. To her mind, something was wrong with society when a widow like herself was forced to find a means of supporting her family alone. Although she was an accomplished, creative, and well-educated writer, she most likely would have been the first to say that her proper place was at home—tending to the needs of her family. In the *querelle de la rose*, what she was arguing for was the basic goodness of womankind against de Meun's characterization of females as lustful, wicked seductresses.

Perhaps in part as a response to this misogynistic feeling, many men and women elected to engage in chaste marriages, in which they remained married but pledged before a priest to abstain from sexual intercourse. In some instances, the husband and wife might enter monastic orders. Margery Kempe, whom we've discussed several times previously, persuaded her long-suffering husband that—after 14 children and numerous visions of Jesus, Mary, and the saints—she and her husband should enter into a chaste marriage. Interestingly, one way that she gets her husband to agree to this is that she offers to settle any debts he owes—a fact that suggests that she owned property or had money that was her own, separate from her husband's possessions. Toward the end of the account of her life story, she relates that in his old age and after a fall, her husband became like a child again. They had been living in separate households, and she relates that many in the community blamed Margery for her husband's condition—as they thought that if she had been home at the time of his fall, he might have gotten help sooner. But according to her, she then tended to him for the rest of his life. Although it was a great deal of trouble to her always to be changing his diaper and washing the clothes that he soiled, she took pleasure in performing this work—as she considered it just penance for what she calls "the great joy" she and her husband had taken in each other's bodies when they were first married.

So in Margery, we can see a broad spectrum of medieval marriage. Her husband, she tells us, was a "worshipful burgess" of the town of Lynn, and as the daughter of the mayor, this match, she suggests, was a good and sensible one. Her discussion of status underscores the economic and practical nature of medieval marriage—even as her many references to the sexual life she had at one point enjoyed with her husband demonstrates the possibility for real affection in medieval wedlock. Finally, her desire to live chastely reflects medieval concerns about salvation, sex, and sin. Fitting marriage and the family into these issues could be complicated.

Without a doubt, there were many marriages in the medieval world that could be considered true partnerships—in which husband and wife worked side by side to provide for the household. Usually this would be through a division of labor, with the wife attending to one set of tasks—usually cooking, sewing, taking care of the house and children—while the husband engaged in labor that would bring in income for the household. In other marriages, husband and wife literally worked side by side—in peasant communities, this might be the case in the fields during harvest time, but in towns and cities, we also see spouses who both take an active role in a business. For example, Richart and Jeanne de Monbaston were husband and wife who both labored as scribes and copyists in their workshop in 14th-century Paris. When Richart died, Jeanne carried on with the business—demonstrating that this had, indeed, been a true partnership.

The work that Richart and Jeanne performed—copying and illustrating manuscripts—is just one of the areas we are going to explore in our next lecture—which examines medieval art, artists, and artisans. When we come back, we'll explore the various means and methods of creative and artistic expression in the medieval world—and we'll see that like modern art, medieval art embraced a wide spectrum of subject matter, execution, media, and emotion.

Art and Artisans
Lecture 32

The Italian Peninsula was exceptional in many ways during the Middle Ages. It had a more continuous urban life than the rest of Europe, more extensive trade networks—especially with the Byzantine, Islamic, and Asian worlds—which meant that it was in many respects more cosmopolitan than the rest of the West. For these and a variety of other reasons, it also saw one of the most dense, and concentrated, and amazing periods of artistic production ever known in the Western world.

Although the early modern period (also called the Renaissance) is often heralded as a watershed in the development of Western art, the Middle Ages saw the production of many beautiful, skillfully executed, and whimsical artistic works. Much of the art that survives from the medieval world is religious and is most often to be found in one of two media: stone and parchment. Cathedrals and other religious structures were filled with many kinds of art—statuary, frescoes, mosaics, rood screens, misericords, and stalls—and were themselves, as a whole, great works of art. They offered craftsmen a chance to display their skills and, occasionally, their sense of humor.

Everyday objects—such as spindles, keys, chess pieces, and candlestick holders—reveal an appreciation for art and beauty in the most unlikely places.

Book production was the other major area of artistic expression in the medieval period. Some of the most stunning displays of artistic talent are found inside medieval manuscripts such as the *Book of Kells*, their images painstakingly executed by hand, rendered in brilliant colors, and containing intricate design elements. Before a word could be written or a single image drawn, animal hide was converted into a workable surface, known as parchment or vellum. From there, several people—or occasionally one multitalented individual—laid out and filled in the contours of each page, indicating where text and images should go. Illustrated, or illuminated, manuscripts contained three types of image: pictures corresponding with the text, whimsical margin images that had little or nothing to do with the subject matter, and glorious and often breathtaking whole-page images called carpet pages. Book production was originally the domain of monasteries and monks, but as time passed, more and more nonreligious people became involved.

Other artisans and craftspeople produced objects that combined artistic sensibility with functionality. Everyday objects—such as spindles, keys, chess pieces, and candlestick holders—reveal an appreciation for art and beauty in the most unlikely places. Glassblowers produced everything from everyday utensils to stained-glass cathedral windows. Wood- and metalworkers crafted a range of objects from furniture to candlestick holders to reliquaries and other religious objects. Although few textiles have survived from the period, those who worked in the clothing industry—from dyers to weavers to seamstresses and tailors—produced clothing that could be considered works of art, especially vestments for religious leaders and rulers.

© 2009 JupiterImages Corporation, a Getty Images company.

Medieval glassblowers produced everything from everyday utensils to cathedral windows.

The pride medieval artists and artisans took in their work is reflected in the rise of workers guilds, which functioned as crosses between a social club, labor union, and fraternity. The guild movement was especially strong in medieval Italy, which also had comparatively more urban centers than the rest of the medieval world. Eventually, the power of guilds throughout Europe would increase to the point that their leaders became major social and economic players on a national scale. ∎

Suggested Reading

Clanchy, *From Memory to Written Record.*

Stokstad, *Medieval Art.*

Questions to Consider

1. How could works of art become important communal representations of the identity of a society or group of people?

2. How did medieval artisans and craftspeople think of functional pieces that displayed an artistic sensibility? Was a difference between pure works of art and artistic objects perceived, or did medieval aesthetics operate more like a continuum than a divide?

Art and Artisans
Lecture 32—Transcript

Welcome back. In our last lecture, we talked about marriage and the family in the medieval world, exploring—among other things—how marriage evolved from a primarily secular institution to one that was considered primarily religious in nature—a shift that gained momentum when the Fourth Lateran Council in 1215 declared marriage to be a sacrament of the church. We discussed customs surrounding how marriages were arranged, the ages at which most medieval people married, and we explored whether or not there was any love to be found within these unions. For a long time, there was a common belief that love in the medieval world could only be found outside of wedlock, but as a few of the examples we examined last time demonstrate, there were plenty of marriages—at all levels of society—in which husband and wife seemed to have deep and genuine affection for one another. We examined literary representations of love, such as those found in the works of 12th century French writer, Chrétien de Troyes, and the phenomenon that has come to be called courtly love, in which a knight pledges to honor a lady by performing ever greater feats of valor in her name.

But in that relationship, consummation is endlessly deferred, which allows the knight to keep on achieving, and even curry favor with the lady's husband, should he be a powerful lord—without any major concern that the relationship will stray into carnal territory, although that did happen on occasion.

In our discussion of love, marriage, and the medieval family, one lecture was barely enough to scratch the surface. We've been able to identify some of the major contours and issues of marriage in the Middle Ages—but in a 30-minute lecture, we really can't penetrate as deeply as one might like into the subject.

The same will most likely be true of this lecture. Today we're going to discuss medieval art and the people who produced it. While we'll certainly identify some of the major trends and themes when it comes to medieval art, in order to do this topic the true justice it deserves, we should spend 36 lectures on this subject alone. Still, in 30 minutes today we can come to a basic understanding of what art in the medieval world was like and how and why it came to be produced.

It comes as no surprise that much of the art that survives from the medieval world is religious in nature and is most often to be found in two media that we have discussed at some length elsewhere in this lecture series—those media are stone and parchment.

Cathedrals and other religious structures built out of stone are at once filled with many different kinds of artistic works—and, as a whole, are great works of art themselves. Many cathedrals contain hundreds—sometimes thousands—of examples of statuary, frescoes, and mosaics that represent the best of artistic and artisanal talent of a particular region. In many cases, the artists selected to do the work in a cathedral were commissioned based on reputation. Most communities were small enough that everyone knew who the most talented stone workers and craftsmen were—although in some areas and for some projects, a contest might be held between rival artists who were both interested in a particular commission.

Perhaps the most famous contest for the awarding of an artistic project in not only the medieval world but all of Western history, from antiquity to the modern period, occurred in Firenze, or Florence, Italy, in 1401. This was the contest to see who would design and cast the bronze panels of the North Doors of the Baptistery of the Duomo.

At least a brief word is in order here about art in medieval Italy. Although by the temporal boundaries most people use when describing the Middle Ages—from about the year 500 to about the year 1500—this Italian contest took place in the late medieval period, at the very beginning of the 15th century. Most art historians consider this period smack dab in the middle of what they think of as the Italian Renaissance—and further, they trace the origins of this artistic period well back into the 14th or even 13th centuries. In many respects, they are right to do so. As you may have gathered by now from earlier lectures in which we discussed issues of trade, government, and the development of medical schools in the medieval world, the Italian Peninsula was exceptional in many ways during the Middle Ages. It had a more continuous urban life than the rest of Europe, more extensive trade networks—especially with the Byzantine, Islamic, and Asian worlds—which meant that it was in many respects more cosmopolitan than the rest of the West. For these and a variety of other reasons, it also saw one of the most dense, and concentrated, and amazing periods of artistic production ever known in the Western world. Michaelangelo, Donatello, Leonardo da Vinci—these are just a few of the artists who were products of what has come to be called the Italian Renaissance, but which is a period that lies within the bounds of the medieval world.

But to return to the Baptistery Doors—in 1401, a contest was announced by the *Arte di Calamala*, or wool merchants' guild, to see who should have the commission to produce bronze panels with which the North Doors should be decorated. It is a mark of the power of the guild and the general importance of artistic expression in the life of the community that some of the biggest names of the day vied for the chance to cast the Doors. Seven artists—including the aforementioned Donatello, Fillipo Brunelleschi, and Lorenzo Ghiberti—competed for the honor, and in the end, the prize was awarded to Ghiberti—who was only 21 years old at the time! All competitors had been asked to submit a single panel, depicting the biblical story of the sacrifice of Isaac, which a committee of highranking citizens then judged. After winning the contest, it took Ghiberti another 21 years to complete the Doors, but it was well worth the wait. These panels—most of which depict scenes from the New Testament—are wonders of artistic skill, in that they are able to convey depth and distance, multiple layers of people and activities, and they are full of life and energy. One almost forgets, in looking at them, that these are scenes that are cast in metal. So pleased were the city fathers of Florence that Ghiberti received another commission—this time for the East Doors of the Baptistery, and here he depicted several scenes and figures from the Old Testament. No less an artistic authority than Michaelangelo himself dubbed these doors "the Gates of Paradise."

As Ghiberti's example demonstrates, art could be serious business—especially when art was intended to honor God or serve as a demonstration of, or inspiration for, faith. As our lecture on the Gothic cathedral suggested, working on these religious edifices and their decorative flourishes—statues, column decorations, stone tracery—was considered by many to be a form of prayer itself—a sort of Crusade in stone. Those who worked in stone or metal seemed to well-understand the enduring legacy of their work, and usually took it quite seriously.

Less permanent aspects of a medieval cathedral, particularly those fashioned out of wood—such as rood screens, misericords, and choir stalls—offered another chance for craftsmen to display their skills and occasionally their senses of humor. A misericord is the name for the carved wooden seat that clergy would sit in or lean against during religious services, and very often the under part of the seat, which would not typically be seen, became a site for woodworkers to indulge any fits of whimsy. All kinds of animals are romping about underneath misericord seats, from the real—foxes, deer, horses, oxen—to the fantastic—gryphons, and mermaids, and dragons abound. Some misericords also depict some typical leisure activities—one carving shows a man playing a tabor, a type of drum, and a pipe. Another shows two men wrestling. Manchester Cathedral, which has some of the most beautiful and best-preserved misericords in the world, has—among others—carvings showing two knights jousting, and one depicting two men playing backgammon.

Several misericords in various cathedrals show a man, or occasionally a woman, carved so that it looks as if he or she is holding up the seat and its occupant with either his hands or his back. We see examples of this in Ely Cathedral, in Hereford Cathedral, and several others. Wood is obviously a less durable medium than stone, so in some instances, the wooden portions of medieval cathedrals have not survived—although we are lucky to have as many as we do. They certainly reveal a less-serious, light-hearted view of the world than the cathedral proper often does, although there are whimsical moments to be found in the stone as well—from impishly cute gargoyles to smiling saints. Even the stoneworker managed to find a space for levity and humor on occasion.

Book production was another major area of artistic expression in the medieval period. As we've discussed previously, the production of a single manuscript from start to finish was incredibly labor intensive and time-consuming. Several, perhaps dozens of, people were usually involved in the creation of a single manuscript. All that labor, from the modern point of view, would seem to have been worth it—as many medieval manuscripts have survived intact into the modern period. Although susceptible to a few things—fire, in particular, or bookworms (yes, there really are such things as book worms)—the animal hide on which medieval texts were written is generally very tough and durable. In many instances, the wooden covers that held a book closed have disintegrated while the pages within are more or less intact.

But let me back up a bit. Before a word could be written or a single image drawn, animal hide needed to be converted into a workable surface known as parchment or vellum. These two terms are used more or less interchangeably today, but it seems that in the medieval period they might be animal specific, with vellum generally meaning "calfskin"—and parchment signifying the skin of a goat. Today scholars don't tend to make a distinction between the two. Once the animal had been skinned, the hide needed to be stretched, scraped, and generally made malleable—a long process that might involve soaking the hide in a concentration of lime for a period of several days or even weeks. Some of the highest-quality manuscripts from the medieval world were made using newborn or even fetal animals.

There was a logical reason for this, as the younger the animal, the less hair it had that needed to be scraped off the hide. Indeed, when pages from medieval texts were bound together, the binder needed to arrange them so that when the book was laid open, there would be a uniformity of appearance—so the hair side of a piece of vellum would always be bound so that it faced another page turned to its hair side, and two skin-side pages would be bound so that they faced one another when the book was opened. In fact, if you look closely at medieval manuscripts, in many cases you can see the hair follicles on the page. More than one medieval scribe was noted to have complained in the margins of a text he was working on that the quality of the pages were poor and very hairy, something that made his task quite difficult.

After the animal hide was cut into sheets, several people—or occasionally one multi-talented individual—would lay out and fill in the contours of each page of the manuscript, indicating where text and images should go. For most of the Middle Ages, this kind of labor was performed in a monastic scriptorium. Indeed, monks were, as a group, the most literate people in the medieval world, and the copying and preservation of knowledge—especially religious knowledge—was considered a kind of prayer. In the later Middle

Ages, more and more laypeople got involved in the manuscript production business. You'll remember that last time in our lecture on marriage and the family, we discussed Richart and Jeanne de Monbaston—a husband and wife who ran a manuscript copying and production concern from their home workshop in 14th-century Paris. As the university system grew from the High to the late Middle Ages, we find more and more non-religious people involved in the book trade—especially in the major centers of learning, such as Paris. Although books were usually prohibitively expensive, there were still a few key texts that all university students would consider necessary to possess. So, they might go to a copyist and commission a copy of a key text or texts—works by Saint Augustine or Thomas Aquinas were two examples of these kinds of works. Alternately, students could rent portions of important texts for a set period of time. While they had this portion of the text in their possession, they could make their own copy of the work in question—a more laborious but less-expensive option.

But to return to book production—once the leaves were cut and assembled in the order in which they would eventually be bound, the pages would be ruled and pricked—two methods of giving the scribe a guide as he worked. Then the pages might be lightly blocked out, showing where texts and images should go on a particular page. In the margins next to a space where an illustration should go, there might be a notation to the scribe—the word *historia* if there should be a story picture in that spot, or the particular letter that should be rendered as an elaborately decorated capital. Usually, these guidewords in the margins were supposed to be erased—or literally, scratched off. The pages before the final product was assembled might contain all these notes waiting to be removed, but sometimes the scribe forgot—much to the delight of modern scholars, as the little notes in the margins leave clues as to how medieval books were put together.

Once the scribe had the pages of the manuscript, he would begin copying whatever text he had been commissioned to work on. The pages at this point remained unbound, as it was much easier to write on a single sheet than the bound pages of a volume. In order to assist the binder when he went to assemble the pages of the book—and these pages were known as folios—the scribe would often write what's called a catchword in the bottom margin of a page. This word was usually the first word on the page that was to follow.

Again, these were supposed to be removed before the book left the copy shop or scriptorium, but in some instances they remain.

Although the production of the text was in itself arguably an art form, it is the pictures in medieval manuscripts that include some of the most breathtaking examples of artistic skill from the medieval world. Manuscripts that included illustrations were known as illuminated manuscripts. The images they contained were usually of three types: a picture that corresponded with the content of the text, either blocked off from the main body of the writing or cleverly worked into the first letter of a section, known as an illuminated capital; or second, images in the margins that were often whimsical and had little or nothing to do with the subject matter of the text; and third, the glorious and often breathtaking images to which an entire page was devoted—and these were known as carpet pages. We've talked a little about carpet pages in some of our earlier lectures—the famous Chi-Rho page from The Book of Kells, for example. A good rule of thumb is that the ratio of illustration to written text on a given page of a medieval manuscript tells you how much that manuscript was worth. The more pictures, the more spaces between words, and the larger the font size—the more precious the manuscript. We've discussed the *Luttrell Psalter* on numerous occasions already in this course—and as you'll recall, every page has lavish illustrations, decorative flourishes, and large letters with plenty of spacing. If ever a text fit the phrase "luxury manuscript" this is it.

Other artisans and craftspeople in the medieval world produced objects that combined an artistic sensibility with functionality. Glassblowers produced everything from utensils for everyday use to stained glass windows used to decorate churches and cathedrals. The process of making stained glass was tricky, delicate, and difficult. First, glass blowers would take the number-one tool of their trade—a long hollow rod—and dip it into a vat of molten glass that had been colored with various minerals. From here, the glass on the end of the rod would be blown into the shape of a globe. While the glass was still soft and workable, the sphere would have to be opened up and rolled into a cylinder shape—after which it would be cut, laid flat, and worked into the shape of a rectangle. Then the various pieces of glass of different colors would be cut to fit into a scene that had been painstakingly designed by a master craftsmen—who usually drew the scene full-scale on a pattern board in his workshop. This was so that all the craftsmen working in the shop could easily see where the variety of different colored pieces were supposed to fit.

Once all the pieces were laid out, any last details—like faces, clothing, etc.—would be painted on to the scene with a special kind of enamel. The whole thing would then be re-fired, so that the enameled details were set, and then the whole image was joined together by means of dark pieces of metal known as lead cames. These lead cames are the bars that are ubiquitous in stained glass, that seem to break up the image but at the same time which seem to emphasize and separate certain colors from one another. The cames would hold the pieces in place, and then the entire thing would be mounted into an iron frame. The cames were made from a very soft lead, so the stiffer iron framework was necessary to support the whole window. Finally, the entire window itself would be mounted into a specially carved opening in the wall of the medieval church or cathedral. This approach meant that windows could also be removed fairly easily if it became necessary to do so—as each pane did not need to be taken out individually. As I mentioned in an earlier lecture, Chartres Cathedral was used as a German social club by the occupying Nazi forces during World War II. Local French officials removed Chartres's renowned stained class—many colors of which have never been able to be reproduced by modern methods—and they hid the glass for the duration of the Occupation, restoring it to its proper place once the war was over.

Perhaps less durable and impressive, but no less artistically sensible, was the work produced by artisans who worked with wood and metal. We've already discussed misericords—the wooden seats for clergy found in many cathedrals at length—but there were other pieces of both whimsy and beauty executed in the medieval period by artisans working in wood. For example, in France the Musée Nationale de Moyen Age—or the National Museum of the Middle Ages—has in its collection two exquisitely carved and lavishly decorated hair combs made of wood. In addition to carved flourishes, the combs are also decorated with heraldic and religious sayings. The same museum has a late 15th-century box of games—essentially, it's a wooden box containing the pieces and playing boards for six popular board games of the period. Again, this attests to the fact that some people in the medieval world certainly took their leisure time seriously. Such a piece as the box of games certainly involved a great deal of labor to produce, and was most likely quite expensive to procure.

Metalworkers produced necessary items to be sure—pots, pans, candlestick holders, and the like—but along the way they produced several pieces that would certainly be considered artistic apart from their functionality— candlesticks with intricately designed bases, horse bridles with the faces of little mustachioed men decorating the metal. As we saw in one of our earliest lectures in which we discussed artifacts from Anglo-Saxon England found in the famed Sutton Hoo Ship Burial, metalworkers sometimes pushed this idea to its limits—taking a functional item and making it entirely decorative.

Perhaps the most famous piece to come out of the Sutton Hoo Burial is an object known as the Great Gold Buckle. It is a stunning example of the linear endless knot style found in much Anglo-Saxon art, and it looks like a functioning buckle—however, it is purely decorative. Most likely it would have been worn over a very simple, working buckle. Of course, one of the major areas in which we see such works of art executed in metal is in the realm of religion. Chalices used to give Holy Communion, crosses and crucifixes that ornamented churches and cathedrals, reliquaries that held the bones or other body parts of saints—these were all pieces that would be crafted by metalworkers, and these pieces of art from the medieval period survive in abundance.

Although little in the way of textiles has survived from the period, those who worked in the clothing industry—from dyers to weavers to seamstresses and tailors—often produced clothing that could be considered works of art, especially in the form of vestments for religious leaders and rulers. Not surprisingly, like the chalices, and reliquaries, and other objects of religion, what clothing has survived from the medieval period tends to be religious in nature. This would be in part because many such ceremonial robes were often intricately decorated with gold and jewels, and they would have been cared for carefully and not worn for everyday use. Those medieval vestments that have survived give us a good idea why—many of them weigh several pounds so decorated with precious metals and gold are they—and no one could have worn them comfortably for more than a few hours at a time.

The pride medieval artists and artisans took in their crafts and trades is reflected in the rise of medieval workers guilds—which functioned, as we've discussed before, as a cross between a social club, labor union, and fraternity. As we've also noted several times, the guild movement was especially strong in medieval Italy, which also had comparatively more in the way of urban centers than the rest of the medieval world. When a group of craftspeople or artists found themselves wanting the power that came from belonging to a guild but couldn't find sufficient numbers to form their own, they might join up with another guild in partnerships that to the modern eye might, at first, not seem to make a whole lot of sense. For example, in medieval Florence, a group of painters joined up with the guild known as the *Arte dei Medici e Speziale*, which was the Guild of Healers and Apothecaries. Once you consider that medieval painters would need to frequent apothecary houses in order to come by the pigments that they would use to mix their paints, this union seems a little more obvious. Eventually, the power of guilds throughout Europe would increase to the point that their leaders became major players in the social and economic lives of their communities on a national scale.

Not only were the guilds powerful when it came to the arts, but as new technologies were discovered and new scientific advances made—especially from the High to the late Middle Ages—guilds and other organizations sought to exploit and control these advances for their own benefit. In our next lecture, we're going to talk about some of the most important developments in terms of science and technology in the medieval world. Unsurprisingly, many significant changes occurred in the areas most critical for survival—food production, clothing, and building or shelter. But even as medieval people focused the bulk of their energy on the basic necessities of life, as today's lecture has demonstrated they still found time to produce breathtaking works of art. In some cases, we have practical implements and items that are crafted with a whimsical artistic touch—as is the case with a misericord depicting a man sniffing the rear end of the occupant sitting in it—and in some cases, the art was purely art for art's sake. The advances in science and technology that we'll discuss in our next lecture meant day-to-day survival was becoming more manageable—something that meant there was more time and resources for those who wished to produce art. As we'll see next time, by the end of the Middle Ages, art, science, and technology had advanced sufficiently to dramatically impact medieval society and create an enduring foundation and legacy for the early modern world.

Science and Technology
Lecture 33

We see—not surprisingly—the greatest attention and innovation occurring in the area of food cultivation and preparation, as sustenance is perhaps the most basic of human needs. But as we move into the High Middle Ages, we begin to see a real growth—for the first time since the end of the Roman Empire—in urban life and a corresponding expansion of people specializing in trades and crafts that were not necessarily directly linked to the production of food.

Over the course of the Middle Ages, there were significant developments in science and technology. As was the case with medicine, the medieval world lagged a bit behind the Byzantine and Islamic worlds when it came to science and technology. By far its most significant developments were in areas crucial for survival: food, clothing, and shelter. The population was 90 percent rural, so changes in agriculture were of huge significance.

While some scholars talk of an agricultural revolution in the 10th century, most now think this significant increase in food production resulted from technologies that had been developing for some time. Heavy, wheeled plows made the planting process much more efficient. A new kind of horse collar—first used near present-day Germany in the late 8th or early 9th century—and greater use of horseshoes meant that horses, which were easier to care for and control than oxen, could be put to the plow. Over time, farms moved from a two-field to a three-field system, allowing the third field to lie fallow. Peasants also discovered the benefits of rotating crops. Usually built along rivers, mills took advantage of water power to grind grain into flour that could then be baked or otherwise transformed into foodstuffs.

Clothing production also saw important advances as the Middle Ages progressed, from more efficient technologies to organizations such as guilds to protect the craftsmen. In the 1100s, a new loom, with foot treadles, made weaving more efficient and comfortable. After weaving, cloth was fulled to shrink loose threads and achieve uniform consistency. This process was long, laborious, and noisome, involving chemically potent components such as urine (human and animal) and a type of clay called fullers' earth. Dyers needed to be part chemist, part botanist, and part laboratory technician to impart color to the cloth.

After food and clothing, shelter is the next most important component in survival. Although surviving medieval structures are mostly stone, the most abundant building material was wood. Although nails did exist, they were used infrequently, so medieval builders developed wood joints such as the mortise and tenon and the lap joint. The construction of cathedrals might take centuries and would require the skilled labor of thousands of workers.

The construction of cathedrals might take centuries and would require the skilled labor of thousands of workers.

Besides food, clothing, and shelter, transportation advances were fundamental to the growth and shape of the medieval world. The most common way to travel was overland and on foot. Improvements to the equipment used for horse travel and wheeled conveyance helped bring distant communities in contact with one another. Although it could be dangerous, travel by water was in fact the fastest way to move. Advances in ship construction brought once far-flung and exotic locales within reach.

Warfare, it seems, affected most of the population of the medieval world at one time or another. Advances in weaponry and defense contributed to the ways in which the medieval world shaped and allied itself. ∎

Suggested Reading

Glick, Livesey, and Wallis, *Medieval Science, Technology, and Medicine*.

White, *Medieval Technology and Social Change*.

1. What medieval inventions or technological innovations seemed to have the widest impact on the societies of the Middle Ages?

2. How did literary representations of mechanical marvels reflect real developments in medieval technology, and in what respect did they influence particular inventions and innovations?

Science and Technology
Lecture 33—Transcript

Welcome back. Last time we discussed the world of medieval art and the artists and craftspeople who produced pieces beautiful, whimsical, and sometimes even practical. Today we're going to come at the topic of object production from the other end of the spectrum and focus on the practical and scientific—and we'll talk about devices and technologies that improved the living conditions of the medieval world.

As with medical learning, the medieval West lagged somewhat behind the Muslim and Byzantine worlds for much of the Middle Ages. Although there are many developments in the area of technology in the medieval period, today I want mainly to focus on three areas, and this is because these are by far the most fundamental elements of human survival—and these are food, clothing, and shelter. At the end of the lecture, we'll also spend a little time talking about a fourth important element—transportation.

By far the most important area in terms of technological development was in the area of agriculture, as over 90 percent of the population of the medieval world were peasants who lived a very rural life and depended upon the crops they sowed and harvested for their very survival. Advances in the technology of farming and agriculture would have the most profound impact on the well-being of people in the Middle Ages.

Historian Lynn White, Jr., has argued that around the 10th century we start to see what one might call an agricultural revolution. This idea was based on three key developments: first, the invention of the heavy, wheeled plow. Second was the development of a specially designed horse collar and horse shoes, which meant that horses could be put to the plow—whereas previously, slower, less-efficient oxen had been used to do the job; and third, there was a shift from a two to a three-field system of planting. While many scholars agree that there was an increase in food production in the 10th century, most are hesitant to label this period as one of agricultural revolution, as archaeological evidence suggests that the development of the horse collar, the heavy plow, etc., were all developments that occurred gradually, over time, and not suddenly—over night. One reason for the relative abundance of food production in the 10th century might have less to do with these advances in farming techniques and more to do with the fact that Viking and other types of invasions had declined. The European climate entered what has come to be known as the medieval warm period, or the medieval climate optimum, which seems to have begun in the 10th century, and the effects of which were felt for a couple of hundred years afterward. These two things in combination—climate change and the decrease in attacks—meant that people had more time to focus on food production, and a more hospitable context in which to do so. This helped promote a significant increase in food production throughout the medieval world.

As the medieval period progressed, peasant farmers began to employ more productive planting techniques. The most basic planting system was called the infield-outfield system, whereby each peasant household had a small plot of land—essentially what we would think of as a vegetable garden—right next to the main family dwelling.

Basic staples—like onions, or carrots, or greens—might be grown here, making it easy for whoever was cooking to simply walk out the door and pick something for dinner. Further away from the household, usually as part of a large plot of land that surrounded a village, there would be land planted with more substantial crops—for example, wheat and cereal grains—which, confusingly, are often called corn in medieval texts. Corn, as in corn on the cob, properly called maize, comes from the Americas and doesn't actually exist as part of the cuisine of the medieval world—nor, as we discussed in our lecture on food and drink, does the potato. As we mentioned in that lecture, the foodstuff most important to the medieval world was bread—called the staff of life. A large portion of agricultural space was given over to the growing of grains that would eventually be ground, made into flour, and baked into bread.

Usually the outfield was divided into several strips, and each household in the village would have a certain number of strips—about half of which they would plant in any given year, and the other half which they would allow to lie fallow. I'm often asked by students, when we look at aerial evidence that shows medieval farmland divided into so many very narrow plots of land, why medieval people would want really skinny pieces of farmland that were often separated from one another, rather than one larger, more equally proportioned piece of land. The answer has to do with the nature of medieval plowing. Turning a plow, whether you were using oxen or horses, was rather difficult—so you wanted to have to turn your plow as infrequently as possible—hence, the preference for long, narrow strips of land, and the preference also for having many of them spread out rather than clustered all together.

So, in addition to the basic infield-outfield division, there was also a basic two-field planting system, as it was clear to medieval people that the land needed time to recuperate after producing a crop. We have evidence from as early as the 8th century, however, that in some parts of the medieval world people were beginning to go to a threefield system—although as standard practice this doesn't seem to have been the norm throughout the medieval world until about the 14th century. In the three-field system, one field was allowed to lie fallow; one was planted with a crop such as wheat, which could be harvested in the summer; and another was usually planted in the spring with a nitrogen-producing crop like legumes. Although medieval people didn't fully understand the science behind it, they came to recognize that planting along these lines helped to keep the soil "in good heart."

From time to time, it was necessary to bring new land under the plow, either because the population of a community had grown so more farmland was needed, or because the traditional fields were exhausted from having been in use for so long—and they needed a rest. As we've already discussed, the most common way of going about this was something called *assarting*, which means "to clear forest land"—a backbreaking job, if ever there was one—and make that land ready for plowing.

The fruits of these labors—the harvested crops—were transformed into foodstuffs for the community by perhaps one of the most important pieces of technology in the medieval period—the mill, which had been in relatively common use throughout the West from the time of the Roman Empire. Although some mills were powered by harnessing the energy of animals, most were powered by water—and thus, usually built over a fast-moving part of a river. There were several types of mills. There was a vertical mill, which stood upright in the water and could be either an undershot mill—meaning the water hit the bottom of the wheel and turned it from that position—or an overshot mill, which, as you might guess, means that the water came over the top of the wheel to turn it. Horizontal mills, in which the wheel was essentially turned on its side in the water, were more frequently used than vertical mills. Although vertical mills were more powerful, horizontal mills were easier to construct and maintain. Whatever its position, the wheel in the river was connected by a shaft to another wheel inside the millhouse, where there were usually two millstones—one that stayed stationary, and one that was turned by the water power acting on the wheel out in the river. Grain was usually poured between the two stones, and that's how the majority of the peasant population had the fruits of their harvest converted into a form that could be used to make a variety of foods. Most peasants would bring their grain to a miller for grinding, and as payment they would give him a portion of that which was ground—the now infamous soke.

Thus, we see—not surprisingly—the greatest attention and innovation occurring in the area of food cultivation and preparation, as sustenance is perhaps the most basic of human needs. But as we move into the High Middle Ages, we begin to see a real growth—for the first time since the end of the Roman Empire—in urban life and a corresponding expansion of people specializing in trades and crafts that were not necessarily directly linked to the production of food. Cloth-making became one of the most important crafts—and about the 12th century, there was a real change in its development. The most significant advancement was a change in the style of loom used to produce cloth. In the early medieval period, those who operated a loom—usually men whose wives spun and prepared the yarn for weaving—had to perform this work standing up, moving a tool known as the heddle bar forward or backward in order to arrange what weavers call the warp threads in a certain position. In the 12th century, a mechanized loom comes into use, which allowed the weaver to sit and work the thread using foot pedals. He could use his hands to pass the shuttle from side to side, which drew the weft threads into a pattern.

Weaving the cloth was just the first step in the process of preparing it for sale in its unfinished form, or for creating garments that could be sold. The next step in the process was something called fulling, which helped shrink any loose fibers in the weaving—producing a more uniform piece of fabric. This was a specialized trade, and those who were known as fullers could often be identified by the strong smell that surrounded them—even when they were not engaged in their trade. Fulling had several steps—most of which involved some kind of washing process. The cloth would usually be placed in a trough filled with water, urine—this could be from people and/or animals and was used because of its ammonia-like properties, and in addition a clay mixture known as fuller's earth would also be added to the trough. Then, the cloth would be pummeled—sometimes with tools, sometimes with the hands and feet of the fullers. The cloth would be rinsed and then the process repeated—sometimes several times. The wet cloth was then placed on tenters, which stretched it just a bit—because as it dried, it would tend to shrink. Once the cloth had been gotten into a workable form by fulling, it would usually be dyed.

Sometimes dyeing might happen earlier in the process, before the wool was even woven into a piece of fabric—and it's from this practice that we get the phrase "dyed in the wool." Those who were less well-off might wear clothing of undyed wool, as it was cheaper, but those who wished to purchase dyed clothing usually had a few options—with red and blue being the most commonly used colors. By the 12th century, the dyeing of cloth had become a highly complex process and very specialized, as a dyer needed to be part botanist, part chemist, and part laboratory technician. He needed first of all to understand which plants produced which colors; the most commonly used were madder root, which could produce reds; and woad leaf, which produced blue. The cloth to be dyed was placed in a large tub with the right mixture of water, dye, and color fixative, and it needed to be poled—or turned—on a regular basis. Like fulling, this, too, could be a rather pungent process. From this point, cloth might be purchased by tailors who would turn it into clothing for purchase, or it might be bought by individuals who might make their own clothes—or who might bring it to a tailor to have a custommade outfit.

Wool was by far the most commonly used material for clothing, although linen—spun from flax—existed. By the end of the High Middle Ages, cotton and silk were being produced in substantial quantities—especially in Italy, which had a bustling trade with foreign and exotic ports in the East. So specialized had the production, treatment, and sale of these fabrics become that Fabric- Industry Guilds gained in power, influence, and prestige at this time. There was a guild for almost every occupation, and each guild—as we've already noted—had strict rules about apprenticeships, working hours, production standards, and sales. As we discussed in our last lecture, it was the Cloth-Makers Guild in the city of Florence who commissioned the Duomo Baptistery Doors executed by the artist Ghiberti—a sign of the status and power of this particular guild.

As the example of cloth-making suggests, many occupations or trades were parceled out in their various phases to different workers who were skilled in different areas of production. An important thing to remember about the majority of the population in the Middle Ages is that although they lived a primarily rural, agricultural life, it would be wrong to think of them in similar terms to early pioneers in the United States. In other words, the image of, say, Ma from *Little House on the Prairie*—a woman who made all the family's clothes; raised, planted, and cooked all the food; etc., etc.—is not necessarily the proper image one should have of a medieval woman. Food, clothing, and other goods might be purchased or bartered from craftspeople who specialized in that particular trade. While medieval people, as a rule, were certainly more capable at a variety of necessary activities in the running of a household than we are today, there was also more specialized division of labor than one might think.

After food and clothing, obviously the next most important component of survival is shelter. Without a doubt, wood was the most abundant building material available in the medieval world, as most of Europe was forested at this time. It is most likely an exaggeration—but not too much of one—to say that in the High Middle Ages, it was possible to travel from modern-day France to what is modern-day Poland and never see the light of day, as the whole journey could be conducted through forestland.

So, wood was the most common material used, even in the building of those structures—such as castles and churches—that we might immediately picture as being built of stone. In many instances, as we've noted, a wooden structure might be built first and then later replaced with a stone one. This was the case, as we've discussed, after William of Normandy conquered England. The first thing he did after his victory was to fill the land full of motte-and-bailey style castles, and most of these were initially built in wood—although many were later rebuilt in stone. The great loss for modern scholars lies in the fact that wood is a material that decays, so there is very little that remains in terms of wholly medieval structures that are made of wood. Because stone is durable and survives much longer, it is no wonder that when most of us imagine the medieval world, we tend to imagine a world filled with buildings made of this most durable of materials.

As we discussed in our lecture on life in a medieval village, the homes of many of the common folk were built using what has come to be known as the wattle and daub method of building—in which relatively slender pieces of wood were woven together, almost like a basket, fastened between support beams, and then covered over—or daubed—with a kind of clay to fill in the gaps. The relatively—by modern standards—insubstantial nature of the walls of medieval homes meant that when someone's home was robbed, the thief might very literally break in—simply make a hole in the wall and force his way inside, something we discussed in an earlier lecture as well. Many buildings, however, were more substantially built. Surviving drawings from the medieval period demonstrate that carpenters in the medieval world were quite skilled at erecting secure buildings that were remarkably sturdy—especially given the limited use of nails and other metal fasteners, although they did exist in the Middle Ages. The two most common joints used by medieval carpenters were something called the mortise and tenon joint, and the lap joint.

A mortise and tenon joint necessitated the shaping of one end of a beam into a squared-off shape usually smaller than the main part of the beam. This little tab was called the tenon, and it would then be slotted into a space of the corresponding shape on another beam—this was called the mortise. The idea behind lap joints resembled those toys known as Lincoln Logs that many of us played with when we were young. Notches were cut in two beams, and then those beams would be crossed and locked together right at that position. While wooden construction was the most common to be found in the Middle Ages, obviously the most impressive structures were those made out of stone. In some cases, these were castles, but as we've discussed, castles were quite frequently built out of wood. It is cathedrals, a subject of another earlier lecture, that remain the most impressive edifices from the

Middle Ages. The construction of a cathedral might take many years—in a few cases, centuries. As we've already seen—both in the earlier lecture on pilgrimage and that on churches and cathedrals—these religious sites would not only serve the local community, but would also frequently function as an important draw for travelers from afar.

This brings us to the next issue, which essentially deals with how people might get from their home communities to the sometimes quite distant destinations to which they traveled. Pilgrims such as Margery Kempe, whom we met in an earlier lecture, might travel all the way from England to Jerusalem. Members of the merchant class built much of their wealth on the import and export of goods. Their profession meant that they often had to travel significant distances as well.

Without a doubt, the most common way of moving about in the medieval world was simply to use one's feet and walk from one location to another. Other options for getting about included riding on horseback or in some sort of wheeled conveyance. For long distances, travel by ship might be dangerous, but it was also the quickest way of getting anywhere in the medieval world. There is a formula to which medieval scholars sometimes refer, and it is usually rendered as something like 1 to 7 to 23. What this formula suggests is that if it takes you 23 days to walk somewhere, covering that same distance will only take you 7 days if you were to go on horseback, and just 1 if you were to travel by ship. An increase in urbanism and longer-distance trade in the 12th and 13th centuries meant that oxen—while strong—were no longer desirable as beasts of burden, at least for covering any great distance, because they moved so slowly. Horses, which were quicker and lighter, came into more frequent use—and wheeled conveyances and harnesses were adapted for them.

If one looks at a map of the medieval world, bodies of water—such as the North Sea, the English Channel, and the Mediterranean—might at first seem like huge barriers that divided areas of the medieval world from one another. On the contrary, given the relative speed of sea travel, bodies of water should more properly be thought of as connecting the medieval world—as moving over water took much less time, as a rule, than traveling overland.

There were essentially two basic types of ship in the medieval world—one was what is known as a clinker-built ship, and the other originally used a mortise and tenon construction, similar to that found in many medieval buildings. The clinker-built style of ship predominated in the North of the medieval world—and in this type of construction, the hulls of ships were built with overlapping planks, which were then usually sealed with pitch or tar. These ships tended to be durable, flexible, and quite fast in the water, and it was this style of ship that was favored by the Vikings.

In the South, the mortise-and-tenon style of shipbuilding was dominant in the early medieval period. In this style of shipbuilding, boards were painstakingly crafted and joined together, with the further step of the security of a dowel used to hold them in place. In about the 10th century, shipbuilders in the European Mediterranean started to first craft a skeleton hull—to which they simply nailed boards that were placed flush against one another. In this type of construction, gaps were filled in with some kind of caulk—and although these ships were cheaper and quicker to produce, they also tended to leak more. The trade-off of economy for security is one that merchants and other medieval travelers constantly had to negotiate.

Starting in the 13th century, the northern and Mediterranean shipbuilding traditions began to make serious advances—in part due to increased contact between these two parts of the world. One of the most important advances in terms of travel by sea was the addition of a second sail near the stern of the ship on seagoing vessels. At the end of the 14th century, shipbuilders were able to make even more effective use of wind power by adding a third sail—this one near the bow. These fully rigged ships were, by the end of the 15th century, the vessels of choice—especially over long distances. They were more maneuverable, and the shape of their construction meant that more goods could be transported with fewer relative crew members than had been the case previously—making them much more efficient and cost effective.

Arguably, the developments in seagoing technology that occurred during the Middle Ages made possible European voyages to the Americas and other parts of the world, ushering in what has come to be known as the age of exploration—one of the most important contributing factors in the development of what some scholars have called a renaissance of learning and education, and which most of us working on the period today prefer to think of as the early modern period.

In addition to technological developments in the most basic and pressing areas of food, clothing, and transportation, several technological advances came about as a result of military conflict. Warfare, it seems, impacted most of the population of the medieval world at one time or another. Technological advances in weaponry and defense contributed positively to the medieval world, in that advances in this area could also reap benefits in other, more peaceable aspects of medieval life. At the same time, war disrupted trade routes and could cause precious crops to be lost if fields happened to lie in the path of an invading army or a marauding military band. Development of new and more effective and efficient military techniques and strategies would end up dramatically changing the face of medieval society, as members of the noble classes—the first order, those who fought—soon found themselves unnecessary and unwanted, as advances in weapons technology would began to make them and their style of fighting unnecessary and obsolete. The development of medieval weapons, war tactics, and the long-range effects of these developments will be the subject of our next lecture.

Weapons and Warfare
Lecture 34

That warfare was an omnipresent fact of life in the medieval world should come as a surprise to no one. … The reasons for waging war and the entities that did so, however—from countries declaring war on one another to individuals skirmishing with their neighbors—varied immensely throughout the period.

War was a dominant aspect of medieval life; even those not directly involved in a conflict might be caught up in fighting due to association with one of the parties or an accident of geography. For a time, many scholars viewed medieval warfare as a haphazard enterprise that involved little in the way of long-range planning or military theory. In fact, evidence suggests a longstanding tradition of military theory that reached back into the Roman period and Vegetius's text *De re militari* (*On Military Matters*).

Broadly speaking, there were three types of medieval warfare: land combat, siege of a castle or fortress, and naval warfare. When it came to armed conflict between two groups of soldiers, actual fighting was usually a last resort, although the numerous recorded conflicts throughout the Middle Ages would seem to suggest otherwise. Often one party engaged in raiding, or *chévauchée*, a tactic designed to weaken the enemy's resources. Pitched battles might include a variety of personnel, from foot soldiers to archers to mounted knights. Although some battles were little more than free-for-alls, several major armed conflicts in the medieval world were decided by shrewd military strategy and tactics.

Siege warfare was much longer and more involved than pitched battle, as both sides might refrain from fighting while waiting for the supplies of one or the other to run out. Starving the opposition was often the most successful tactic in siege warfare, as was convincing the opposition of the abundance of one's own resources. Special equipment such as siege towers, ladders, catapults, and trebuchets were necessary to mount an attack on a castle, fortress, or walled city. Those within the structure used ingenious methods to repel invaders.

Naval warfare was the least common form of fighting in the medieval world. Until about the 13th century, the sea was most commonly used to move military personnel around; battles, when they did happen, resembled pitched battles on land, with two boats side by side acting as the battlefield. In the 1400s, new technology—including gunpowder—changed conflict at sea so that it came more to resemble naval warfare as we know it today.

Medieval developments in military technology and weapons would profoundly alter the way war was waged. Without question, the single most important development was the stirrup, developed in the 8th century. It made mounted cavalry much more efficient and deadly. For most of the period, the armed, helmed, and mounted knight on horseback was one of the most formidable weapons in the military arsenal. The longbow played a significant role in English victories during the Hundred Years' War between France and England at the battles of Crécy, Poitiers, and Agincourt. By the end of the Middle Ages, gunpowder and long-range cannons combined to render knights on horseback almost obsolete. Germ warfare, long considered a modern weapon, was perhaps invented at the Siege of Caffa in 1348, when attackers lobbed plague-infested bodies into the fortress.

For most of the period, the armed, helmed, and mounted knight on horseback was one of the most formidable weapons in the military arsenal.

The main place where medieval military training took place was the tournament ground. Tournaments initially served a practical function in that they kept nobles in fighting form while providing an outlet for aggressive energy and entertainment for others. By the end of the medieval period, tournaments were almost solely for entertainment, rather than training. In the late Middle Ages, a knight might have two sets of equipment—one for actual fighting, one for tournaments. Tournaments were idealized in and popularized by many medieval romances, so by the end of the period, nobles hosted tournaments deliberately modeled after the stories of King Arthur and the like, further removing them from reality and locating them in the realm of entertainment. ∎

Suggested Reading

Prestwich, *Armies and Warfare in the Middle Ages.*

Verbruggen, *The Art of Warfare in Western Europe during the Middle Ages.*

Questions to Consider

1. How might the mind-set and worldview of a medieval man-at-arms have differed from that of the modern soldier?

2. What were the most important developments in medieval military strategy and technology over the course of the period?

Weapons and Warfare
Lecture 34—Transcript

Welcome back. In our last lecture, we talked about medieval science and technology, focusing on those areas that were most necessary for survival in the medieval world—namely food or agriculture, shelter or construction, and travel. One area that we didn't cover in any great detail were technological and scientific advances that came about due to the need to wage war or defend yourself from someone who was waging war against you. That warfare was an omnipresent fact of life in the medieval world should come as a surprise to no one. As the last 33 lectures have suggested, again and again armed conflicts dramatically affected medieval societies and the people living in those societies.

The reasons for waging war and the entities that did so, however—from countries declaring war on one another to individuals skirmishing with their neighbors—varied immensely throughout the period. In fact, what we tend to think of as typical war—two huge armies facing each other on the battlefield and fighting until one side or the other was the clear winner—was not typical at all in the medieval period. What was much more common was a type of warfare known as siege warfare, in which one party was usually holed up in a castle, or walled city, or other strong defensive structure, while the opposing party hung around outside—sometimes for months—waiting for thirst or starvation to drive the other side out. But as we will see in today's lecture, this was just one type of warfare. Over time, weapons and strategies for this and other types—the pitched battle, the raid, and others—would be developed and change how war was waged in the medieval world. In turn, the medieval world itself would be irrevocably changed.

For a time, many scholars viewed medieval warfare as a haphazard enterprise that involved little in the way of long-range planning or military theory. In fact, evidence suggests that there was a longstanding tradition of military theory that reached back into the Roman period. Books from the Classical period that had survived into the medieval world were considered required reading for many leaders, especially young royals. Even if their technologies were out of date, the strategies and philosophies were still considered useful lessons for the leaders of the medieval world.

One of the most important texts on military strategy in the Middle Ages was Vegetius's *De re militari* (or *On Military Matters*), which, while popular, included advice that was long out of date by the medieval period. Vegetius—full name, Flavius Vegetius Renatus—was a Roman military officer of the 4th century A.D., and the huge popularity of his text in the medieval world is attested by the number of copies that survive—well over 300, and we can assume that there were certainly more than these made. Its various forms also underscore its widespread popularity. We find it in the libraries of many royals and nobles, in luxury form, but we also find it in more compact versions—easily portable, presumably so that it could be carried and consulted while on a campaign.

Using Vegetius's text as a base, many writers—among them the late medieval Italo-French woman writer Christine de Pisan—wrote more contemporary military manuals that were highly prized, although evidence of their practical use is limited. You may recall that we've discussed Christine de Pisan in an earlier lecture on love, marriage, and the family. In that lecture, we explored a bit how, widowed at the age of 24 with a family to support, Christine turned to writing as a source of income. Because her father had been appointed to the court of Charles V of France when Christine was still a young girl, she had access both to an education, unusual for women of her day, and she had access also to a library that was extremely varied in its contents. Philosophical tracts, romances, and military manuals all were available to her, and when she turned to writing as a means of earning money, she was able to draw on this base of texts for source material. Christine was clearly a practical woman, and she chose texts to copy that were likely to be popular—and thus, earn her the largest return for her labor. In 1408, she produced a text based on Vegetius's *De re militari*, which she entitled the *Livre des faits des armes et de chevalerie* (or the *Book of Feats of Arms and Knighthood*). The book was widely circulated in the medieval world, and in 1489, King Henry VII of England asked William Caxton—the first printer in England, whom we've encountered in several earlier lectures—to translate Christine's book into English and print it, so that Englishmen would have access to the knowledge contained therein. Caxton himself felt compelled to comment on the importance of this book, noting in his introduction that it was necessary reading for all people who might be involved in the activity of war—no matter whether they came from high or low estate.

Broadly speaking, there were three types of warfare commonly practiced in the medieval world: combat on land, either in the form of raiding or in the case of two armies facing off against each other; the siege, in which a castle or fortress was attacked, and which we've already mentioned; and the least common form, naval warfare. As a general rule, when it came to armed conflict between two groups of soldiers, actual fighting was usually a last resort—although the numerous recorded conflicts throughout the Middle Ages would seem to suggest otherwise. More frequently, each side would make raids on the other, trying to diminish the opposing parties' supplies and their will to fight. Actual face-to-face combat usually only occurred if the raiding didn't succeed in forcing one side or the other to give in to the other's wishes.

One of the more infamous raiding techniques came to be called the *chévauchée*—a tactic designed to wreak as much havoc on one's enemies' resources as possible, thereby weakening his position. The *chévauchée* was a favorite technique of the English soldiers in France during the Hundred Years' War, and essentially the idea was to absolutely destroy the countryside in a particular region—straining the economic stability and the resources of a particular leader. Entire villages, fields of crops, were set afire. The army felt free to plunder whatever they wished, and the people who bore the brunt of this tactic were, in fact, not the nobles who were actively waging war, but rather any unfortunate peasants who happened to find their homes and fields in the path of an advancing army.

The impact of a *chévauchée* was not only physical but psychological, and for those peasants whose lords knew of an approaching enemy force but did nothing to help them—perhaps because he couldn't, perhaps because he wouldn't—those peasants might be persuaded that their lord did not care for them, and perhaps switch sides. It might seem odd for people to join the side of the people who had just torched their homes and crops, but the *chévauchée* was a recognized and expected military strategy, and many peasants accepted it as part of life in the Middle Ages. Self-preservation would, in this case, prevail above all else—and the common populace would want to be affiliated with whatever party was most likely to offer the greatest degree of protection.

The allowance of plundering and looting was what persuaded many men to participate in military maneuvers like the *chévauchée*, as they were able to acquire significant wealth by stripping armor and other valuables from any enemies they encountered. But much more desirable was to capture a high-ranking member of the enemy army and hold that person for ransom. In some cases, the men would not be held at all—rather, after the soldier who had been lucky enough to capture a nobleman showed his prize to his commander and any other officials, very often the captured warrior would be given safe passage to return home and collect the specified amount of ransom—which he would return and pay at an agreed upon time. Other captured prisoners were held hostage until their ransom could be paid by family members or the government.

This was one of the prime ways of financing medieval warfare and for defeating one's enemy. For example, at the Battle of Poitiers between the French and English in 1356, the French King, Jean II, was captured. The country of France was able to raise half the ransom the English demanded, and then Jean himself was granted safe passage to return home and raise the rest of the money. He failed to do this and ultimately handed himself back over to the English, where he died as a prisoner a few months later. France was thus decimated economically and psychologically, and for a time, England had the upper hand in this long-running conflict—which we'll discuss in a little more detail in our next lecture.

If the *chévauchée* or capture of an enemy did not cause one side to capitulate to the other, then a pitched battle between two groups of soldiers might take place. Such a conflict might include a variety of different military personnel—from foot soldiers to archers to mounted knights on horseback. These were usually arranged in three groups: the vanguard, or front wave; the main guard—often foot soldiers and some archers; and the rear guard. For most of the Middle Ages, the vanguard consisted of mounted, armored knights on horseback. Usually grouped together in bands of about 30 or so, they would most frequently follow the commands of a single leader put in charge of their unit. A popular strategy in a pitched battle was for each unit to charge in succession, so that pressure was continuously applied to the enemy. Support would come from archers—and in more than a few instances, it was archers who would decide the outcome of a battle.

For example, Henry V of England arguably won the Battle of Agincourt in 1415 because of his use of the Welsh longbow. This battle was fought on a narrow piece of land, which limited the ability of either side to try and outflank the other. The French were more heavily armored than the English, and the terrain was freshly plowed and muddy. In their armor, the French thus moved slowly, fell down often, and proved easy targets for the English bowmen. Soon, dead and dying Frenchmen clogged the way forward for the rest of the French army, and the English pressed their advantage. It's estimated that the French outnumbered the English by at least 3 to 1—some historians put the figure as high as 10 to 1—but at the end of the day, it is estimated that as many as 10,000 Frenchmen were dead and as few as 100 Englishmen.

More typical than the pitched battle or the raid was siege warfare, which usually was much longer and involved than pitched battles—as both sides might refrain from actual fighting while waiting for the supplies of one or the other to run out. Starving the opposition was often the most successful tactic in siege warfare, as was convincing the opposition of the abundance of one's resources—as numerous examples from the medieval period attest, like the quasi-mythical story of the siege of the French walled town of Carcassone. The story goes that the town got its name after enduring a particularly long siege by an enemy force. The people in the city were starving and on the brink of surrendering to the army, which had been camped outside its walls for months, when one Madame Carcas had an idea. She took the last of the grain in the city and fed it to the last pig, against the vehement protests of her hungry neighbors. She then had the pig catapulted over the walls of the city toward the enemy army. When the pig landed, it split open, and the enemy leaders could see not only that the pig was plump, but that it had recently been fed copious amounts of grain. Assuming that the city must be incredibly well supplied and nowhere near starvation if they were able to cavalierly jettison pigs over their walls, the attacking army gave up and left. When the bells of the city rang out in triumph, the population cried out "Carcas sonne! Carcas sonne!" meaning that the bells were ringing in honor of Madame Carcas—and that is how the city got its name. While this event most likely never actually occurred, the popularity of the story and its details point to the fact that most of the medieval populace was familiar with the particulars of siege warfare.

If an army didn't feel like waiting for the inhabitants of a walled city or fortress to succumb to starvation, they might launch an attack against its walls. Special equipment such as siege towers, ladders, and catapults—also sometimes called *trebuchets*—were necessary to mount such an attack within the structure under the attack while those within the structure under attack often used ingenious methods to repel would-be invaders. One of the first lines of attack would be the *escalade*, or the use of ladders to scale the walls of a castle or fortress. This could be successful if the attacking army had archers to lay down supportive fire, but also relatively easily repelled if the defenders were able to dislodge the ladders—and the men climbing them—from the walls and tip them over backward. People in the castle might also throw rocks, stones, and other heavy items down onto the heads of those attempting to scale the castle walls.

While this was happening at the top of the walls, near the base, men known as sappers would be working to undermine the foundation of the castle wall, or make a hole in it with pickaxes and similar devices. Sometimes the sappers would work under a moveable cover, which would deflect missiles and other deterrents—like boiling oil—that were dropped from above. Once the sappers had a big enough opening, they would pack the hole with explosive agents and then set them off—a tactic that usually undermined the strength of the wall and occasionally brought the whole thing down, allowing the enemy entrance into the stronghold.

Another approach was to aim projectiles at castle walls, and one of the most efficient means of accomplishing this was to use a catapult or a trebuchet, both of which utilized the principle of pivot action to accomplish their aims. A trebuchet had a long, hinged arm with a sling on one end and a counterweight on the other. The counterweight was held in place while the projectile was placed in the sling. Then, when the counterweight was dropped, the arm of the trebuchet would swing up, and then the upper-hinged part would release the projectile in its sling with remarkable force and accuracy. As we saw in our lecture on the Black Death, the forces besieging Italian merchants holed up in the city of Jaffa in the 1340s defeated those within the city by loading their catapults with the dead bodies of plague victims and flinging them over the walls.

Entrance could also be gained to a stronghold by means of battering rams—these were usually heavy pieces of wood or stone suspended by ropes within a moveable frame. The ram would be drawn backward in its frame and then let go—and its own weight would propel it forward until it crashed into the entrance to the fortress. If this was done enough times, even the stoutest entrance would usually eventually give way.

Another piece of equipment used in attacking a castle was the siege tower. This would be a tall, wooden structure with openings through which attackers could observe the enemy from a strong vantage point, or they could fire weapons as well. Some towers seem to have been built simply to allow the attacking forces a good view of the conflict, while others seem to have been intended to be moveable and wheeled right up to the castle walls with the attackers inside. Often the sides of the siege tower were covered with animal hide or treated in some other fashion so as to repel fire and other defensive tactics. Sources relate that during the Siege of Lisbon during the Second Crusade, the English built a siege tower that was 95 feet high. One of the drawbacks of this type of equipment became evident when they began to wheel it toward the city walls, and it became stuck in the mud—and essentially useless.

Naval warfare was the least common form of warfare in the medieval world, and until about the 13th century, the sea was most commonly used as the easiest and quickest way to move military personnel around. Battles, when they did happen, resembled pitched battles on land—with two boats side-by-side acting as the battlefield. Until the late Middle Ages, there were no ships built for the express purpose of warfare—so two ships that wished to engage would simply pull up alongside one another, and grappling hooks would be thrown from one vessel to another. The fighting that would then take place was violent hand-to-hand combat, with the losers usually being thrown overboard. As naval battles became more common toward the end of the Middle Ages, some sailing vessels might be retrofitted for war, with wooden towers erected on either end of the vessel. These would provide some cover for those men shooting arrows or other missiles at the enemy vessels. In the 1400s, the development of new technology—including the use of gunpowder—changed conflict at sea, so that it came more to resemble naval warfare as we know it today.

Developments in military technology and weapons would profoundly alter the way in which war was waged throughout the medieval period. In some cases, developments in the realm of weapons and warfare would have long-range implications for the social order of the medieval world as a whole. Without question, the single most development in terms of military strategy and combat was the use of the stirrup. The stirrup made its way into Western Europe from the East starting around the 8th century, but was not in common usage throughout the medieval world until a couple centuries later. It had been the case prior to the widespread use of the stirrup that you would ride to the battle, get off your horse, fight—and if you survived, get back on your horse after the battle and ride back home.

With the advent of the use of the stirrup in warfare, mounted warriors on horseback became much more efficient and deadly than had previously been the case. They were now able to use the force of a galloping horse and what is called a couched lance—one that is tucked under the arm in such a way as to cause the most damage to one's enemy and the least potential harm to one's self. The deadliness of the lance was enhanced multiple times when it was paired with the speed and strength of a horse—and this meant that the mounted warriors at the front of a charge could take down much more of the enemy more efficiently and quickly than had previously been the case. So, for most of the period the armed, helmed, and mounted knight on horseback was one of the most formidable weapons in a military arsenal. Some scholars have gone so far as to suggest that the use of this small piece of metal and the way it changed military techniques, in fact, helped give rise to the medieval social structure known as the three orders, or the three estates—or what has also been called feudalism. Those who fought—the nobles—were at the top, valued for their military might. Some scholars think that without the stirrup, this situation would never have come to be.

But if one piece of military technology could arguably be said to have given rise to a particular social structure, other developments in terms of weapons would also change that social structure dramatically. For example, the development of the longbow would play a significant role in key English victories during the Hundred Years' War between France and England at the battles of Crécy, Poitiers, and Agincourt—as we've already discussed. While mounted knights on horseback played an important role in these conflicts, new technology—which gave rise to bows that could shoot further and more precisely—was obviously much more efficient. The benefits are obvious: With a longbow, you can attack your enemy from a great distance, while the mounted knight on horseback has to get up close and personal with the enemy to cause any damage—an obvious disadvantage.

By the end of the Middle Ages, gunpowder and long-range cannon combined to render the knight on horseback almost irrelevant and obsolete in warfare. In turn, this affected the social order of the medieval world. We can see this shift taking place with the increased use of scutage—a tax that a knight could pay in order to get out of the days of military service he owed his lord as a vassal, and which we've already discussed at some length. It was much more efficient for a lord to accept payment from the knight and release him from his obligation, and then use that money to hire soldiers to do his fighting. But even though, by the 15th century, the mounted knight on horseback was pretty much obsolete, there was still a knightly class who felt entitled to the honors and status that they had previously earned by military service to their lords. If the stirrup was the means by which medieval warriors had vaulted to the top of the social order, then gunpowder and cannon was the means by which that position was undermined. As William Caxton's preface to his edition of Christine de Pisan's *Book of Feats of Arms and Knighthood* suggests, the subject of war was, by the 15th century, a matter of some importance for people from the non-noble classes as well as those who occupied the traditionally elite positions of society.

We can see this shift in the importance of knights in battle as compared to the ordinary foot solider if we examine the change in the main arena in which military training took place in the medieval world: the tournament ground. Initially, tournaments served a practical function in that they kept nobles in fighting form while providing an outlet for aggressive energy. On the tournament field, knights practiced becoming proficient at jousting, or using the lance to unhorse an opponent. The tournament was also the place where mock battles took place. At the same time that the warrior class was honing and maintaining their battle skills, they provided entertainment for other members of the noble classes. By the end of the medieval period and beyond, tournaments were almost solely focused on entertainment rather than training. As I've already noted, by the late Middle Ages, a knight might have two sets of equipment—one for actual fighting, and one for participating in tournaments. The latter set might be largely useless in real combat, a fact that emphasizes how far tournaments had moved from their original function. They had become idealized and popularized in many medieval romance texts. By the end of the period, nobles began to host tournaments that deliberately modeled themselves after those depicted in stories of King Arthur, with participants playing the parts of famous figures from literature, like Sir Lancelot or Sir Gawain, on the tournament field— something that further removed tournaments from the realm of the real and located them in the realm of entertainment. As we saw in our lecture on the Black Death, the proliferation of tournaments—and the general feeling that these were frivolous activities; a waste of time, money, and other resources— was identified by some as one of the potential causes of the Black Death, in that these lavish entertainments, in their excessive qualities and lack of usefulness, had incurred the wrath of God.

But even as tournaments used the tactics and techniques of war as a form of amusement in the later Middle Ages, real war was still being waged—and the 14th and 15th centuries saw a number of conflicts that would dramatically change the landscape of medieval society. From localized uprisings—like the Peasants' Revolt in England, the Jacquerie Rebellion in France, and the Ciompi Revolt in Florence—to national internal conflicts—like the Wars of the Roses in 15th century England—to international conflicts that embroiled almost all of the medieval world—like the Hundred Years' War between France and England—the later Middle Ages was a time when advances in weapons and warfare were put to use on what might have seemed to be almost a daily basis. These conflicts will be the subject of our next lecture.

Revolts, Uprisings, and Wars
Lecture 35

The Hundred Years' War is important for our understanding of certain aspects of the medieval world in part due to the development of new kinds of weapons, battle tactics, and patterns of taxation—all things that fostered great change in the three-estates model of medieval society.

In the late Middle Ages, a series of revolts, uprisings, and wars transformed the medieval world in new and unexpected ways. Perhaps the longest-lasting of these events—both in duration and impact—was the Hundred Years' War. This conflict between England and France was actually a series of conflicts rather than a single, sustained engagement, and it lasted more than 100 years—from approximately 1337 to 1453.

When William of Normandy conquered England in 1066, nobles now owned lands on both sides of the English Channel. To whom should they do homage—to the king of England or France? Furthermore, this technically made the king of England vassal to the king of France, a situation intolerable to the English. The situation was exacerbated by the marriage of Eleanor of Aquitaine to King Henry II of England in the 12th century. Their marriage brought the French duchy of Aquitaine under English control, a blow to French territorial interests.

To break the will of the French, King Edward III of England employed *chévauchée*. English raiding parties burned and slaughtered their way through the French countryside, avoiding any formal, pitched battles and demoralizing the French. The English also achieved considerable success after developing some advanced weaponry, particularly the Welsh longbow. To pay for the war, monarchs levied kingdom-wide taxes, sometimes more than once in a single year, and largely abandoned the chivalric ideal of vassals giving military service in favor of a paid army.

During the duration of the Hundred Years' War, smaller revolts in France, England, and Italy further strained the power structures of medieval society.

The Jacquerie uprising occurred in France in 1358, in and around Paris. The English captured the French king after the Battle of Poitiers, encouraging French peasants to overturn a system that kept them at the bottom of the social order. Within Paris, the uprising was mainly the merchants, led by Etienne Marcel, against the royals and government. In the countryside, peasants rose up against nobles, slaughtering many of them and sacking their estates. Although the revolt was quickly put down, the status quo of absolute royal power was no longer viable, and change was needed.

Around the same time, across the English Channel, the seeds of a similar uprising were sown. After the first major wave of the plague swept through Europe, the surviving peasants found their labor in high demand. To curb the movement of peasants and a steep climb in wages, Parliament passed the Statute of Laborers in 1351, freezing wages at preplague levels and tying peasants to their manors. In addition, the English king levied taxes to help pay for the war with France in 1377, 1379, and 1380. In 1381, a general uprising began with attacks on royal tax collectors and soon became more widespread and violent. Although called the Peasants' Revolt, it involved a large proportion of the population who could more accurately be called merchant class. Although the revolt was finally put down by King Richard II, it was clear that old policies derived from the three-estates model no longer served medieval society.

A similar situation began in Italy in 1378, but unlike the Peasants' Revolt, the source of the discord was in an urban center—Florence. Due to postplague depopulation, many artisans were compelled to work directly for merchants rather than as independent artisans-cum-merchants, a dissatisfying situation for most craftspeople. This issue was felt particularly strongly in the cloth industry, whose workers, the Ciompi, were all governed by a single guild, the Arte dell Lana, which allowed only cloth merchants to be members. This guild also lengthened apprenticeships and refused to allow those in related industries—such as dyers, fullers, and weavers—to have their own guilds. In 1378, the Ciompi uprising ousted the sitting Florentine government and placed a wool-carder in charge of the city. Within a few short years, infighting between the various Ciompi factions brought the rebellion to an end, although the impact would be felt long after.

No sooner had the Hundred Years' War between France and England come to an end than a new, internal conflict broke out in England that led to a new royal house coming to power—ushering out, in the view of many historians, the medieval period and bringing in the early modern. The roots of the Wars of the Roses are to be found in the Hundred Years' War. After his victory at the Battle of Agincourt in 1415, King Henry V of England took, among other things, the French princess Catherine for his bride. Henry V died when his infant son, Henry VI, was only nine months old, thus throwing English government into turmoil. Adding to this difficulty, as an adult Henry VI had no real inclination to be king and had inherited the insanity of his grandfather, the French king. During two of his bouts of insanity, Henry's cousin, the duke of York, was named protector of the realm and served as regent, a situation that many English people would have liked to become permanent. This conflict—between the royal houses of Lancaster and York—would come in later years to be known as the Wars of the Roses, as each house supposedly had either a white or red rose as its emblem. After 32 years, the conflict ended when Henry Tudor, a distant Lancaster cousin with an equally distant claim to the throne, defeated the Yorkist king, Richard III, at the Battle of Bosworth field and took as his bride Elizabeth of York. ∎

> No sooner had the Hundred Years' War between France and England come to an end than a new, internal conflict broke out in England that led to a new royal house coming to power—ushering out, in the view of many historians, the medieval period and bringing in the early modern.

Suggested Reading

Allmand, *The Hundred Years' War*.

Carpenter, *The Wars of the Roses*.

1. What factors combined to produce so many revolts, wars, and uprisings in the later Middle Ages in multiple geographic locales and between so many varied groups of people?

2. How might European society have developed differently if the lower classes had not revolted against their superiors in England, France, and Italy?

Revolts, Uprisings, and Wars
Lecture 35—Transcript

Welcome back. In our last lecture, we discussed technological advances in weaponry and changes in military strategy throughout the Middle Ages. The impact of these developments was far-reaching—extending beyond the battlefield and into the everyday lives of most of the citizens of the medieval world in one way or another, and at one time or another. Today we are going to talk about some of the conflicts in which these new technologies and strategies were used, their causes, and the aftermath that would irrevocably change medieval society—and would have a hand in the gradual transformation of the medieval world into the early modern one.

As we enter the late Middle Ages, a series of revolts, uprisings, and wars would impact the medieval world in new and unexpected ways. Perhaps the longest lasting of these events—both in duration and impact—was the so-called Hundred Years' War. This conflict between England and France was actually a series of conflicts—rather than a single sustained military engagement—and it lasted well over 100 years: from approximately 1337 to 1453. A warning is in order here before we begin to go much further with our discussion today: In the period under examination today, there is a ton of what we might call back-and-forthing of the English throne, and your head might start to hurt from trying to keep all the monarchs straight. You are not alone in this, and you should feel comforted that any number of historians who have long worked on this subject still need to consult history books and notes themselves in order to keep everything straight in their minds.

The initial source of the Hundred Years' War can be found in William of Normandy's Conquest of England in 1066, which we discussed in Lecture 12. When William became king of England, he still held control of Normandy—but as a duke, not a king. Technically, then, the king of England was thus a vassal of the French Crown. Since William had stripped all the Anglo-Saxon nobles of their lands and titles and bestowed them on his own vassals, he put his own noble subjects into a legal bind similar to that in which he found himself. The Norman Conquest of England created a situation in which nobles owned lands on both sides of the Channel, and this led to some confusion as to whom lords should do homage—to the Kings of England or to France?

While in the early years, there was not too much concern over this, as time went on, understandably, the idea that the king of England should have to do homage to the king of France for anything became intolerable in the minds of the English people—as to do so would essentially be saying that the king of France was above the king of England in the feudal hierarchy—rather than that as rulers of sovereign nations, they were, if anything, equals.

This tense situation was exacerbated by the marriage of Eleanor of Aquitaine to King Henry II of England in the 12th century. As her dowry, Eleanor brought to the English the French duchy of Aquitaine, which was a huge piece of land and a blow to French territorial interests. Aquitaine, Normandy, and other lands that Henry managed to claim during his reign—he pushed north and west into what had largely been Celtic realms—gave the world what has come to be termed the Angevin Empire—and this included England, most of what we think of as France today, and Ireland. Although as I've noted before, the term "Angevin Empire" was never used during the Middle Ages, it's still a handy descriptor for the large territory that was under England's control, and which extended far beyond the bounds of what we think of as England itself today. Even though England's holdings on the Continent were hugely enlarged with the acquisition of Aquitaine, this did not at all resolve the issue of homage to the French king, as Aquitaine was technically a duchy of France—and arguably, this meant that the English king was yet again bound to the French monarch as one of his vassals, a subordinate.

In 1328, the last Capetian king of France died without an heir, and many contenders—including King Edward III of England—made a claim for the French throne. The ultimate winner of this dispute was Philip of the House of Valois, who became King Philip VI. Tensions were already running high, then, when in 1337, Philip claimed that Edward had not done homage in the proper fashion for some of his holdings. On this basis, the French then tried to capture the Englishheld realm of Gascony, saying that Edward had forfeited his right to hold it by not properly doing his homage to the French Crown. It was this move that led to the first outbreak of the Hundred Years' War.

As we discussed last time, the Hundred Years' War is important for our understanding of certain aspects of the medieval world in part due to the development of new kinds of weapons, battle tactics, and patterns of taxation—all things that fostered great change in the three-estates model of medieval society. As you'll also recall from our last lecture, in order to break the will of the French, King Edward III of England employed a military strategy known as the *chévauchée*, in which English raiding parties burned and slaughtered their way through the countryside—thereby demoralizing the French, decimating their supplies, and avoiding any formal pitched battles. The English also achieved considerable success after making some technological advances in terms of weaponry, particularly with the Welsh longbow. Again, as we discussed in the last lecture, this was what was the deciding factor at the Battle of Agincourt in 1415, when King Henry V of England with a small army—what Shakespeare famously immortalized as "we few, we happy few, we band of brothers"—not only decisively defeated, but also killed the majority of the French nobility.

A conflict that lasts well over 100 years is, obviously, going to get expensive after awhile. In order to pay for the war, the monarchs of both kingdoms took to levying kingdom-wide taxes, sometimes more than once in a single year. They also largely abandoned the chivalric ideal whereby a vassal performed a certain number of days of military service for his lord. We could spend several lectures just discussing how the Hundred Years' War itself dramatically altered medieval society, but during the course of the 116 years that it lasted, many smaller revolts impacted the societies of France, England, and Italy—further testing and straining the power structures of medieval society. It's worth our time to focus on some of those for a moment.

The first revolt we're going to talk about—the uprising known as the *Jacquerie*—is directly related to the events of the Hundred Years' War. This occurred in France in 1358 in and around the city of Paris. The initial impetus for this revolt was the capture of the French king by the English after the Battle of Poitiers in 1356. This situation seemed to encourage French peasants to believe that now was their chance to overturn the power structure that had kept them at the bottom of the social order. Within the city of Paris, the uprising was mainly one in which merchants, led by one Etienne Marcel, revolted against French royals and the government. In the countryside, peasants rose up against nobles—slaughtering many of them and sacking their estates.

It was not only the nobility who were attacked. Many members of the church suffered during this uprising, as the church was regarded as supporting the nobility and their policies. The rebellion at first seemed to be succeeding, but in the end, the townspeople and peasants were simply no match for the might of the French army. Although the revolt was quickly put down by the French nobility, it was clear that the status quo in which the royal government had held absolute power over the citizenry was no longer viable, and change was needed.

At the same time, it became clear that the French government was going to have to negotiate with England. These negotiations resulted in the Treaty of Brétigny, signed in 1360, which temporarily brought hostilities between France and England to a halt. Among its provisions were some real boons for England—namely, that English kings would no longer be considered vassals of the French throne, and that in order to secure the release of the French king, France was going to have to pay an enormous ransom. But, while England got to keep most of the contested territories on the Continent, the English monarch had to renounce any claims to the French throne—something that would come back as an issue of contention as hostilities between the two nations broke out again and again. Around the same time this was happening, across the Channel in England, the seeds of an uprising similar to the *Jacquerie* were being sown. Indeed, the *Jacquerie* itself is significant at least in part because it served as a kind of model for rebellion for the rest of Europe.

As we discussed in our lecture on the Black Death, immediately after the first major wave of plague swept through Europe, those peasants who had survived found their services in high demand from nobles who needed laborers to work their lands. In an attempt to curb the movement of peasant families throughout the countryside and to halt the steep climb in wages they demanded for their labor, the English Parliament passed the Statute of Laborers in 1351, which froze wages at pre-plague levels and tied peasants to the manors with which they had long been affiliated. Essentially, Parliament tried to do an end-run around the laws of supply and demand. Adding insult to injury, the English king levied taxes on the population to help pay for the war with France, and he did this in 1377, 1379, and 1380. In 1381, those who made up the majority of the English population had had enough. When tax collectors attempted to perform their jobs, in May of that year, they were attacked and a general uprising—long called the Peasants' Revolt—occurred. In the beginning, this revolt involved attacks on royal tax collectors, but it soon became more widespread and violent. Although called the Peasants' Revolt, it involved a large proportion of the population who more properly should be thought of as belonging to the merchant class. Lead by peasants Wat Tyler and John Ball, the Peasants' Revolt—more properly called the Uprising of 1381—also had a religious component, as many of those who were followers of John Wyclif and the movement known as Lollardy—which we discussed in a previous lecture—joined in as they saw this as an opportunity to resist not only the power of secular authority, but that of the church as well.

Before they were done, the rebels had, among other things, executed the archbishop of Canterbury and burned down the Savoy Palace, home of John of Gaunt—a son of King Edward III, patron of Geoffrey Chaucer, and the wealthiest man in England. At the time, Gaunt was also acting as regent for his nephew, the 14-year-old King Richard II. According to some reports, this was young Richard's finest hour, as it was he who met with the rebel leaders and eventually quelled the uprising. Although order was finally restored, it was clear that, as with the aftermath of the *Jacquerie*, old policies derived from the ideal of the three-estates model could no longer serve medieval society. Serfdom was on its way out, and the hold of the church over matters of religious doctrine was eroding.

A similar situation was occurring in Italy, starting in 1378, but unlike the Peasants' Revolt or the initial wave of the *Jacquerie*, the source of the discord was located in an urban center—the city of Firenze, or Florence. Like the Peasants' Revolt, the aftermath of the plague played an important role, in that with the depopulation of the community, many artisans were compelled to work directly for merchants rather than as independent artisans-cum-merchants—a situation that was dissatisfying for most craftspeople. The issue was felt particularly strongly in the cloth industry, whose workers, the Ciompi, were all governed by a single guild—the *Arte dell Lana*, which allowed only cloth merchants to be full members, although it dictated rules about the industry as a whole. The Arte dell Lana also lengthened apprenticeships and refused to allow those in industries crucial to cloth-making—such as dyers, fullers, and weavers—to have their own guilds.

In 1378, the Ciompi, the wool-carders, rose up. Wanting to break the stranglehold-like control the more powerful guilds had over the city government, the rebels also demanded higher wages and a position in government for members of the minor guilds. They ousted the sitting Florentine government and placed a wool-carder in charge of the city—managing to control the city government until 1382. The Ciompi Revolt established one of the most democratic governments in medieval Italy—setting up a new Florentine constitution that gave rights to new guilds and to unskilled workers. This marvelous new experiment in government failed, however, when in 1382 the elites of the city hired a band of mercenaries to put the rebel leaders in their place. The mercenaries surrounded the slums of the city, which housed the largest portion of the cloth workers—and thus the major part of the support base for the Ciompi government—and this band effectively crushed the Ciompi movement with bloody house-to-house fighting.

Ultimately, though, this attack was not the main cause of the failure of the Ciompi government—then, as now, deciding factors in a situation such as this were economic. The real problem was that the Ciompi government—as fair, and just, and forward-thinking as it had been—hadn't managed to bring prosperity to Florence. Had the economic picture improved for the city between 1378 and 1382, the rebel government might very well have been left in place. As it was, even though the revolt was effectively quashed, the ideas it had embraced had taken root in the consciousness of the populace—and the Ciompi uprising would continue to bear fruit long after it had been put down.

While all of this was happening, the Hundred Years' War was continuing to go on, and on, and on. While the Treaty of Brétigny had brought England much that it had wanted, the rest of the Hundred Years' War was going to tend to favor France, with a couple of key exceptions. Fighting between the two nations broke out again in 1369 and didn't stop until 1396, when another treaty was signed. This treaty, unfortunately, didn't address the matter of the duchy of Aquitaine or English claims to the French throne, and both sides regularly violated it until fighting flared up again full-force with the Battle of Agincourt in 1415—which we've already discussed. With the decisive victory here, it seemed that the French Crown was almost within the grasp of the English. The victorious Henry V took as one of his prizes the French Princess Catherine—and as part of the treaty of Troyes that was made soon after, the French king named as his heir the son of Henry V and Catherine. Understandably, most of the citizens of France liked this idea not at all, and there was widespread resistance to the Treaty of Troyes.

When Henry V died unexpectedly in 1422, he left behind the ninemonth-old Henry VI. One can imagine that even in the most stable of times, an infant on the throne is not what one would choose, and French resistance to an English claim to the French throne increased—with war breaking out again. This time, the French were hugely successful in chipping away at English holdings on the Continent, in large measure due to the efforts of the French crossdressing peasant girl, Joan of Arc—who, claiming she was guided by angels, led the French to a series of victories over the English. Eventually captured and burned as a heretic, Jeanne d'Arc, as she is called in France, continues to loom large in the French popular imagination as a national heroine.

By 1453, England had lost all of its holdings on the Continent—save the port city of Calais—and the Hundred Years' War had effectively come to an end. No sooner had this happened than a new internal conflict broke out in England that led eventually to a new Royal House coming to power and ushering out, in the view of many historians, the medieval period and bringing in the early modern. This internal conflict between Royal Houses of England came to be called the Wars of the Roses. The plural is important here, as—like the Hundred Years' War—this conflict was actually a series of military conflicts that varied greatly in scale and outcome. Its roots are to be found in the Hundred Years' War—specifically with the aftermath of the English victory at the Battle of Agincourt in 1415. As we discussed a moment ago, Henry V died when his infant son, Henry VI, was only nine months old—thus, throwing medieval English society into some turmoil. Adding to the difficulties surrounding Henry VI's claim to both the English and French thrones was the fact that, as he grew up, it became quite clear that Henry VI had no real inclination or desire to be king—and he had also inherited the insanity of his grandfather, the French king.

During two of his bouts of insanity, Richard, duke of York, was named protector of the realm. The protector served as regent, a situation that many English people would have liked to have become permanent. Richard served as protector from 1453 to 1455, until Henry recovered from his first period of insanity. From this point on until 1485, however, the hostilities between these two Royal Houses of York and Lancaster would flare up again and again. We should back up here and say a little bit about why it is that these two royal lines were in conflict. Both houses descended from King Edward III, who was succeeded by his 10-year-old grandson, Richard II, upon his death in 1377. As you might imagine, the cards are pretty well stacked against anyone who becomes ruler of a nation at such a young age—as poet William Langland wrote in his 14th-century poem *The Vision of Piers Plowman*— "Woe to the land when the king is a child." Richard was ousted by his cousin Henry Bolingbroke in 1399, and most likely Richard was probably murdered in Pontefract Castle shortly thereafter. Henry Bolingbroke was also a grandson of Edward III by his father, John of Gaunt, and when he took the throne he became Henry IV. It is his son, Henry V of England, who won the glorious victory for England against the French at the Battle of Agincourt in 1415—but as we've already seen, Henry V died unexpectedly, leaving an infant to rule.

If a 10-year-old king is no good, then a nine-month-old one is much worse. It is this royal line that are known as Lancastrians, so-named because John of Gaunt, from whom they descend, was also duke of Lancaster. The lines of the Dukes of York also descend from King Edward III—so in effect, this was a feud among cousins, a family conflict writ large, which would embroil almost every noble house in England before it was over. It is only in later years that this conflict would come to be known as the Wars of the Roses, as each house supposedly had either a white or red rose as its emblem. At the time, it wasn't called any such thing.

In 1461, the barons of the realm, fed up with the instability of Henry VI and his unpleasant, aggressive wife, Margaret of Anjou, put Edward duke of York on the throne as Edward IV. Edward would rule from then until 1470, when

Lancastrian powers restored Henry VI. This second reign of Henry's did not last long. In 1471, Edward came back to the throne and Henry—imprisoned in the Tower of London—was most likely murdered there shortly thereafter, so that there would be no figure around which his supporters could rally. Edward then ruled until his death in 1483.

What is more important for our purposes today is not the back-andforthing of the English throne, but the impact this dispute had on the rest of society. The time of the Wars of the Roses was one of conflict and scheming, with each side desperately trying to shore up and confirm alliances, break enemy alliances—and it was marked by a series of so-called private wars among various noble houses, many of which occurred far from the main dispute happening in the major centers of power. It was a period when many social ideals collapsed. The honorable and chivalric aspects of knighthood were nowhere to be seen, as it was every man for himself—and many knights and nobles regularly changed sides, depending on which royal line was in power.

One such turncoat figure, as we discussed in our lecture on King Arthur, was the minor nobleman Sir Thomas Malory—who seems to have been a Yorkist at first, but then switched to the Lancastrian side. It was his implication in a Lancastrian plot that most likely landed him in prison in the 1460s, although he was accused of myriad crimes—including cattle stealing, rape, and assaulting an abbot. While he was in prison for such un-knight-like behavior, he did a very curious thing. He wrote the manuscript we have come to know as *Le Morte d'Arthur*, which is the most comprehensive and thoroughly rendered treatment of the legend of King Arthur before the modern age. In his massive opus, Malory essentially writes a hymn to all those chivalric ideals absent from his own age—loyalty, honor, steadfast friendship, service to ladies—notably, many qualities that he himself seemed to be lacking. At the same time that Malory praises those values, however, his work also seems to acknowledge that it is impossible for mere mortals to adhere to such lofty goals consistently. Thus, the Arthurian community—and by extension, Malory's own world—seems doomed to failure from the beginning, despite the valiant efforts of its king and his knights to uphold honor, and justice, and virtue.

In many respects, *Le Morte d'Arthur* is the last great literary work of the English medieval world, although the values that it espouses and the world of knights, and damsels, and noble kings it describes would continue to be popular and serve as the subject for some of the greatest literature the world has ever come to know for at least two centuries afterward.

It may have seemed that with the death of Henry VI and the second reign of Edward IV, the conflict of the Wars of the Roses was essentially over, but there was more drama yet to come. Once again, upon the death of an English monarch, an adolescent inherited the throne—this would be the 11-year-old Edward V—who, along with his younger brother, Richard, duke of York, were given into the care of their father's brother—Richard, duke of Gloucester. Their uncle, under the guise of protecting them, put them in the Tower of London while he assumed the throne in his nephew's stead. The young king and duke of York—known to readers of Shakespeare as the princes in the tower—never emerged from their imprisonment and were most likely murdered on the orders of their uncle.

Thirty-two years after it began, the family conflict that came to be known as the Wars of the Roses would finally end when Henry Tudor, a distant cousin from the Lancastrian line with an equally distant claim to the throne, would defeat Richard III at the Battle of Bosworth Field in 1485. Richard lost his life there after his horse was killed beneath him—a moment that has become famous due to claims that as he stood on the battlefield facing certain death, Richard roared: "A horse! A horse! My kingdom for a horse!" No horse was to be had, and Richard met his end.

To shore up his claim to the throne, Henry Tudor, now Henry VII, took as his bride Elizabeth of York, sister of the ill-fated princes in the tower—and thus, ushered in the Tudor Dynasty, which would produce England's King Henry VIII and Queen Elizabeth I. For the sake of convenience, many historians point to 1485 as the end of the Middle Ages in England—more as a matter of convenience really than anything else. Although there were some significant changes in society that year, the changing of thrones from one dynasty to another is less significant in terms of social changes than the long-lasting impact that the extended Wars of the Roses—along with the Hundred Years' War and the uprisings and revolts like the *Jacquerie*, Ciompi, and

Peasants' Revolt—would have on the medieval world as a whole. For almost 200 years, war would touch all corners of the medieval world—profoundly undermining certain ideals of social order and noble behavior that had been pervasive. Arguably, this is what would help to usher in that period known as the early modern, or Renaissance. But as we'll see in our next and final lecture, the roots of the Renaissance lie deep in the medieval world, and the early modern has more things in common with the Middle Ages than it has distinctions from it.

Toward the Early Modern Period
Lecture 36

> The term "Renaissance," which literally means "rebirth," was long used by those who saw the 16th century as a period of enlightenment and learning after the long, dark, and uninteresting period known as the Middle Ages. ... Instead of a gap or divide between the medieval and early modern period, I tend to see bridges that connect the two in important ways.

The Renaissance, spanning roughly from the late 15th to the 17th century, has been simplistically defined in terms of its difference from—and by extension, its superiority over—the medieval period. Advances in artistic technique and production, a rediscovery of lost Classical texts, a new valuation of the individual, and dramatic religious reforms are all considered the hallmarks of the Renaissance. Yet all of these developments have their root in the Middle Ages. Where once scholars spoke of the differences between the periods, we now tend to see much greater continuity of ideals and values as the medieval world slowly transformed into something new.

One of the defining elements of the early modern period, or Renaissance, was the explosion of interest in Classical texts that had been lost or unknown to the Middle Ages. In fact, the gathering of manuscripts by Charlemagne and Alfred the Great laid the foundation for the rediscovery of works of classical antiquity. In addition, trade relations with the east—particularly through the Italian city-states—brought other undiscovered or lost texts into the European orbit.

© 2009 JupiterImages Corporation, a Getty Images Company.

The Gutenberg Bible was the first book printed in the west using movable type. About 40 copies survive.

The exponential increase in literary production during the early modern period was made possible by the development of moveable type and the printing press in combination with paper, which was much easier to produce than parchment or vellum. Although probably not the inventor of moveable type, Johannes Gutenberg was responsible for its initial and eventual mainstream use in the medieval world. Printers such as England's William Caxton exploited the printing press to great advantage while still participating in the luxury manuscript book trade, which points to the continuity between the medieval and early modern.

The Teaching Company Collection.

Johannes Gutenberg most likely did not invent movable type, but his printing press brought the innovation to the mainstream of medieval printmaking.

Although the Protestant Reformation is often described as beginning when German religious reformer Martin Luther nailed his 95 Theses to the door of a church in Wittenburg in 1517, its origins actually lie in the medieval world. In England in the 14th century, reformers such as John Wycliff, associated with the Lollard movement, argued for a greater emphasis on the individual's relationship with God and vernacular translations of the Bible. Wycliff's ideas greatly influenced Czech theologian John Huss, who took up the cause of church reform in the late 14th century. Although Huss was eventually excommunicated and executed for his efforts, his ideas about religion lit a spark in the imagination of the medieval world.

The major literary and artistic developments of the early modern period can be traced to 14th-century Italy, which produced a plethora of writers and artists. A new, more realistic style of artistic representation was introduced in Italy by the great artist Cimabue and his pupil, Giotto; their influence on other painters and sculptors such as Donatello, Leonardo da Vinci, and Michaelangelo, would be profound. From a literary perspective, the early modern period arguably began with late 13th- and early 14th-century Italian poets such as Dante and Petrarch. In England in the 14th century, Chaucer's

Canterbury Tales followed Dante's lead by using the vernacular—English—rather than the Latin of scholars and monks and in turning traditional character types into individuals.

The early modern period is often known as the age of exploration, as nations such as England and Spain sent explorers to the New World. Such expeditions were made possible in part by advances in naval engineering developed during the medieval period. The impulse to look west began as early as the year 1000 with Leif Erikson's journey to North America. The explosion in journeys of discovery was fueled in part by demand for natural resources unavailable in most of Western Europe, a taste for which had begun with the exotic spices and goods that trickled west with the advent of the Crusades.

William Caxton exploited the printing press to great advantage while still participating in the luxury manuscript book trade, which points to the continuity between the medieval and early modern.

Medieval people were more like us than they were different. We would do well to remember the medieval world and its people—their world gave rise to ours, and in our most sacred institutions of government, houses of worship, and social ideals, the shadow of the medieval looms large. ∎

Suggested Reading

Füssel, *Gutenberg and the Impact of Printing*.

Lambert, *Medieval Heresy*.

Questions to Consider

1. How useful is a term like "Renaissance" in describing what most scholars now call the early modern period? What medieval institutions, ideas, and inventions gave rise to the early modern?

2. Although most scholars argue for assuming a greater degree of continuity between the medieval and the early modern worlds than was once the case, there are some striking discontinuities. What produced these notable breaks with tradition?

Toward the Early Modern Period
Lecture 36—Transcript

Welcome back. In our last couple of lectures, we discussed how late medieval society was impacted both by a series of wars, uprisings, and revolts—and by advances in military technology. Together, these events and developments reshaped national boundaries and identities as well as undermined the ideal of the three orders or estates—which had long held sway in the popular imagination as the primary organizing principle of society in the medieval world. The first estate, the nobles, had risen to the top of medieval society because they were those who fought, who protected the second estate—the church—and the third—the peasants, or "everyone else." Their status was directly linked to the fact that the most powerful weapon in the medieval world had long been the mounted knight on horseback, and that in order to maintain horse, weapons, and armor, one needed significant amounts of wealth. This situation became unstable in the High and late Middle Ages, as—particularly after the Black Death—many nobles found themselves short of cash, and the concomitant rise of the merchant class meant that many people who were technically peasants were accruing wealth that had once only been possible for those in the nobility. Add to this technological developments in warfare, such as cannon and gunpowder, and the mounted knight on horseback was quickly becoming obsolete—and in turn, losing status and power.

Military conflicts—such as the Hundred Years' War between England and France and the Wars of the Roses that divided the ruling powers in England—further increased the precariousness of the position of those in the noble classes, as did popular uprisings of commoners—such as the Ciompi Revolt in Florence, the *Jacquerie* in France, and the Uprising of 1381 in England. All of these things in combination signaled a world in turmoil and transformation—and what it was transforming into is what has usually been called the Renaissance, or early modern period. Although it may seem like splitting hairs, there is a good reason for preferring one of these descriptors over the other. The term "Renaissance," which literally means "rebirth," was long used by those who saw the 16th century as a period of enlightenment and learning after the long, dark, and uninteresting period known as the Middle Ages. The term "Renaissance" was used to signal the contrasts between the two periods. More recently, scholars have tended to see more continuity than division between these two periods. Such scholars tend to prefer the term "early modern," as it does not as emphatically suggest a stark difference and division between these periods as was once commonly thought to be the case. As you might have guessed by now, I find myself in the camp that prefers the phrase "early modern." As we'll discuss today, just as the Roman world transformed, rather than collapsed, into the medieval one—so, too, did the medieval world gradually become the early modern. Instead of a gap or divide between the medieval and early modern period, I tend to see bridges that connect the two in important ways.

One of the defining elements of the early modern period has long been considered the explosion of interest in Classical texts that had been lost or unknown to the Middle Ages. Many of these manuscripts made their way into the late medieval and early modern world from the Greek and Arab worlds, where they had been preserved. But in fact, the gathering of manuscripts by Charlemagne during the Carolingian Renaissance of the 8th and 9th centuries and Alfred the Great's program of collection and translation of important texts into English during the Alfredian Renaissance of the 10th century laid the foundation for the rediscovery of works of Classical antiquity—as did contact with the Arab world and other realms to the East during the period of the Crusades. In addition, trade relations with the East—particularly in terms of the Italian city-states, many of which had become impressive maritime powers during the Middle Ages—brought other undiscovered or lost texts into the European orbit. It is true that many manuscripts were lost to the medieval world—sometimes due to the ravages of invaders like the Vikings, who plundered numerous monasteries, the main repositories for learning. In some cases, memory of a text would remain, even when the text itself was lost. For example, the works of Homer were unknown in the medieval world, even though medieval writers such as Geoffrey Chaucer knew his name and the general subject matter on which he wrote.

The exponential increase in literary production during the early modern period was made possible by the development of moveable type and the printing press in combination with the use of paper—a much easier writing surface to produce than the parchment or vellum made from animal hide. Although probably not the inventor of moveable type, Johannes Gutenberg was responsible for its initial and eventual mainstream use in the medieval world. Originally trained as a goldsmith, the family occupation, Gutenberg set up his printing press in Mainz, Germany, by 1450. He is perhaps best known for the 42-line Bible he produced—which has come to be known generally as the Gutenberg Bible.

As far as we know, Gutenberg's press turned out 180 copies of this Bible—some printed on paper, and some on animal hide. Almost 50 copies of this Bible survive. There had been experiments with printing prior to Gutenberg's foray into the business, but in these earlier experiments pages were usually printed using the woodblock method—in which the words of a single page would be carved in mirror image into a block of wood, which could then be inked and pressed onto a surface. This was fairly labor intensive, but it was still quicker than copying out texts by hand if one wanted to produce several copies of a particular text. Faster still was printing using moveable type, which is what Gutenberg did. The name "moveable type" refers to the fact that individual metal letters could be moved or assembled into whatever order someone wished—and thus, could be used over and over for a variety of different texts, an obvious advantage over entire pages carved into a block of wood. Because the letters were made using what is called the metal punch method, they were also fairly durable.

Printers such as William Caxton in England—a figure of particular interest to me and one whom we've already talked about some—exploited the printing press to great advantage while still participating in the luxury manuscript book trade, a fact that points to the continuity between the medieval and early modern. As I noted in an earlier lecture, Caxton learned printing on the Continent, probably in Germany, and he first turned his hand to printing in the Belgium town of Bruges. After returning to his native country, England, he set up that nation's first printing press in the town of Westminster around 1476. His life and career is a wonderful example of the continuity between the medieval and early modern—of how the one was transforming into the other, rather than there being an abrupt division between the two.

A commoner, Caxton came from the countryside of Kent into London where he was apprenticed to a mercer, or someone who dealt in cloth. In this business he traveled to the Continent, where he was first exposed to printing.

While there, he advanced to a senior position in the town of Bruges of a group known as the Company of Merchant Adventurers of London—sort of an expatriate group of businessmen who had found it more profitable to remain on the Continent to conduct most of their business. He advanced to this position through hard work and intelligence, and it was this post that brought him into the orbit of the noble house of Burgundy, whose duchess, Margaret, was sister to the king of England. Caxton was a shrewd attainer of patronage, able to gain Margaret's good favor and that of other nobles back in England—especially after he returned. It was always a good idea, if you were an author, a scribe, or a printer of books, to dedicate them to someone powerful and high-ranking. Caxton dedicated any number of books to members of royal and noble families, but he also mentions several well-connected commoners in his prologues and epilogues—among them several powerful but non-noble London merchants. Caxton recognized the power that remained with the traditional social elites as well as that which was increasing among the bourgeoisie, and the output of his print shop suggests he was a shrewd businessman who cleverly exploited the potential of both groups of consumers.

Similarly, he recognized and catered to traditional interests when it came to the output of his print shop. He is perhaps best known for printing the works of Geoffrey Chaucer, but he also took the initiative when it came to many works—often translating texts out of Latin or French on his own impulse, and then printing them for an audience that he gauged would be receptive to them. He also, as I've noted before, continued to participate in the luxury book trade—importing, buying, and selling handwritten manuscripts for wealthy clients. While the luxuriously illuminated manuscript was still a status symbol in the late 15th century, the ease and quickness with which printed books could be produced and circulated, in combination with an increasingly literate and educated population, helped fuel the explosion of writing that has come to be associated with the early modern period.

It is a similar story with the Protestant Reformation, long considered by many as one, if not the, defining event of the early modern period. The origin of the Protestant Reformation is often described as beginning when German religious reformer Martin Luther nailed his 95 Theses to the door of a church in Wittenberg in 1517. Luther had been a monk, but he became dissatisfied with what he saw as the corruption of the papacy, and he held that the Bible was the only infallible source of God's word on earth, essentially stating that the pope, being human, was prone to errors and misunderstandings of God's word—and thus, he refused to acknowledge the authority of the papacy. He also challenged the secular authority of the Holy Roman Emperor Charles V, and when he would not submit, the emperor had him excommunicated from the Roman Catholic Church. From this conflict, it has been argued, Protestant Christianity was born, but its roots actually lie a bit further back in the medieval world.

In England in the 14th century, reformers such as John Wycliffe, associated with the Lollard movement, argued for a greater emphasis on the individual's relationship with God. No one is quite sure where the word "Lollard" comes from, but it may come from a similar Dutch word that was used to refer to people who mumbled or muttered—or from the English "loller," which was used to refer to lazy lie-abouts. Derogatory names were often used of Wycliffe and his followers, and it's possible that some combination of meanings came together to produce the term as it came to be used in the 14th century. Wycliffe and his followers supported production of English translations of the Bible, something vehemently opposed by the clergy, who felt that the Latin Bible was the most accurate version of the word of God, and accessibility of scripture to the mainstream population could result in dangerous errors of faith—leading people to sin and damnation. One of Luther's main concerns had been that the Bible be available to everyone, and over 100 years after the Wycliffite movement, Luther would translate the Bible into German.

Lollard communities also had argued that anyone, even women, could be allowed to preach—one of their tenets that led to Wycliffe's posthumous condemnation as a heretic. Later on, Martin Luther would similarly reject many of the foundational elements of Roman Catholic monasticism—prominently among them the commitment to celibacy. Luther married a former nun, setting an example of a new kind of clerical marriage. They had six children, and in his writings Luther referred to her with a great deal of respect and affection, saying he would not trade their poverty-stricken life for any amount of wealth—demonstrating a respect for women and the spiritual role they could play that had been one of the more interesting and controversial ideas of Wycliffism.

Wycliffe's ideas also greatly influenced Czech theologian John Huss, who took up the cause of church reform in the late 14th century. Huss took many of Wycliffe's ideas back to the Continent—where, in turn, they came to influence Martin Luther a bit later. Huss himself was excommunicated by the church in 1411 and then burned at the stake in 1415 after being declared a heretic by the Council of Constance—which we discussed in an earlier lecture on the Papal Schism of the 14th and early 15th centuries.

So, as we can see, the late medieval world was a place of new ideas, particularly when it came to religion—and it was that medieval invention, the printing press, that arguably helped to circulate and disseminate these ideas in ways that could not have been possible just a century earlier. So, many changes in the early modern world, then, have their beginnings securely rooted in the medieval. For example, many of the major literary and artistic developments of the early modern period can be traced to 14th-century Italy, which produced a plethora of poets, prose writers, and artists near the end of the medieval period. In fact, as we've already noted, although for the sake of convenience most scholars think of the medieval world in Europe as lasting from about 500 to 1500, most scholars who speak of an Italian Renaissance date it from the early 14th century. Indeed, some scholars even point to the exact moment when the Italian Renaissance began—April 8, 1341, when the Italian poet Petrarch crowned himself Italy's first poet laureate since antiquity. Petrarch himself studied writers of antiquity, becoming a poet of some fame and acclaim. It is ironic that Petrarch himself seems to have contributed to the idea of the Middle Ages as a dark age, as he on more than one occasion referred to the period before his own as one of darkness. But it was the medieval world that produced Petrarch, along with a slew of other poets and artists who would transform the medieval into the early modern. I'm not sure what was in the water in 14th-century Italy, but here we see a true explosion of art and literature of a kind heretofore unknown in the medieval world.

A new, more realistic style of artistic representation was introduced in Italy by the great artist Cimabue and his pupil, Giotto. Their influence on other painters and sculptors—such as Donatello, Leonardo da Vinci, Michelangelo, and others—would be profound. Paintings and sculpture that had previously been generally representational, somewhat flat and emotionless, now seemed to come to life. Cities, such as Florence, were filled with what modern people would think of as museum quality pieces in public squares, on bridges, as decorative objects on buildings, in private gardens. The Ghiberti Doors on the Baptistery of the Duomo, which we discussed in our lecture on art, are a prime example of this. From a literary perspective, the early modern period arguably began with late 13th and early 14th-century Italian poet Dante, even though Petrarch was the one named poet laureate. In choosing to write his great *Divine Comedy* in the vernacular language of the Florentine dialect rather than in Latin, Dante Alighieri was breaking with the traditions of the medieval world and making an almost unimaginably bold move towards what we tend to regard as modern ideas about literature. The presence of the "I," the narrator in Dante's *Divine Commedia*, also strikes one as particularly modern in his sense of self.

In England, in the 14th century, Geoffrey Chaucer's *Canterbury Tales* followed Dante's lead by using the vernacular—English—rather than the Latin of scholars and monks, and in taking his character types and turning them into individuals. Both Dante and Chaucer were writing for an audience that may not have had the benefit of a Latin education—in other words, the up and coming merchants, craftspeople, and bourgeoisie who were beginning to become educated and wealthy. As Alfred the Great had suggested back in the 10th century, it made more sense to teach people how to read in their common tongue, their native language, and then if they desired further education, they might go on to study Latin. Both Dante and Chaucer were capable of writing in Latin—they were both certainly able to read it quite well. But in choosing to write in the vernacular, they were—perhaps innocently—signaling that the medieval social order and the usual audience for the written word was undergoing transformation as it headed toward the early modern period.

The early modern period is often known as the age of exploration, as nations such as England and Spain sent explorers to the New World. Of course, this world wasn't new at all to the people who had been living there for thousands of years, but to the European world it was. To quote Shakespeare, who was himself influenced by the interest in the Americas, it was a "brave new world," filled with possibilities and potential freedoms not to be found in the medieval world. Such expeditions to places such as the Americas were made possible in part by advances in naval engineering developed during the medieval period. One of these was the development of a type of ship known as a caravel, which had both square and triangular sails—affording it both speed and maneuverability, and making it ideal for longer voyages than had typically been the norm.

As we've seen in earlier lectures, the impulse to look to the West had begun as early as the year 1000, with Leif Erikson's journey to North America. Although Scandinavian sailors had gone so far as to establish settlements in North America—most notably at the site known as L'Anse Aux Meadows—the effort it took to travel to the Americas and establish a community there was seen as not being worth the potential trade benefits. What the native Americans at the time had to offer by way of trade—furs, and the like—were all things the Vikings could procure for themselves for the most part. The gold and especially silver they tended to plunder on their forays was not easily to be found in the Americas at this time. So, trade routes between Scandinavian powers and American peoples were largely abandoned.

Almost 500 years later, there would be an explosion in journeys of discovery to the west, but that movement toward the Americas, which so many tend to think of as a 16th-century Renaissance phenomenon, actually has its origins in the early 15th century on the Iberian Peninsula. Fueled in part by demand for natural resources unavailable in most of Western Europe, a taste for which had begun with the exotic spices and goods that trickled west with the advent of the Crusades in the 12th century, Spanish and Portuguese sailors began making longer and longer journeys down the coast of Africa—eventually rounding the Cape of Good Hope in 1498, and thereafter establishing a solid and dominant trade presence in the Indian Ocean. Given their proximity to the African continent, it made sense that it would be the Portuguese and Spanish who would first venture beyond the typical nautical routes of the medieval world. The original goal of such voyages had been to bring those exotic spices and other goods that Europeans so desired by the 14th century—but more importantly, they were driven by a desire to cut out the middle men who were taking a portion of the profits to be had.

Eventually some sailors turned west, conquering and settling in the Canary, Madeira, and Azore Islands and establishing sugar plantations and the like there. But it would be the voyage of Christopher Columbus—an Italian who had come to the court of King Ferdinand and Queen Isabella of Spain— that would dramatically reshape the medieval world and contribute to the momentum of transformation that was turning it into the early modern. It's quite well-known that Columbus was not trying to reach the Americas at all, and that he thought he had arrived in the Indies. Until his dying day, he would contend that the continent that he had set foot on was Asia—not the *Mundus Novus*, or "New World," that fellow explorer Amerigo Vespucci had named it.

As we enter the early modern period, a series of exchanges of food, livestock, and (unfortunately) disease would alter both the European and the American worlds. Europeans were introduced to new foods, including corn and potatoes—and to tobacco and chocolate, which quickly became huge concerns in early modern trade. The Americans were introduced to some new foods as well—coffee, for example, which had its origins in the Middle East. But it was the diseases European visitors brought with them—particularly the Spanish who conquered the Aztec and Inca Empires—that had the most lasting impact. Smallpox, syphilis, and other diseases decimated the population of the Americas. Some scholars estimate the native populations were reduced by about 70 percent. Further altering the ecology and social structures of the Americas was the introduction of domesticated horses, sheep, pigs, etc. This exchange between the Americas and the medieval world has come to be called the Columbian Exchange, but it hardly seems like a fair deal. The European world gained new foodstuffs, lands to extract a profit from, and more—while the native populations had their societies conquered and their people killed off by diseases to which they had little or no immunity.

But once again, the origins of this impulse for exploration lie far back in the medieval world—with the daring voyages of the Vikings and the profitable ventures of the Italian city-states along the Mediterranean coast standing as some of the earliest evidence of the desire to go beyond the boundaries of one life to see what lay beyond.

In so many ways, the medieval world is utterly alien to our modern sensibilities. Ideas about class and the theoretical impossibility of moving between classes are far removed from the idea of the American dream—in which anyone can become a success from nothing if he or she simply works hard enough. The omnipresence of religion in all aspects of life is also strikingly different from our modern world, in which the line separating church and state is often fought over vociferously. The medieval world could be a time of seemingly unending violence, a time when a peasant minding his own business might have his home and crops burned to the ground because of a dispute between his lord and another—a dispute in which he would have no real voice, and that fact he would usually accept as part of life. Legally speaking, with a few exceptions, women were considered under the jurisdiction of their fathers and then their husbands. For most of the population, the labor to stay alive and decently fed was arduous, and a twist of fate like an early frost or a rainy spring could bring a family to the brink of starvation. Plague regularly ravaged the entire medieval world, sparing no one—no matter degree or estate—and killing up to half the population of 14th-century Europe. Facing such a threat without benefit of modern medical knowledge or cures would strike fear into the heart of any one of us.

But for all the differences of the world in which they lived, medieval people were more like us than they were different. They fell in love. They told jokes. They played board games and ball games to amuse themselves. Many were kind and generous to those less fortunate than themselves. They liked a good party with plenty of food, drink, and music. They stood up against the elites of society to make a claim for what they felt was right. Plenty of medieval commoners used their intelligence, cunning, and hard work to advance up the social ladder—despite a system that sought to keep them in place.

They were, above all, resilient. They had to be—with threats of war, plague, disease, infant mortality, and starvation looming—they lived, laughed, and loved just as modern people do. We would do well to remember the medieval world and its people. It is their world that gave rise to ours—and in our most sacred institutions of government, houses of worship, and social ideals, the shadow of the medieval looms large.

Timeline

285–305 .... Reign of Emperor Diocletian.

312 .... The Battle of Milvian Bridge; Constantine becomes emperor of the Western Roman Empire.

313 .... Constantine issues the Edict of Toleration.

325 .... Council of Nicaea, presided over by Constantine.

378 .... Battle of Adrianople.

410 .... Goths sack Rome; Alaric becomes emperor.

c. 449 .... Anglo-Saxons, led by brothers Hengest and Horsa, invade Britain.

c. 480 .... Clovis becomes king of the Franks.

c. 480–547 .... Life of Saint Benedict of Nursia.

c. 500 .... Probable date of the Battle of Mount Badon, at which the legendary King Arthur defeated the invading Anglo-Saxons, curbing their incursion into Britain for a time.

531 .... Franks attack and slaughter the Thuringians.

622... Muhammad makes the Hejira, fleeing
from Mecca to Medina; Muslim
calendar begins.

632... Death of Muhammad.

664... Synod of Whitby reconciles the date of
Easter between the Celtic and
Roman Churches.

687... Frankish mayor of the palace, Pepin
of Heristal, defeats the Neustrians,
consolidating power through his
domination of Burgundy and the
surrounding region.

711... Arab conquest of Spain begins.

731... Venerable Bede completes his
*Ecclesiastical History of the
English People*.

597... Augustine of Canterbury heads the
Christian mission to the Anglo-Saxons.

789... Vikings sack Lindisfarne Abbey.

800... Charlemagne crowned emperor by Pope
Leo III on Christmas.

814... Death of Charlemagne.

843... Treaty of Verdun divides and dissipates
the power of the Carolingian Empire.

871... Alfred the Great crowned king
of Wessex.

874.. Settlement of Iceland begins.

899.. Death of Alfred the Great.

c. 900s .... Composition of the *Exeter Book*.

911–919... Carolingian dynasty ends; rise of the
Ottonian dynasty.

930.. First meeting of the Althing, arguably
the medieval world's first parliament,
on the plain at Thingvellir, Iceland.

991.. The Battle of Maldon.

c. 1000... Composition of *Beowulf*.

1000.. Leif Erikson reaches North America.

1013.. Swein Forkbeard, king of Denmark,
declares himself king of England.

1042.. Edward the Confessor crowned king
of England.

1054.. Great Schism between Eastern
(Orthodox) and Western
(Catholic) Churches.

1066.. William of Normandy
conquers England.

1095.. Pope Urban II preaches the First
Crusade at the Council of Clermont.

1098.. Robert Molesme founds Cistercian
monastic order.

1099 .... Western forces capture Jerusalem.

1136/38 .... Geoffrey of Monmouth composes his
History of the Kings of Britain.

c. 1140 .... Beginning of gothic architecture.

1170 .... Thomas à Becket killed by four
knights of King Henry II in
Canterbury Cathedral.

1187 .... Battle of Hattin; Jerusalem falls to
Saladin and his army.

1204 .... Sack of Constantinople by Crusaders.

1215 .... King John of England compelled
to sign the Magna Carta;
Fourth Lateran Council.

1290 .... Expulsion of the Jews from England.

1291 .... Fall of Acre, the last Western-controlled
outpost in the Holy Land.

1309 .... Pope Clement V takes up residence
in Avignon, beginning the
Babylonian Captivity.

c. 1337 .... Hundred Years' War begins.

1348 .... Plague begins to ravage Europe.

1351 .... English Parliament enacts the Statute of
Laborers, freezing wages at preplague
levels and limiting peasant movement.

1358	Jacquerie breaks out in Paris.
1377	Papacy returns to Rome.
1378	Ciompi Revolt in Italy.
c. 1380s	Geoffrey Chaucer composes *The Canterbury Tales*.
1381	Peasants' Revolt in England.
1415	English defeat the French at the Battle of Agincourt.
c. 1450	Johannes Gutenberg introduces moveable type and printing to Europe.
c. 1455	The Wars of the Roses begin.
1476	William Caxton sets up his printing business in England.
1485	Defeat of King Richard III of England at the Battle of Bosworth Field; Henry Tudor crowned Henry VII of England.

Timeline

Glossary

Althing: Arguably the medieval world's first parliament. It convened on the plain of Thingvellir, in Iceland, in the year 930.

Arianism: Heretical movement popular during the early Middle Ages that held that although Jesus Christ was divine, he could not be as divine as God the Father because he had been human for a time. Stamping out Arianism was one of the major concerns of early church councils.

Articella: Literally, "little thing"; refers to the standard texts used for study at the medical schools of Bologna, Salerno, and later, Montpellier.

assarting: Process by which forest land was cleared and brought under the plow.

Babylonian Captivity: Period during the 14th century when the pope resided in Avignon, rather than in Rome, conveying the sense that the papacy in some sense was held captive during this period. It alludes to the captivity of the Hebrews by the Babylonians during the 6th century B.C.

Black Death: A 16th-century term describing the waves of plague—bubonic, pneumonic, and septicemic—that devastated the population of Europe starting in 1348. At least a third and perhaps as much as half the population of medieval world succumbed to the plague, with episodes recurring once a generation or so well into the 18th century.

Byzantium: Political entity that developed from the eastern half of the Roman Empire; also at times the name of the capital city, which was rebuilt and renamed Constantinople in the early 4th century (c. 330) and was later called Istanbul, it's original Turkish name. Compared with the West, the Byzantine Empire was more stable and advanced for much of the Middle Ages.

Catharism (a.k.a. **Albigensian heresy**): Heresy found primarily in the south of France in the 12th and 13th centuries. Cathars were dualists—holding that ideas such as good and evil, God and the Devil needed to be held in balance—and they refused to acknowledge as significant the moment of the Crucifixion. They were largely wiped out during the Albigensian Crusade of 1208.

chévauchée: Military strategy employed with great frequency during the Hundred Years' War, particularly by Edward, the Black Prince, heir to the throne of England. It involved pillaging, setting fire to, and generally laying waste the territories—including farmland and homesteads of innocent peasants—under control of one's enemies.

Ciompi: Florentine clothworkers who revolted against guild restrictions in 1378 and seized control of the government of Florence, maintaining it until 1382.

comitatus: The most important element of Germanic society, a band of loyal retainers, or thanes—usually young men—who acted as the personal war band of the leader or king.

danse macabre: Literally, "dance of death"; artistic motif, often depicting a skeleton engaged in the act of leading people into the afterlife, that became a common element of literature and art in the wake of the Black Death.

Drang nach Osten: Saxon "push to the east" that began in the 10th century, in which commoners and lords were encouraged to move east and settle on unoccupied lands, thereby enlarging German borders.

estates satire: Tradition of writing in which representatives of the three orders or three estates of medieval society were caricatured. Geoffrey Chaucer's *Canterbury Tales* is an example.

feudalism: Much-disputed but still useful term to describe medieval social structure and relations. Although the term was first used in the 16th century, it derives from the Latin word feudum, which in the Middle Ages referred to a "fief," or piece of land that a lord might bestow on a vassal in return for service and loyalty. A feudal society may be described as hierarchical and dependent on bonds of loyalty and service for its organization.

flagellant movement: Self-penitential movement in which participants whipped themselves, punishing the flesh to perfect the spirit. The practice became widespread and public during the Black Death, when groups of flagellants would travel from town to town, publicly whipping themselves in the belief that the plague was a punishment from God and their behavior might help atone for whatever sins humankind had committed that resulted in the plague.

Germania: Territory to the north and west of the Roman Empire—beyond the Rhine and Danube rivers—populated by Germanic tribes who were not members of the Roman world.

Gregorian chant: Although named for Pope Gregory the Great, this monophonic religious plainchant was popularized by the Emperor Charlemagne as part of his move to reform religion and standardize church services.

gothic: Style of architecture found primarily in churches and cathedrals that came into use in the 12th century near Paris. Its signature elements included the pointed arch, high vaulted ceilings, and flying buttresses.

Hejira: Flight of the Prophet Muhammad from Mecca to Medina in the year 622 to escape persecution. This event marks the beginning of the Muslim calendar.

Hundred Years' War: Conflict between England and France over the right to the French throne that continued from about 1337 to 1453, with occasional truces and cessations in fighting.

Jacquerie: Rebellion by French peasants against nobles that erupted in 1358. Angry at being asked to rebuild noble houses destroyed in the Hundred Years' War, the participants joined with another rebellious group, led by Étienne Marcel, who had seized control of Paris. The rebellion was relatively quickly put down.

Lollard: Followers of John Wycliff, whose heretical teachings were of great concern to clerical leaders in England in the 14th and 15th centuries. Lollards (or Wycliffites) believed that every individual should have access to the Word of God and that the use of priests as mediators and explicators of the Bible was unnecessary. They thus believed strongly that the Bible should be translated into English, something to which church leaders were violently opposed.

mark of cadency: Distinguishing mark on a coat of arms that identifies the bearer as junior member of that particular family.

mayor of the palace: Political office of great importance during the Merovingian dynasty of the 7th and 8th centuries. Eventually the position became hereditary, and in 751 Pippin III took the crown from the Merovingians, founding the Carolingian dynasty. The son of Pippin III was Charlemagne, king of the Franks and later Holy Roman Emperor.

motte and bailey: Style of castle building favored by conquerors—such as William of Normandy—to establish a defensive position in occupied territory. The motte is a raised earthen mound surrounded by a ditch, for added security; the bailey is a courtyard below and in front of the motte where most of the daily life of the castle took place.

ofermod: Old English word meaning "excessive pride" or "excessive assurance/self-confidence." In the poem about the Battle of Maldon, which took place in 991, the poet tells the reader that it is because of his ofermod that the English leader Byrthnoth makes a fatal tactical mistake, leading to the defeat of the English forces.

Pelagianism: Heresy based on the teachings of a 5th-century monk named Pelagius. Pelagianism held that one could earn one's way into heaven by doing good works, a position deemed heretical by church officials, who upheld the teaching that only God's grace determined whether one would go to heaven or not.

quadrivium: Four of the seven liberal arts, consisting of arithmetic, astronomy, geometry, and music.

Reconquista: Series of efforts, beginning in the 8th century, to re-Christianize those territories in the Iberian Peninsula that were under Muslim rule. With the conquest of Granada in 1492, the Reconquista was complete.

Romanesque: Style of architecture marked primarily by the use of the rounded arch and barrel vaulting; this style preceded the gothic.

romanitas: Literally, "romanness"; as the Roman Empire expanded, its military and citizens sought to recreate Rome wherever they went, attempting to maintain an essential quality of romanness.

three estates (a.k.a. **three orders**): Ideal division of medieval society into three groups: those who fought (the nobles), those who prayed (the clergy), and those who worked (the peasants). Although a tripartite division, the estates were in no way equivalent. The nobles and the clergy—most of whom also came from the noble class—made up about 10 percent of the population, while the workers—everyone else—comprised 90 percent.

trebuchet: A military weapon very similar to a catapult.

trivium: Three of the seven liberal arts, consisting of grammar, logic, and rhetoric.

Wars of the Roses: A series of dynastic conflicts beginning in 1455, fought between factions loyal to the English houses of Lancaster and York. The conflict lasted until 1485, when the Lancastrian Henry Tudor, who had only a very distant claim to the throne, defeated the Yorkist King Richard III at the Battle of Bosworth field. The new Henry VII then married the only surviving Yorkist, his cousin Elizabeth, thereby cementing his claim to the throne and beginning the Tudor dynasty.

Biographical Notes

Alfred the Great (848–849): The most unlikely of kings and the only English monarch to bear the title "the Great," Alfred was the fifth son of the Anglo-Saxon king of Wessex and came to the throne in 871 after the deaths of his older brothers, most of whom met their ends in armed conflicts with the invading Vikings. Famously forced to flee into hiding in the Atheleny marshes, Alfred regrouped and defeated the Vikings, becoming king of the Anglo-Saxons and setting the stage for his grandson to eventually become the first king of England. During his reign, Alfred instituted defensive measures such as the Burghal Hidage and the first English navy, and he promoted education and the church.

Arthur (c. 500?): The legendary ruler of Britain, most likely based on a real historic personage who rallied the Britons against the invading Anglo-Saxons in the late 5th and early 6th centuries. Probably never called king in his own lifetime, he was most likely a Romanized Briton who came to power when the Roman legions withdrew after the sack of Rome in 410. The fact that the origins of this hero are lost in the mists of time is likely why he has become such a popular figure of legend; his story has lent itself to appropriation and elaboration by any number of groups and peoples throughout the last 1,500 years.

Bede, the Venerable (672–735): Were it not for the Venerable Bede's masterpiece, *The Ecclesiastical History of the English Language*, completed in 731, we would know next to nothing about pre-8th-century England. A monk who spent most of his life in the monastery of Monkwearmouth-Jarrow in Northumbria, Bede also composed many other religious tracts that had great influence on the development of Christianity in early England.

Charlemagne (a.k.a. **Charles the Great**; 747–814): A scion of the Carolingian dynasty, Charlemagne became king of the Franks in 768. A conqueror, state builder, defender of the faith, and promoter of education and the arts, he is regarded as the instigator of the Carolingian Renaissance, a period in the 8th and

9th centuries that saw an unprecedented flowering of scholarship and the arts. On Christmas Day in the year 800, he was crowned emperor by Pope Leo III, an act that would give rise to the idea of the Holy Roman Empire, which would remain potent in the figurative sense long after it had ceased to have any real relevance. After his death, Charlemagne's kingdom was divided among his heirs after much squabbling; 60 years after his death, the power of the Carolingian empire he had built had almost completely disappeared.

Chaucer, Geoffrey (c. 1343–1400): English poet best known for *The Canterbury Tales*, written in the 1380s. This text provides a unique view of the various strata and occupations of medieval society, from highest to lowest. Although writing in an established genre known as estates satire, Chaucer made brilliant innovations to produce a kind of writing that was in many respects utterly new. Associated with the household of John of Gaunt, the wealthiest man in England and one of the sons of King Edward III, Chaucer was an example of the kind of upward mobility available to the middle classes in the wake of the Black Death.

Constantine (c. 272–337): Emperor of Rome from 306 until his death, Constantine the Great is perhaps most important in terms of the development of the medieval world for his Edict of Toleration, issued in 313, which protected Christians from persecution. There is some debate as to whether or not Constantine himself was a Christian, but his protection of Christians paved the way for Christianity to go from the most persecuted religion of the empire to the most favored within the span of just a century.

Gutenberg, Johannes (c. 1398–1468): Goldsmith who is credited with introducing the printing press and moveable type to the medieval world. The spread of printing helped pave the way for the explosion of learning and exchange of knowledge that would mark the early modern period.

Henry II (a.k.a. **Henry Plantagenet**; r. 1154–1189): King of England who, with his marriage to Eleanor of Aquitaine, enlarged England's continental holdings to the largest they would ever be. His reign was marked by a dispute with his former friend, Thomas à Becket, archbishop of Canterbury, that resulted in Becket's murder at the hands of four of Henry's knights. Toward the end of his reign, he was embroiled in numerous disputes with his wife and sons, particularly Richard the Lionheart and John.

John (1167–1216): King of England. As a younger son of Henry II and Eleanor of Aquitaine, John was initially given the nickname "Lackland," as it seemed likely that he stood to inherit very little in the way of estates or titles. After succeeding his brother Richard as king in 1199, John's rule became famously inept. He lost almost all the territories his father had amassed and was forced to sign the Magna Carta in 1215 by 25 of his most powerful barons.

Justinian (c. 482–565): In 597, Justinian ascended to the throne of the eastern half of the former Roman Empire—also known as the Byzantine Empire—and sought to restore the unity of Rome by reclaiming territories that had been lost. He also was a great promoter of the arts, and during his reign the magnificent Hagia Sophia was constructed. The most important legacy of Justinian's rule, however, was his legal code, known as the Justinian Code or the Corpus Juris Civilis, which clarified and affirmed the Roman legal code and which remains a foundational element of many law codes today.

Muhammad (570–632): Revered as the founder of Islam and regarded as the prophet of God by its followers. Around the age of 40, he began conveying messages given to him by God while he meditated in a cave outside the city of Mecca. Although he gathered many followers, he was also subject to persecution by the tribal leaders of the area, who saw him as a threat to their power. In 622, he made the Hejira, or flight, to the city of Medina. Eventually, the various tribes of the Arabian Peninsula and beyond united as a single Muslim polity; this unity allowed a flourishing of education, science, and the arts in the Islamic world that far exceeded what was happening contemporaneously in the medieval world. Islam would play a vital role in influencing and shaping European society throughout the Middle Ages.

Saladin (1138–1193): One of the most remarkable figures in history, Saladin was a Kurdish Muslim who led the resistance against Crusaders in the Holy Land. His honorable behavior toward those he captured and defeated, his scholasticism, and his attempts to work with Frankish leaders to find peaceable solutions in the Levant earned him the respect of his enemies, and he became a central figure (along with Richard I of England, the Lionheart) in medieval stories of chivalry and knightly activity. After his capture of Jerusalem in 1187, he famously freed most of those held captive in the city and allowed the Jewish population to resettle there. He died of fever in Damascus.

Urban II (c. 1042–1099): A monk and reformer, Urban became Pope in 1088. He is best known for preaching the First Crusade in 1095 at the Council of Clermont. The leaders of the first units of Crusaders answered directly to him, and it was forbidden for any to "take the cross" and go on Crusade without his approval. He died in July 1099, two weeks after Crusaders had captured the city of Jerusalem but before news of the victory could reach him.

William of Normandy (a.k.a. **William the Conqueror** or **William Bastard**; c. 1027–1087): King of England. Cousin to the last Anglo-Saxon king, Edward the Confessor, who was childless. When Edward died in 1066, the king's brother-in-law, Harold Godwinson, claimed the throne; William maintained that Edward had promised the crown to him and so invaded England in October 1066. He defeated Harold's troops and killed Harold at the Battle of Hastings. Within a few short years, English society was profoundly and radically transformed by Norman rule.

Wycliffe, John (c. 1330–1384): English scholar and theologian who is considered one of the leaders of the religious movement known as Lollardy. Many of Wycliffe's teachings—including that the Bible should be translated into English and that the intercessory efforts of a priest were not necessary for individual salvation—were condemned by church officials, who saw his beliefs as threatening to their power and status. In his argument that the church should not own property and his other beliefs, he anticipated the coming Protestant Reformation.

Bibliography

Abels, Richard. *Alfred the Great: War, Kingship, and Culture in Anglo-Saxon England*. London: Longman, 1998. A thorough history of the life and times of the only English monarch to be called "the Great."

Allmand, Christopher. *The Hundred Years' War: England and France at War c. 1300–1450*. Cambridge: Cambridge University Press, 1988. Engaging and readable text that concisely discusses the causes, contexts, and effects of the Hundred Years' War.

Berkey, Jonathan P. *The Formation of Islam: Religion and Society in the Near East, 600–1800*. Cambridge: Cambridge University Press, 2003. Carefully written and thoroughly researched study of the development of the Muslim world.

Bloch, R. Howard. *A Needle in the Right Hand of God: The Norman Conquest of 1066 and the Making and Meaning of the Bayeux Tapestry*. New York: Random House, 2006. Engaging and absorbing work that places the Bayeux Tapestry in its historical context.

Bouchard, Constance Brittain. *Strong of Body, Brave and Noble: Chivalry and Society in Medieval France*. Ithaca: Cornell University Press, 1998. A solid examination of how chivalry developed in medieval France.

Breay, Claire. *The Magna Carta: Manuscripts and Myths*. London: The British Library, 2002. Clear, concise, and accurate, there is no better short, accessible introduction to the events of 1215 at Runnymede.

Brundage, James. *Law, Sex, and Christian Society in Medieval Europe*. Chicago: University of Chicago Press, 1987. A compendious and groundbreaking work.

Cantor, Norman. *The Civilization of the Middle Ages: A Completely Revised and Expanded Edition of Medieval History: The Life and Death of A Civilization*. New York: Harper Perennial, 1993. A great general introduction to the topic by a master scholar.

Carpenter, Christine. *The Wars of the Roses: Politics and the Constitution in England, c. 1437–1509*. Cambridge: Cambridge University Press, 1997. Often used as a textbook in courses that treat any part of late medieval English society; a reliable and thorough overview of the subject.

Chaucer, Geoffrey. *The Canterbury Tales*. Edited and translated by Nevill Coghill. Harmondsworth: Penguin, 2003. A readable translation of the medieval masterpiece.

Chibnall, Marjorie. *Debate on the Norman Conquest*. New York: St. Martin's Press, 1999. An excellent overview of the competing scholarly positions as regards William of Normandy's conquest of England.

Clanchy, Michael T. *From Memory to Written Record: England 1066–1307*. 2nd ed. Oxford: Oxford University Press, 1993. Thoroughly revised and updated edition of Clanchy's groundbreaking study on royal administrative practices in England.

Collins, Roger. *Charlemagne*. Toronto: University of Toronto Press, 1998. A solid biography of the emperor.

Fox-Davies, A. C. *A Complete Guide to Heraldry*. New York: Skyhorse Publishing, 2007. A reissued edition of an old classic, Fox-Davies' text contains every detail one could want to know about the "science" of heraldry and coats of arms.

Frugoni, Chiara. *A Day in a Medieval City*. Translated by William McCuaig. Chicago: University of Chicago Press, 2005. Vibrantly illustrated, this book is useful for the way in which it illuminates life in one of the most thriving urban areas of the Middle Ages.

Füssel, Stephen. *Gutenberg and the Impact of Printing.* Burlington, VT: Ashgate, 2005. An excellent overview of the development and impact of the printing press in the medieval world.

Ganshof, F. L. *Feudalism.* New York: Harper and Row, 1964. The place where all recent studies of the controversial topic begin.

Geary, Patrick J. *The Myth of Nations: The Medieval Origins of Europe.* Princeton: Princeton University Press, 2002. This book confronts and disputes popular theories about European ethnicities and the formation of national identities in the Middle Ages.

Gies, Frances, and Joseph Gies. *Daily Life in Medieval Times.* New York: Black Dog and Leventhal, 1999. Lavishly illustrated text that includes the Gies' three classic popular texts on life in a medieval village, a medieval city, and a medieval castle.

Glick, Thomas, Steven J. Livesey, and Faith Wallis, eds. *Medieval Science, Technology, and Medicine: An Encyclopedia.* New York: Routledge, 2005. A thorough compendium on all things having to do the elements mentioned in the title; indispensable for those interested in the scientific life of the medieval world.

Grant, Edward. *The Foundations of Modern Science in the Middle Ages.* Cambridge: Cambridge University Press, 1996. This work traces scientific developments from the medieval to the modern period.

Hanawalt, Barbara. *The Ties That Bound: Peasant Families in Medieval England.* A fascinating glimpse into the everyday life of the commons in the Middle Ages, this book relies heavily on legal documents and coroners' reports to make the claim that medieval peasant families enjoyed warm and affectionate relationships.

Herlihy, David. *The Black Death and the Transformation of the West.* Edited by Samuel J. Cohn Jr. Cambridge, MA: Harvard University Press, 1997. A provocative study that argues against many commonly held beliefs about the plague that ravaged Europe beginning in the 14th century.

Hieatt, Constance B., and Sharon Butler. *Pleyn Delit: Medieval Cookery for Modern Cooks*. Toronto: University of Toronto Press, 1976. Includes recipes updated for modern preparation with full explanations of ingredients and processes.

Horrox, Rosemary. *The Black Death*. Manchester, UK: Manchester University Press, 1994. This book contains a wealth of primary documents and contemporary accounts, all translated into English and helpfully placed into historical context.

Jones, Terry. *Medieval Lives*. London: BBC Books, 2004. A companion to Jones's acclaimed BBC series of the same name, this book is full of fascinating facts that help bring the medieval world to life.

Keen, Maurice. *Chivalry*. New Haven, CT: Yale University Press, 1984. Still the definitive book on the subject.

Lacy, Norris J., Geoffrey Ashe, Sandra Ness Ihle, Marianne E. Kalinke, and Raymond H. Thompson, eds. *The Arthurian Encyclopedia*. New York: Garland, 1986. Organized alphabetically by subject, this volume covers almost every conceivable aspect of the legend of King Arthur.

Lambert, Malcolm. *Medieval Heresy: Popular Movements from the Gregorian Reform to the Reformation*. 2nd ed. Oxford: Blackwell, 1992. The indispensable resource for anyone interested in heretical movements of the Middle Ages.

Lewis, Suzanne. *The Rhetoric of Power in the Bayeux Tapestry*. Cambridge: Cambridge University Press, 1999. A thorough introduction to the topic.

Linehan, Peter, and Janet L. Nelson, eds. *The Medieval World*. New York: Routledge, 2001. A thematically organized collection of essays by some of the top scholars in the field dealing with the topics of identity, power, social structures, and groups. Nicely complimented by maps and illustrations.

Mango, Cyril, ed. *The Oxford History of Byzantium*. Oxford: Oxford University Press, 2002. A thoroughly researched collection of essays by leading scholars in the field.

Mayr-Harting, Henry. *The Coming of Christianity to Anglo-Saxon England*. University Park: Pennsylvania State University Press, 1991. A careful examination of how the Anglo-Saxon world became Christianized.

McKitterick, Rosamund, ed. *Carolingian Culture: Emulation and Innovation*. Cambridge: Cambridge University Press, 1994. A collection of essays that gives depth and breadth to our understanding of the Carolingian world.

Moore, R. I. *The Formation of a Persecuting Society: Power and Deviance in Western Europe, 950–1250*. Oxford: Blackwell, 1987. A rigorously researched work on heresy and persecution in the High Middle Ages.

Nirenberg, David. *Communities of Violence: The Persecution of Minorities in the Middle Ages*. Princeton, NJ: Princeton University Press, 1996. Focusing mostly on Spain and southern France, this book examines the rise of persecution of minority groups in the 14th century.

Orme, Nicholas. *Medieval Children*. New Haven, CT: Yale University Press, 2001. A book at once rigorously scholarly while remaining accessible to the general reader, Orme's work is the definitive word on the subject of childhood and the medieval world.

Piponnier, Françoise, and Perrine Mane. *Dress in the Middle Ages*. Translated by Caroline Beamish. New Haven, CT: Yale University Press, 1997. More than just a survey of medieval fashion, this book explores materials, sources of information, and social status.

Pollard, A. J., ed. *The Wars of the Roses*. 2nd ed. New York: Palgrave Macmillan, 2001. A collection of essays by leading scholars on the conflict between the houses of York and Lancaster.

Prestwich, Michael O. *Armies and Warfare in the Middle Ages: The English Experience*. New Haven, CT: Yale University Press, 1996. An absorbing introduction to the experience of medieval warfare.

Reynolds, Susan. *Fiefs and Vassals: The Medieval Evidence Reinterpreted*. Oxford: Oxford University Press, 1994. This book argues that the term "feudalism" is incorrectly used to describe medieval social structures and conventions. It sparked a firestorm of controversy in academic circles when first published.

Riché, Pierre. *Daily Life in the World of Charlemagne*. Philadelphia: University of Pennsylvania Press, 1978. Examines life in 8th- and 9th-century Francia.

Riley-Smith, Jonathan. *The Crusades: A History*. New Haven, CT: Yale University Press, 2005. The definitive history by the leading authority on the topic.

Rosenwein, Barbara H. *A Short History of the Middle Ages*. 2nd ed. New York: Broadview Press, 2004. An excellent introduction, this book is often used as the main textbook in college courses on the subject and is commendable for its extensive coverage of the Islamic and Byzantine worlds and its many illustrations, maps, and timelines.

Sawyer, Peter, ed. *The Oxford Illustrated History of the Vikings*. Oxford: Oxford University Press, 2001. This thoroughly researched volume provides depth in its coverage and its beautiful illustrations.

Scully, Terence. *The Art of Cookery in the Middle Ages*. Woodbridge: Boydell Press, 1995. A detailed study of medieval food preparation and gustatory habits.

Shahar, Shulamith. *Childhood in the Middle Ages*. New York: Routledge, 1990. Shahar confronts and disputes the argument of scholar Philippe Aries that there was no real conception of childhood in the Middle Ages.

Snyder, Christopher A. *The World of King Arthur*. London: Thames and Hudson, 2000. This work traces the development of the Arthurian legend from its 5th-century origins to its present enactments. It includes the latest archaeological discoveries and numerous color illustrations.

Stokstad, Marilyn. *Medieval Art*. New York: Harper and Row, 1986. A breathtakingly ambitious overview of artistic creation ranging from painting to architecture to everyday objects, spanning more than 1,000 years and covering the broad geographical sweep of Western Europe in the Middle Ages, from England to Spain, Denmark, France, Italy, and beyond.

Sumption, Jonathan. *The Age of Pilgrimage: The Medieval Journey to God*. New York: Hidden Spring, 2003. A reprint of the compendious 1975 *Pilgrimage*, covering just about every aspect of this medieval activity.

Verbruggen, J. F. *The Art of Warfare in Western Europe during the Middle Ages: From the Eighth Century to 1340*. New York: North-Holland/Elsevier, 1977. An excellent introduction to the subject with copious amounts of detail on weaponry, division of labor within a medieval army, and battle tactics.

Waley, Daniel. *The Italian City-States*. 3rd ed. New York: Longman, 1988. A short and concise introduction to a difficult topic.

Webb, Diana. *Pilgrims and Pilgrimage in the Medieval West*. New York: I. B. Tauris, 1999. An excellent overview of the medieval pilgrimage experience.

Wemple, Suzanne. *Women in Frankish Society: Marriage and the Cloister, 500–900*. Philadelphia: University of Pennsylvania Press, 1981. An important study of women in medieval society.

White, Lynn, Jr. *Medieval Technology and Social Change*. Oxford: Oxford University Press, 1962. White explores three major areas of technological development in the medieval period: warfare, agriculture, and mechanical devices for everyday use. Still the best book on the subject.

Whittow, Mark. *The Making of Byzantium, 600–1025*. Berkeley: California State University Press, 1996. One of this book's great strengths is the way in which in contextualizes Byzantium in relationship to its neighbors. It also contains excellent maps.

Wilson, Christopher. *The Gothic Cathedral: The Architecture of the Great Church 1130–1530.* London: Thames and Hudson, 2005. A readable, engaging book that still pays scrupulous attention to the mechanics and realities of the gothic architectural process.

Notes

Notes

Notes